Argument: - too much emphasis placed on (commerce)
during "long durée"
- importance of _urbanization_ + _agency_
- How did Ming polity (constellation of
self-governing natural villages) accommodate existence
of cities?

4 Case studies
Chapter 1: "We must be taxed"
↬ grassroots mobilization to create urban tax
in place of labor services
→ discussion of resistance by residents of
imperial mandate of wall construction
↳

* ways in which late-Ming natives of Nanjing present locality
1) prospects "jing" ~ epitome of city per elites
2) Ketan (conversations w/ guests)
- direct evidence of what contemps find interesting
~ Nanjing elites uneasy about effects of urban life
* Author's arg. → Nanjing _not_ unique, part of broader phenomenon
~ late Ming cities face common problems + deal w/ them
in similar ways
→ too much emphasis on _conflict_ btw state +
society inste   two
* existence of dynastic ur
* dynasty's institutional arr   ing negotiations
btw state, society

D1087372

* dynasties differed in ways cities are treated, this influenced
how cities functioned

Negotiating Urban Space

Urbanization and Late Ming Nanjing

Harvard East Asian Monographs 320

NEGOTIATING URBAN SPACE

Urbanization and Late Ming Nanjing

Si-yen Fei

Published by the Harvard University Asia Center
Distributed by Harvard University Press
Cambridge (Massachusetts) and London 2009

Printed in the United States of America

The Harvard University Asia Center publishes a monograph series and, in coordination with the Fairbank Center for Chinese Studies, the Korea Institute, the Reischauer Institute of Japanese Studies, and other faculties and institutes, administers research projects designed to further scholarly understanding of China, Japan, Vietnam, Korea, and other Asian countries. The Center also sponsors projects addressing multidisciplinary and regional issues in Asia.

Library of Congress Cataloging-in-Publication Data

Fei, Si-yen, 1971-

Negotiating urban space : urbanization and late Ming Nanjing / Si-yen Fei.

p. cm. -- (Harvard East Asian monographs ; 320)

Includes bibliographical references and index.

ISBN 978-0-674-03561-4 (cl : alk. paper)

1. Urbanization--China--Nanjing Shi--History. 2. Urban policy--China--Nanjing Shi--History. 3. Cities and towns--Growth. 4. Nanjing Shi (China)--Social conditions. I. Title.

HT384.C62N364 2009

307.760951'136--dc22

2009030935

Index by Hung-ken Chien

∞ Printed on acid-free paper

Last figure below indicates year of this printing
18   17   16   15   14   13   12   11   10

Acknowledgments

As I was finishing the final draft of this book, I realized that although prospective readers might consider it a study of Nanjing or Ming urbanism, for its author, it is also a scrapbook filled with markings and entries evoking specific memories: a footnote reference that came from a good friend; a document that called back the long days spent in the Stanford East Asian Library at its former home in the Hoover Institute and the beautiful Japanese maples in front of the building; a particular turn in a chapter's argument that evolved from a prolonged discussion over the phone (and later Skype). As I read on, I recognized the parts that were first developed after my husband and I took a cross-continental trip to the East Coast and lived in the center of Philadelphia above a huge convenience store. The manuscript later underwent another major makeover during our European sojourn in Bonn and Cologne in northwestern Germany and in Antwerp in Belgium.

Indeed, buried among the heavy references to late Ming culture and society is a map of my life's path. When the project began, I was a graduate student at Stanford University struggling with the art and science of living alone in a foreign country. As the manuscript approaches its final version, I have started working at the University of Pennsylvania and just welcomed the birth of our daughter, Zoe. Reflecting on the long journey this manuscript has traveled, I cannot help but feel deeply indebted to the teachers, friends, and colleagues who touched the life of this book and its author in so many different and yet equally profound ways. The foundation of this book, my Ph.D. dissertation, grew out of the care and attention of Harold Kahn and Timothy Brook. Both epitomize the ideal *jingshi* 經師 and *renshi* 人師 as teachers of both knowledge and character. The specific interest in Nanjing came from a collaborative seminar that led to a mini-exhibition of seventeenth-century Nanjing art organized by Richard Vinograd and his graduate students. Working with a group of excellent young art historians such as Mei Yun-chiu and Ma Yachen gave me invaluable insight and much-needed courage to embark on a chapter on visual Nanjing. The main portion of the research was conducted at the Kyoto Institute of Humanities under the warm guidance of Professors Fuma Susumu and Iwai Shigeki. The repeated references to work done by my teachers and friends from Taiwan such as Hsu Hong, Chiu Peng-sheng, Chiu Chung-lin, Wu Jen-shu, and Wang Hong-tai attest not only to the significance of their works but also to their lasing influence on me as a scholar. The two anonymous reviewers of the manuscript for the Harvard University Asia Center also provided invaluable insights that allowed me to overcome a myopic bias as an author. Finally, this book could not have been finished without the encouragement and generous advice from my friends, especially the unfortunate Stanford gang of Tobie Meyer-Fong, Lisa Claypool, Shari Epstein, Erica Yao, Janice Kam, and Colette Plum who had to read numerous drafts of the same chapter and came up with sharp and inspiring comments every single time. If graduate school is one's native-place identity in the academic world, I certainly have benefited tremendously from the bond of sisterhood. Also essential to the completion of this project was the financial support I received from the Chiang Ching-kuo Foundation, Stanford Humanity Center, Center for East Asian Studies at Stanford University, and Academia Sinica in Taiwan. In particular, Li Xiaoti, my generous host at the Institute of History and Philology, organized a team working on Ming-Qing urban culture reminiscent of the literati salons described in this book: filled with banquets, feasts, excursions, and random and yet inspiring conversations that form the major inspiration for the final stage of this manuscript. It is difficult to put into words my gratitude to those who lent me endless support during this time period when my preoccupation with this manuscript made me chronically less attentive and occasionally(?) irritable. To my dear sister Chen Wenyi, my parents, my husband, and my daughter Zoe, this acknowledgment marks a new chapter of my life with you.

S.-Y.F.

Contents

Figures, Maps, and Table   ix

Introduction: A New Approach to Chinese Urbanism   I

1 "We Must Be Taxed"   29

2 To Wall or Not to Wall   76

3 Imaging Nanjing: A Genealogy   124

4 Nanjing Through Contemporary Mouths and Ears   188

   Conclusion: Toward a New Perspective on Late
   Imperial Urbanization   239

APPENDIX

Gu Qiyuan's *Fengsu* Treatise   259

REFERENCE MATTER

Notes   265

Works Cited   319

Index   351

Figures, Maps, and Table

FIGURES

3.1 Components of the 1624 edition of *Jinling tuyong* 127

3.2 Sources of the 1624 edition of *Jinling tuyong* 129

3.3 *Hongwu Atlas*: government offices 136

3.4 *Hongwu Atlas*: temples and shrines 137

3.5 *Hongwu Atlas*: streets, markets, and bridges 138

3.6 *Hongwu Atlas*: entertainment buildings 139

3.7 *Hongwu Atlas*: mountains and rivers 140

3.8 Map of Nanjing in the Three Kingdoms era, *Jinling gujin tukao* 142

3.9 Map of Nanjing during the Southern Dynasties, *Jinling gujin tukao* 143

3.10 Map superimposing historical sites of Nanjing, *Jinling gujing tukao* 144

3.11 Adaptation of *Hongwu Atlas* in *Sancai tuhui* 147

3.12 Tour map of Nanjing city in *Hainei qiguan* 148

3.13 Qing map of Nanjing, *Jiangning fuzhi* 148

3.14 Qingxi youfang, *Jinling tuyong* 174

3.15 Changgan li, *Jingling tuyong* 175

3.16 A kick ball game, *Jinling tuyong* 176

3.17 Sword practice, *Jinling tuyong* 177

3.18 People carrying goods outside the city gate, *Jinling tuyong* 178

3.19   Working in the fields, *Jinling tuyong*   179

3.20   Archery practice, *Jinling tuyong*   180

3.21   *Nandu fanhui tu*, details   181

3.22   Qingxi, *Jiangning fuzhi*   182

3.23   Changgan li, *Jiangning fuzhi*   183

4.1   Nanjing imperial observatory   203

MAPS

2.1   Gaochun City, *Gaochun xianzhi*, 1683   90

2.2   Nanjing Metropolitan Area; Chen Yi, *Jinling gujin tukao*, 1516   116

2.3   Nanjing Metropolitan Area in the Ming dynasty   122

4.1   Official demarcation of five Nanjing boroughs   218

4.2   Gu Qiyuan's neighborhoods   219

TABLE

4.1   Gu Qiyuan's Conception of Nanjing Neighborhoods
       in Terms of *Fengsu*   216

NEGOTIATING URBAN SPACE

Urbanization and Late Ming Nanjing

A New Approach to Chinese Urbanism

Over the course of three centuries, the spatial outlook of Ming China (1368–1644) underwent a drastic change that probably few historical empires have experienced. Founded by the peasant emperor Zhu Yuanzhang (1328–98; AKA Ming Taizu or the Hongwu emperor), the Ming dynasty began as an agrarian state, conceived and institutionalized around the ideal of self-governing rural communities. Yet by the close of the dynasty, cities had impinged on the everyday reality of Chinese life. Through extensive urban networks, even staple grains and commercial crops such as cotton were integrated into empire-wide long-distance trade. For those in the succeeding dynasty, the Ming would be remembered for its urban glamour and material decadence. For historians today, the transition from an empire of villages to one of cities, though fraught with conflicts and confusion, marks the triumph of commercial power that defied and eventually prevailed over the oppressive grip of the state. The ascendancy of economic forces, however, is only one side of the radical transformation of the Ming empire. Equally important, albeit less dramatic, are the concurrent institutional reforms and cultural negotiations that bridged and reconciled the early Ming rural ideal and late Ming urbanization. After all, commerce could not have transformed Ming China without accommodations that enabled the dated imperial infrastructure to continue to function and that rendered disruptive social change meaningful. Many urban historical studies have illumined the rich economic, cultural, and social life of late Ming towns and cities. Few, however, have focused on the corresponding changes in state regulations and cultural interpretations of cities prompted by the growing influence of cities. This book is a study of urbanization that explores how the expanding roles and functions of cities led the idea of city to be reinvented, contested, and reconceived in the late Ming empire.

I approach this macro-transformation from a micro-perspective, using four case studies from a particular city—Nanjing—as entry points to observe changes in it as a walled community, as a metropolitan area, as an imagined space, and, finally, as a discursive subject. This vantage point allows us to see what was at stake for the urbanites during the transition. The unraveling of their endeavors further brings to the fore the centrality of urban space in the process. Most interestingly, although we might expect Nanjing residents to be drawn to issues such as street plans and the built environment essential to the workings of urban life, the concerns of locals extended far beyond the physicality of urban space. In each case study, we find great social efforts to negotiate the ways in which urban residents' lived space was regulated by state institutions and rendered through cultural works. The active involvement of Nanjing residents created a unique moment in Chinese history when urban space was not only a geographic location but also a point of social contention, open to political negotiation and cultural creation—a development that constitutes the core of this book.

Located in the northwestern corner of the lower Yangzi delta, Nanjing, literally the "Southern Capital," served as the primary capital for the first half-century of the Ming dynasty (1368–1421). During this period, the city underwent significant physical expansion with population growing to over half a million. In many ways, Ming Nanjing was a product of a great political undertaking.[1] Under the auspices of the founding emperor, Nanjing's walled space was significantly expanded and its metropolitan area (Yingtian prefecture) restructured. The expansive reconstruction entailed massive labor conscription and forced immigration from throughout the empire to materialize Zhu Yuanzhang's ideal capital, one that featured broad streets, grand palaces, and state-made residential quarters in service of government offices. This ideal vision for Nanjing was articulated in a series of printed urban plans the emperor personally and explicitly commissioned to provide an "imagined capital" for his subjects, most of whom would never see the grandeur of the capital in person. Political power, therefore, dominated not only the physical but also the imaginary cityscape of early Ming Nanjing.

The urban character of Nanjing, however, changed greatly in the following centuries. After a military coup d'état staged by a prince enfeoffed in northern China and his victory in the subsequent civil war at the beginning of the fifteenth century, the center of gravity of the imperium shifted to Beijing in 1421. Nanjing became a secondary capital, its population was halved, and its economy declined. Yet with the general prosperity in the sixteenth century and the city's prime location in Jiangnan, the most culturally and economically advanced area at the time, Nanjing revived as the Southern Metropolis (Nandu 南都). The transition from political capital to commercial metropolis was palpable in the city's everyday life. The influx of sojourners and their housing needs fractured Zhu's residential ward system and created a flourishing real estate market. Vendors encroached on the broad streets that had once been the pride of Nanjing, and the newcomers illegally occupied many government buildings.[2] The collision between commercial power and Zhu Yuanzhang's urban vision—a highly politicized, state-controlled space—transformed the cityscape of Nanjing, radically reshaping the lived space for urbanites.

The ramifications of this clash, however, extended far beyond the physical cityscape. As will be apparent from the four case studies, a distinctive social activism challenged the administration and conceptualization of urban space. In 1609, residents of Nanjing collectively volunteered tax information under one another's supervision in order to realize their long-term demand for a tax reform (Chapter 1). This reform led to the creation of an urban property tax for the first time in this dynasty. The action of the urban community redefined the inhabited space in fiscal terms. Nor was this political activism bound by the walls of Nanjing; it resonated within the greater metropolitan area. A traditional Chinese city did not constitute a formal political unit. Rather, it served as the administrative center of a greater region. The name Nanjing, as was true of Suzhou or Yangzhou, also referred to the prefectural region, a mostly rural area governed from the metropolis through a group of lower-level walled cities. In this extended sense of Nanjing, urban space was physically marked by a system of city walls symbolizing the state presence in the area. Yet such official demarcation of urban space was visibly compromised in 1597, when a popular protest in one of Nanjing's subordinate counties, Gaochun, dramatically overturned an imperial edict mandating construction of a city wall (Chapter 2).

In addition to political actions that challenged state-imposed definitions of urban space, there also appeared cultural products aimed at remolding the imagination and conception of the city. For instance, an illustrated guidebook, *Jinling tuyong* 金陵圖詠 (Illustrated odes on

Nanjing), depicts forty scenic spots and gives specific instructions on the ways the city was to be viewed (Chapter 3). This vision, as advocated by a group of native Nanjing elites, grew out of the cultural practice of landscape appreciation. It formed a stark contrast to the imperial vision of Zhu Yuanzhang. Not only was Nanjing being reimagined through visual projection, but the city was also becoming the subject of discourses at odds with the glorified accounts found in official local gazetteers. Two early seventeenth-century *ketan* 客談 (conversations with guests), for example, record conversations among urban elites about the city they inhabited (Chapter 4). Drawing largely on street news and gossip, these conversations present a vernacular rendition of Nanjing as a lived space. Widely circulated through a booming publishing industry and avidly consumed by the rapidly growing reading public, these well-received texts and images powerfully reshaped the popular imagination of Nanjing.

Although probably not deliberately, the actions and imagination of Nanjing residents in effect called into question the institutional prescription and cultural interpretation of urban space. How to determine if urban space was taxable or its boundary wallable? Given the changing role and function of the city, how should the heterogeneity of urban space be construed through images and texts? Although these challenges and responses studied in this book bear the distinct signature of the particular environment of Nanjing, in the final analysis they were driven by the transformations occurring in the Ming empire. By examining the institutional and cultural conjunctions at the heart of the Nanjing cases, this book hopes to uncover a new dimension of late Ming development, one deeply rooted in the mid-dynastic commercial boom and yet centered on cities.

AN UNTOLD STORY OF
LATE MING PROSPERITY

The Nanjing episodes took place at a remarkable moment in Chinese history marked by the advance of a monetarized economy supported by an influx of silver from Japan and the New World. It has been estimated that toward the end of China's "silver century" (1550–1650) at least 250,000–265,000 kilograms of foreign specie were exchanged for Chinese goods each year. China had become a major participant in the global economy. Monetization prevailed in the rural economy as cash crops and market-oriented specialization became dominant. Urban and rural handicraft production continued to grow, as did the labor market. Eventually even the government fiscal system became monetized when labor conscription was commuted into silver payments. The triumph of the market economy left such a profound imprint on a wide array of social and cultural developments that it has become an obligatory preface to late imperial Chinese studies.[3] With prosperity came expanded cultural horizons that liberated people from the rigorous hierarchies of gender and social order and created new opportunities to stake out domains of individual or corporate autonomy.[4] This newfound freedom, in Jonathan Spence's vivid phrase, epitomizes the "energies of Ming life."[5]

Contemporary elite observers, however, were much less enthusiastic about the rise in material wealth. The social energy unleashed by economic development profoundly challenged the prescribed social norms for an agrarian community. The clash between political and social forces created a fluid social scene, or the "floating world" in Dorothy Ko's words:

Traditional social distinctions—between high and low, merchant and gentry, male and female, respectable and mean—were idealized constructs best suited for a self-sufficient agrarian society. By the sixteenth century, these binary oppositions seemed at odds with the complexity of human relationships in the highly commercialized region. The ideal Confucian norms, devised to instill social harmony by perpetuating hierarchies and distinctions, became more prescriptive than descriptive, although they were no less powerful because of that.[6]

The erosion of cultural norms stirred deep anxieties among those less receptive to change. Grave concern over "corrupted social customs" was so prevalent that the general tone of contemporary social criticism and self-perception during this period was a strong sense of confusion.[7] In some extreme cases, the frequent transgressions of boundaries in public and private life were considered an indication of a monumental crisis. Indeed, in comparison with similar social critiques in the Song and Qing dynasties, scholars find that late Ming exhibited a far deeper sense of anxiety over social disorder and cultural crisis—"the whole country has gone mad," announced the editor of one gazetteer as he lamented that the reversal of social status had become the norm.[8] In response to the fear of impending social and moral collapse, the late

Ming witnessed a surge in publications aimed at reversing social disorder and re-establishing the proper boundaries between superior and inferior and between men and women. Voluminous records and biographies of chaste women and filial sons were published and widely circulated.[9] Manuals of genteel taste attempted to reclaim social distinction through the display of true refinement.[10] Paradoxically these cultural artifacts facilitated emulation of scholarly and social elites while further deepening anxiety over blurred social boundaries.

Yet, at the same time, intensifying social mobility and interaction also prompted extraordinary developments previously unknown in Chinese history, such as the prominent role played by "public opinion" in public affairs and an eccentric cultural scene with a strong populist undertone. The most radical strain of late Ming Neo-Confucianism, for example, announced that *dao* resides in the common people's everyday life and that sagehood is attainable by anyone regardless of social class or profession.[11] These trends were further enhanced by a flourishing publishing industry, through which political posters and pamphlets were easily produced and circulated and vernacular novels became so influential that "fiction" was said to rival the three teachings (Confucianism, Buddhism, and Daoism).[12]

The economic-social-cultural nexus of change that emerged from this period has marked the late Ming as an extraordinary chapter in Chinese history. This characterization of the late Ming moment—full of energetic, sometimes contradictory, changes—is at odds with an earlier view of the Ming as a downward turning point for Chinese civilization. Under this view, the drastic expansion of imperial autocracy under the Ming led to an inward-looking age of intellectual and technological stagnation in sharp contrast with "early modern" Europe spanning the Renaissance, the age of discovery, and the Reformation. With the surge of new literature in the field,[13] scholars have begun to regard late Ming developments as symbolizing the "sprouts of capitalism"[14] or as reflecting an indigenous early modernity in China.[15] Ongoing debates over nomenclature notwithstanding, a revisionist scenario centered on commerce-driven challenges to the prescribed order of social hierarchy in late imperial times appears to have gained firm ground.

The four case studies examined in this book both confirm and challenge the silver-driven late Ming narrative. The social and cultural de-

velopments prompted by the commercial boom did indeed play a critical role in these events. The tax movement was part of the empire-wide
fiscal reform that converted all levies into silver payments, a movement
that attests to the relentless tide of the silver economy. The anti-city-
wall protest echoes the surge of social conflicts, protests, and uprisings
resulting from the disruptive effects of the market economy on the prescribed social hierarchy. Similarly, the published images and discourses
about Nanjing are a product of the lively late Ming cultural industry.
The Nanjing tour guide—an example of the lifestyle guidebooks that
emerged during this period—embodies the intrusion of commercial
wealth into cultural life, as elites and their emulators sought guidance in
navigating the burgeoning consumer culture. At the same time, even as
greater social mobility created the need to reassert social distinction,
many literati began to look to the common people's world for inspiration. The newfound interest in popular culture was manifested in the
enthusiastic pursuits of novels and dramas based on current events, a
trend that led to the publishing of gossip in its most immediate form,
ketan, which featured juicy conversations in printed texts.

Closer examination shows, however, that the familiar elements in the
Nanjing cases also played out along unfamiliar lines: the grassroots tax
reform, in an effort to lessen the fiscal burden, strove to *create*, instead
of oppose, a new urban property tax; the popular protest against the
court's demand that Gaochun wall itself was directed not only at the
onerous fiscal and physical impositions from the state but also at what
a city wall symbolized—the status of an official city normally associated
with power and prestige. In the other cases, current historiography
proves to be similarly insufficient. For example, the editor of *Jinling
tuyong*, immediately after its well-received first publication, published a
second edition that included dozens of additional poems as well as a
historical atlas of Nanjing city, an editorial move that deviated drastically from the book's original format as a lifestyle manual for the aspiring newly wealthy. Furthermore, compared to the singular focus of
contemporary *ketan* on entertainment, the two Nanjing *ketan* studied
here appear to be more ambitious. They incorporate a significant
amount of discussion on urban administration and cultural explications
of the idea of "Nanjing." In other words, although the narrative woven
around the commercial boom can account for the occurrence of these

popular actions and creation of cultural products, it falls short of explicating their unique agendas.

The unraveling of the Nanjing cases brings into focus the limitations of the narrative of the late Ming triumph of commercial powers. Closing this historiographic gap requires a separate treatment of urbanization and its impacts apart from the generalized sweep of commercialization. Therefore, instead of folding the Nanjing cases into the wholesale changes wrought by late Ming prosperity, I focus the analysis on the new challenges to the administration and conceptualization of urban space faced by an urbanizing rural empire. For example, the lack of urban land tax in effect prevented the late Ming fiscal reforms from being extended to urban inhabitants, and this drove the popular demands for taxes in Nanjing. Yet why was urban space—in its most mundane form of land and property—deemed not taxable by the early Ming state? What problems did this absence of taxation cause for urban administration and how did urban residents campaign for a tax reform when the existing fiscal system recognized no urban taxes? Moreover, in light of the persistent state demand that official urban space be demarcated by city walls, it is not surprising that the protest against city-wall construction in Gaochun would provoke debates among residents on the very nature of their space and a challenge to the state decision to promote their market town into a county seat. It brought to the fore the underlying tension between the official urban hierarchy and market towns, whose proliferation in the sixteenth century prompted a new-found sense of identity for town dwellers. How did this development affect the management of commercial and official city systems in the Ming empire?

By the same token, only by viewing the Nanjing images and texts as part of the shared cultural responses to an expanding urban society can we fully appreciate the rich messages embedded in them. In light of the rising importance of cultured sightseeing in major late Ming cities, the expanded edition of *Jinling tuyong* exemplifies the continuous efforts of native Nanjing elites to detach the imaginary of Nanjing from Hong-wu's grand vision and reanchor it to local landmarks. The unusually rich contents of Nanjing *ketan*, I will argue, reflect the growing interests and concerns of a new breed of urban elites toward their lived space as a result of the influx of rural gentry into cities. The questions to ask are:

Why did urban literati choose these particular formats to articulate their perceptions of urban life and what new conceptualization of urban space arose from these cultural works?

These questions are of central concern in this book. Taken together, they challenge the current view of urbanization as an automatic by-product of commercialization and the city as the site in which many of the silver-driven social and cultural developments materialized with higher frequency and greater density. Above all, the case studies of Nanjing indicate that the ramifications of urbanization cannot be reduced to the mere intensification of commercial influences.[16] This distinction is particularly relevant to Ming China, an empire initially conceived and institutionalized around the ideal of self-governing rural communities. Because of urbanization, the growing number and increasing size of cities brought enhanced commercial efficiency, social mobility, and cultural interaction, all contrary to the expectations of the dynasty's institutional infrastructure and ideological premises. The chasm between the original system and the emerging social reality became the source of widely felt discontent and confusion: How to reinvent the fiscal foundation for an urbanizing rural empire? How to effectively manage and balance the proliferation of commercial towns with the official walled cities? How to render the heterogeneity of urban space through images and texts when the function of the city could no longer be defined only in political/administrative terms? In the wake of the sixteenth-century boom, the Ming empire confronted a host of increasingly pressing "urban questions," each requiring revision of the idea of the city.

Viewed from this perspective, the story threading through the four case studies of this book relates how Nanjing residents responded to and negotiated with these urban questions. The advantages of this approach is manifold. First, it allows us to consider urbanization as a willed process, in which local initiatives play a key role.[17] The emphasis on the reactions of historical actors to their time further makes it clear that what we observe in Nanjing is both general and unique. General in that the developments in Nanjing were ultimately driven by urban questions as the Ming empire strove to cope with the ramifications of urbanization. Yet at the same time unique, as repeatedly demonstrated in the following chapters, the responses and reactions in Nanjing were only part of a wide spectrum of possibilities created by urban residents at the time.* That is, Nanjing is representative not because other contemporary cities adopted the same courses of action but because the same challenges and demands similarly motivated urban residents elsewhere to respond and react, albeit in their own terms. The search for common ground, I believe, does not have to be confined to locating uniform patterns of behavior, for this assumption undervalues the innate creativity of human agency. What ties members of society together is not the replication of actions but the shared circumstances that prompt them to act in the first place—in this case, the problems facing cities. Finally, the focus on the interplay between micro-developments in Nanjing and the macro-transformation of the Ming empire foregrounds the fact that the nature of and responses to these urban questions are in many ways unique to the Ming dynasty, a finding that sheds new light on the nature of urbanization and urbanism in late imperial China.

A DYNASTY-CENTERED APPROACH

In highlighting the urban transformation of the late Ming empire, this book restores the concept of dynasty to the study of Chinese cities. This analytical framework calls attention to the impact of institutional infrastructure and shared cultural trends on the nature and consequences of urbanization in a centralized, rural empire. Such an approach is particularly relevant to the field of Chinese urban history since urbanization is rarely considered in the context of a particular dynasty.[18] This tendency is curious in view of the rather disparate attitudes toward cities of the various dynasties of the past millennium. For instance, in contrast to the institutional centrality of rural communities in the early Ming system, cities served as the governing base for the ruling minorities (Mongols and Manchus) in the multiethnic colonial empires

---

*This is not to suggest that Nanjing's developments are always one of a kind but, rather, to advocate a more nuanced and accurate case-by-case evaluation of Nanjing's scenarios. In some cases (such as the creation of urban land tax in Chapter 1), Nanjing does represent the most typical solution—but by no means *the* solution—at the time. Such comparison also enables us to better identify the truly innovative in Nanjing (such as the significance of the populist measures in Ding Bin's *huojia* reform, also discussed in Chapter 1).

of the Yuan and the Qing. And the state-driven economic activism practiced by the Song, like the Ming a Han-centered dynasty, resulted in a much more intensive urban taxation scheme than the Ming imposed.[19] Despite these differences, however, little attention has been paid to studying and comparing how these factors affected urban developments in different dynasties.

This oversight is to a great extent rooted in the persistent pursuit of a China-centered urbanism (i.e., the particular form and dynamic of Chinese urban development).* Interest in the idea of "the city" and its specific formulation in China can be traced to Max Weber's studies in the early twentieth century. Grounded in his unique definition of "the city," Weber's thesis contended that the essence of Western modernity lay in its distinctive urban societies. Challenging the conventional definition of cities according to population density or the fulfillment of specific political or military functions, Weber maintained that only from the presence of autonomous urban communities could we ascertain the existence of cities—or, rather, the ideal type of cities. Under this criterion, imperial Chinese cities, dominated by particularistic social relations (attached to native villages) and the administrative needs of imperial governance, were deemed the antithesis of the occidental cities that had served as precursors to the modern era.[20]

Provocative and polemical, Weber's verdict on Chinese cities has been very influential in shaping the *Problematik* of the field.[21] Weber's *longue durée* perspective, which considered cities as a benchmark not for individual dynasties but for Chinese civilization as a whole, influenced even his most vehement opponents such as G. William Skinner.[22] Countering Weber's portrayal of Chinese cities as marginal to state power and irrelevant to historical development, Skinner's thesis successfully reclaimed a place for cities in late imperial China and remapped the country around a nested urban hierarchy.[23] Skinner's model not only reformulated the spatial conceptualization of Chinese empires

---

*There appears to be no clear consensus among scholars on the use and connotations of the term "urbanism." This book adopts a historicized view of urbanism, referring to a particular form and nature of urbanization at a specific time and space; see, e.g., "Baroque Urbanism" in Lees and Hohenberg, *The Making of Urban Europe*, pp. 137–78. In other words, although "urbanization" refers to quantitative changes in urban settlement, "urbanism" emphasizes the qualitative development of the process.

but also revolutionized the narrative of urban history, establishing a timeline of Chinese urbanism independent of dynastic chronology. In Skinner's schema, Chinese cities underwent the most significant transformation rather early, between the tenth and thirteenth centuries. Before this change, Chinese cities were mainly administrative centers populated by officials and their families as primary consumers. During this time period, a shift in the primary role of Chinese cities from political to economic demolished the previously rigorous city planning that had created controlled marketplaces and segregated quarters. What emerged were major metropolises with as many as a million residents. The second important change occurred during the sixteenth-century commercial boom, when domestic commerce began to progress beyond interurban exchanges of luxury goods to intraregional markets for daily necessities such as grains and commercial crops. As a result, cities came to penetrate Chinese life at a much deeper level, playing central roles as nodes of commodity exchange, social interaction, and cultural exposure. Yet even though Skinner's thesis successfully rescues Chinese cities from Weber's Europe-centered teleology, it still measures the nature and changes of Chinese urbanism against the *longue durée* development of a market economy spanning several dynastic boundaries.

The influence of Skinner's thesis could not be more profound. It refutes the essentialist characterization of "the city" in Chinese civilization by considering the development of urban space as an active and ongoing historical process. Demonstrating that market-driven urbanization indeed redefined the spatial order of imperial China, Skinner successfully destroyed Weber's dichotomy between the Occidental and Oriental city. This insight allows scholars to re-evaluate the historical role of Chinese cities and revisit issues regarding the political and cultural ramifications of late imperial urbanization. First, embedded in a vast agrarian empire, did cities command the same level of cultural centrality in Chinese life as their European counterparts? In particular, can we identify a coherent and sustaining "urban tradition" in Chinese cultural practice? Second, essential to Weber's characterization of the ideal type of city that served as the precursor of modernity is a self-identified urban community pressing for political rights from the monarchy. Were Chinese cities, buttressed by their commercial clout, able to develop a special power relationship with the imperial state?

In sharp contrast to Skinner's optimism regarding continuous urban growth, scholars find that, despite the strong tides of market-driven urbanization, the increasing presence of cities in Chinese life in the past millennium did not formally factor into institutional and cultural practices. The conceptualization of urbanity was subject to an enduring rural-centered cultural paradigm, and urban autonomy took on a highly situational form outside state institutions. These findings lead to the inevitable conclusion that the nature and consequences of urbanization in a vast, centralized, agrarian empire such as China are so different from those in Europe that historians should acknowledge the Chinese case as a distinctive form of urbanism in its own right rather than a matter of deficiencies and flaws.[24] However, although highlighting the particularity of Chinese urbanism, this formulation also inadvertently suggests that enduring cultural and institutional inertia toward the expanding urban realm was the norm prior to the advent of Western influence in the modern era. The pursuit of a China-centered urbanism has thus led the field to a conceptual impasse.

This dilemma, this book argues, derives from the fact that the seemingly continuous urban expansion was punctuated by a wide variety of "dynastic urbanisms." Instead of being an automatic byproduct of *longue durée* commercialization, urbanization in late imperial China was a process shaped by institutional and cultural practices particular to each dynasty. This insight allows us to move beyond the dichotomy of Chinese- and European-style urbanism and focus on the specific terms of Chinese urbanism in each dynasty. Studying urbanism under a more nuanced time frame, however, is not just a matter of reorganizing historical sources; it requires a new methodology for approaching the cultural and political effects of late imperial urbanization. The following section reviews the development of these two lines of inquiry in the field so as to establish a proper analytical scheme for this book.

The Cultural Effects of Urbanization

The Urban-Rural Continuum Thesis. The centrality of cities in economic development—well established by Skinner—does not extend into the cultural realm. On the contrary, many scholars are convinced of the persistence of rural dominance over Chinese urban culture. This view can be traced to Weber's conjuncture that, measured against European cities, Chinese cities exhibited a high degree of rural dependence that perpetuated "rural attitudes" and hindered the formation of an urban merchant class.[25] With a much firmer command of Chinese culture, Frederick Mote reformulated Weber's dim assessment into a unique rural-urban continuum that distinguished China from the world's urban traditions. Mote's thesis conceives a Chinese city as culturally and politically an "open institution" that displayed no distinct boundaries from the countryside in terms of administration, lifestyles, architecture, and the like.[26]

Mote's characterization of the urban-rural continuum, as indicated in the title "A Millennium of Chinese Urban History," aims to offer a sweeping generalization of Chinese urbanism since the Tang-Song urban revolution.[27] The signature of this urbanism, ironically, lies in its dependence on rural culture. Mote goes as far as to state that "the rural component of Chinese civilization was more or less uniform, and it extended everywhere that Chinese civilization penetrated. It, and not the cities, defined the Chinese way of life."[28] As a result, despite the continuous urbanization of late imperial China, the "urban" still failed to register in the political, social, and, above all, cultural realms. In Mote's opinion, "there may have been a trend toward concentration of the elite in cities as places of domicile in the later imperial era, but it was at best a trend; throughout the traditional period in Chinese social history, the elite was widely diffused in space, and psychologically oriented toward as many rural ties as urban ones."[29] In other words, despite the increasing concentration of elite residents and cultural and economic resources in Ming-Qing cities, the urban-rural continuum prevailed in the Chinese psyche and prevented the development of a distinct urban tradition in imperial China.

The Urban-Rural Continuum Revisited. Since the appearance of Mote's thesis in the 1970s, the academic landscape has undergone drastic changes. Above all, the great cultural divide described by Mote has been shrunken considerably from both sides by new scholarship. The European urban-rural dichotomy cited by Mote has been much modified by revisionist studies that emphasize the interconnectedness of cities and countryside in the early modern era.[30] At the same time, the many social and cultural studies on Ming and Qing cities have also demonstrated that the "urban concentration" in late imperial times involved not just quantitative congregations of people and resources but also significant alterations in the fabric of life. For example, contrary to Mote's claim, new studies on material culture and urban consumption have forcefully established the importance of cities in creating fashions and consumption patterns at the time. Most prominent was the city of Suzhou. Under its sway, the term *Suyang* 蘇樣 (Suzhou style) became synonymous with taste and fashion in contemporary minds. The rising importance of urban consumption lent additional cultural valence to taste as a form of status distinction and ultimately prompted radical thinkers to advocate spending on luxuries as a spur to overall economic development.[31]

The new role of cities as centers for commercial activity and cultural consumption attracted a broad spectrum of visitors seeking career opportunities or simply entertainment. The influx of sojourners gave rise to an increasingly active social scene in major cities in the empire. Public spaces such as urban gardens, teahouses, temples, and courtesan salons provided physical grounds for heightened social interactions through which new ties were developed outside traditional kinship or native-place affiliations. For the well-educated, the abundant opportunities for networking and cultural activities in cities even created alternative careers outside the prescribed path to officialdom through the civil service examinations. Even the less cultivated became increasingly connected through a shared world of print news and gossip, the circulation of which was greatly enhanced by the flourishing printing industry.[32] The informed and oftentimes politicized urban mass formed the social base for the growing frequency and scale of collective action in Ming and Qing cities, which ranged from food riots, protests against fiscal policies, wage disputes, and strikes to open opposition against the tenure of controversial local officials.[33] Although formally granted political rights were still far off, the opinions and actions of the urban public began to play a visible role in contemporary politics.

In many ways, although cities were not official administrative units, they indeed developed into de facto social and political entities operating on very different principles from the countryside. The unique social structure of cities provoked administrative concerns that were distinctly urban in nature and required solutions different from those used for rural problems. The uniqueness of "urban" issues was clearly recognized by contemporary elites. As more and more gentry moved into nearby towns and cities and became absentee landlords, they began to play an active role in urban affairs. In many case studies, scholars are repeatedly struck by the "specific preoccupation of both urban elites and urban administrators with *urban* problems, both groups being completely accustomed to assuming the discreteness of the municipal unit as a locus of managerial responsibilities."[34] In other words, the institutionally perpetuated rural bias was not as inhibitive of political awareness among urbanites as Mote thought.

Urban Identity Vs. Urban-Rural Distinction.   The new findings in the field, interestingly, have not rendered Mote's thesis obsolete but prompted an updated revision from a very different branch of scholarship, one that combines archival work and anthropological field research. This approach has proved fruitful in understanding popular perception of the swift commercialization and urbanization that in so many respects remolded the lives and livelihood of Chinese people. Drawing together works by scholars from Europe, the United States, and China, the edited volume *Town and Country in China: Identity and Perception* renews Mote's thesis from the perspective of popular religions by extending the concept of the urban-rural continuum from architectural styles and elite aesthetics to ritual performance. The editors contend that urban-rural distinctions did not become a significant part of an individual's identity in China until the twentieth century when "political reforms separated cities and towns as agents of social change, [and] an ideology emerge[d] that looked upon villages as the source of backwardness." The urban-rural distinction was so external to traditional Chinese thought that "the search for the urban tradition within traditional China ends in anachronism."[35] Fully aware of the commercial developments in late imperial times that rendered cities a distinct realm for social practices, scholars in this volume find it necessary to distinguish between social history and cultural paradigm.[36] That is, the apparent urban-rural differentiation in social reality had no recognizable impact on Chinese identity. What dominated Chinese people's view of their lived space, argue the editors, was an all-pervasive paradigm, defined by the administrative structure of the bureaucracy, that denied the distinction between urban and rural areas.

The dominance of a state-centered view of space, however, does not necessarily imply the triumph of the suppressive power of the state. On the contrary, by adopting the language of the state, David Faure argues, township leaders were able to keep power in local hands. Yet also because of this, the growing importance of market towns did not give rise to an ideology highlighting town-country differentiation.[37] In addition to the functionalist explanation, Henrietta Harrison suggests that we should consider the seemingly curious obliviousness to the urban-rural distinction in the larger context of boundary-making. In her case study of Taiyuan (Shanxi), she finds that the urban-rural distinction generated by social and economic developments paled in comparison to other territorial divisions (i.e., the urban-rural division was subordinated to the differences between Taiyuan and other counties or between mountain and plain areas in Taiyuan). The obscured sense of urban-rural division, in other words, arose from the fact that the communal boundaries generated by religious practices substantially crosscut marketing and administrative hierarchies, resulting in a society in which "political, marketing, and religious centers could all have social characteristics which we would define as urban, but the clear differentiation between the different types of hierarchies meant that they were not perceived as such."[38] Contrary to Mote's argumentation, Harrison argues that it was not the lack of an urban-rural distinction but rather an overabundance of such divisions that constituted the urban-rural continuum in traditional China.

These expositions of the obscuring of urban identity in late imperial China, albeit compelling, do not inherently exclude any form of cultural articulation of urban sentiments or experiences. It is curious, then, that the editors of this volume argue for the incompatibility of an urban-rural distinction and traditional Chinese thought. As the title of the volume rightly suggests, "identity" and "perception" are two related and yet separate components of Mote's urban-rural continuum thesis. To be sure, identities in China often manifest themselves through a matrix of competition, and there might well be a hierarchy of spatial identities in place in which, for strategic or ideological reasons, the urban-rural division was not a dominant factor.[39] Yet it is quite a different matter to claim a collective apathy toward the urban—to insist that a rural-centered cultural paradigm (for Mote, it is part of a national psyche) consistently prevented the perception and articulation of urbanity in an age of rapid urbanization. To better distinguish the two, we need to take a close look at the substance of this proposed cultural paradigm. Similar to Mote's emphasis on the rural lifestyle and pastoral aesthetic found in Nanjing or Suzhou, David Faure and Taotao Liu contend that despite the seemingly distinct appearance of great administrative cities, "when one searches in towns and villages for the rural tradition, one finds very much the same beliefs and customs as in the administrative cities."[40] In other words, the most tangible evidence for this paradigm lies in the unity of cultural performance across the urban-rural continuum.

However, this cultural unity proves superficial and deceptive—not only for historians but also for contemporaries as well. Although the idealization of rural life remained a recurring theme in literati painting and literature in the late Ming, a well-developed urban-based elite community added a new twist to the rhetorical yearning for rural life. As one Nanjing luminary, Gu Qiyuan, observed, urban glamour had evidently prevailed on his peers. Many reconciled this conflict between the draw of the metropolis and their bucolic yearnings by building a garden in their grand urban mansions as a gesture toward the rural ideal (as Gu himself did). Even the so-called *shanren* 山人 (mountain inhabitants), who flaunted a reputation as lofty rural eremites, used their rural residences as facades to mask frequent trips into town.[41] The novel *Tale of Marriage Destinies* 醒世姻緣傳 is another case in point. It portrays the fall of a utopian self-contained agricultural community, Mingshui, as it develops into a market town and becomes engulfed by material indulgence and moral decadence. Daria Berg, however, finds that beneath the didactic lamentations over the fall of Mingshui lie rather mixed emotions. The spectacle of human depravity also provides a way to escape the lethargic boredom of the rural utopia. Although the rural idyll still retained its utopian lure, late Ming literati found themselves increasingly entangled in city life and torn between escapism and an addiction to the cosmopolitan world.[42]

These examples foreground the importance of reading cultural texts and images against contemporary social praxis. One telling example is the development of the genre of *yongjing* 詠景 (textual and visual appre-

ciation of scenes), which had developed into a prominent representational mode in late imperial times. *Yongjing* distill a place into a series of
scenic snapshots—*jing* 景 (prospects). Dictated by literati aesthetics that
idealized a bucolic lifestyle, *jing* almost always are pastoral. Just as the
urban-rural continuum thesis predicts, the production of *jing* largely
failed to register cityscapes and urban glamour of even major cities.[43]
Despite the weight of tradition, however, details of bustling city life still
found their way into *jing* representations. For example, *Hainei qiguan*
海内奇觀 (Fantastic spectacles within the realm), a collection of empire-
wide tourist attractions published in 1609, includes one urban scene depicting the night market in Beiguan, a busy marketplace in Hangzhou.
More significantly, the appreciation of scenic sites, when conducted in
cities, became a practice that created solidarity among urban elites, a
development first brought to light by Tobie Meyer-Fong's study of
Yangzhou. Through her vivid portrayal of this major port city in the
late seventeenth century, we learn that Yangzhou, in the wake of a
highly disruptive dynastic transition, became a popular venue for leisure
touring and social gatherings. The reconstruction and celebration of the
city's famous sites allowed its elite sightseers—men of divergent political allegiances—to present themselves as members of a single class of
urban elites. What Meyer-Fong observes in early Qing Yangzhou is in
fact the continuation of a late Ming development—touring as a means
for urban literati to form social ties.[44] What appears to be a rural-
centered aesthetic was appropriated as a constituent element in the
formation of urban society.

By the same token, the lack of definitive architectural differentiation
between the city and the countryside does not necessarily imply no differentiation between urban and rural spaces.[45] For instance, recent studies such as Yinong Xu's work on Suzhou demonstrates that although
the seemingly indistinguishable appearances of flat buildings and court-
yards constitute the basic units of Chinese built environments, ostensibly similar spaces could still be appropriated for different functions.
The most telling example can be found in the Xuanmiao Guan (a Daoist temple) complex at the center of Suzhou city, which served as a site
for worship, association meetings, business, entertainment, and other
aspects of social life. The versatility of a single site was realized not
through formal prescription but through social practice.[46]

Indeed, these new studies effectively contest the efficacy of an all-powerful cultural paradigm that refused to grant urban space formal recognition by embedding it in a rural-dominated cultural unity. As this review has proposed, with an influx of human and material resources, qualitative changes arose in perceiving the "city" as a political, social, and, above all, conceptual entity distinct from the countryside. What misleads us is that these changes were registered in a cultural language shared across the urban-rural divide. The seeming uniformity in architectural styles or art genres such as *yongjing*, when applied in the urban environment, could also serve as effective vehicles for the articulation of urbanity. In other words, instead of creating a separate urban cultural tradition, urbanites appropriated the shared cultural language to express their spatial experiences. It is thus the underlying social practices, not the formats used to embody them, that dictate the meaning of urbanites' cultural expressions. To fully appreciate the messages conveyed in city images and urban literature, as demonstrated in the second half of this book, we need to take into account the social activities that led to their creation. This approach, moreover, allows us to see that the articulation of urbanity was far from an exercise in philosophical abstraction. Through the reinventing of existing literary genres and cultural practices, new social ties were formed and a sense of society articulated.

The Political Effects of Urbanization

The Issue of Urban Autonomy.   A second line of post-Weberian scholarship focuses on the formation of urban communities and their power relationship to the imperial state. The most important work on urban autonomy is William Rowe's two-volume work on Hankow, which traces the development of the city between 1796 and 1895.[47] Rowe found a surge of urban institution-building efforts in Hankow during the nineteenth century as merchants assumed increasing responsibilities in public affairs and achieved more and more latitude to regulate their own economic activities. The growth in number, functional range, and systemic linkage of these institutions amounted to the popularization of local governance. Moreover, this spontaneous and intense participation in public life facilitated a sense of solidarity and an impetus to communal self-nurturance that transcended kinship and native-place ties.[48] This development, Rowe argues, attests to the emergence of an autonomous urban community indigenous to traditional China.

This finding powerfully refutes Weber's dichotomy between Occidental and Oriental cities, placing China back on the map of global moder-nity. In Rowe's view, an indigenous form of early modernity emerged in China between the increase in long-distance trade in the late sixteenth century and the advent of factory-based industry in the last decade of the nineteenth century. During this time period, many Chinese cities "shared a sufficient number of basic features with their Western counterparts to justify [viewing] the two as comparable social units."[49] Hankow, for example, exhibits the main traits of early modern European cities such as "the steady development of organized, corporate-style civic action and the proliferation of a wide range of philanthropic and public service institutions."[50] The conscious process of urban institution building in Hankow yielded increasingly formalized autonomous groups and organizations, ranging from guild federations to benevolent halls to fire brigade networks to local defense militia. Rowe argues that the advent of these community groups marked the emergence of a "public sphere"[51] in late imperial China, a monumental development despite its unfortunate demise in the twentieth century.[52]

The appearance of Rowe's claim of a public sphere in the wake of the 1989 Beijing Tian'anmen Square massacre provoked great interest and controversy in the China field. The scholars who participated in this debate came from various disciplines, and the periods investigated ranged from the early seventeenth century to contemporary China.[53] Although observers generally agree that corporate groups and voluntary associations were plentiful in premodern China and that public participation was an essential element of late imperial Chinese urban life, there appears to be no consensus whether such affiliations can be identified as signs of a public sphere in late imperial China.

In particular, central to the public-sphere debate is an assumed antithesis between autonomy and collaboration and between state and society. After all, how autonomous could Hankow elites be if the privileges they enjoyed depended largely on official patronage?[54] The insistent presence of the state in the elite managerial public sphere is observable in many other areas, such as community granaries and charity schools.[55] Thus in comparison to the situation in European cities, the interests of gentry and officials were more complementary and their relations less antagonistic.[56] The intertwining state-society relations have led scholars to seek alternative schemata.[57] Philip Huang, for example, suggests that a hybrid category between the state and society might better capture the actual historical dynamics in China where the continued collaboration between the state and society seems more striking than either growing societal autonomy or increasing bureaucratic control. He proposes to characterize the public sphere by a trinary structure, rather than the state-society dichotomy implied in the original model, to allow for the concept of a "third realm," one that is between state and society and yet one in which both participated.[58] In a similar vein, Frederic Wakeman urges a more fluid view on state-society relations in China, that the field "might gain a better sense of political legitimacy in late imperial China by devoting less attention to the appearance (or absence) of autonomous, norm-shaping institutions outside of government, giving greater consideration instead to activities along the ever-shifting boundary between 'public' and 'official' during several periods of literati political participation under the Ming and Qing dynasties."[59] In particular, social activism should not be conceived along the dividing line between "public" (*gong* 公) and "official" (*guan* 官) but as nested hierarchies whose domains were determined by social practice.[60]

  From Public Sphere to Public Space. In brief, these revisionist efforts reflect the emerging view in the field that the energetic public life[61] of late imperial cities was undergirded by a persistent state presence whose power and authority were never formally conceded to social groups but which could in practice be negotiated and appropriated. They call for a new conceptual protocol that acknowledges such ambiguity while still retaining analytical efficacy. A new trend in the field is to move away from fixed conceptual constructs such as "public sphere" toward a greater focus on the actual operations of urban "*public* spaces." Two new studies on Beijing exemplify this development.

  The first work is Susan Naquin's *Peking: Temples and City Life, 1400–1900*. As Philip Kuhn aptly points out in a review, what Naquin demonstrates in this detailed study of urban life in Beijing is that "the public had 'spaces' but no 'sphere.'"[62] The word "temples" in this work is defined broadly to include other urban institutions such as guildhalls and native-place lodges that often conducted their own ritual observances. Naquin establishes the connection between temple spaces and the mosaic-like social landscape of Beijing (composed of sojourning compatriots, ritual associations, occupational groups, foreign ethnics, and the like) by showing that urban public spaces accrued different meanings through social practice. For example, during the Qing, of the Beijing temples patronized by the Ming court, at least 34 served as sites for festivals, 22 for charitable activities (official or nonofficial), 12 for markets, 10 for pilgrimages, 89 for popular tourist attractions, and at least 7 for informal political organizing. One third of them later acquired private sponsors, including merchants, religious associations, or ordinary people.[63] The versatility of these sites allowed them to serve as the "focus for community-building and identity-defining activities. . . . Their relative autonomy from family or state control was reflected in—indeed in important ways constituted through—use of this space."[64] The latitude Beijing urbanites enjoyed in their appropriation of public spaces was never formally granted; rather, it was acquired via political negotiation and social practice. For the most part, negotiation was accomplished through informal ties to the state; social practice simply added another layer of activity to temple spaces by using them as marketplaces and entertainment sites.[65]

Such liberty in appropriating public spaces does not imply a public sphere independent of the state. The prescriptive boundaries between state and urban society were too ambiguous and unstable for us to reach a conceptual conclusion.[66] Instead, Naquin suggests, "The formal precariousness of these organizations, the participation of people who were part of the state structure, and the absence of language of independence or opposition makes teleological comparisons with a later and ostensibly autonomous European 'public sphere' dangerous and probably inappropriate."[67] Still, it is clear that even without formal official sanction, the public spaces that played a crucial role in urban life could be appropriated through political negotiation and social practice.

In other words, in clear recognition that Chinese cities did not enjoy institutionally sanctioned legal rights, scholars are looking for a more nuanced and situational approach to untangle the complicated issue of urban autonomy. Richard Belsky's work on native-place lodges in Ming and Qing Beijing is a case in point.[68] Moving beyond the debate on the communal or particularistic nature of native-place lodges, he shifts the focus to the area hosting these native-place lodges and examines it as a public space mediating the political center and localities. Belsky finds that this particular public space served different functions at various junctures in history and its political influence peaked during the late nineteenth-century reform era. What emerges from these studies is a vision of a much more fluid relation between the state and cities, contingent on the particular public space carved out by individual groups and associations at different moments and places.

During the long journey since Weber first put forth his characterization of Chinese cities, historians have come to see that, despite the lack of well-established legal boundaries, we can still locate urban autonomy and agency in imperial cities, even if they took on highly situational and amorphous forms. However, although this localized approach provides a historically grounded concept of power and social agency, by relegating urban autonomy to informal arrangements and institutional ambiguities, it ironically perpetuates the Weberian argument that the Chinese imperial state was so bound by its rural base that political changes in cities could be made only outside state institutions. After all, the fact that the state did not grant formal legal status to the city does not necessarily preclude institutional adjustments to accommodate the growing presence of cities in the empire. The first half of this book, therefore, hopes to demonstrate that the demands of governing an increasingly urbanized society indeed prompted institutional reformulation of urban space. That is, while following the argument of China historians that urban autonomy does not reside in formal independence from state authority but rather in the negotiations between state agencies and urban residents, this investigation will take the further step of looking into how local initiatives prevailed at the institutional level.

URBANIZATION IN A RURAL EMPIRE: OVERVIEW AND ORGANIZATION

The preceding review has positioned the argument of this book in relation to the main approaches to late imperial urbanization. Either inspired by Weber or motivated to prove him wrong, scholars have made significant headway in uncovering the side of Chinese urbanism that eluded Weber's attention: one that features a continuously expanding urban realm emerging on the economic, cultural, and political landscapes. As historians move away from Weber, it becomes clear that cities should not be reified as an index for Chinese civilization. As such, the significance of urbanization can be measured only through the particular ways by which cities registered in Chinese society. In this direction, Skinner's model explicates how late imperial urbanization spawned a market-driven spatial hierarchy that fundamentally restructured economic activities. In contrast, our understanding of the effects of urbanization on Chinese cultural and political life is much less clear.

On one hand, in light of the complex ties between cities and the countryside in an agrarian empire such as China, Mote's "urban-rural continuum" thesis contended that, despite urbanization, the supremacy of rural culture prevented a well-defined perception of the "urban" from taking shape. As this review has made clear, however, the preponderant attention to the countryside, even in the extreme case of the Ming, did not prohibit the emergence of cultural practices expressing sentiments and needs unique to urban environments; it was only that they were registered through the same cultural vocabularies across the urban-rural division. Thus, the questions this book asks are: How did urbanites reinvent existing cultural forms to articulate their spatial experiences? What was the conceptualization of urbanity that emerged from such cultural practices?

On the other hand, the central issue regarding the political ramifications of urban growth also remains unresolved: Did cities develop a new power relationship with the state? The debates on public sphere and civic society have made clear that China did not develop institutionally sanctioned spaces for cities. New studies have found the distinctive social composition and functions of cities indeed prompted urban residents to seek compromises and strike bargains with the government over the use of their lived spaces. Thus, the interaction between the imperial state and urban society is best characterized as continuous negotiation in response to the changing nature and needs of urban society. This book takes this view a step further, arguing that such social initiatives did not stop at informal arrangements such as the appropriation of public spaces but in fact forced changes and adjustments at the institutional level.

Taken together, the two main lines of analysis in this book foreground the singular importance of social praxis in negotiating the meaning of urban space. The goal of such praxis, most important, was not to create novel developments of urban autonomy or a well-defined urban tradition as prescribed by Weber or Mote, but to effect changes in the idea of the city through *existing* institutional and cultural schemes. Furthermore, this process appears to have progressed under a different time frame than the conventional view of *longue durée* urbanization. Under the influence of Skinner's periodization of Chinese urbanization, studies on late imperial cities tend to view urban development between the Song and the Qing as continuous—only with qualitative vicissitudes according to economic conditions. However, the development observable in Ming Nanjing argues that the nature and consequences of urban growth cannot be measured only by the expansion of commercial capacity; rather, institutional and cultural adjustments also need to be taken into account. A full appreciation of late Ming urbanization, as this book demonstrates, requires a dynasty-centered approach, since its particular course of development was fundamentally shaped by a host of institutional and cultural preconceptions established at the very inception of the Ming dynasty.

The dynasty-centered view, finally, shifts the analytical center of the book from the polarity between the state and society. Instead, the discussion focuses on the tension between the early Ming rural ideal and late Ming urban development and the resultant urban questions that compels *both* the society and the state to respond and adjust with available institutional and cultural resources. This process, in turn, helped define the specific terms and characteristics of late Ming urbanism—a unique feature that I revisit and develop further in the Conclusion.

To unravel the process of re-envisioning the late Ming against the early Ming vision of cities, nevertheless, is a more complicated task than it appears. The enduring influence of the founding emperor, Zhu Yuanzhang, in shaping the trajectory of the Ming empire has attracted great scholarly attention. Yet most studies have focused on his policy of self-sustained agrarian communities, which formed the basis of the last native empire in Chinese history. Indeed, other than Zhu's distrust of urban residents and his well-known apprehension concerning the social value of their means of livelihood, the "Ming constitution" instituted by Zhu betrays little of his urban vision.[69] To uncover the urban plan of the Ming empire, we must substitute artifacts for texts. In the absence of urban policies in court directives and official memorials, Nanjing, the capital city Zhu Yuanzhang built for his empire, becomes the best available source.

In this light, Nanjing, in addition to its rich visual and textual materials, offers a precious vantage point for us to study the characteristics of Ming urbanism. Guided by the action and imagination of Nanjing-ness, the chapters that follow explore the continuous negotiation over the institutional (Chapters 1 and 2) and the conceptual (Chapters 3 and 4) constitution of urban space engaged in by both the state and the society. In brief, Chapter 1 looks closely at the Nanjing tax reform, examining how challenges to the administration of urban space during the late Ming fiscal reforms brought the residents together in the same cause. Chapter 2 expands the focus to the Nanjing Metropolitan Area, studying the management of city systems under the jurisdiction of Nanjing. Chapter 3 approaches the issue of "imagined Nanjing" through the production and social uses of city images, especially the ways in which Nanjing elites countered the state-imposed vision of their city by producing manuals advocating their own ways of looking at Nanjing. Finally, Chapter 4 directly confronts the idea of the "city" by exploring the conceptual ties between urbanites and the space they inhabited through a close reading of two early seventeenth-century *ketan*, collections of recorded conversations among urban elites about the city that they inhabited.

The analysis throughout the book is dictated by the constant interplay between the microcosm of Nanjing and the underlying macro-developments as the empire strove to cope with the ramifications of urbanization. The dialectic between the micro and the macro allows us to keep sight of the agency of historical subjects in shaping the course of their own history while exploring general trends in the Ming empire that made their innovations possible. The Conclusion draws on the macro-trends emerging from the four chapters and develops a more historically grounded approach to cities and urbanism in late imperial China.

"We Must Be Taxed"

On a momentous day in 1609, the streets of Nanjing were thronged with people engaged in an unusual activity—they were voluntarily supplying information to the government so that they could be taxed. For decades, locals had unsuccessfully petitioned the government to launch an urban fiscal reform that would rescue many people from bankruptcy and jail. Finally, Nanjing residents decided to take matters into their own hands. Since the main barriers to reform cited by the government were the lack of local consensus and urban tax registries, community leaders proposed that each neighborhood supply a registry to the government. Over the period of a few days, over a thousand tax registers were compiled and submitted. Soon thereafter, more than a thousand Nanjing residents gathered before Nanjing officials and pledged their support for tax reform. The persistence of Nanjing residents had at last led to the implementation of a new urban property tax.

The scale of popular participation and the key role it played in the success of the reform demonstrate an extraordinarily high level of civic solidarity and political activism. Yet, rather than trying to reduce payments, this "tax reform" sought to create a new tax. From our present perspective, when "tax cuts" are a perennial favorite of politicians, this episode indeed seems bewildering. Why were Nanjing residents so eager to be taxed?

According to the two leading petitioners, Li Zixin 李自新 and Liu Mingxiao 劉鳴曉 (neither of whom appears to have held an official title or degree), the impetus for this collective action was a particular form of urban levy known as "neighborhood captain and firewatchers" (*zongjia huofu* 總甲火夫 or *huojia* 火甲), which had evolved into a great source of suffering for Nanjing residents.[1] As the name suggests, *zongjia huofu* aimed to provide night patrol and fire-watching services. It was imposed through a neighborhood organization called *pu* 鋪.[2] The captains on duty regulated residents' activities during the night, using as their physical base a shed (also called *pu*), which sometimes served as a police station to hold suspects in custody temporarily.[3] The operation of this organization relied on conscripted labor via a system known as *yanmen lunpai* 沿門輪派. As one contemporary account relates, "Every day [the duties of] one neighborhood captain and five firewatchers were rotated among residents door by door";[4] that is, the duty to serve in these positions fell on each residence within the precinct of each *pu* in turn. Unlike conscription for the regular corvée, which was tied to the household registration system, *huojia* drafted not only native residents but also the sojourning population.[5] Hence its failing had an even wider impact in a major city such as Nanjing.

According to the official description of the system, *huojia* was about patrolling only. The supply and maintenance of equipment were the responsibilities of designated craftsmen's households known as *jianghu* 匠戶. However, patrolling involved substantial legal liabilities even though the fire captains were not salaried state officials. Despite their marginal role in assisting criminal investigation, those on duty could easily fall victim to extortion from yamen clerks and thus face the possibility of bankruptcy and even imprisonment. To make the situation worse, the range of duties was considerably expanded by *feichai* 飛差 (extraordinary official duties). Draftees were not only sent out to patrol at night but also summoned during the day to perform numerous government tasks. Since gentry households were exempted to various degrees from serving, the remaining candidates, mostly laborers and petty peddlers, were forced to be on call at a fairly high frequency.[6]

To address these problems, the petitioners asked that the *huojia* service be converted into a fixed cash payment. In other words, the call for taxes was in fact driven by a desire to eliminate corvée conscription, a demand that resonated strongly across the late Ming empire. The Ming fiscal system consisted of two tracks: *fu* 賦 (the land tax) and *yi* 役 (labor service). Since the middle of the fifteenth century, growing problems with corvée conscription had occupied a central place in policy discussions. The subsequent waves of reform gradually converted elements of labor conscription into fixed tax payments and eventually led to the creation of the Single Whip reform. This empire-wide reform fundamentally restructured the fiscal system around a uniform tax payment in silver, a radical change now generally considered the final triumph of the flourishing silver economy.[7]

However, the widely accepted narrative of the Single Whip movement does not fully explain the collective pursuit of taxes among Nanjing residents. Besides volunteering to produce a tax registry, city residents were also repeatedly polled for their opinions; in fact, their support and collaboration were aggressively solicited by officials throughout the Nanjing reform project and played a central role in the reform's success. These phenomena give rise to two sets of questions. First, why did Nanjing's reform rely so heavily on grassroots participation instead of bureaucratic fiat? What were the political nature and social basis of this reform activism? Was it uniquely urban? To what extent does the case of Nanjing represent other cities in the late Ming? Second, if taxation was indeed the favored solution to repair the failing fiscal system, why were there no urban taxes in place before the reform movement? What was the fiscal relation between the state and urban residents prior to the reform, and how did urban tax reform proceed in such a peculiar institutional setting?

Although both sets of issues are intrinsically related to the striking urban solidarity demonstrated by the Nanjing community, they belong to two separate developments during the late Ming fiscal reform that is of central concern to this chapter. This distinction is essential to the interpretation of the event: although it is tempting to view the mobilization of Nanjing residents as an indication of a burgeoning urban public, the enthusiastic grassroots support was in fact part of a general development of expanded political participation during the fiscal reform.[8] What made Nanjing's tax reform uniquely urban, this chapter argues, were the demand to create a new tax and the challenges that arose from this, problems facing many cities at the time.

In spite of their different trajectories, both lines of development can be traced to the early Ming ideal of a rural empire. After centuries of division and alien rule, the founding of the Ming dynasty marked a return to native Chinese rule. The political rhetoric of the "native turn" found institutional expression under the founding emperor, Zhu Yuanzhang (r. 1368–98), who envisioned an empire based on the construction of self-governing village communities. The ideal rural communities would not only assume substantial moral and legal authority but also serve as nodes of operation for the allocation and collection of state revenues. The intent was to keep local government intervention to a minimum. This was indeed an extraordinary development. Although China had always been an agrarian country, Zhu's vision elevated economic fact into institutional mandate. Under this design, the operation of the fiscal system was predicated on the stability of self-governing rural communities. Cities were so marginalized in imperial governance that urban space (land or property) was left outside the purview of fiscal administration.

The rural-centered nature of the Ming fiscal system becomes particularly evident when compared with the urban administration of the two preceding dynasties, the Song (960–1280) and the Yuan (1280–1368). In sharp contrast to the Ming, the Song government defined urban and rural residents as separate categories in the state fiscal system. Of the five major tax categories under the Song summarized in the opening statement of "Shihuo zhi" 食貨志 (Chapter on economics) in the official history, one, the *chengguo zhi fu* 城郭之賦, was a tax on urban housing and land. The Song state administered a sophisticated assessment program that ranked the wealth of urban residents into ten grades based on the possession of real estate (*wuye* 屋業) and liquid assets (*yingyun wuli* 營運物力 or *fudong wuli* 浮動物力).[9] Real estate, which included housing and land within cities, was further differentiated into four categories: *chong jin xian man* 衝緊閒慢 (critical, busy, slow, idle). This progressive taxation scheme allowed the assessment of urban estates to be based on location. At the same time, the state also took into account liquid assets such as those used in business operations and rental incomes. Furthermore, as urbanization progressed, the state expanded the concept of "city" from administrative centers to commercial towns and even temporary marketplaces called *caoshi* 草市 (straw markets). Under heavy fiscal pressure from the frequent military campaigns against its nomadic neighbors, the Song resorted to aggressive urban taxation to take full advantage of the prospering urban economy.

The Song-style administration of urban space underwent drastic changes in the subsequent Yuan dynasty. The unprecedented creation of a separate urban institution called Lushi si 錄事司, the Municipal Affairs Office, marks the Yuan system as an exception in the history of

Chinese urban administration.[10] Except during this time, Chinese cities never functioned as independent political units but were embedded in larger, mostly rural jurisdictions. Important cities were usually the seat of multiple administrative offices.[11] Ming Nanjing, for example, housed not only the court and central government but also one prefectural and two county offices. The nomadic conquerors of the Yuan regime, however, adopted a very different approach toward urban administration. The Mongolian rulers prioritized the acquisition of materials produced by agricultural China, and cities were the perfect places to realize this goal. Therefore, in contrast to the traditional dividing and embedding of cities within the administrative hierarchy, major Yuan cities were separated out as individual units under the direct control of the central court. By securing unmediated control over cities, the minority Mongolian rulers were able to effectively govern the vast conquered land of China. This unique style of urban governance distinguishes the Yuan as a predominantly city-based regime.[12]

At the beginning of the Ming, the administration of urban space underwent another major shift. Dedicated to restoring a native Chinese world order, Zhu Yuanzhang established an administrative system that contrasted sharply with those of the Song and the Yuan. The difference was particularly evident in cities, which were no longer governed separately from the countryside. In fact, the Ming system was so centered around rural communities that agricultural landholding played a predominant role in determining both taxes and corvée requirements. As a result, the financial obligations of the landless were left undefined. In the countryside, where the primary occupation was farming, this omission spared landless tenants from further fiscal burdens. However, the same criterion, when applied to cities, in effect shifted the tax burden from the wealthy residents with fewer assets tied up in land to those of lesser means. In sharp contrast to the Song dynasty, a clear standard for assessing urban wealth was never formally established in the Ming era.[13]

The rural-centered early Ming system indeed facilitated impressive economic recovery following the years of warfare that led to the establishment of the Ming; however, extensive commercialization over the course of the fifteenth century gradually eroded the social foundation of the community-based fiscal system. The consequent rift between the institutional ideal of self-governing rural communities and the social reality of a mobile and commercialized society allowed the rich and the privileged to profit at the expense of local communities. As a result, rural society became increasingly polarized, and the consequent social instability posed a serious threat to the survival of the Ming. The crisis prompted a series of reforms that would last for the remaining years of the dynasty's existence.

The clash between commercial forces and Zhu Yuanzhang's rural ideal has been well studied by historians; for the most part, however, the early Ming institutional design is considered the cause of Ming fiscal reform, rather than an active force shaping the nature and course of these changes.[14] The extraordinary activism of Nanjing residents and their demand for a new urban tax allow us to move beyond the silver-centered narrative of the Single Whip reform and bring to light two developments in late Ming reform that bear clear imprints of the early Ming legacy: expanded popular participation and an emerging urban-rural division.[15] At the same time, a deeper appreciation of the greater structural changes also provides the parameters necessary for evaluating the significance of Nanjing's reform, an event that runs counter to our modern intuition in many ways. The analysis of the Nanjing tax reform in this chapter, therefore, is grounded in two new facets of the late Ming fiscal reform.

First, despite the clear consensus on the need for change, officials found themselves facing the difficult task of filling the void left by the disintegration of self-governing rural communities. As discussed in the next section of this chapter, reformers had little confidence in the corruption-riddled local offices and resorted to grassroots collaboration with the state's agents as an alternative to the problematic expansion of local bureaucracy. Some officials, such as Ding Bin 丁賓, who presided over the Nanjing reform, even incorporated public polls into the policy-making process. When measured against contemporary practices, what truly stands out in the Nanjing reform is not so much the grassroots support it enlisted but the systematic consensus-building mechanism created during the process.

Second, since the Single Whip reform aimed to convert corvée obligations into a monetary tax, the lack of urban taxation in the existing system forced reformers to take a different tack in cities from that taken in the countryside. This de facto urban-rural division is particularly striking given the native Chinese tradition of urban administration, which did not differentiate between cities and the countryside. The final section of this chapter therefore considers the Single Whip reform from an urban perspective and examines the urban-rural discrepancies that arose during the process of implementing it. Although the urban-rural fiscal divide was never formally addressed by the court, the political activism inspired by the fiscal reform turned such institutional ambiguity into an open ground for local interpretation and negotiation. In an ironic turn of history, as the empire of villages underwent a fundamental fiscal restructuring, its institutional bias brought urban residents together under an unlikely banner—the pursuit of a tax. Furthermore, despite the city's special status as the secondary capital, fiscal reform in Nanjing, as in many other late Ming cities, resulted in a new tax on urban real estate. The invention of urban taxation placed urban property under the purview of state administration for the first time in the Ming dynasty. Eventually, in an effort to confront the embedded rural bias, urban residents precipitated a newfound appreciation of urban space in the fiscal regime of the Ming empire.

POPULISM IN THE LATE MING FISCAL REFORM

Late Ming Fiscal Reform and Early Ming Social Legislation

Community-Based Labor Conscription. The political activism of Nanjing residents during the *huojia* reform is not unique to the former capital city but indicative of the expansion in political participation engendered by the late Ming fiscal reform. This development is intrinsically related to the early Ming reliance on self-supervising rural communities. Indeed, central to the early Ming design was a state-engineered social organization called the Village Tithing (里甲 *lijia*) system, through which labor conscription was implemented.[16] The Village Tithing system organized households into groups of 110, with each of the ten wealthiest charged with the leadership of a tithing composed of ten households. Despite its critical role in tax collection and labor conscription, the *lijia* was by no means merely an accounting unit; rather, it was a fully functioning social entity. Under the leadership of local wealthy households, *lijia* provided the state with the goods and labor it needed; more important, they were expected to bring about social stability, communal cohesion, mutual aid, and moral transformation with minimal local governmental control. Indeed, the creation of *lijia* epitomized Zhu Yuanzhang's social vision, one that considered self-supervising rural communities the foundation of a native Chinese empire arising after centuries of division and alien rule. For Zhu, the empire builder from a humble background, this ideal had a particularly strong appeal because it promised to transform society without expanding the power of local government, which Zhu held in deep suspicion. Thus in place of civil governance, Zhu resorted to administrative communities such as *lijia* as the cornerstone of his social planning.[17]

The emphasis on self-governing rural communities shaped the infrastructure of local governance in many ways. The allocation of fiscal duties, for example, was community based and determined by the grade assigned to each household. Household ranking was in turn based on the number of adult males in the family and the family's general wealth (land, valuables, capital, houses, cattle, carriages, boats, and the like). Those deemed affluent were to serve in a ten-year rotation as community leaders (*lizhang* 里長, *jiashou* 甲首) and were primarily in charge of collecting and delivering taxes. In the event of unexpected public expenses, ad hoc labor conscription might also be assigned at the discretion of local officials based on each household's ranking. With communities providing manpower to do most of the government's work, the function of the local bureaucracy was reduced to a minimum.

Despite his faith in grassroots power, Zhu Yuanzhang was not an egalitarian. His policies demanded that hierarchical distinctions, in terms of both age and wealth, be clearly recognized, and he expected those with age, wealth, and learning to provide local leadership.[18] To achieve this goal, community leaders such as *liangzhang* 糧長 (tax captains) or *lizhang* 里長 (village heads) were assigned a variety of social, economic, moral, and cultural responsibilities. Toward the end of his reign, after decades of trial and error, Zhu further expanded the authority of the Elders (*laoren* 老人) system by granting juridical powers to several elders in each rural community. These powers could be exercised independently of county (*xian* 縣) officials and clerical staff.[19] This move, unprecedented in Chinese history, allowed village communities to fend off the intrusion of local government (except in cases of major crimes). With the right to bypass local administration or even to petition the court directly, village communities would become an effective counterweight to the imperial bureaucracy. In some extreme examples recorded in the *Da Gao* 大誥 (The great pronouncement), the founding emperor even called on commoners to arrest corrupt officials, especially in matters involving taxation and labor conscription.[20]

Although Zhu's ideal was to promote the welfare of peasants, the success of his system depended largely on particular economic and social conditions: first, the determination of labor assignments was based not on absolute wealth but on a household's relative financial standing in the administrative community *lijia*. Therefore, the wealth that could result in assignment as the village leader (*lizhang*) in one community might lead to a ranking as a medium household in another. In other words, the system was premised on an empire of homogeneous villages, each with a similar financial profile. Moreover, fair and efficient revenue collection was essentially dependent on the accuracy of the land surveys and household census conducted every ten years. The system did not anticipate rapid population growth, extensive migration, or frequent land transactions, much less the emergence of a commercialized rural economy in which absentee urban landlords exercised power over resident villagers. As a result, with the growth of the monetized economy beginning in the middle of the fifteenth century, the gap between Zhu's ideal and the reality of rural society became increasingly apparent. This fostered a wide range of tax-evasion tactics—such as breaking landholdings up among several different administrative units to lower the grade of households, or registering landholdings under the names of degree holders, who by law were to varying degrees exempt from labor conscription. Incapable of accommodating the fast-paced commercialization, community-based corvée conscription soon failed to uphold fiscal justice. In addition to legal loopholes, corruption among local clerks and community leaders' abuses of power were rampant. As a result, rural society became increasingly polarized. Powerful families availed themselves of legal loopholes or conspired with clerks to evade their corvée obligations, and the less privileged simply fled and disappeared from the government registration rolls. The social foundation of the Ming fiscal system—immobile, self-sustaining village communities—disappeared from the landscape with alarming speed.[21]

At the same time, the ideal of minimal local governments operating on small budgets also proved untenable. It had resulted in an extremely conservative revenue policy that permitted little leeway for local government and oftentimes left officials with no choice but to impose irregular levies to meet their operational needs. Therefore, the conscription of labor services, originally intended for the purpose of tax collection and local security, soon became a means of carrying out daily bureaucratic operations, such as the postal service, local militias, and the ordinary tasks necessary to run local offices (runners, watchmen, doormen, coolies, scribes, guards).[22] In addition, local governments also conscripted labor for ad hoc construction work, such as building yamen offices or city walls. Such contingency measures did substantially lower public expenses, but, not surprisingly, the corvée was also exploited for personal gain. In the eyes of contemporary critics, illicit labor conscription accounted for a main portion of the rampant abuse and corruption in local government. Regulating and curtailing these excessive ad hoc requisitions became one of the most pressing issues in fiscal reform.

The Progression of Reform Movements.   Beginning in the middle of the fifteenth century, signs of the rural crisis began to draw public attention and inspire a stream of reform proposals. The first major reform scheme was called *junyao* 均徭 (equalized labor service). Various localities had experimented with *junyao* since the 1430s, but this method did not gain the court's recognition and full endorsement until 1488.[23] To curb irregular levies, *junyao* formally regulated the ever-increasing labor conscription by instituting a specified budget for local governments. To complement the changes in budgeting practices, *junyao* also converted part of the labor-service requirement into a fixed cash payment (*yinchai* 銀差) while allowing local governments to solicit service from people in the name of *lichai* 力差 (labor service).

Within only a few decades, however, *junyao* proved incapable of curbing fiscal malfeasance; in retrospect, it was a transitional measure in the full-scale overhaul of the fiscal practices, namely, the Single Whip reform. Similar to *junyao,* the Single Whip reform also grew out of local experiments and exhibited a high level of local variation.* These variations differed only in detail and shared a host of core features. In essence, the Single Whip method converted the rotating labor corvée obligation into part of one's annual tax payment; the duty of collecting and transporting the single silver tax payment was transferred from community leaders to local officials.[24] In other words, the Single Whip method abolished labor corvée in form, if not in reality, and combined the double-track system of *fu* (land tax) and *yi* (labor service) into one silver payment.

Although the adoption of payments in silver attests to the power of the flourishing silver economy, the impetus for the reform was not merely economic. Driven by mounting social tensions over tax evasion and corruption, the late Ming fiscal reform sought to devise not only a new tax scheme for greater fiscal efficiency but, more important, new procedures of tax allocation, collection, and transportation to enhance accountability and the transparency of fiscal transactions. Achieving this goal required a viable replacement for the collapsing village organization. After all, under the early Ming design, the fiscal health of the country was predicated on, among other things, the continued existence of self-governing rural communities defined by highly stable membership and landownership. As the economy became commercialized and population grew fluid, the *lijia* organization ceased to provide a proper social base for revenue allocation and collection. However, instead of expanding the reach of local government, the reformers resorted to popular collaboration to replace the functions of community leaders. This trend is clearly observable in new procedures for tax allocation, collection, and transportation as well as measures to regulate local governments' budgets. The effort to redress the failure of community-

---

*The late Ming fiscal reform movement under discussion in this chapter was practiced primarily under the direction of the Single Whip method. The consensus of historians is that this "method" was simply a general guideline and deliberately kept flexible in order to take into account different local needs, among which the south-north variation was a primary consideration. This chapter argues that urban-rural variation should also be considered. In the following discussion, these general guidelines are referred to as the "Single Whip method," and the actual fiscal reform movement conducted under the guidance of this method is termed "Single Whip reform." "Method" indicates an ideal rising above the intricacies of local politics, whereas "reform" embodies local variations resulting from negotiations between the old and new practices.

based labor conscription while maintaining the early Ming ideal of minimal governance, as demonstrated in the following section, opened up a new space for popular participation during the late Ming fiscal reform.

The Expansion of Popular Participation

Collection and Transportation of Tax Payments.   Among the first signs of rural crisis were the difficulties community leaders (*lizhang* or *liangzhang*) faced in fulfilling their duties. In the *lijia*-based fiscal system, community leaders played a central role and shouldered most of the duties of collecting and transporting tributary taxes and goods. Their burden was further exacerbated by the ever-increasing ad hoc conscriptions. Although in theory these duties were collectively shared by the administrative community, in the absence of any laws stipulating the means of allocation, local offices counted on community leaders to apportion the duties and, in the case of default, to fulfill these requests themselves.[25] As a result, community leaders either were bankrupted by the excessive burdens or became oppressors when they passed the burden on to local residents. As the paternalistic authority that the system presumed and relied on gave way to abuse and exploitation, the cohesion of village communities was irreparably damaged.

With the implementation of the Single Whip reform, the collection and delivery of tax grain were removed from villagers and became the responsibility of officials. At the same time, efforts were also made to retain the early Ming ideal of minimal governance. As a result, we find innovative procedures instituted to seek the collaboration of local taxpayers. Most representative is the *zifeng tougui* 自封投櫃 (self-seal and self-deposit) system, which mandated a "silver chest," or "land tax chest," to be placed in a public location (usually in front of a county office).[26] On tax collection day, the government would send supervisors to oversee the dropping of payments by locals into the silver chest. Community leaders no longer had to pay on members' behalf even if they defaulted. In addition, by eliminating middlemen, direct payments also effectively prevented such exploitations and abuses as substituting fake for real silver, the levying of surcharges, the practice of extortion, and theft.

To coordinate tax collection without drafting community headmen or expanding local bureaucracy, the government began to issue collection notices called *yizhidan* 易知單 or *yizhiyoudan* 易知由單 (easy-to-understand slip) before the due date to facilitate the drop-off process for taxpayers.[27] The merit of this new procedure, according to Qi Biao-jia 祁彪佳, a famed late Ming cultural icon who later died as a Ming loyalist martyr, lay in its simplicity.[28] In Qi's opinion, the old tax collection system had been significantly compromised by its complexity: the convoluted tax procedure not only created confusion for both taxpayers and the collecting officials but also made the system vulnerable to clerical abuse. To solve the problem, Qi standardized the collection procedure in the Jiangnan area by issuing *yizhiyoudan* that stated the amount due. The intent to facilitate popular participation was made even clearer in the demand by the regional inspector (*xun'an yushi* 巡按御史) for Guangdong that all notices be printed in large type and in the most accessible language so that "as soon as the slip meets [taxpayers'] eyes they will know what it means."[29]

The creation of collection slips or boxes undercut the role of community leaders and yamen clerks in the collection and transportation of state revenues. In the reformed system, all that was needed were simple printed notices, a collection box, and supervisors dispatched from the central government. Widely adopted across the empire, these measures embodied the core spirit of the Single Whip method and substantially empowered local residents; by simplifying the process of collection, the taxation system became much more comprehensible and transparent to the uneducated masses. As a result, it was more difficult to take advantage of them. Ultimately, by drawing on popular participation and print media—readily available in the late Ming—the reformed system was able to lessen the duties of community leaders without entailing further bureaucratic expansion.

Written in Stone: Regulating Local Government Budgets. The same approach was also extended to regulating local governments' ever-increasing demands for conscripted labor, one of the primary goals of the fiscal reform. To ensure the operation of local government within the bounds of legal budgets, reformers worked to institute itemized local budgets to prevent ad hoc surcharges or illicit levies. More important, the process was often accompanied by a new documentation system openly inviting the scrutiny of the general public.[30] Stone steles were erected and registers of tax and corvée published, sometimes in multiple editions, specifying every single expense, all with the aim of ensuring effective regulation of local budgets.

The efficacy of these public records was clearly recognized and appreciated by reform officials and local residents alike. Statements attesting to enthusiastic implementation of such measures can be found not only in core areas of the Ming empire like Nanjing, but also at its fringes. Nanning 南寧, an area in the southwestern borderland, is a case in point. Having finally implemented the Single Whip method, the presiding reform official in Nanning proposed that a permanent and public record of the reforms be made: "I fear that the reform might be aborted by wicked conspiracies when I leave this office. . . . [In order to prevent this,] all the agreed-on measures should be inscribed on a stone stele to be erected outside the county office."[31] Regional Inspector Gu, in a memorial entitled "A Plea That Mercy Be Granted to People in the Border Regions in Order to Save Them from Deep Misery," concurred in this sentiment. In addition, Gu further ordered that numerous copies of the details of the statutes that could not be carved on the stone stele be printed and distributed among local villages. Should future officials refuse to honor the agreement, locals could refer to these public documents as a means of legal recourse (*zhu wei lingdian* 著爲令典).[32] The benefit of public documentation was so apparent that, as discussed below, Nanjing residents even collectively petitioned to erect stone steles to ensure that the reforms would endure.

The proliferation of public documentation of local fiscal reforms again confirms the growing importance of popular participation in the late Ming fiscal reform. The well-publicized new tax rates and governmental budgets invited public scrutiny to pre-empt future increases and curb encroachment of local government on the people's labor and resources, goals reminiscent of the aims of Zhu Yuanzhang's *lijia* system. Yet, as we have observed, in contrast to Zhu's emphasis on community elders as counterweights to local bureaucrats, the late Ming fiscal reform solicited locals' support in a very different manner—through public media and grassroots collaboration.

The Apportionment of Fiscal Duties. The need to publicize re-formed procedures in order to ensure their continuance reveals the highly contentious nature of the fiscal reform. In fact, these reforms not only were controversial among officials but also provoked divided opinions among locals. A systematic overhaul of this scale must have immediately pitted its beneficiaries against those with vested interests in the status quo. This was especially true when it came to the apportion-ment of fiscal duties. Indeed, as repeatedly pointed out by contempo-rary observers, the core issue of the Ming corvée system lay not so much in its being onerous as in its being unfair (*bujun* 不均). Therefore, in addition to regulating government budgets, reformers also endeav-ored to assure a fair allocation of levies based on the ranking of house-holds, for which a procedure called *bianshen* 編審 (inspection and regis-tration) was the key.

However, despite the vital role of *bianshen* in determining the burden of individual households, this process was ridden with confusion and, often, corruption. Not only was the process determined solely by local officials and clerks, but the criteria to be employed in assessing house-hold wealth were also unspecified. The ambiguity provided a breeding ground for manipulation and abuse. In fact, toward the end of the fif-teenth century, it was well known that the official registry of house-holds had become so detached from reality that many powerful families were able to transfer most of their tax burden to the poor. The situa-tion was vividly captured in the popular phrase *maifu chaipin* 賣富差貧, "the rich buy themselves out while channeling the entire levy burden to the poor."[33] The corruption was so severe that people were said to dread *bianshen* as much as if they were to be thrown into boiling water.[34] By the late Ming, *bianshen* had become a process that precipitated social strife. In his memoirs, Zhu Guozhen 朱國楨, a member of the elite ac-tive during the late Ming fiscal reform movement, described how per-sonal experiences, especially events that he witnessed in his hometown, Huzhou 湖州, drove him to become a reform activist. Zhu recalled that, after the 1601 *bianshen*,

I heard endless crying in the neighborhood. People were so miserable that they could not even figure out a way to die. The neighbors to our north, a father with his two sons, made their farewell calls to all the neighbors and fled the area. Within a hundred steps around my house, I heard of numerous suicides taking place. However, in the midst of misery, the devious local bullies were celebrating their victory [i.e., favorable ranking from the inspection] with hands clapping and their wicked wishes satisfied. They were so thrilled that they were throwing drinking banquets and temple festivals to show gratitude for the blessings from local deities.[35]

This account vividly portrays the harsh reality in Huzhou as well as in many other places where the *bianshen* inspection had become a life-or-death event for local community members.

Clearly, the most problematic element of the *bianshen* lay in its heavy dependence on the discretion of the local authorities in the apportionment of fiscal duties. With no objective standards to ensure the fairness of inspection, corruption and abuse became difficult to control, thus turning corvée conscription into systematic oppression of the underprivileged. In an effort to redress the inspection process, some areas introduced the practice of *mianshen* 面審, or "in-person inspections." A state representative less invested in local interests would meet with people directly and confirm their ranking in person. In some cases, these in-person inspections were even complemented by a process of communal consent and supervision. For example, during the 1601 inspection, the magistrate of Haiyan 海鹽 county sent a *yidan* 議單 (discussion sheet) to each community in his jurisdiction asking them to publicly decide the apportionment of corvée service based on the amount of land owned. If there was no one capable of serving alone, locals could elect the ways in which they served (rotating, sharing the same service, etc.) and note their communal decision on the sheet to be approved upon official review.[36] In a similar spirit, in the Zhejiang area, the implementation of the Single Whip method stipulated that the results of *bianshen* were to be printed and distributed to each household so that locals could confirm that their ranking was accurate and that no one was evading taxes or hiding assets. By rewarding those who reported fraud, the government was able to further utilize locals' intimate knowledge of the community to ensure an accurate assessment and fair apportionment of labor service.[37]

Again, in an effort to improve the quality of fiscal surveys and inspections, grassroots collaboration was utilized to ensure the accuracy of the information the government collected. However, despite these innovative procedures, it was still painfully clear to contemporary observers that moderate changes were not sufficient to redress the problems of the failing fiscal system. Eventually, reformers came to realize that, in order to ensure a fair apportionment of fiscal duties, they needed to reformulate the criteria for allocating corvée radically. Instead of an allocation based on the estimated overall wealth of individual households—a figure difficult to estimate and thus vulnerable to clerical abuse—there would be a fixed-rate payment based on the amount of land owned and the number of able-bodied adults, both of which were publicly visible and easier to supervise.

Indeed, over the course of two centuries of fiscal reform, a consensus gradually emerged among reformers that the corvée should be replaced by a tax payment. However, the commutation rate remained a major controversy until the end of the Ming era, especially the relative weights to be given landholding (*liang* 糧) and capable male labor (*ding* 丁) in calculating the new tax. As a result, the new Single Whip taxes were determined by a wide range of combinations between *ding* and *liang* in different places. For example, in Tongzhou (in modern Shaanxi), the rate was set in 1594 based 80 percent on *ding* and 20 percent on *liang*. Yet in Fujian province, the rate generally was calculated as 60 percent *ding* and 40 percent *liang*. Even the same locale might shift these proportions at different points in time. In one of Nanjing's metropolitan counties, Shangyuan, the percentage based on *liang* in the new tax went from 20 percent (1430–51) to 50 percent (1536–39) and to 75 percent (1567–70). Surprisingly, the high level of local diversity was in fact endorsed by the court. In 1577, Guang Mao 光懋 at the Ministry of Revenue memorialized the court about social unrest in Shandong owing to the improper introduction of the Single Whip method, which based the new corvée-turned-taxes on landownership alone. According to Guang, this change in policy provoked widespread panic among locals, who rushed to sell their land in order to lower their new tax rates. He believed that although excluding *ding* from the calculation of the new tax rate might work in the south, in northern China, this move would only devastate the already declining rural economy. Representing a rather typical view at the time, this memorial was well received by the minister of revenue, who in turn suggested that separate regulations be applied in northern and southern China. However, the court did not accept the proposal:

The value of the law lies in its ability to improve people's lives, under which principle there is no need to distinguish north and south. It is the duty of the regional inspectors to adjust the application of the law in order to best fit the conditions of each individual locality. They should follow the needs of the locals and not enforce the law uniformly.[38]

Such leniency toward local conditions in fact dictated the progression of the reform process. Although in 1581, after decades of regional experimentation, the court formally recognized the Single Whip method as an official policy for empire-wide implementation, the pace of adoption differed from place to place. On encountering local resistance, some local officials even petitioned to withdraw their jurisdictions from participation in the program. For those who joined the reform, the court also tolerated great latitude for local modifications. The lenient attitude of the court toward local variation made the Single Whip method more of a general guideline open to local negotiation than a set of strictly enforced court directives. It also raised such questions as, How was the "suitability" of each locality for the Single Whip reform to be determined? Who was entitled to make decisions regarding local modifications? Although local officials were granted the political authority to make these decisions, they did not necessarily possess the required local knowledge, since the law of avoidance mandated that they be nonnatives of the jurisdiction in which they presided. Under these circumstances, as discussed in the following section, consultation with locals became critical in adapting general fiscal reform guidelines to specific localities. This further extended popular participation in the policy-making process.

The Rising Importance of Public Opinion

Scholars have pointed out that consultation in the name of *difang gongyi* 地方公議 (local public opinion) gained increasing importance in local governance during the late Ming.[39] However, "public opinion" was usually confined to the educated members of the community and did not extend to the general public. Therefore, in practice, *difang gongyi* was virtually indistinguishable from *shiren gongyi* 士人公議, political advocacy by governing elites, ranging from incumbent and retired officials to the lowest rank of degree-holders, the *shengyuan*. The intertwined relationship between *difang gongyi* and *shiren gongyi* can be seen in the following letter written by the famed late Ming gentry Qian Qianyi 錢謙益 (1582–1664). Addressing the upcoming tax inspection (*bianshen*), Qian explicitly urged the magistrate of his home county to consult public opinion: "For your benefit, it would be better not to act despotically but trust the matter to public discussion (*gongyi*)." Why? "Corvée service is a public matter concerning the whole county, not the private affair of the magistrate." Hence, Qian continued, "The incumbent magistrate should consult *jinshen gongyi* 縉紳公議 [the public opinion of the gentry], and the gentry should share their concerns with the magistrate."[40] Here, as in many similar examples, "public discussion" in fact refers to *jinshen gongyi*, a collegial conference between local elites and officials.[41]

The highly contentious conflict of interests during the fiscal reform, however, made such elite-dominated public forums inadequate for arbitrating issues regarding taxes or corvée. In fact, one of the most controversial issues in the corvée reform focused on elite exemptions from corvée conscription.[42] Abuse of this privilege in effect transferred most of the burden from the landed gentry to people of moderate or even lesser means. In some areas, it was reported that the ownership of more than half of all landholdings was hidden under "fraudulent trusteeships" (*guiji* 詭寄) and the land had hence become levy-free. The collusion between the privileged and the wealthy proved fatal to the rural economy: it bankrupted peasant households in the countryside and eventually the corvée system at large. It also divided rural society into the privileged and the deprived. In fact, the appearance of the term *xiangshen* 鄉紳 (rural gentry) in the mid-Ming is a clear indication of deteriorating social relations in the countryside.[43] This contrasts sharply with the early Ming, when rural landlords served as village heads in the *lijia* system and enjoyed moral as well as political authority. The organic ties of rural communities were gravely disrupted by the mid-dynastic urbanization, as many of these landlords relocated into towns and cities, becoming absentee landlords. The urbanized landed gentry ceased to be involved in local affairs and had little knowledge of or interest in the devastating consequences of their evasion of labor services. The benevolent local leaders formerly known as *minwang* 民望 (lit., "those looked up to by the people") had morphed into self-interested, if not malicious, *xiangshen*.[44]

Although the problems caused by the gentry exemption privilege were well recognized at the time, with class interests at stake, late Ming elites were highly divided among themselves on this issue.[45] As a result, the practice of *gongyi*, which delegated the articulation of public opinion to the educated class, became highly problematic. How could the privileged classes accurately represent the public interest when they themselves were under attack as part of the problem? Given the highly contentious nature of fiscal reform, it is not surprising to find that some reform-minded officials circumvented the educated classes' mediation and opted to canvass the less privileged directly.

For example, in Shaoxing prefecture in Zhejiang, the prefect openly solicited public opinion during a heated debate over fiscal reform. He stated, "Since the reform will deeply affect people's livelihoods and is critical to governmental operations, we cannot take it lightly and completely rely on the words of the petitioners." He then requested that local offices publicize the statutory changes under consideration and urged all concerned gentry or locals to submit their opinions in writing on the matter within five days of the announcement.[46]

A similar episode took place decades later, when a proposal by the Zhejiang provincial surveillance commissioner for transportation (*Zhejiang anchashi* 浙江按察使), Jin Zhijun 金之俊, was accepted by the emperor. The court's approval allowed Jin to shift the duty of transporting tributary rice from conscripted laborers to local officials. In preparation for launching a large-scale provincial-level reform, Jin took the precautionary measure of gathering information on local conditions. In order to solicit feedback from the locals, Jin ordered magistrates to print his approved memorial and distribute copies in front of their yamen in the hope of attaining an accurate measure of local opinions.[47]

In some cases, the solicitation of public opinion was executed in a very aggressive manner. In Jiangxi, in order to convert postal labor service into fixed payments, one local community (De'an li 德安里) petitioned the prefect, who met with community leaders and approved their proposition. But before he put the reform in place, he wanted to confirm that the village heads accurately represented the wishes of the local public. He asked county government officials to post a board in front of the office with detachable slips. All 180 residents of this community were to fill in their names and vote on whether or not they considered this reform convenient and to return the slips within five days.[48] In some places, the polling was conducted in person at the regular *xiang-yue* 鄉約 (community compact) meetings so that officials could communicate with the public directly regarding reform-related issues.[49] In contrast, as discussed in the following section, to accommodate the fluid urban environment of Nanjing, instead of polling residents at regular meetings, Ding Bin took a more aggressive approach. He conducted a series of both public hearings and home visits to solicit public opinion about the proposed reforms.

Taken together, these developments bring to light the overlooked populist dimension of the late Ming fiscal reform. Although the reform was largely prompted by the failing of community-based corvée conscription, the solutions still reflected a certain level of communal autonomy. In recognition of the difficulty of devising a plan suitable for a country as vast and varied as China, the Single Whip reform provided general guidelines centering on a uniform annual silver payment, leaving great room for local initiatives. Not only was there no mandated timetable for implementing these policies, but adjustments made by individual communities were largely tolerated. Most significantly, many local modifications were based on mutual agreements between local governments and their people. The open-endedness of the Single Whip method, in other words, created a new space for political negotiation between locals and their presiding officials. The question was: Whose voices should be heard and whose interests should be represented? On one hand, the flexibility of the fiscal reform lent additional weight to the established role of elite consultation in local politics. On the other hand, the contentious corvée-exemption privilege of the gentry and its prevalent abuse made that class a primary target of criticism. The escalating social tension in many areas made it clear that the interests of the gentry were not necessarily those of the general public. In an effort to circumvent the gentry, we find officials actively polling local community members, pursuing the "people's will" in the most immediate manner through methods such as town hall meetings or direct balloting.

In view of the social tensions engendered by the fiscal reform, it is not surprising that popular participation was also widely solicited to further cement the reform agreement. Multiple editions of tax registries were published and stone tablets erected so that key components of the reform such as itemized government budgets and the rules by which revenue was apportioned and collected were made transparent and open to public scrutiny. Public documentation provided legal recourse for locals to pre-empt attempts to alter the newly instituted statues, ensuring that the reform policies were honored regardless of changes in personnel. From the battle against an obsolete fiscal system, therefore, emerged a renewed realm of public participation, one that expanded from the early Ming reliance on community leaders to a more far-reaching solicitation of grassroots support.

A Ming-Centered Perspective on the Fiscal Reform

All in all, the Nanjing reform reveals a new dimension of the late Ming fiscal reform closely connected to the early Ming legislation. The empire-wide implementation of the Single Whip reform and the changes it wrought are generally considered a pivotal event in late imperial Chinese history.[50] Economically, not only did this reform further encourage the development of the silver economy, it also emancipated much of the labor force from state control and conscription. From a social standpoint, it also entailed a fundamental revision of imperial governance as the primary focus of state taxation shifted to land; with the eventual abolition of corvée labor, household registration and migration control were significantly relaxed.[51] Nevertheless, these grand assessments tend to view the significance of the reform from a *longue durée* perspective across dynastic boundaries. In contrast, the developments emerging from this discussion bear clear witness to the enduring influence of the imperial infrastructure created at the inception of the dynasty.

That is, as late Ming society outgrew the institutional framework born out of a postwar economy, the ideal of self-governing villages became the source of systemic malfunction. The consequences were severe: this malfunction not only impoverished the state but also significantly polarized rural society. The process of reconciling the idealized rural vision of the Ming founder with a flourishing commercial economy concluded with the Single Whip reform, which featured the complete commutation of labor conscription into a fixed tax payment. The move was both realistic and accommodating: it acknowledged the inevitable monetization of imperial finance as well as the need to modify the early Ming ideal of self-governing rural communities.

In spite of the struggles against the early Ming legacy, Zhu Yuan-zhang's distrust of the government and bureaucracy continued to reso-nate until the end of the dynasty. Even in the face of the collapse of self-governing rural communities, there was little effort to expand the reach of local bureaucracies.[52] Instead, reformers utilized print technol-ogy readily available in the late Ming and solicited popular collaboration at the grassroots level to facilitate the adoption of reform measures. The unlikely continuity notwithstanding, we should also keep in mind that, in contrast to the early Ming emphasis on the internal hierarchy of local communities, the late Ming reform replaced reliance on community leaders with far-reaching grassroots participation. The public participa-tion sometimes even extended into the process of policy-making. The open-ended nature of the Single Whip reform called for local consulta-tion to determine the appropriate local formula for implementing fiscal reform. Although public opinion was often represented by local elites, the division of interests inherent in the fiscal reform sometimes com-pelled presiding officials to pursue the "people's will" by aggressively polling local residents, a development best illustrated through the pro-gressive reforms of Ding Bin in Nanjing.

Ding Bin's Reform

Initiation and Obstacles. The preceding discussion has estab-lished that the popular support witnessed in the Nanjing *huojia* reform was not an isolated phenomenon but part of the expanding trend of popular participation during the late Ming fiscal reform. This par-ticular form of political activism was shaped not by antagonism be-tween the state and society but by the need for state agents and the general populace to collaborate in order to justify and ensure the im-plementation of reform measures. This feature requires us to unpack the "state"–"society" dichotomy and in its stead focus on negotiations between different agents and social groups driven by their specific in-terests in a particular policy issue. Such an approach is especially crucial in analyzing Nanjing's *huojia* reform since disagreement over the feasi-bility of its implementation not only divided the local community but also the officials in charge. Only against this background can we understand why Ding Bin, the presiding official for Nanjing's *huojia* reform, created one of the most systematic and progressive consensus-building mechanisms in the Ming.

A Zhejiang native, Ding Bin spent over thirty years in various offices in Nanjing.[53] His lifelong commitment to the city is reflected in a long list of reforms and achievements that won Ding the ultimate recognition by the Nanjing community: a shrine dedicated to him was built in central Nanjing three years before he passed away.[54] Probably due to his reputation, soon after Ding Bin took office at the Nanjing Censorate, residents launched another petition drive to convert the *huojia* corvée into a standardized monetary payment and relieve the draftees from legal liability. This proposal did have a legal basis, especially the precedent of Beijing, which began to convert *huojia* into fixed payments as early as 1421.[55] Due to Nanjing's status as the auxiliary capital, this precedent was particularly relevant.[56] Nevertheless, as far as Ding Bin was concerned, legal merits were not the most decisive factor in the success of the reform. After Ding Bin received the petition, he checked whether similar petitions had been filed in the past and found that the same proposal had been submitted several times. However, according to the records, a lack of "public consensus" had stymied the proposal, pending further investigation by the Nanjing Censorate. Nonetheless pro-reform gentry and urban residents persisted in submitting similar petitions for reform.[57] This situation must have alerted Ding that although the demands for change might appear strong enough to warrant official action, reform would not be uncontested. To ensure the success of the reform, it was imperative for Ding to pre-empt all potential disputes before the reform was launched. But how was such a public consensus to be attained as well as ascertained? In the absence of modern polling technology, the building of public consensus was not a simple matter.

What Did the People Really Want? Ding's Pursuit of Public Consensus. Feeling compelled to ascertain that this course of action indeed represented the will of the general public, Ding Bin decided to communicate with local residents directly in order obtain firsthand confirmation of the collective will of Nanjing residents. With this goal in mind, he started an unusual and prolonged pursuit of "public consensus" (*gongyi* 公意) in its most literal sense. This elaborate consensus-building mechanism consisted of five stages:

Face-to-Face Interviews

The first stage of investigation was conducted at the Censorate in Nanjing. Each *pu* in Nanjing delegated three to four representatives, including both rich and poor residents, to meet with Ding in person on a designated date. Ding then conducted face-to-face interviews, making inquiries on such points as: Were all properties correctly registered? Were all waivers of corvée requirements justly applied?[58] Were the listed corvée payments for 1608 accurate? And was each property accurately assessed according to the ranking of its location (heavy traffic or remote)? Based on the information collected in the interviews, Ding adjusted the household rankings.[59] After all were adjusted and confirmed, the information was then officially archived.

A Public Hearing with the Five Ward Censors

In the second stage, Ding asked the five borough censors to hold a meeting at the Office of Convergence (Huitongguan 會同館) in order to investigate concealment or abuses in waiving privileges, uneven apportionment of payments, unjust rankings, and reluctance to pay the tax. This investigation was publicized in advance through posters displayed throughout the city. The posters clearly indicated that anyone unwilling to pay his assessment could petition the censors in person at this meeting. Once the petition was heard and approved, payment would be waived immediately. However, even with such a generous offer, according to Ding, not a single complaint was filed during the second stage of the investigation.

A Public Hearing with Central Officials

Even so, Ding was still not satisfied, and he summoned all the most important central government officials as well as more than a thousand Nanjing residents to a public hearing at the Office of Convergence. At this conference, high central government officials from the six ministries, supervising secretaries, and censors first asked the residents in attendance whether such a reform would be appropriate. The reply was a unanimous "yes." Residents of lesser economic means were specifically asked the same question, and the answer was still a resounding "yes." Suspicious of this answer, officials further asked, "Since you do not have money, why would you favor hiring with cash payments over serving in person?" The poorer residents explained that although they did not possess substantial property, they still had to serve their turns as the head of a neighborhood unit and might incur serious legal liabilities. When problems arose, their lack of financial means to bribe the clerks made the situation worse. Even if they were not subject to extortion, involvement in lawsuits would prevent them from earning a livelihood and taking care of their family. They therefore preferred to pay a fixed fee in exchange for peace of mind.

Home Visits

Because of the unprecedented nature of the reform, Ding was still concerned whether every resident had been properly heard, especially in a densely populated city like Nanjing. So he sent out censors to visit underprivileged residents (e.g., the poor, widowed, orphaned, and disabled) at home to find out more details about these destitute households and make appropriate adjustments accordingly.

Accounting and Final Confirmation

Only after every detail had been confirmed to Ding's satisfaction did the accounting process began. Since the wages for government services had already been standardized,[60] Ding Bin's goal was to match people's payments with the budget set by the Register of Corvée to eliminate room for bureaucratic manipulation and corruption. After making detailed calculations, Ding found that the collection of payments for the year 1608 actually exceeded the projected budgets. Therefore he reduced the payment in the five boroughs proportionately. He then publicized the new payment assignment list by posting it in each neighborhood *pu* and again summoned the original petitioners in the five boroughs for their opinions on the results of the reform.

Supervising the Implementation of the Reform. After the extensive public opinion survey and the accounting process were completed, each household received a ticket from the Censorate in Nanjing. True to the conventions of the Single Whip reform, it stipulated that on the first day of the fifth month, all residents were to deposit their payments into a box at a designated station in each neighborhood. In Ding's account, the enthusiasm with which Nanjing residents poured into the streets to pay their dues made the tax-paying stations as lively as marketplaces. There was no delay whatsoever. Moreover, Ding set up three inspection offices outside the city gates so residents would be able to lodge complaints about the procedure any time they needed.

To further facilitate public supervision, the details of the reform were widely publicized in print and stone tablets. At the end of his report to the emperor, Ding Bin announced that after the reform received approval from the court, he would have the details published as an official record to ensure that the fruits of the reform would be maintained. In fact, in addition to the publication of Ding's official report, we find numerous editions of the new tax registry printed privately with prefaces by prominent Nanjing elites testifying to the accomplishments of the reform. The most notable of these are Jiao Hong's 焦竑 "Paimen tiaobian bianmince xu" 排門條編便民冊序 (The preface to the Single Whip manual) and Gu Qiyuan's 顧起元 "Difang fuchaice xu" 地方夫差冊序 (Preface to the local corvée book).[61]

The seemingly excessive documentation of the Nanjing reform reflects the anxiety among local residents that their hard-fought reform might be revoked in the future. In fact, Nanjing residents were so concerned that they rallied to have the reform "inscribed in stone" and displayed as a public monument, a task accomplished three years later. The inscription on the stele states:

It is the people's concern that as time passes, succeeding officials will not be familiar with the motivation and purpose of the corvée reform and might easily alter the system, placing an additional burden on the people. Further, without a public testament as firm and clear as a stone inscription, rumors and confusion might hamper the reformed system. In our minds, the best way to pre-empt this potential problem is to erect stone tablets so that no unwelcome changes can be slipped in without public notice.[62]

Such a deep sense of insecurity came from long-term frustration. Reform in Nanjing did not come easily but was the result of a series of failed campaigns that exhibited a recurring pattern: as soon as the reform-minded officials left for other posts, the changes in the system were abolished. After numerous thwarted attempts with short-lived improvements, Nanjing residents came to realize that the best way to safeguard the new system was to publicize every stipulation in as many ways as possible, leaving no room for future officials to rescind the changes. As a result, not only were tax registers published in multiple editions but even stone steles were erected in multiple locations—five in each district and one in front of the office of the Nanjing Censorate.

Grassroots Power, Collective Action, and the Formation of an Urban Public.

The high level of civic solidarity manifested during the Nanjing *huojia* reform is striking. According to Ding Bin, the whole reform was propelled by the determination of Nanjing residents: it was initiated by residents' petition; it was legitimized by a thorough investigation of residents' intentions and willingness to participate; it was implemented by residents' voluntary submission of information and compilation of tax registers and by their cooperation in paying their taxes directly to the government. Finally, Nanjing residents supervised the implementation of the reform.[63] By all indications, the success of the Nanjing reform points to the appearance of an urban public bound by a specific cause. How should we understand this political activism? Was it uniquely urban? To what extent did Nanjing represent other late Ming cities?

The grassroots power Nanjing residents collectively demonstrated is beyond dispute. Whether it indicates the emergence of an "urban public" is, however, debatable—or at least needs to be strictly qualified. As demonstrated in this section, the central roles of local initiatives and grassroots activism in the Nanjing reform were made possible by the expansion of public participation during the Single Whip reform across the empire, a development closely related to the collapse of the early Ming rural ideal. Yet although the political activism found in Nanjing was not uniquely urban, the agenda—creating a new urban property tax—was truly exclusive to urban residents at the time. Indeed, the rural-centered bias of the early Ming system presented an additional challenge to reform activists in cities. Despite all the local variations and changes, from *junyao* to the Single Whip reform, the trend was to shift the basis of taxation to agricultural land. Yet clearly this method could not be applied in cities—What happened to urban residents who did not own such land? Surprisingly, not only was there no institutional foundation for urban taxation, but throughout the reform there also appeared to be little discussion of the subject. In order to be free of the corvée, urban residents needed to devise an alternative means of financing the commutation of labor services. Having surveyed the political ramifications of the fiscal reform, I now turn to the de facto urban-rural divide and explore how urban reformers overcame the structural rural bias in the Ming system. The overall trajectory of urban reform in the Ming dynasty also allows us to see how *huojia*—originally created for communal self-surveillance—became the focus of contention in late Ming cities, including Nanjing.

THE MING URBAN
CORVÉE REFORM

The Unique "Urban Question" of the Ming Empire

Negotiating Urban Taxation: Ward Corvée Reform. As discussed above, one curious legacy of the rural-centered social vision of the early Ming legislation lay in its ambiguity toward urban taxation. In sharp contrast to the previous dynasties, not only were cities no longer defined separately from the countryside in the administrative hierarchy, but no clear standard for assessing urban wealth was ever formally established. Composed of an agricultural land tax and rotating corvée services, the early Ming fiscal system never officially stipulated taxes for urban residents.[64] As a result, although both urban and rural residents were liable for corvée services, only rural farmland was subjected to taxation.[65]

This institutional ambiguity for cities was a unique product of the Ming ideology. This "benevolent neglect" of urban residents, however, turned out to be a double-edged sword: it could work either for or against the interests of urbanites. To begin with, the lack of a formal distinction between *lijia* and *fangxiang yi* 坊厢役 (ward corvée) did not prevent local governments from imposing different levies on urban and rural residents. Such de facto rural-urban inequality in corvée systems is apparent in a gazetteer for Taiping prefecture 太平府 (modern Anhui):

The residences within the city walls are called *fang* wards, and the ones in the rural areas are called *li*. Each one has its leaders to head the community according to the routine regulations of the Ming. Although urban residents do not own land and live by their trades, such livelihoods should be given the same status as farming under a polity that treats its people with no discrimination regardless of whether they live inside or outside the city walls. Alas! For urban residents who live close to the county and prefectural governments, their corvée is twice that of rural people.[66]

The sympathies of the gazetteer editor clearly lay with urban residents. Their heavier levies were said to be a function of geographical expedience. Since they lived close to local government offices, urban residents were convenient targets for extra corvée conscription. In Jianchang prefecture 建昌府 (in Jiangxi), the burden was so great that "the wiser" people started to move out of the city.[67]

In the Suzhou area, however, the scale seemed to tip in the opposite direction. There, as in Jianchang, rural-urban differences in local corvée conscription began during the Xuande reign (1426–35). During this period, urban residents answered calls for labor services from the local office, and rural peasants were in charge of the collection and transportation of the tribute grain. This system, however, underwent a series of changes and reforms, and by the time of the Jingtai reign (1450–56) urban households were liable neither for corvée nor for any replacement payments. Seizing on the loophole, many rural landlords falsely registered themselves as residents of Suzhou in order to evade labor service conscription.[68]

The rural bias also affected the implementation of the *junyao* fiscal reform. In Nanchang 南昌 prefecture (Jiangxi), for instance, reformers tended to focus on regulating rural inhabitants' corvée obligations according to landownership. As a result, the burden shifted to urban residents. One gazetteer from late Ming Nanchang describes this unfair allotment and the consequent suffering of urban residents:

Both urban and rural residents are like children of the state. For rural residents, as soon as they complete the four types of corvée service, they can rest for the remainder of the tax period. However, such a blessing was never bestowed on urban residents, who are responsible for responding to the demands of both the yamen and visiting officials, as well as for supplying all the equipment and miscellaneous necessities for all official occasions, ranging from sacrificial rituals to banquets. The corvée imposed on urban residents is unfairly harsh.[69]

Clearly, since the implementation of *junyao* focused on relieving the burden on peasants, urban residents were left to fulfill the remaining demands of local government. The exclusion of urban residents from the benefits of the fiscal reforms appears to have been a relatively common phenomenon. It could be found in the southernmost reach of the empire, Qiongzhou 瓊州 prefecture (in Hainan).[70] Even those urban residents included in the reform plan tended to get the short end of the stick. Since *junyao* converted only part of local corvée into a cash payment (*yinchai* 銀差), local governments could still solicit labor services in the name of *lichai*. *Lichai*, the part considered relatively burdensome, was often specifically assigned to urban residents. Again, spatial expedience was cited to justify the apparently unfair division of labor—because urban residents were geographically close to government offices, it was more convenient and less burdensome for them to serve in person.[71]

In the middle of the fifteenth century, *junyao* was supplanted by the Single Whip method, which converted all corvée requirements into silver payments. Yet the rural bias continued to affect the succeeding reform movement, and in some areas the reform measures were not extended to cities. For example, the editor of a 1609 Anhui gazetteer indicated that ward corvée had become even more onerous since the successful implementation of the Single Whip method. The irony, again, is a product of the rural bias. Under the forceful execution and close supervision of grand coordinators (*xunfu* 巡撫) and regional inspectors (*xun'an yushi* 巡按御史), local governments were unable to levy corvée on rural areas and all labor services fell on ward residents.[72] Even in places where cities figured in the considerations of reformers, the absence of an urban taxation system rendered the assessment of monetary payments in lieu of corvée highly problematic.

Local solutions varied widely, with different consequences. For example, in order to level the rural-urban inequality, Nanchang prefecture converted both urban and rural corvée into a fixed silver payment based on *ding* (adult males) and *liang* (agricultural output). This solution obviously favored urban residents with no agricultural land. Both rural and urban residents paid the same poll tax in place of previous corvée service, but peasants were still liable for land tax assessed by *liang* to subsidize the operations of local offices. Previously these offices had relied solely on contributions from urban residents, and the implementation of the Single Whip method substantially reduced the fiscal burden on urban residents.[73] The reduction was so dramatic that in Xiaogan (Hubei), the shift toward silver payments provoked complaints that urban residents paid as little as half the amount of taxes levied on peasants.[74]

If land was not a fair means to determine the rate for commutation of corvée, then what was? Indeed, the pros and cons of different tax bases provoked heated debates. As noted above, the chief reason for using land taxes as a substitute for corvée service lay in the fact that, unlike other measures of financial capacity, agricultural land, owing to its immobility and relatively stable output, was difficult to hide and less susceptible to clerical manipulation. But it was also recognized that if labor services were converted into land taxes, those whose income was not fully generated by rural land received an undeserved tax break. This problem was exacerbated when more and more rural landlords moved to cities during the economic boom of the sixteenth century. Particularly in the south, the conflict of interests between landowners and merchants appears to have been most intense since the economy was more commercialized and yet the reformers tended to convert labor service requirements into agricultural land taxes. As the main Single Whip advocate in Jiangxi, Liu Guangji 劉光濟, pointed out in a memorial in 1588, when determining the commutation rate, local governments in the north used a composite index of *men* 門 (household), *ding* 丁 (male adults), *shi* 事 (liquid assets), and *chan* 產 (property), whereas those in the south tended to use only *tianliang* 田糧 (agricultural out-put). The reliance on land as the basis for corvée conversion not only exempted the increasingly affluent merchant class from taxation but also drove peasants to abandon their land, further damaging the already declining rural economy. Indeed, many contemporary critics observed that the heavy Single Whip tax placed on land had caused peasants to abandon farming and pursue frivolous professions such as trade (*qi ben zhu mo* 棄本逐末), which in turn led to land depreciation in rural areas.[75]

The complexity of this issue and the social tension it generated are best exemplified by two prefectures in Jiangnan, Jiaxing 嘉興 and Huzhou 湖州. In both regions the fiscal liabilities of urban residents provoked heated debates, but the outcomes were very different.[76] In Jiaxing, the controversy surrounding urban taxation had become so

charged that it made a pro-reform magistrate's top-ten list of urgent local issues. According to him, locals were torn between two propositions
regarding the corvée reform. One side pressed the local government to
equalize the burden among all landholders, especially between gentry
(meaning their exemption privileges had to be modified or even abolished) and commoners; the other side contended that greater social justice lay with the creation of urban property taxes for urban residents
who owned no land. Supporters of urban taxation argued that this issue
had particular salience in Jiaxing because the local economy had allowed people to get rich without investing heavily in land. Therefore,
even if the reform equalized the converted corvée rate among landowners (the so-called *juntian juanyi* 均田均役), the result still would not
satisfy locals' demand for fiscal justice. In the end, the magistrate sided
with the second position and proposed a new tax on urban residential
property. He emphasized that the measure was not intended to exploit
the wealth of urban residents. Rather, it aimed to redress the loophole
in the current system that allowed wealthy merchants to escape the
reach of the Single Whip reform.[77]

In Huzhou, however, this debate took a different turn. Zhu Guozhen, an active participant in the local reform movement, made a different argument in his "Shihu yi" 市戶議 (A proposition regarding urban households).[78] A closer look at Huzhou's economic practice, Zhu
asserted, would show that there were few rich people in this area who
did not invest in agricultural land. Therefore, a separate urban property
tax was unnecessary. The more pressing issue, Zhu believed, was to
limit the generous exemptions of the gentry class. Zhu's point was
elaborated by another Huzhou reform activist, Ding Yuanjian 丁元薦
(1563–1628), who contended that the conservative gentry's support for
urban taxation was just a ruse to deflect the attack on their privileges.[79]
This tactic appears not to have been unique to Huzhou. For example, a
gazetteer for Quanzhou prefecture (Fujian) noted local criticism of the
Single Whip reform as favoring wealthy merchants with no landholdings. The editor, however, dismissed this opinion as a self-serving claim
by local gentry whose interests were compromised by the reform. While
not denying that the current reform plan indeed benefited wealthy merchants, the editor remained strongly convinced that the issue of gentry

privileges should take priority: not just because this move was critical in rescuing the peasant economy from collapsing, but, more important, because it would eventually secure the welfare of the rural landholding gentry class.[80] Whether this point is valid or not, the conservative gentry's tactic of using merchants as a scapegoat may have had more profound consequences than intended. With the opposition to gentry privileges on the rise, the perception that taxing the urban rich and reducing gentry privileges were mutually exclusive options may to some degree have prevented urban taxation from becoming a mainstream measure in corvée reform.

In the end, the "urban question" received very localized treatments in the late Ming fiscal reform. Even areas inclined to tax the urban rich adopted solutions other than creating taxes on urban property. One was to have urban residents establish *yitian* 役田 (corvée fields) and use the rental proceeds from these lands to fund the hiring of labor services. In the Suzhou area, for example, the most affluent residents were urban merchants who rarely invested in land. Therefore the assignment of corvée fell unfairly on the much less well off peasants. In the mid-sixteenth century, magistrate Song Yiwang 宋儀望 successfully raised money from the urban rich to establish public corvée fields.[81] The same measure, however, was employed in nearby Songjiang 松江 for an opposite purpose: since urban residents there bore a heavier share of government labor requisitions, they raised money and established corvée fields to relieve the burden on themselves.[82]

In sum, the rural bias of the Chinese administrative system developed to its strongest degree in the Ming era. The absence of urban taxation in the Ming, for example, was a unique product of that dynasty's ideology. Like rural villagers, urban residents were liable for corvée, but no specific taxes were levied on urban assets or properties. As a result, despite the increasing importance of cities in Ming society and culture, their fiscal capacity went untapped. This bias became even more problematic when the corvée system underwent a fundamental overhaul beginning in the fifteenth century, and land taxes began to figure more prominently in the fiscal system. The failure of the original fiscal scheme to take urban land into account, however, was never redressed systematically at the central level. Rather, it was confronted on a case-by-case basis. As observed above, some sought to hold urban residents liable by creating a new urban tax, and others chose to prioritize other issues in the fiscal reform (such as abolishing gentry privileges). Yet amid the diverse policy positions, the growing recognition of the problematic urban-rural divide in the early Ming fiscal design opened room to renegotiate the fiscal value of urban space.

From Ward Corvée to Huojia: *The Expansion of Urban Corvée Conscription.* Although the fiscal reform faced a much more complicated situation in urban settings, to an extent it reduced the burden of ward corvée in many cities. However, success, albeit limited, bred new problems for urban residents. Unfilled government requisitions were now channeled into other forms of labor service, especially through security organizations such as *huojia*, as we have seen in the case of Nanjing. This development is not surprising because *huojia* was not tied to the now-obsolete household registration system and thus proved a more efficient venue for labor conscription. Since the original purpose of *huojia* was to provide local security, the expansion of government levies into other areas of labor service was deemed illicit and widely seen as a sign of official corruption. However, recent scholarship has shed new light on this popular view and found a deeper structural root for the abuse of labor service in the promotion of frugal governance.

Dictated by the ideology of "low taxes / light corvée" (*qingshui bofu* 輕稅薄賦), this emerging governing style was in line with the early Ming ideal of minimal governance. The resultant conservative fiscal practice often led to budget shortfalls, forcing underfunded local governments to impose illicit requisitions on an ad hoc basis in order to support routine operations. This tendency was aggravated at the height of the Single Whip movement, a reform initiated at the local level and encouraged under the auspices of Chief Councilor Zhang Juzheng 張居正 (1525–82). Granted, thrifty governance was consistent with the goal of the Single Whip reform in regulating local budgets. Nevertheless, as was true of Zhang's many measures to centralize the imperial bureaucracy, his championship of this policy was driven by the interests of the central government. In order to survive the military threat from the north, the court needed to secure more revenues, which had shrunk seriously over the course of the two hundred years of the Ming's existence. To avoid unpopular measures, such as imposing new or higher taxes, Zhang opted instead to recover taxes in default. Since the court competed with local governments for the same pool of revenues, as long as local offices continued to cut their budgets, they would be able to remit more tax revenues to the state treasury. Thus by emphasizing "thrifty governance" in evaluating the performance of local bureaucrats, Zhang was able to channel more revenue to the state treasury.[83]

Frugality, however, was detrimental to the fiscal health of local governments since it encouraged bureaucrats to radically reduce local budgets in order to score political points. The faults of this policy were not lost on contemporary observers. Sun Chengze 孫承澤 (1592–1676), a late Ming–early Qing high official, for example, found policy-makers' glorification of "light taxes" during the Single Whip reform highly problematic. Sun was particularly averse to the extreme reduction of local budgets (*jiesheng zhishuo* 節省之説). He believed that this ideal of frugality had led local officials to engage in self-deceiving political rhetoric that would serve only to destroy local financial stability.[84] Indeed, we find that as ambitious officials eagerly campaigned for budget caps far below operational costs, the resulting deficits were relieved either by channeling funds from other sources or by imposing illegal taxes or corvée requisitions. With the collapse of the *lijia* organization in both cities and countryside, local governments sought to fulfill their unmet needs by imposing further demands on the security organization. This tendency proves to be the key to understanding the impetus for *huojia* reform in Nanjing.[85]

Coping with the "Urban Question" in Ming Nanjing

Ward Corvée Reform in Nanjing. Corvée reform in Nanjing shared the general features of the late Ming fiscal reform, but it was also shaped and conditioned by its unique setting. As an imperial capital, Nanjing was a heavily bureaucratized city that housed three levels of government: the county, prefecture, and central court. From early on, two corvée systems, namely ward corvée and *huojia*, were put in place to serve the numerous government offices in the city.

The heavy demand for corvée drastically declined when Chengzu 成祖 (the Yongle emperor, r. 1402–24) moved the capital to Beijing. Following the example of forced migration set by Taizu, Chengzu also moved 27,000 households to Beijing. As a result, the population of

Nanjing dropped by half, as did ward requisitions. In fact, demand was so low that ward corvée was sometimes funneled to support *lijia* operations in rural areas (Nanjing wards were under the jurisdiction of two metropolitan counties, Shangyuan and Jiangning, which governed both the city of Nanjing and its neighboring villages). In 1437, metropolitan governor Kuang Ye 鄺埜 consolidated the existing 318 wards into 79 and set an upper limit of 300 taels of silver for each season of the year to cover the expenses of hiring out ward corvée services.

The light burden of government requisitions, however, did not last long in Nanjing. As the economy of the empire continued to prosper, population increased and the bureaucratic workload expanded, causing the burden on ward residents to grow heavier and heavier—one source estimates that it multiplied by forty.[86] As elsewhere in the empire, a vicious cycle began: the heavier the burden became, the more people evaded registration. The fewer residents on the roll, the heavier the fiscal burden for the remaining ones. When the ward funds became irreparably deficient, county clerks abolished the fixed payment, and ward residents were again on call for unlimited government requisitions of labor services. Every season, "wealthy households" were appointed to make good on the deficits either by collecting the sum from fellow ward residents or paying the difference from their own pockets. Assignment of those responsible for the arrears was completely at the discretion of local county clerks. There were no objective property assessment standards whatsoever. Naturally this system was open to abuse and corruption. To make things worse, beginning in the Hongzhi reign (1488–1505), requisitions from the central government skyrocketed. In bleak language and meticulous detail, Gu Qiyuan described this dark age for his hometown:

More labor service is requested from [the Ministry of Revenue] for the nine storehouses, eight domestic custom houses, and five boroughs [in Nanjing]. Other extra requests include: purchase and transportation of firewood in place of the Ministry of Works for the Court of Imperial Entertainment; providing the Court of Imperial Sacrifice nine kinds of fresh food; paying for document copiers as well as building maintenance for all yamens [in Nanjing]. From 1539 on, [the Nanjing ward levy] started to be responsible for providing [labor and supplies] for yet another eight yamens. This does not yet include all the expenses spent on banquets, festivals, and lanterns. Furthermore, emissaries or messengers [passing through Nanjing] issued tickets drafting services including running errands, supplying food, and even escorting marching bands on their way in and out of the city of Nanjing. On top of everything else, officials, clerks, and lesser functionaries abused the system to satisfy their personal needs by way of extortion and intimidation. These practices became such a problem that that many people on duty went bankrupt. Every day suicides were reported. People were on the verge of collapsing.[87]

The situation apparently continued to deteriorate until the 1570s, when a local *shengyuan*, Zhao Shanji 趙善繼, initiated a campaign to reduce government requisitions.[88] Zhao's uncle had died on corvée duty, probably from imprisonment due to a failure to fulfill his assigned work. Zhao's family originated in Henan and was one of the "wealthy households" forcibly relocated to Nanjing at the beginning of the Ming. Despite the Hongwu emperor's prohibition against the involvement of students at county schools in local politics, Zhao organized students from local families to join his cause. Their primary goal was to reduce the extra requisitions, the *feichai*, imposed by government offices in Nanjing. Indeed, as Zhao observed, even if each yamen requested only a few items at a time, the cumulative burden far exceeded the means of Nanjing residents. His strategy was to use personal persuasion by showing officials how their seemingly innocuous requests were severely impoverishing Nanjing's ward residents.

Zhao's biography describes in vivid detail what it took to accomplish a fiscal reform that involved the interests of every Nanjing yamen. Along with his fellow county school students, Zhao first rallied public support through a campaign of printed petitions submitted to gentry and officials of all ranks in Nanjing. After receiving a green light from the metropolitan governor, students lobbied individual offices to join the reform. Their efforts met with many different reactions.[89] Some bureaucrats were resistant to change; others deliberately used "requisitions" as favors to grease their way up the bureaucratic ladder; still others were simply too vested in the corrupt system to contemplate change. Many times their petition was accepted and then overturned the very next day, and they had to start all over again. Nevertheless, because of their persistence, consciousness of the problems of the ward corvée system grew, and officials began to take a more sympathetic attitude toward their petition. With extraordinary determination, Zhao Shanji went from office to office pleading his cause. This personal approach to reform, however, also led to its quick demise after Zhao passed away at the end of the sixteenth century. The transience of Zhao's personal approach might have encouraged Ding Bin to take a more aggressive approach to building public consensus.

True to the general pattern of Ming fiscal reform, Zhao Shanji's campaign sought changes in Nanjing by regulating the demands of government offices. However, it was also clear to contemporary observers that as long as ward residents were subject to unlimited requisitions from government, the root cause of their suffering remained intact. Therefore, another stream of ward corvée reforms was initiated to convert on-call service liabilities into fixed tax payments. In 1567, the Longqing era's first year (always a prime time to initiate reform), the regional inspector and metropolitan governor decided to restore the rules of the Zhengtong reign and removed ward residents from the on-call roster of the county yamens. Once a set quota of silver had been paid in by city residents, they were relieved of their official obligations. The tax revenues, which were just 10 percent higher than the amount set in the mid-fifteenth century, were used to hire laborers and buy supplies for the Nanjing offices. Soon after the governor left, however, his successor restored the old system of on-call conscription. From this point on, Nanjing's ward corvée seesawed between fixed payments and in-person service. The struggle continued at least until the early seventeenth century.[90]

One reason for the constant shifts in policy may have been the court's increasing appreciation of frugal bureaucrats. In 1575, after numerous setbacks, the reform effort began again when a new metropolitan governor took office. After reviewing the account books of the two metropolitan counties, the governor realized that the heavy burden on ward residents was caused by the inclusion of private expenses from the yamens. To curb this abuse, he cited a precedent from Beijing and set 540 silver taels per year as the upper limit for ward corvée. This measure gained great support and collaboration from County Magistrate Lin Dafu 林大輔, who is said to have excelled in frugal governance. However, soon after Lin left his post, four-fifths of the annual budget was already spent within the first season. A subsequent proposal to restore corvée conscription stirred such a public outrage that it almost resulted in an urban riot. The government relented under public pressure: county funds were used to cover budget shortfalls in the city, the clerks involved were punished, and, most astonishing of all, the ward corvée budget was further cut by 100 silver taels to appease the angry crowd. Despite the inflation that accompanied the economic boom, population growth, and bureaucratic expansion, the ward corvée fund was less than half of the amount set more than 150 years before! The plummeting budget may also reflect the sharp decrease in registered ward members during the fifteenth and sixteenth centuries, which is not a surprising development given the excessive burden imposed on ward residents.[91] These factors aside, however, the needs of local offices did not diminish. With ward corvée increasingly regulated, the unmet government requisitions morphed into *feichai* levied through the *huojia* organization.[92]

From Ward Corvée to Huojia.   The abuse of *huojia* developed into a major issue when Hai Rui 海瑞 served as the Nanjing censor-in-chief (1586–87). As he pointed out:

Huojia were established for the purpose of local defense. For all the hundreds of officials in the capital, clerks and runners are appointed to be at their disposal. However, this is not the case in Nanjing. [All the extra burden] imposed on local residents was so unbearable that they had to appeal to the officials above. . . . The people suffered for a long time under this *huojia* corvée. Nonetheless, as soon as such an issue was raised in a memorial and the resolution was approved, the same problem [illicit conscription] recurred. Soon after, the same proposal was raised in another memorial again [and the situation continued as before]. It is because the officials in charge took a lenient attitude and never really intended to deal with it. All the memorials were nothing but lip service.[93]

It seemed as if Nanjing residents would never see an end to their miseries: the same issue had been brought to the attention of the court over and over again, but any changes were soon abandoned. From Hai's point of view (typical throughout Hai's famous but controversial career), most of the problems could have been resolved if the officials in charge had acted with sufficient determination and moral commitment.[94] However, human failing was only partly responsible for the misery caused by the *huojia* system. As discussed in the previous section,

Nanjing's malfunctioning fiscal system suffered from a much deeper structural flaw: a disproportionately low statutory budget for bureaucratic operations repeatedly forced local officials to impose nonstatutory levies on locals.[95] Still, Hai Rui's view was typical of the general perception at the time: the fiscal crisis was attributed to moral, rather than structural, failings.

To solve the problem, Hai declared his determination to enforce a set of new regulations to prevent further abuses by yamens at all levels in Nanjing. Hai also compiled *Fuchai ce* (Register of corvée), a comprehensive list of all the labor services for which Nanjing residents were to be responsible. Any official requisition beyond those listed in the register would be deemed illegal and subject to chastisement. Interestingly, Hai's reform did not seek to restore *huojia* to its original form as a security service. Instead, his compromise realistically acknowledged urban corvée as an alternative source for government operations. The aim of this reform, therefore, was to protect the status quo from further deterioration. The *Register of Corvée* listed five main categories of yamen work, further broken down into more than a hundred types of labor service:

> Yamen hall watchers (more than 50 types)
> Palace and yamen cleaners (12)
> Night watchers for officials' personal residences (24)
> Yamen lantern holders (28)
> Yamen nonroutine laborers (12)

This lengthy list of duties provides concrete proof of how extensively the *huojia* system had been expanded into a complementary labor supply system for government offices in Nanjing. Because of the special status of Nanjing as the secondary capital, the list was unusually long compared to that of regular prefectural government. Indeed, Nanjing hosted offices for the palace, the six ministries, one prefecture (Yingtian 應天), and two county governments, all of which required staff to run their daily operations as well as to help on ritual occasions. When insufficient funding prevented these government offices from recruiting an adequate workforce, the burden was transferred to local residents by way of *huojia*. In fact, so much of this workload had been channeled through the *huojia*, even a list as meticulous as Hai's could not meet all the government's needs. As a result, a dual "ticket and book" system was put in practice. Any request outside the corvée register needed an officially approved ticket to be fulfilled. This expedient opened the floodgates for even more irregular demands on Nanjing residents and paved the way for a more radical reform during Ding Bin's tenure.[96]

Reinventing a Taxable Urban Space

It should be clear by now that despite Nanjing's unique status as the auxiliary capital, the trajectory of its urban corvée reform was typical of that of many cities at the time. On one hand, officials recognized the urgent imperative to regulate local government's excessive impositions by converting levies into fixed silver payments. On the other hand, because of the ever-present shortage of local funding, illicit conscription in the form of *feichai* survived the end of the Ming dynasty and continued to haunt the new Manchu empire.[97] One of the most common reincarnations of the old corvée conscription was made through the local security system, *baojia* 保甲. The abuse appears to have been so rampant that it compelled the court to take action. In 1603, the Ministry of Revenue memorialized the emperor to further stipulate the implementation of the Single Whip method, emphasizing that *baojia*, the local security organization, should not be exploited as a venue for illicit levies.[98]

Although the malfeasance was not confined to cities, urban residents probably felt its impact the strongest since *baojia* was based not on official household registration but on a residence-by-residence rotation called *paimen* 排門.[99] Thus it reached a more extensive social base, including sojourning merchants and new migrants, who evaded levies based on the outdated household registration.[100] In an urban environment with a constant influx of new population, *paimen* was clearly a far more productive method for local governments to allocate levies. As *huojia* became more widely adopted as a security organization in cities, however, the problems of its abuse grew. In 1609, in Jianchang prefecture (Jiangxi province), a censor forbade all forms of *paimen* urban labor conscription such as *huojia* or *zongjia* 總甲, which emerged *after* the implementation of the Single Whip method had nominally abolished in-person corvée services.[101] Apparently, *huojia* was exploited as an alternative to the recently abolished ward corvée, a development also observed by the editor of the Qiongzhou gazetteer:

At the beginning of the [Ming] dynasty, other than the statutory *lijia* conscription, people were not bothered at all. This situation changed drastically later on, when people were burdened with all kinds of extra-statutory conscriptions. . . . The position of *zongxiaojia* 總小甲 (also called *huofu* 火夫, *zongjia* 總甲, *baozhang* 保長) was originally set up to inspect wrongdoings, and yet whoever is on duty is often harassed with onerous requisitions.[102]

Indeed, as Lü Kun 呂坤 (1536–1618) stated, the rampant exploitation of *huojia* had made it a de facto official levy, *chai wai zhi chai* 差外之差 (an extra corvée that was not a part of the prescribed labor services).[103]

The abusive conscription of *huojia* led Nanjing, as well as many other cities, back to the same quagmire as with ward corvée. On one hand, the ever increasing extra-statutory requisitions from local offices had pushed the system to the verge of collapse; on the other hand, the wealthy and the powerful were able to evade conscription, leaving the urban middle and lower classes to shoulder the burden alone. Therefore, it is not a surprise to find that calls for reforming the *huojia* system were often voiced by members of the urban lower middle class who were not sheltered by the exemptions built into the system for the gentry. Shouldering burdens far beyond their means, these unfortunate city residents were obliged to respond to all daytime service calls and material requisitions as well as nighttime patrol requests. The high number of urban uprisings, especially in places such as Hangzhou and Suzhou in the economic center of Jiangnan, gives clear evidence of the mounting frustration among the urban middle class.[104] The threat of imminent urban unrest precipitated another wave of urban *huojia* reforms, including the one in Nanjing.

Nevertheless, compared with the way in which *huojia* reforms unfolded in other cities, the reform process in Nanjing was remarkably peaceful, probably because of the leadership of the presiding official, Ding Bin. As discussed above, the key to Ding's success in preventing open confrontation between supporters and opponents of the reform lay in the process he developed to establish public consensus. Before he officially implemented the reform, Ding Bin personally met with the petitioners, dispatched officials to interview residents in their homes, held public hearings, and posted notices urging dissenting residents to speak their minds. The oft-cited Confucian ideal of "respecting the people's will" was aggressively pursued in the most literal terms. Although Ding Bin explained his repeated surveys as cautionary measures to assure public consensus, in view of the contentious history of Nanjing's fiscal reform, they might well have served to create effective public pressure. Indeed, compared to the personalized reform strategy of Zhao Shanji, the conspicuous display of public consensus in Ding Bin's reform proved to be a much more successful tactic both to force officials into cooperating and to appease the agitated urban public.

Yet, as with earlier urban corvée reforms, the conversion of the labor services of the *huojia* system into silver payments was not as straightforward as it was in the countryside: it required reformers to create an urban equivalent of agricultural land to determine the tax rates. To solve this problem, Ding Bin again resorted to the support lent by the community leaders. The petitioners put forth an innovative proposal, calling on Nanjing residents to voluntarily register on the tax rolls:

Since we [Nanjing residents] have been hiring substitutes to serve for *huojia* on our own, there is a going price for each household to share. Since the price is based only on a tacit agreement among residents [no prices are written down], we volunteer to compile a book on the exact share for each household, rich or poor, in the year of 1608. Every *pu* [the neighborhood unit for the *huojia* system] will meet to collect and compile this information into a list named *Wucheng puce* 五城鋪册 (Neighborhood almanac for the five boroughs of Nanjing), and together we will send it to the government to be used as an official reference.[105]

To forestall any lingering hesitation on the officials' side, residents further volunteered mutual surveillance to assure the accuracy of the collected data: "Since each book is to be compiled in public in every neighborhood, no one will dare to cheat by recording a lesser amount than their actual portion, nor will anyone report more than they are bound to pay."[106] According to Ding's account, within a few days more than a thousand levy registers were compiled and sent to him directly. This information was then used as the basis for the new graduated urban property tax (*fanghao yin* 房號銀).

Although similar measures were found in other cities, property tax was not the only possible answer to the problem.[107] Some localities opted to convert labor service into existing tax categories such as the stamp tax (*tianfangqi* 田房契) or store franchise fees (*mentan* 門攤). Some revived elements of the Song urban tax system, which used the size of a person's house, rental income, or real estate value to determine tax rates.[108] As noted above, some cities established *yitian* (corvée fields).[109] In one case, the revenue generated by charity houses was used for this purpose.[110] The diversity aside, in the end *fanghao yin* emerged as the favorite choice for converting urban corvée into silver payments. It was widely adopted in Shanxi during Lü Kun's tenure as regional inspector[111] as well as in Shandong, where it was reported that merchants in Linqing avoided local registration in order to evade this new tax.[112]

Here we find an unexpected return—though not fully—to the Song system of urban taxation. Instead of being driven by state economic activism, however, the revival of an urban land tax was prompted mainly by popular demands to overcome the obstacles posed by a rural-based fiscal system. In an ironic turn of history, the system that marginalized the place of cities inadvertently brought urbanites together.

The Urban Dimension of the Late Ming Fiscal Reform

To be sure, a fiscal reorganization of the magnitude of the Single Whip reform was bound to provoke conflicts of interest and power struggles on multiple fronts. Traditionally the reform movement was deemed a battle against bureaucratic corruption and the abuse of gentry privileges. Recent studies also point out another factor contributing to the lengthening of the reform process: competition for revenue between the central and local governments. By promoting frugal governance, the state was able to recover revenues that had been absorbed by the ever-growing local expenses. Yet the unrealistically low caps set by ambitious officials further strained the finances of local governments, sometimes forcing local offices to resort to illicit conscription.

This chapter brings to light yet another important, but often overlooked, dimension of this grand war for fiscal justice—the spatial. As land taxes emerged as the favorite solution to fiscal injustice, urbanites, through numerous petitions and sometimes even uprisings, endeavored to overcome the de facto urban-rural division in the fiscal reform. In order to be included in the Single Whip reform movement, many cities, like Nanjing, reinvented their cities as a taxable space by installing a graduated property tax. With urban space being redefined in fiscal terms, new perceptions of the "city" emerged on the political landscape of the empire.

CONCLUSION: STATE, SOCIETY, AND A POPULIST URBAN REFORM

We now return to the question with which this chapter began: Why did Nanjing residents, after repeated petitions, pour into the streets to register to be taxed? How can a seemingly incongruous populist movement *for taxes* possibly be explained? This chapter has given us two insights for understanding this puzzle. On one hand, it argues that the active role of Nanjing residents was a product of the expansion of political participation in the fiscal reforms. On the other hand, the implementation of fiscal reform proved to be particularly challenging in cities where no specific taxes had been imposed. What drove the impressive civil solidarity in Nanjing, it turns out, was the particular agenda of late Ming urban residents to reinvent a taxable urban space.

Indeed, the Nanjing *huojia* reform took place at a time when, in the wake of a collapsing fiscal system premised on self-supervising rural communities, both state and society were preoccupied with fiscal justice. The intense anxiety gave rise to a series of reform efforts and eventually culminated in the creation of the Single Whip method, which converted all labor service obligations into fixed silver payments. The adoption of silver as the fiscal currency marked a monumental change in Chinese history but did not fully resolve the problem of fiscal inequalities. The ability to restore fiscal justice rested on two other factors: just criteria to measure financial capacity and a well-designed procedure impervious to malfeasance. Taxes, especially when based on the most concrete, visible, and hard to hide form of property—land—proved to be an ideal candidate for both the state and the people. In the long run, the trend toward land taxes prevailed in the early eighteenth century when corvée was officially abolished and rural landownership became the primary basis for taxation.[113] Public demand for a tax in place of corvée—as in the case of Nanjing—was an important element of this collective effort to formalize and publicize fiscal transactions between the state and its people.

Furthermore, in order to create new procedures for tax apportionment and collection, grassroots power was widely enlisted to circumvent bureaucratic expansion. Since the Single Whip method allowed for a wide range of local modifications, officials sometimes appealed to the general public to determine reform-related policies, to confirm the results of property inspections, and to supervise the implementation of reform statutes. The active engagement of the Nanjing community was thus no accident: with the voluntary cooperation of urban neighborhoods, the local government was able to undertake a new tax system. The power demonstrated by urban residents was so impressive that it may have inspired Ding Bin to present his reform in the same spirit. In his accounts, Ding characterized his reform as the persistent pursuit of public consensus coupled with enthusiastic grassroots participation.

Although the expansion of public participation was a general trend during the fiscal reform, the form it took in cities differed from that in the countryside. Thus, the second part of this chapter treats the important, and often overlooked, spatial dimension of the Single Whip reform movement. The urban-rural divide arose from the ideal of self-governing rural communities in the early Ming fiscal system. As a result, no specific statute regulated the fiscal responsibility of cities to the state, even as the empire underwent energetic urban development. This omission, however, did not necessarily work to the advantage of urban residents; rather, in some cases, it exposed them to further corruption and exploitation. Above all, the lack of urban tax registries made the conversion of corvée into silver payments especially difficult. As traced in this chapter, the path of fiscal reform in Ming cities was convoluted. The lack of institutional attention continued throughout the late Ming, and the reform of urban corvée tended to proceed on a case-by-case basis and never became a formal component of the Single Whip method. However, the shared effort to define urban wealth for tax purposes is of great consequence. It forced institutional recognition, albeit limited, of the inadequacy of the rural-centered bias of the Ming system and the need to administer cities in a separate manner. The creation of new property taxes in cities such as Nanjing, in this sense, reinvented the idea of urban space for a Ming political geography originally defined by idealized rural communities.

CHAPTER 2

To Wall or Not to Wall

The focus of investigation in this chapter is Nanjing as a region, a cityscape defined by a network of city walls. Indeed, for Ming contemporaries, Nanjing, often under its cultural sobriquet, Jinling 金陵 (Golden hills), referred to both the walled city and the prefectural region (Yingtian prefecture, or the Nanjing Metropolitan Area)* under its rule. This spatial ambiguity resulted from the fact that a Chinese city did not constitute a formal political unit. Rather, it served as the administrative center of a greater region, most of which was rural. In this extended sense, the actual "urban space" of Nanjing was composed of a network of administrative cities (*cheng* 城) and commercial towns (*zhen* 鎮). However, only the government seats were physically bounded by city walls.[1] Trading towns, despite their rapid growth during the mid-Ming urbanization, were neither institutionally nor architecturally distinguished from villages at this time.

City walls, in this sense, not only were the most prominent architectural feature of the Chinese cityscape but also marked the boundary between two city systems, one symbolizing the state's presence and the other commercial vitality. Yet the walled boundary itself was by no means permanent. In the case of Ming Nanjing, changes were precipitated by the city's elevation in status to imperial capital and the consequent extensive territorial restructuring of the Nanjing Metropolitan Area. The expansion took place in two stages. At the beginning of the dynasty, Taizu incorporated Luhe 六合, a county across the Yangzi River, into the jurisdiction of Nanjing and then carved a new county, Jiangpu 江浦, out of Luhe to strengthen the defensive ring around the

---

*The term "Nanjing Metropolitan Area" refers to *jingzhao* 京兆, the unofficial designation of the prefectural area surrounding the imperial capital. It differs from *zhili* 直隸 or *Nan zhili* 南直隸 (after 1421), the Southern Metropolitan Area, which was roughly composed of modern Jiangsu and Anhui provinces. See Hucker, *Dictionary of Official Titles.*

capital. Later, in the fifteenth century, another new county, Gaochun 高淳, was established and placed under Nanjing's rule. Both of the new county seats had been unwalled trading towns prior to the creation of the new counties, and with the change in status came the task of city-wall construction. Although dissent was voiced in both counties against the wall-building projects, in the end not one but two walls were built around Jiangpu city. Following a heated protest, however, Gaochun city remained unwalled. This outcome drastically redefined the cityscape of the Nanjing Metropolitan Area, and the striking contrast between Gaochun and Jiangpu is the central issue in this chapter.

Unlike the preceding Song and Yuan dynasties, the Ming court was adamant that all administrative cities should be walled.[2] This policy was emphatically enforced in the wake of pirate attacks in the sixteenth century, leading to a revival of the wall-building movement. Yet despite the general frenzy for city-wall construction, the popular response to wall building varied considerably. In areas threatened by the pirates, the locals often took the initiative, petitioning for permission to construct or expand city walls in order to defend themselves more effectively.[3] Yet for residents in other areas, city walls, the most symbolic spatial feature of the Chinese cityscape, were luxuries that consumed money and labor at public expense, and opposition to their construction was often vocal. Nevertheless, in most cases, local dissent was managed or quelled, and the imperial project of wall building proceeded. The success of the Gaochun anti-wall campaign is even more unusual given its location within the Nanjing Metropolitan Area. Since city walls had come to play a critical role in regional defense and security plans in the sixteenth century, it is curious that, in a strategically significant area such as Nanjing, the anti-wall protest not only went unpunished but even succeeded.

The Gaochun protest, as it turns out, drew heavily on a long-term campaign by local residents to restructure local finances after a major defeat in a water dispute. The scope and efficacy of Gaochun lobbying clearly refute the conventional wisdom that the Ming dynasty was the epitome of Chinese despotism.[4] To be sure, under the Ming founding emperor, monarchical power expanded significantly. Most notable of all was the abolition of the office of prime minister in 1380, a move that drastically undermined the autonomy of imperial bureaucracy.[5] Yet further studies have also demonstrated that the monarch's power was far from absolute. The emperor, his officials insisted, was still bound by constitutional precedents.[6] Moreover, in an empire of China's scale, the state's authority was inevitably far removed from its subjects, and commands had to be filtered through not only the imperial bureaucracy but also the local gentry before they reached their targets. As intermediaries, the elite played a critical role in social control and state governance, and not necessarily always in conformity with the state's goals.[7]

This complicated interaction, as Timothy Brook has recently suggested, allowed great space for negotiation, and as a result, the Chinese state's power was strongest only when it successfully integrated the interests of these mediating groups, a unique feature that Brook eloquently terms the "capillary effect." This analogy vividly captures the social embeddedness of the Ming state: "percolation from above with no guarantee of where the moisture of state influence might reach, and capillary action from below with potentially no limit on the capacity of society to remake the state."[8] This delicate play of power and the rough equilibrium between state and society depended greatly on the capacity of local elites to mediate and keep underlying tensions from erupting into conflict.[9] Sarah Schneewind's work on the development of community schools throughout the Ming era similarly testifies to the Ming state's precarious control over local society. As she remarks, "State personnel and those they ruled not only served and thought about the state, but also turned it to their own uses. The Ming state was built from below as it was from above; as people colonized government institutions and documents for their own aims, they lengthened the reach of the state."[10]

Indeed, the works of Brook, Schneewind, and other scholars have significantly modified, if not subverted, the view of the Ming polity as despotic and supplied ample evidence of local resistance and manipulation. Nevertheless, the state is still perceived in these studies as a repressive power with which social agents had to contend. In contrast, the previous chapter highlights collaboration between government agencies and local residents during the fiscal reform and presents a very different view of the tug-of-war between state and society. The case of Gaochun further brings to light the overlooked space of local lobbying and political negotiation in the implementation of seemingly incontestable state policies. By shifting the analytical focus from contention to negotiation, we will find that what was at stake was not just the power struggle between state and society but, more important, the issues and concerns that informed and shaped the course and outcome of such political negotiations. Indeed, central to Gaochun's campaign against the wall mandate was the new identity of Gaochun city. Gaochun, for the first time in the town's history, had been promoted from trading town (*zhen*) to county city (*cheng*), a change of status locals normally embraced with enthusiasm for the political clout and other benefits it brought.[11] The resistance of Gaochun residents, therefore, throws into sharp relief the growing tension between the official and the commercial city systems in the wake of the sixteenth-century boom. In the previous chapter, we saw how the rediscovery of the fiscal value of urban land during the Single Whip reform challenged the state's prescription of urban space. This chapter presents another challenge to that notion, one physically marked by the construction of city walls.

THE GAOCHUN
CITY-WALL PROPOSITION

The Plot

The story of Gaochun's legendary wall protest opens in 1597 with a scene of mass panic. Immediately after Magistrate Ding Rijin 丁日近 announced his plan to build a city wall, more than four hundred people ran, as one account had it, "in tears" to Regional Inspector Li, one of the three regional inspectors of the Southern Metropolitan Area.[12] Although Li's statutory duties were to supervise the conduct of local officials and report directly to the emperor, since the mid-Ming these inspectors had come to be increasingly embroiled in local governance.[13] In this case, Li's intervention was particularly justified by an earlier wall-construction edict.[14] To be sure, a crowd of four hundred was a considerable turnout in a county of some 6,000 registered male adults, especially since many of those lived in remote areas and thus were unable to show up at the petition site in such a timely fashion. Even though official population data in the Ming are notorious for being low, since only registered males would be drafted for the construction of city walls, the figure happens to be meaningful in measuring the significance of the size of the crowd.

This was not the first time that wall building became a public issue in Gaochun. Two decades earlier, in 1573, then-magistrate Xia Daxun 夏大勳 also proposed building a city wall following an edict mandating that all government seats be walled.[15] This action stirred such an uproar among locals that the plan was shelved. Yet after the 1597 protest, the tension between locals and county government over wall construction appears to have been resolved. For example, in 1635, upon receiving another edict reiterating that all unwalled county and provincial capitals had to build walls, the county magistrate immediately sided with the locals and reported back to the emperor that Gaochun could not follow the edict because of geographical and financial difficulties, the same conclusions as reached in the 1597 wall controversy. The wall proposition was dropped again, and Gaochun was never walled.

The sharp contrast between heated contention in 1573 and firm consensus in 1635 indicates that the 1597 protest was indeed decisive. The local gazetteers, however, record the event without comment, as if a popular protest that succeeded in defying a state mandate were a normal occurrence needing no further explanation. Yet this narrative, smoothly slipping over the contours of the incident, is deceptive. The success of Gaochun's anti-wall campaign *was* unusual, especially in view of the aggressive wall-building policy in the wake of pirate attacks. After all, city walls safeguarded not only individual cities but also the whole region by interrupting the supply lines of pirates. They constituted effective inland defense frontlines. Thus, it is not surprising that one of the main defensive tactics to counter the pirate incursions was to have more cities walled or, rather, properly walled.[16] In fact, as early as the fourteenth century, the founder of the Ming dynasty recognized the threat posed by pirates and launched a wall-building campaign on the southeast coast himself.[17] However, despite repeated edicts throughout the dynasty reaffirming the court's position on wall construction, the policy had never been thoroughly implemented because of the tremendous cost of building and maintaining city walls.[18] Thus when pirate attacks peaked in the mid-sixteenth century along both the coastal area and the lower Yangzi region, the court was dismayed to find that most city walls needed substantial reconstruction. The unexpected turmoil inflicted by pirate attacks made the Ming state once again recognize the vital role of city walls in regional security, leading to what

Japanese scholars refer to as the "reviving of the inland regional defense policy"[19] and a new wave of city-wall building.

The court's much stronger intent to enforce the wall policy is apparent in the 1573 edict. Announced in the first year of the Wanli reign, this edict called for "vital" local constructions (*xingjian yaohai* 興建要害) with the building of city walls as one critical item:

Walls and moats are intended to protect people and are especially critical in coastal and frontier areas. Although the court has issued numerous edicts, they have been ignored by the authorities. As a result, all cities and settlements [without the protection of walls and moats] are easily seized when attacked by pirates/bandits. The Ministry of War now asks all superior commanders, military superintendents, regional commanders, grand coordinators, and regional inspectors to inspect every city wall and moat in their jurisdiction, distinguishing the ones that are defensible and those that are not, and then propose budgets and possible sources for financing repair. Furthermore, determine what to do with the cities which are not walled. The above assignment needs to be accomplished in three months, with a report back to the emperor.[20]

Although earlier wall-building edicts also expressed the court's frustration regarding the lack of wall maintenance and construction, they paled in comparison with the urgent tone in the 1573 edict, which specifically delegated responsibilities for wall construction and expressively stated the court's determination. Pressed by a series of defeats by pirates, the emperor launched a new wall-building campaign that demanded the involvement of military units at all levels. But although the strongly worded edict for the most part put military officers in charge of the inspection process, when it came to the actual building, the burden of labor recruiting and fund raising still fell on local civil officials.[21]

This larger background helps explain the timing of wall controversies in Gaochun: the first wall-building proposal was a response to the 1573 edict. Governing one of the two counties in the Nanjing Metropolitan Area that were not walled (for the other county, Jiangpu, see below), the magistrates of Gaochun may have felt this top-down pressure acutely. In response, Magistrate Xia Daxun proposed to finance construction of a city wall in part by selling horse pastures, the Shuiyang Granary, and military exercise fields, to relieve the burden on local people. However, this proposal still met with vehement local opposition and eventually fell through. Under pressure from the court, it is not surprising that the same proposal was made again in 1597. What the political context fails to explain, however, is the leniency granted to Gaochun in the middle of an intensive wall-building campaign. As discussed above, the local outrage was so strong that it not only derailed the current proposition but also pre-empted future attempts. Why was the 1597 protest so powerful in settling the wall issue in Gaochun? To answer this question, I examine the event from both the locals' and the state's perspectives. The following section looks first at the anti-wall campaign in Gaochun, especially how locals perceived the issue of wall construction. As to why the state would allow Gaochun's anti-wall initiative to prevail, given the lack of sources detailing the official decision-making process, I place Gaochun's wall protest in the context of contemporary wall-building politics to identify the factors that contributed to its unusual success.

Wall-Building Debates and the Anti-Wall Discourse

Pro-Wall Opinions.   How did Gaochun locals perceive the issue of wall building? The "local construction" chapter (*jiangzhi* 建置, a common place in local gazetteers for documenting the construction of city walls) in the 1683 Gaochun gazetteer offers some clues. Under the rubric of *guanfang menlou* 關防門樓, "watch towers and guardian gates," the editor states that Gaochun had never been walled. Only after a serious theft in 1526 at the county treasury did the magistrate decide to build seven gates at strategic points to safeguard the county office. The entry refers readers to a group of three essays on wall building, two by local literati and one by a magistrate, who by the law of avoidance was not a native of Gaochun county. All three essays express strong anti-wall sentiments. Their consensus, however, should be regarded not as proof of local unanimity, but as a result of the suppressing and silencing of dissent. The opinions of Magistrate Ding and his reasons for proposing a wall-building plan, which triggered the protest, for example, do not appear in the gazetteer.

It is noteworthy that although historians consider gazetteers the most authoritative sources regarding local history, they were also contemporary forums of local politics; the politics of local gazetteers is often subtly reflected in such matters as the titles used to refer to locals.[22] Thus it is not surprising to find the heated wall debates in Gaochun became a one-sided anti-wall discourse in the gazetteer. Yet the source's bias is not insurmountable since the pro-wall opinion survives in the presentation of arguments against specific plans and proposals. Four possible wall locations, for example, were recorded. Two plans, one in which the walls were confined by the river and the other in which the wall enclosed it, were the main targets of attack in the anti-wall essays and portrayed as unrealistic, if not physically impossible. The others were mentioned only in passing and involved the alternative of moving the county seat or enwalling a market town in the northern part of the county named Xunzhenpu 尋眞鋪 in lieu of walling the county seat. Some specific funding plans, such as requesting aid from nearby counties or selling government property, were also mentioned and refuted in the anti-wall essays. Taken together, beneath the deliberate effort to present a "local consensus" are traces pointing to a heated debate that provoked broad attention and active involvement from locals.

The Anti-Wall Discourse.   Despite the contentious nature of the argument, it is clear that anti-wall opinion prevailed in 1597 and put an end to further debate. Playing a critical role in shaping local consensus, the anti-wall essays collected in Gaochun gazetteers warrant a close examination:

> Han Zhongshu 韓仲叔 local (*yiren* 邑人) and Han Zhongxiao 韓仲孝, *shengyuan* 生員, "Nan cheng shuo" 難城説 (On the difficulty of building a wall).[23]
>
> Xiang Weicong 項維聰, magistrate, 1606, "Jiancheng lun" 建城論 (A thesis on wall building).
>
> Huang Bingshi 黄秉石, local (*yiren* 邑人), "Cheng Gaochun yi" 城高淳議 (A discussion on walling Gaochun).[24]

The focus on these three essays in the local gazetteers is no accident. The biographical information on the authors is scanty, but it appears that they were connected to the local elite circle behind the compilation of the 1606 gazetteer.[25] Magistrate Xiang, in his preface celebrating the completion of the Gaochun gazetteer, proudly described the accomplishment as a group effort involving intensive participation from locals. The compilation sprang from a meeting between the magistrate and two local literati, Qin Shangbin 秦尚賓 and Chen Yuling 陳毓靈, who convinced Magistrate Xiang to undertake the project. After the meeting, a special bureau was set up to collect information, and arrangements were made to interview village heads (*lizhang* 里長) for information on taxes and levies, students for stories about local schools, and gentry for past and present local issues.[26] The activists Qin and Chen were county students (*shengyuan*) and noted for their literary talent. Their tightly knit literati circle included both Huang Bingshi and Han Zhongxiao.[27]

The close relationships among the authors did not preclude personal idiosyncrasies in the anti-wall essays. Huang's essay is the most radical. He began by stating: "Walls are built to protect people. But if today Gaochun is forced to build a wall, then it [Gaochun] will end up with no people and thus defeat the whole purpose of wall building. Why? Please hear me out before condemning me to death."[28] Huang's plea for immunity alerts us that the anti-wall discourse consciously ran counter to imperial policy. Considering the political atmosphere, Huang's forthright objection to wall construction as well as his implicit suggestion of popular defiance should this unwelcome policy go forward make his treatise the most radical and outspoken of the three. In comparison, although Han's essay also speaks with similar urgency, his criticism is skillfully muted with multiple allusions to the *Chunqiu* 春秋 (Spring and autumn annals). On the conservative end is the piece by Magistrate Xiang, whose status as an imperial bureaucrat prevented him from enjoying the same level of liberty as his fellow authors. Xiang acknowledged the importance of building walls for the purpose of guarding Nanjing, but he also admitted the difficulty of wall construction in Gaochun and proposed the short-term compromise of walling the county office in lieu of the whole city.

Despite differences, the three essays not only share the same position on the wall-building issue but also exhibit a strong structural resemblance. A passage in Xiang's essay nicely summarizes their core message:

The *Yijing* 易經 (Book of changes) calls for geographical/physical barriers in order to guard a county and multiple gates to protect against violence. Therefore, establishing fiefdoms and developing the realm requires not only moral inculcation but also the strength of city walls. However, circumstances sometimes force this ideal to be either restricted by space or limited by time. Even with a strong desire to reinforce the defense system, the situation simply does not allow it to happen.[29]

In essence, the authors conceded that the court's insistence on wall construction was justified and in line with classical ideology. However, as desirable as this ideal was, sometimes reality simply just did not permit its materialization. Indeed, these essayists did not dispute the legitimacy of wall policy; rather, they aimed to establish that Gaochun in 1597 was neither the time nor the place for a city wall. Not only was the county struggling with near-bankruptcy, but its topography made the plan of a city wall infeasible.

Judging from the determined local opposition, the argument was well received in Gaochun. Since the three essays exhibit such strong affinities of content, authorship, and influence, it is appropriate to treat them as one "anti-wall discourse." As becomes apparent in the following discussion, this discourse consists of two main elements: first, a detailed cost-benefit analysis calculating all the gains and losses, both social and financial, to attest to the impracticability of wall building in Gaochun at that time; and second, a discussion of Gaochun's local topography illustrating the city's virtual "unwallability."[30]

"The Wall of Public Will": Cost-Benefit Analysis of Wall Construction. If the main impetus for the top-down political pressure for city-wall construction was to prevent recurrences of the massive destruction inflicted by pirate attacks, in the eyes of Gaochun locals the edict for wall construction came too late to be of any use. As Han points out, if the aim of the wall-building project was to repel the pirate attacks plaguing southeast China, then timing was crucial. However, since Gaochun had no pre-existing wall structure to expand or repair, a solid *li* of wall would require at least several months of work. The project could never be finished in time to address the urgent crisis. Even for the sake of improving local security against bandits arriving by water, Gaochun stood to lose more through wall construction than it risked by being unprotected. Indeed, Han argued, if the purpose of wall construction was to protect the county treasury and prison, then one had to wonder if it were worthwhile to spend tens of thousands of taels to guard a treasury not even worth one thousand, or to sacrifice the lives of hundreds of thousands of people just to make sure that a handful of prisoners stayed in jail. The costs and benefits of the project just did not balance.

The scale tipped further away from wall construction when the social costs were considered. Not only did the wall offer little in the way
of protection, but the pressures and financial burdens of construction
might have turned the residents of Gaochun into rebels. Han cited the
ancient adage "People's minds will become walls";[31] that is, local defense ultimately depends on people's willingness to take part; no matter
how tall and thick the wall, it still relies on people to function. In this
sense, Han argued that it was pointless to build a physical wall at the
cost of the "wall of public will."

To substantiate the point that wall construction would indeed be an
unbearable burden, Han presented two types of cost-and-benefit calculations. First, building a wall would cost tens of thousands of piculs of
tax rice in a county that produced annual revenues in the amount of
forty thousand piculs. Therefore, for every picul of rice produced in
Gaochun county, an extra tax of 20,000 copper cash would have to be
added. Since 90 percent of Gaochun households paid taxes of roughly
one picul of rice every year, this meant that 90 percent of the local
population would have to shoulder an extra tax burden of 20,000 copper cash! Such heavy supplementary tax rates, argued Han, would take
every penny that peasants made from the most productive land, not to
mention that most land in Gaochun land did not reach that level of
productivity. As a result, peasants would have to sell their land to pay
for the wall tax. And if the majority of Gaochun residents went broke
and lost their land, Han asks, what was the point of having a city wall?
There would be no people and no land left to be protected.

Huang Bingshi, in his "Cheng Gaochun yi,"[32] offered his own calculation based on the price of bricks and the proposition to assess a wall
tax of 40 bricks for every *mu* (6,000 square meters) of land. According
to brickmakers, every brick cost 0.02 tael of silver, and therefore for
each *mu* an extra 0.8 tael of silver would have to be added to the regular
tax to pay for the 40 bricks. Further discussion with local craftsmen revealed that building the proposed 11.2-meter-high wall would require an
additional levy of 4 taels of silver on each *mu*. The problem was, even
the most fertile land in Gaochun was worth only about 4 taels per *mu*!
Not to mention the fact that most fields were worth much less. For the
poorest land, the yield was not enough to pay the regular tax; the land
value was so low that sometimes people had to beg others to take their

land for free in exchange for clearing their tax debts. To make things worse, although in theory the county could rank agricultural land based on its productivity and thus even out the burden of wall tax, in reality every land inspection, when executed by clerks, was fraught with bureaucratic abuse and extortion. In the end, as Huang forcefully pointed out, the poor would suffer most from the wall project.

Even if we set aside the problems of corruption, the two budgets provided by Huang and Han make it clear that Gaochun was in no fiscal shape to support the building of a city wall. In theory, it was possible to channel funds into the county through the practice of *xieji* 協濟 (collaborative fund-in-aid), a fiscal procedure in which the state transferred funds from elsewhere (usually nearby counties or prefectures) to areas suffering from severe deficiencies. However, as Huang pointed out, given the floods and droughts in the Jiangnan area in recent years, every nearby county office was already struggling with deficiencies. Sharing the construction costs would exacerbate the problems of neighboring counties and yet do little to relieve Gaochun locals since they would still be liable for the labor services of wall building. The locals would, Huang predicted, either starve or run away. In a time of peace and general prosperity, Huang asked, how could this catastrophe possibly be justified?

Indeed, the desolate picture of Gaochun painted by anti-wall authors stands in sharp contrast to the general prosperity during the sixteenth-century boom. Why was this the case? The financial difficulties of Gaochun only hinted at by the authors were extensive and arose from a specific local context: namely a flood-control project that benefited downstream residents at the expense of Gaochun (discussed in detail below). As a result, most of Gaochun's fields were submerged by the flood-control lake.[33] According to Magistrate Huang, Gaochun's economy had deteriorated to the point that locals had to sell their houses, land, and even children to meet regular tax dues.[34] The sense of imminent fiscal crisis is echoed in Han's opening statement: "Gaochun, a tiny, small county, is located in the Three Lakes area (Map 2.1a). With much farmland ruined and many harvests failed, people are destitute and buried in deep debt. All high officials with a kind heart would look at such poverty that had reduced people to bare survival with sympathetic eyes. . . . Given these conditions, how could Gaochun afford a city wall?"[35]

In the end, the wall was a financial problem. Gaochun simply could not afford to build it. Many cities faced similar obstacles, but the issue in Gaochun appeared to run deeper and was symptomatic of greater financial failings. The bottom line was, even without an expensive project like city wall construction, Gaochun was already approaching bankruptcy. Although the authors did not expand on the root cause of Gaochun's fiscal crisis—probably because it was so well known among locals that it needed no elaboration—the particular circumstances that led to Gaochun's impoverishment, when combined with a problematic decision to make Gaochun a county seat, significantly shaped the course and outcome of Gaochun's anti-wall movement.

The Unwallable City of Gaochun. As if financial ruin alone was not sufficient to abort the wall project, the authors used local geography to further illustrate the unwallability of Gaochun. Although topographic difficulties were commonly cited in contemporary oppositions to wall construction, Gaochun authors took an unusual step in attacking the "city-ness" of Gaochun and, ultimately, the decision to promote Gaochun from trading town to county seat.

What kind of city was Gaochun to be deemed "unwallable" by its residents? In the words of Magistrate Xiang, Gaochun city was in reality more of a trading town than a county capital: "Gaochun is designated a county despite its being virtually a town." In Xiang's estimate, the county seat ranged only one *li* (117.7 m) from north to south, and one-half *li* east to west, rather small by the standards of the time. Most residents were concentrated in the southwest corner, which had started with a few reed shacks scattered around the lakeside. Only recently had the city witnessed development and population growth. The whole city population was home to a couple hundred households, more than half of them in the lakeside area. The northeast section was mostly hills, and people there had settled along a dirt wall built earlier as a temporary defense measure after the theft of the county treasury occurred. The rest of the hill area was packed with one tomb after another. Such was Gaochun "city," Xiang lamented.

Exaggerated or not, this self-effacing image was repeated throughout the anti-wall essays and geographically grounded the anti-wall discourse.

For example, in Han's estimate, the "city" (or as the Gaochun people preferred, the "town") was just two streets intersecting in the middle of this topographically marked space. Each street was only tens or a hundred *wu* (no more than 80 meters) long.[36] How could such a humble and undersized settlement be responsible for a wall? After all, as the three authors reiterated over and over, "Does Gaochun even qualify to be a county seat? It is merely a trading town along the lake. Historically there was never a county unit in this area."[37] The emphasis on Gaochun's identity as a trading town is no mere rhetorical tool concocted for the purpose of the anti-wall argument; rather, as we shall see, it is a highly politically charged statement closely intertwined with Gaochun's ongoing economic problems. For now, I focus on the role of this identity in the anti-wall discourse.

Based on their analysis of local topography, the authors further contended that not only was Gaochun not qualified to be a walled city, but also there was simply no place to build a wall within Gaochun county. In Huang Bingshi's vivid description, Gaochun county

to its four directions is nothing but polder fields facing rivers. In the north spread a few mountains and woods, beyond which is still nothing but polders [farmland reclaimed from lakes]. People build burial grounds on the upper land and houses in the lower, which then become the core of this newly made county. Since all the trading profits come from water [transportation], the urban settlement is closely built along the river, and every inch of the riverside land is developed.[38]

The crowded landscape had to do with locals' dependence on waterways. As is apparent in a seventeenth-century map (Map 2.1), Gaochun county is topographically defined by the Three Lakes and numerous rivers. Not only do these waterways structure transportation and commercial activities throughout the area, but they also play an important role in local agriculture, which relies heavily on polders. In Huang's description, the polders largely dominate Gaochun's built environment. Amid the interlacing polders are settlements on the lowlands (along the lake and dirt wall) and burial sites on the higher ground. Typical of southern China, Gaochun people exhausted every possibility the land offered.

Clearing space for a city wall in such a crowded landscape would significantly disrupt the balance between land and inhabitants. To begin

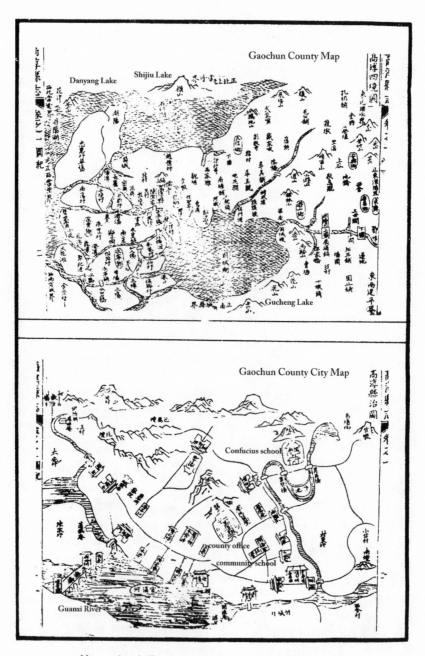

Map 2.1a (*upper*) Gaochun county; Map 2.1b (*lower*) Gaochun city
(SOURCE: *Gaochun xianzhi*, 1683)

with, a fair number of the manmade structures would have to be moved or demolished, be they human settlements or burial grounds. As Huang pointed out, "After all these years, the high ground is fully occupied by tombs row after row. Seeing the density of land use here, once we start building city walls, half the buildings would have to be torn down and countless tombs dug out and corpses exposed. It would be as if the place had been severely hit by a war—only there would be no war, just a city wall being built."[39] The damage would affect the living and the dead alike since the prospective wall would not only destroy the locals' property but also violate their ancestral burial grounds.

Despite the staggering social cost, the wall could still be justified if it brings compensatory benefits. Thus Huang further asks: What would Gaochun make of the destruction of numerous people's homes and family tombs? What would the proposed city wall look like? According to Huang's estimate, which somewhat corresponds with that of Magistrate Xiang, the prospect would be barely worth the sacrifice:

Look at Gaochun's topography: from south to north it extends no more than the distance one arrow can reach [about 190–240 meters]; between east and west there runs a street, people built their houses face to face. . . . The scale of Gaochun city cannot even compare with an off-wall city ward in other counties. Should a wall be built, Gaochun would look more like a passageway than an actual city. Is this the "city" we are looking for? It does not even have the shape of what we call a "city."[40]

The image of a city wall looking like a corridor is indeed appalling. Yet compared to other plans, the corridor-shaped wall turns out to have been one of the better choices for wall. In a city defined by rivers, Gaochun's wall plans had to take into account some remarkable topographical restriction. According to Han, there were two alternative sites for the wall (apparently relocating the county seat altogether, another proposal, was too expensive to even consider): one would enclose only that portion of the city inside the river and use the river as a natural moat; the other would enclose the whole city within it by placing the walls outside Gaochun. In the first plan, the wall would be placed on an elevated area between the river on the south and hills to the north. Due to the population density (both alive and dead), half the residences on the street as well as eight- to nine-tenths of the burial grounds would have to be destroyed in order to make way for the new walls. The east gate area would be half-deserted in order to build a river dike, whereas to the west, the Yongfeng Granary would be outside the city wall. Han questioned the actual amount of land that would be enclosed and asked, "What is the purpose of building a wall to protect such a tiny piece of land?"

On the other hand, should Gaochun go with the second plan, incorporating fields and the river into the walled city, then "it would damage the geomantic channels on the north side of the city."[41] In a cultural environment that considered it imperative to position county offices and schools so that they aligned with auspicious geomantic veins, this flaw was unacceptable. Further, the east and west sides of the wall would be built on polders, forcing residents to lose their livelihoods. Finally, the south walls would be set along the river and exposed to flooding. And because the walls would cut through the river, there would have to be two water gates, adding further costs of tens of thousands of taels. However, even with such a heavy investment, the water gates might not be sturdy enough to tame the lake. During a flood, the surrounding polders would be inundated. To make things worse, in the summer flood season, the water might extend up the walls to a height of three *ban* (a *ban* 版 is 0.64 m × 2.56 m) and it would take endless work to simply keep the wall standing. In view of the potential problems, Han concluded, "could there be anything more harmful than building a city wall?"

This powerful exposition of the unwallability of Gaochun raises the inevitable question: Why even establish a county seat on such an impossible site? Indeed, such was the underlying sentiment embedded in the anti-wall discourse, pointedly articulated by the outspoken Huang Bingshi:

Gaochun was divided from ancient Lishui county. Seeing the prosperous fields and houses in Lishui, locals already wish that they could have just carried their children to reside within the territory of Lishui. How can we in Gaochun afford another expensive project like wall building? . . . After all, what city walls are really about is to protect powerful gentry families who stick together in big cities. It is not meant for a place like Gaochun, which is no more than a small village.[42]

The message here is astonishing. Above all, it questions the wisdom of dividing Gaochun off from Lishui as a new county in 1491.[43] Being a county meant becoming part of the official administrative system, representing the state at the grassroots level, and thereby being subject to expenses and duties much heavier than those of towns—for example, the building of city walls. Ironically, for Gaochun, the burdens of promotion appear to have been so onerous that they destabilized the newly imposed identity and led to nostalgia for the pre-separation era.

The Said and Unsaid. In brief, the anti-wall discourse used detailed budgets and textual maps to illustrate the financial and spatial unwallability of Gaochun city. Yet when read closely, their message seems to be more than the impracticability of building a city wall in Gaochun. Rather, the authors suggest that the failing local economy, in connection with the problematic decision of making a county out of Gaochun, were the underlying causes of locals' discontent. The subtlety of this undercurrent, however, should not belie its importance to the success of Gaochun's wall campaign. As demonstrated in the following section, despite the compelling arguments presented by Gaochun's anti-wall discourse, such strong vocal dissent was not uncommon during the late Ming wall-building movement. In fact, even this celebrated popular protest pales in comparison with many much more intense and heated contemporary controversies over walls, which ended with the walls being constructed. The remarkable efficacy of Gaochun's anti-wall campaign, as it turns out, drew on the particular context of Gaochun hinted at by the anti-wall authors, namely, a failing economy burdened by separation from Lishui county. The resultant local activism transformed the state's perception of Gaochun's wall protest and eventually allowed the locals to prevail during the height of the wall-building movement.

The Public Forum for City-Wall Debates

Despite the frenzy of the wall-building movement, it was not unusual to hear locals voice hostility toward such socially and financially expensive public projects for reasons similar to those of the residents of Gaochun. Case studies of the social responses to wall building have concentrated mostly on coastal areas such as Fujian and Zhejiang, since they had long suffered from pirate attacks.[44] According to these studies, the opposition was mostly financial, since wall construction often inflicted a painful tax spike that continued long after the construction was completed. Residents who lived close to the planned wall site were also concerned about the confiscation of private property and the prospects for receiving fair reparation from the government. Sometimes the dispute broke out along urban-rural lines, since city walls were usually funded and built with the labor and taxes of rural residents but the security benefits belonged mostly to those who lived in the city.[45] Yet even urban residents sometimes opposed wall construction on the grounds that new walls would further enclose urban space and constrain traffic in and out of the city. The wall plan in Suzhou, the economic capital of the sixteenth century, is a case in point. As commercialization spawned urban development beyond Suzhou's walled quarters, the suburban area west of the Chang Gate became the core market of the city. Following several pirate raids, the government decided to expand the western wall to include the newly developed marketplace. However, strong opposition from merchants thwarted this plan—they feared that a wall might hinder commercial traffic.[46]

Many sources testify to the existence of local opposition in general, but the descriptions are rather vague. The story of Lü Kun, however, allows us to look into one such "local complaint" in concrete terms. A famous late Ming scholar, Lü Kun was implicated in a political conspiracy because of his book *Guifan* 閨範 (Virtues in the inner quarters). Lü was exiled to his hometown, Ningling 寧陵 in Henan, where he remained for more than two decades until his death. During this time, Lü participated actively in local affairs, including tax reform and wall building. One of Lü's proposals on wall building was taken as proof of a malicious conspiracy and provoked vehement attacks and criticism. To clear himself and to further advocate his cause, he published two pamphlets clarifying his position. In the first pamphlet, Lü described the intense local reaction that had prompted him to defend his opinion:

The wall-expansion proposal has been in place for years, and I was never the only one who believed that it should be done. Last winter, however, there suddenly appeared anonymous flyers specifically attacking me. The words used were horrifying and the intent malicious. . . . If I did not come out and clear my name, it would look as if I was intimidated by the slander and dared not speak up again. . . . Therefore I wrote this book in the format of questions and answers and give it away to everyone that I know.[47]

The booklet did not have its intended effect. Lü attributed its lack of popularity to his overtly literary writing style, which made it difficult for county folks to appreciate his message, and he decided to produce another, more colloquial version.[48] The "translated" copy relates the politics of Lü's wall scandal more explicitly. Lü recalled that the city-wall proposal began with an encounter with a gentryman surnamed Wang, who was in deep legal troubles and asked for Lü's help. In return, the Wang family promised to pay for the expense of wall construction. Lü and another member of the local elite decided it was worth the effort to help Wang since it would relieve the whole county of the burden of paying for the wall. However, despite Lü's insistence that his action was totally altruistic and that he had no self-serving agenda, the locals did not agree. Once the deal was exposed, the whole county became so outraged that hundreds of folk songs as well as anonymous posters appeared, all targeting Lü Kun. The scandal was even adapted into a drama and staged.[49] The public outcry put an end to the deal, and the city wall remained underfunded. Even those convinced of Lü's good intention suspected that Wang had tricked Lü into the deal without any intention of paying. To dispel such doubts, Lü explained that, to hold Wang to his promise, they had a sworn contract in Wang's own handwriting, and one copy had already been submitted to the local government. Lü concluded by swearing on the lives of his family, "As witnessed by all the deities and ghosts and my county folks, I have said nothing but the truth."[50]

Even with popular protests of this scale, the city-wall project went through. Perhaps Lü's persistence finally convinced the residents of Ningling. In any case, Lü's story offers a vivid example of confrontation among locals on the matter of wall building. Even in the absence of modern media, the communication of views via printed flyers, letters, booklets, folk songs, and even local dramas was impressively active. The growing influence of public opinion in local politics has been well established by scholars, but cases in such a remote town as Lü Kun's Ningling are rarely noted.[51] If the wall debate could develop into this level of engagement in a small, obscure county like Ningling, we can only imagine what kind of turmoil resulted from these "complaints about walls" in more advanced areas such as Jiangnan.

Furthermore, when people started to use mass media like folk songs and dramas to advance their objections, "local" politics became less local. Their words circulated so widely that residents of other areas could compare the implementation of wall-building policies and decide what to make of (or how to interpret) their own situation. The story of Zhuji and Xiaoshan is a case in point. Both were located in pirate-plagued Shaoxing prefecture (modern Zhejiang) where almost every county endeavored to construct or reinforce its city wall. However, when the new Zhuji magistrate announced his plan to rebuild the city wall, he met with strong opposition from locals. Clearly, one cause of the deterioration of the city walls was the habit of locals of building houses against the wall and appropriating sections of the structure into their residences. As a result, in the middle of the Jiajing reign (1522–66), when pirates became a serious threat, only the gates were left intact to protect the city. Since the old walls had virtually become part of locals' residences, however, the new wall proposition provoked strong objection. To appease local residents, the magistrate posted a public announcement declaring: "City walls belong to the state and will not be ceded to the people. However, I assure you that the building of a city wall will not disturb your daily life. You shall not dispute again." Soon the magistrate launched the construction and completed it quickly without harming the residents. A wall fund granted from central government was not even touched. The smooth process formed a sharp contrast to neighboring Xiaoshan county. The magistrate there became so notorious that there appeared a saying, "The city wall in Xiaoshan was 'punched in' [built by force], whereas the one in Zhuji was 'talked in' [built by persuasion]. Ask people which magistrate is better? The city walls are the answer."[52]

These contemporary cases throw the partiality of Gaochun accounts into sharp relief: despite their celebration of the anti-wall protest, local opposition was not uncommon during the sixteenth century's frenzy of massive city-wall building. In fact, the resistance in many places was much fiercer than that in Gaochun yet was still unsuccessful. How, then, did Gaochun manage to frustrate the mounting pressure for wall construction? Clearly the causation was not as straightforward as that presented in the local gazetteer: a popular protest obliged an immediate positive response from the state. Instead, a unique local context generated an extraordinary result.

Local Activism in Gaochun

As we have seen, wall building was a public issue that often ignited heated debate. Although in some areas traumatized residents fought to get governmental help in building or reinforcing existing city walls (as in the case of Songjiang),[53] because of the tremendous investment of resources such building projects demanded from locals, more often than not officials and gentry had to convince people of the urgency of the work. The spirited engagement from both sides took the form of popular protests, political tracts, and even satirical dramas. In view of contemporary wall controversies, it is not surprising that Gaochun residents became so involved in the decision-making process about wall building. What distinguished Gaochun's protest and its unusual success was that the anti-wall protest was not an isolated event but deeply embedded in a history of activism in Gaochun.

Indeed, all the authors of the anti-wall essays belonged to a literati activist group with an impressive track record during the Ming era. In the preface of the 1606 gazetteer (which, as we have seen, was also the product of local advocates), Magistrate Xiang proudly announced numerous reforms in Gaochun county. At the top of the list was the leveling of tax rates between official and private cultivated land. In the Ming system, cultivated land was subject to one of two tax rates, based on type of ownership. The rate for government-owned land was much higher than that for privately owned land. When Gaochun county was carved out of Lishui county in 1491, the division was based on agricultural productivity, not the type of ownership. So on the surface, the division left Gaochun a fair share of agricultural output, whereas in fact, most of the land assigned to Gaochun was owned by the state and therefore subject to a much higher tax rate. This created great economic hardship for Gaochun residents. Thus, when the difference in rates was eliminated, the burden was partially relieved. Another successful reform was the conversion of ranches that supplied horses for state use into taxable farmlands; again this helped to relieve the financial burden of the county government. Third, the obligation to supply tribute grain was commuted into cash payment. This in effect cut taxes, since the conversion rate was favorable to peasants. Fourth, temple lands, which had previously enjoyed full immunity from state taxes, were now taxed at the same rate as privately owned land, and this, too, increased county revenues. Finally, since, as the number of households dropped, fewer people were available for public labor service, the county government adjusted its budget accordingly.

Immediately after these achievements, Xiang noted two disappointing developments in Gaochun: first, the building of East Dam (also called Guangtong Dam) led to the flooding of hundreds of thousands of *mu* of fields; and second, the ever-increasing ad hoc demands from the central government far exceeded the amount set in the original tax system. The first problem was unique to Gaochun; the second was a national fiscal cancer that was eating up virtually every corner of the empire. The combined result was a severe deterioration of local finances. Such difficulties made reform even more urgent and necessary.

The reforms that made Xiang proud aimed at increasing tax revenues and relieving locals' tax burden, both more or less the goals of the Single Whip reform, which gradually spread all over the country during the sixteenth century. However, the scale of the Gaochun reform was unusually wide, ranging from state-owned farms to pasture lands to monastery property. It also included significant reductions in tax and labor services. In the end, Gaochun county's fiscal structure and landownership system were radically transformed in favor of local peasants. The magnitude of the change was extraordinary, even during this time of frenetic fiscal overhaul. Most impressive of all, most of these reforms were initiated by locals under the leadership of the Han family.

The author of one anti-wall essay, Han Zhongxiao, came from this family. Zhongxiao's grandfather (Han Shuyang 韓叔陽), father (Han Bangxian 韓邦憲), and brother (Han Zhongyong 韓仲雍) were Metropolitan Graduates, the highest degree that could be achieved at the time, and all of them were devoted to the welfare of their hometown. Han Shuyang started this family project when he personally funded *yitian yicang* 義田義倉 (charity lands and granaries) in Gaochun.[54] Han Bangxian retired early from the bureaucracy to take care of his father. After returning to his hometown, Han Bangxian worked closely with Magistrate Deng Chuwang 鄧楚望 (who served in Gaochun in 1567–69 and wrote an essay honoring the charity granary Han Bangxian's father built) on the matter of land survey and measurement (*qingzhangliang*

清丈量) for the purpose of fair taxation, a common practice during the Single Whip reform. His most important project was lobbying for tax-grain reduction.[55] This became a Han family enterprise throughout the rest of the Ming dynasty. When Bangxian's grandson Han Bin 韓斌 died in Beijing in 1636, he was still fighting for the tax reduction at court.[56]

The theoretical and moral foundations of this family mission were declared in an article by Han Bangxian on the East Dam, in which he traced the dam's history back to an ancient classic, the *Zuozhuan* 左傳.[57] The dam, which lay on the east side of Gaochun, controlled the waterways in the Three Lakes area, which were the largest source of water for Lake Tai in the Suzhou and Changzhou regions, the most productive region in the empire. However, management of the East Dam soon became a zero-sum battle between eastern Gaochun and the Lake Tai area. If the East Dam closed off the flow completely, the downstream Lake Tai region could be spared the annual inundation. But then the water backed up and flooded much of Gaochun. If, however, the river was unblocked to keep Gaochun county from turning into a lake, then the Lake Tai region would experience serious flooding.

Further compounding this dilemma was the shifting political geography of Nan zhili, the Southern Metropolitan Area. In 1393, when Nanjing was still the primary capital, the state built the Rouge Canal (Yanzhi River 胭脂河) through Gaochun to ship tax grain to Nanjing in order to avoid the high-risk Yangzi River.[58] However, once the primary capital moved to Beijing, the canal was no longer needed and soon became silted up and was abandoned. This significantly undermined the strategic importance of Gaochun and its bargaining power in the subsequent tug-of-war between the Three Lakes and the Lake Tai regions regarding the East Dam. Naturally the upstream (Three Lakes area) lobbied for increasing the flow to relieve flooding in their area, whereas the downstream (Lake Tai area) proposed to lessen the flow to keep their area safe from flooding. Merchants and inland couriers also jumped into the fight to protect their own interest, which was to block water transportation.

In 1512, Gaochun lost the battle. The court ordered the height of the dam to be raised by three *chi* (0.96 m). As expected, the river submerged most of the Gaochun area. Local elders still recalled what a great town Gaochun had been. And these bitter memories were aggravated when the water level dropped and exposed the relics of houses or furniture to remind locals of the long-gone prosperity. The reality was harsh: people knew that either they or the people downstream must bear the brunt of an untamed river, especially since the bottom of the Three Lakes was at the same level as the top of the watch towers on the Suzhou city walls. If the water in the East Dam were released, the most glamorous city of their time would soon be swallowed by Lake Tai.

Because of Gaochun's suffering and sacrifice, the local population soon dropped by 70 percent. However, the tax quota remained the same, and the tax burden on those who remained suddenly surged more than threefold. At the end of his essay, Han Bangxian pleaded: "Ever since Su Shi in the Song dynasty, all the discussion around the East Dam has favored the people downstream. No one ever considered the problem from the perspective of the people upstream. I have been witnessing all the misery the people of Gaochun went through, and therefore I write this." In an important essay entitled "Gaochun shiyi" 高淳事宜 (Four propositions on Gaochun affairs) written in 1569, Han Bangxian extended the scope of the prospective reforms to include a full-fledged cadastral survey and a restructuring of labor corvée and horse ranch regulations (a legacy from Han's father).[59] Han also elaborated his vision in "Jianshui yi" 減稅議 (Discussion on tax reduction) and "Sitian yi" 寺田議 (Discussion on temple lands).[60] But the most influential work was the "Four Propositions." This essay essentially outlined a full-scale reform program for Gaochun. It soon became so popular that Han ran out of personal handwritten copies to be circulated among his friends. He was then prompted to put the essay into print. Han remarked on his work in a tone of courteous modesty, but his ambition in reaching out to the public is clear: "This thesis was not done in an elegant style as my purpose was to make it easy to understand and accessible to the public. It turned out to be rather verbose and lengthy."[61]

Not only did Han Bangxian write prolifically about local reforms, but he and his brother Han Bangben 韓邦本 put their thought into action by "donating a thousand taels to advocate the cause of tax reduction and mobilize people to participate."[62] Their call received an enthusiastic response from locals. In addition to Han's petition for tax reduction, which was granted by the grand coordinator, the residents of

Gaochun also initiated petitions to convert their tax grain obligations into cash payments and to adjust the rents on horse and elephant ranches, temple lands, and the like. According to the documents preserved in gazetteers, Gaochun residents launched five rounds of petitions, each time to different officials, including the grand coordinator, regional inspector, prefectural governor, and even the Nanjing censor.[63] On each petition different names are listed. Some are identified as "county school student," and others as "gentry," but for most the label is "county people." And indeed most of them were too obscure to leave a trace in the documentary record.

These petitions generated not only paperwork but also numerous rounds of field inspections and local interviews by officials sent from Nanjing. Each time a petition was filed, locals had to gather signatures and raise money for travel expenses. In response, Nanjing would send officials to Gaochun, and the locals would mobilize again to receive and meet these inspectors. All this networking and mobilizing of Gaochun residents eventually shaped the way people perceived and reacted to local politics. Indeed, during the latter half of the Ming dynasty, collective petitions and negotiations with the state became the way Gaochun residents survived the catastrophic East Dam decision. The connectedness of the local community is clearly seen in the swift congregation of more than four hundred Gaochun residents at the petition site without any apparent planned coordination. The stream of collective actions not only redefined the local community but also shifted the government's perception of Gaochun's anti-wall protest; rather than open defiance, the government saw it as a new initiative in the campaign for East Dam relief measures.

The Wall Protest in Context.   In brief, the anti-wall discourse in Gaochun presented two arguments: Gaochun was an unwallable city, and the costs of walling it outweighed the possible benefits. The financial burden was a common local objection to the mandate to construct walls. However, Gaochun's local activism gave the anti-wall petition extraordinary meaning and effects. In the eyes of both Gaochun residents and the state, it was not an isolated event but one of a series of petitions and protests attempting to control the damage stemming from the state's earlier decision regarding East Dam. Only from the perspective of local activist politics can we explain why, among so many cities that opposed wall building, Gaochun alone succeeded.

In the same vein, "unwallability" was not merely a fact of natural topography. Since city walls symbolized an official administrative status, an oxymoron such as "unwallable county seat" would make sense only when read against the political undertones. In this light, the "unwallability" of Gaochun ultimately lay in its dwindling importance in the area. The sense of decline and disempowerment is clearly reflected in the repeated emphasis in the anti-wall discourse that Gaochun city was still a town (*zhen*). When Gaochun had been promoted to be a county seat (*cheng*), it was described as a thriving town truly worthy of such a change in status. The quibble between *cheng* and *zhen* was not just a difference over the evaluation of Gaochun's development but referred to the drastic decline precipitated by the construction of the East Dam. The defeat in the dam dispute was closely related to Gaochun's diminished ties to Nanjing following the move of the capital and the growing importance of the Grand Canal as a transportation route for tax grain. With little bargaining power against the empire's financial center (the Lake Tai area), Gaochun residents were forced to make a self-destructive sacrifice that furthered their own decline. Economic hardship, not surprisingly, bred misgivings among Gaochun residents toward the new status they now could not afford. As Huang Bingshi acidly remarked, the people of his hometown could not help but wonder if their life would have been better had Gaochun still been part of prospering Lishui.[64] Underlying the wobbly sense of identity is the despair of a newly created county that had lost two-thirds of its income. No wonder that the tone was distressed and the message poignant.

When the anti-wall discourse is placed in the context of Gaochun's activism, we find that ultimately, it was the political terrain, not the topographical one, that made wall building unfeasible in Gaochun. The central role of political geography in shaping wall politics is further illuminated when considering the story of another county in the Nanjing Metropolitan Area, Jiangpu. As we shall see in the following discussion, the dilemma "to wall or not to wall" was to a great extent determined by each individual county's relation with Nanjing, and the dynamics of regional geopolitics came to define the most conspicuous feature of the urban landscape—city walls.

JIANGPU: A CASE IN CONTRAST

Located north of Nanjing across the Yangzi River, Jiangpu resembled Gaochun in many ways. It had never been a county before the Ming; its riverside location presented topographical difficulties for wall construction; and its residents also strongly resisted city-wall projects. However, in the end, Jiangpu built not one but two city walls in the sixteenth century. What explains the contrast between Gaochun and Jiangpu?

Jiangpu was made the seat of a newly created county in 1371 under the jurisdiction of Yingtian prefecture. Like Gaochun, Jiangpu was a trading town when Taizu promoted it to a county in order to expand the Nanjing Metropolitan Area across the Yangzi River. This move gave Nanjing a military advantage in defending itself from potential attacks along the Yangzi River. Obviously a capital on a major river enjoyed great commercial benefits. At the same time, such openness also exposed Nanjing to more security threats and thus created the need for stronger fortifications.

When Jiangpu was first made a county in 1371, a city wall was built. Yet because of a subsequent northward shift in the course of the Yangzi, the walls were repeatedly attacked by the river and severely damaged. In 1391, the county seat was moved to a higher plain farther away from the river, and no new walls were constructed at that time. After the county seat was moved, the old walled city was renamed Puzi 浦子, and continued to house several central government offices, including such offices as the Wuwei 五衛 (Five Guards), Hubu fensi 戶部分司 (Branch Bureau of the Ministry of Revenue), Sancang 三倉 (Three Granaries, the capital granary), and Shouyufu 守禦府 (Yamen of the Commandant of the Transport Command), all under the jurisdiction of Nanjing. In effect, Puzi became a military bastion directly overseen by Nanjing, and all its wall-related issues were managed by capital-level officials (such as the Ministry of War and the Censorate).[65] For example, in 1503, the Puzi walls collapsed into the Yangzi River. Because of the military importance of Puzi, Nanjing officials mandated a ritual ceremony to appease the spirit of the river. The emperor approved this motion, and one of the highest officials in Nanjing, the *Nanjing shoubei* 南京守備 (grand commandant),[66] was appointed to perform the ritual.[67] Obviously the ritual did not work, since during the Hongzhi reign (1488–1505) the Yangzi continued to encroach on the southern walls of Puzi. The Nanjing minister of war petitioned to relocate the city, but his proposal was not approved.[68] The officials who worked on this matter held the two most important military posts in Nanjing,[69] attesting to the close ties between Nanjing and Jiangpu.

This close link began when Jiangpu county was founded: 2,000 households were taken from Jiangning, the county in which the city of Nanjing was located, and assigned to Jiangpu.[70] Since that time, Jiangpu became visible to Nanjing in both literary and administrative terms. Take the inspection of salt shipments, for example: previously merchants shipping salt via the Yangzi River had to stop at Nanjing and wait to be inspected. Because of the heavy traffic, it often took months to go through the routine procedure, which substantially delayed the shipment. Consequently merchants appealed to have the inspection conducted by the salt-control censor at Puzi, across the river from Nanjing.[71] In other words, since Nanjing could not process all the traffic expeditiously, it in effect extended its jurisdiction across the river into Puzi. The granaries established by the Ministry of Revenue in Puzi were for similar purposes.[72]

Nanjing took full advantage of the open space in Jiangpu as well as its heavy military security. Of the ten Nanjing guard units north of the Yangzi River, six were located in Jiangpu. Because of its geographical availability, Jiangpu came to function as a satellite city and military fortress for Nanjing.[73] It also controlled the overland route between Nanjing and Beijing, over which commuting central officials as well as their clerks constantly shuttled back and forth. Because of such close ties, when the main river route between Nanjing and Jiangpu, the Duijiang River 對江河, was blocked, dredging was initiated and administered directly by the Nanjing metropolitan governor in cooperation with other Nanjing central government officials.[74] Judging from the unusual numbers of ports, custom offices, and military guard posts, it is no wonder that Jiangpu's gazetteer called Jiangpu the most critical corner of the Nanjing Metropolitan Area.[75]

Puzi City Walls

Jiangpu's close ties to Nanjing significantly affected the process of wall building there. The city walls of Puzi were built at the beginning of the Ming dynasty and started to fall apart in the late fifteenth century. As noted above, the court denied a memorial requesting permission to relocate Puzi city. Starting in 1585, the Nanjing Censorate proposed alternatives cosponsored by the prefectural governor, the Southern Capital ministers, and the Capital Training Divisions[76] to repair the walls.[77] After more than thirty years of debate between the two capitals, in 1617 Nanjing finally prevailed. Minister of War Huang Kezuan 黃克纘 supervised the wall building with support from the ministers of revenue and works as well as a powerful eunuch and a few censors from Nanjing. The grand commandant and the minister of rites in Nanjing jointly oversaw the final design of the city wall. To ensure the quality of construction, members of the Nanjing Censorate inspected the work and kept all Nanjing central offices informed of its progress.

Huang Kezuan explained to the emperor the main barriers to building a city wall at Puzi:

In my humble opinion, Puzi is the principal shield of the Southern Capital. Since one side of the walls have collapsed, however, the protection is essentially nonexistent. Although the urgent need to repair the southern side of the city walls is apparent to everyone, there are two reasons why the issue is still unresolved: First, whoever launches the project will provoke strong grievances and even resentment from those whose property is destroyed by the construction. Second, a wall so close to the river is at high risk of collapsing and causing severe consequences.[78]

The obstacles to walling Puzi were certainly reminiscent of those in Gaochun: resistance from locals who had to relocate, and difficulties in maintenance due to the wall's proximity to water. As in Gaochun, two plans were devised: one called for walls next to the river and the other for walling an upland area to the north. Both plans involved substantial relocation. Nevertheless, Huang pointed out, since most of Puzi's residences were built along the river to take advantage of the waterfront, it would be pointless to build a city wall with no people living inside. Therefore, Huang concluded, the well-being of the majority—meaning the security of Nanjing residents—should take priority over the interests of the minority facing relocation. Like many of his colleagues, Huang appealed to the "greater good" in convincing locals of the urgency of the walls. Yet unlike the typical local officials, Huang actually presented a concrete and well-considered plan for reparations:

Regarding the [illegible characters, probably names] 113 households who would be affected by the construction of walls, it was decided at community compact meetings to offer them [a total of] 407.9 taels of silver [to offset] relocation costs. Locals appeared to be eager to collect their share and willing to relocate. In fact, ever since the southern end of the wall was inundated and collapsed, business has gone down so badly that the rich residents moved away long ago. Even most of those staying in small, shabby sheds moved into the city soon after the wall project was announced, leaving no need for us to force these people out. For those required to tear down more than seven *jian* [a measurement for the size of houses] of property, we plan to compensate them with either official land in the city or money if no land is available.[79]

The meticulous attention to reparations is indeed impressive, but, compared with other cases, Jiangpu's wall construction was led by much higher level bureaucrats. With richer resources at hand, officials were able to put a detailed plan into action to appease local opposition.

Jiangpu County City Walls

As in Puzi, influence and intervention from higher offices in Nanjing can be seen in the construction of Jiangpu county's city wall. Following the 1573 Wanli enthronement edict calling for wall construction, a Grand Coordinator Zhou issued a plan for walling Jiangpu. However, this proposal was not received well among Jiangpu residents and officials. As in Gaochun, the locals claimed that such a huge undertaking did not suit their remote small town. A compromise between Nanjing and Jiangpu called for building a *yuan* 垣 (a smaller dirt wall) as a temporary expedient. Soon thereafter, a *yuan* was erected to secure the county office, followed three years later by another *yuan*, further fortified with defensive stations and stockades. Although a *yuan* was not as sophisticated as a *chengqiang* (a brick city wall), it was still built on a stone foundation, had wooden stakes at the top, and was faced with ceramic tiles and thorny caltrop bushes on the face. A *yuan* was, however, much cheaper (by a hundred thousand copper coins).[80]

Unsatisfied with Jiangpu's quasi-city walls, in 1575, Yingtian Prefect Wang, the highest official in the field administration of the Nanjing Metropolitan Area, proposed to build a formal wall for Jiangpu with defensive stations. Although this plan did not materialize, three years later, following a promotion to censor-in-chief at the Nanjing Censorate, Wang again proposed to wall Jiangpu. With his previous failure in mind, Wang was far less sympathetic to local opposition. In a memorial to the throne, Censor Wang made it clear that the strategic importance of Jiangpu should trump local interests:

The territory is grand, and our vision needs to extend much farther. Given this, how can we conceive an important project in collaboration with common folks? In the Jiajing reign, pirates attacked the Lake Tai area and some of them went farther, to the west of Nanjing. The strategic position of Jiangpu not only directly guards Nanjing but also is a pivotal point in controlling the Yangzi River.[81]

He concluded, "Considering that Jiangpu faces Nanjing across the Yangzi River, guarding the most crucial strategic point, it should, by all means, be properly walled."

Wang's argument successfully convinced the minister of war and the grand coordinator, the top military and civil administrators, respectively, in Nanjing, of the urgency of walling Jiangpu. In Wang's plan, part of the funding would come from the sale of confiscated smuggled salt at the disposal of Nanjing authorities. Responsibility for finding the rest of the funding as well as supervising the construction work would fall on the shoulders of the local magistrate. The task was first entrusted to Magistrate Shen Menghua 沈孟化, who had the whole project planned out in detail. However, before Shen could start executing his plan, he was promoted to Beijing and left the wall project unfinished. In light of previous local objections and the heavy-handed management from Nanjing, Jiangpu's wall building became a difficult task for the new magistrate, who was caught between Nanjing and Jiangpu. Because of the strategic importance of the walls, finally the court appointed a former censor, Yu Qianzhen 余乾貞, as magistrate to take on the task.

The whole process was closely observed by Nanjing literati. An essay by Yu Menglin 余孟麟, a prominent Nanjing literatus serving as a junior editor (*bianxiu* 編修) at the Hanlin Academy, commemorated the expansion of Jiangpu's school, another project undertaken by Magistrate Yu at the same time. Yu Menglin recalled that when he first heard the news of the wall construction project in Jiangpu, like many other Nanjing literati he responded with suspicion: "How could a small county like Jiangpu afford to undertake such a huge project?" The suspicion deepened when Yu Qianzhen was appointed magistrate and immediately launched not one but two major projects: the school expansion and the wall. However, to everyone's surprise, Magistrate Yu completed both jobs in one year without any disturbances. According to the somewhat euphemistic description of Yu Menglin, an effective methodology and equitable distribution of responsibilities were the keys to his unlikely success. What, then, was Yu Qianzhen's "methodology"?[82]

As was true of other localities, the hardest part of building a wall lay in the financing. Earlier, Magistrate Shen had done an excellent job of finding extra funding for the construction. Shen successfully overturned a previous denial of a proposal to lease official land reserved for imperial ritual use and hence off-limits to locals. He also made a case at the ministry level that since the walls would benefit both the local civilian and military populations, the costs should be shared by both. In theory splitting the costs appeared to be a fair solution, but working out the details proved to be rather complicated—especially in light of the long-term disputes over jurisdiction between civil and military offices. The tension was heightened by the fact that although three-fourths of the county land was under military jurisdiction, the burden of corvée service was much heavier on the civil side. To everyone's astonishment, Magistrate Yu was able to reconcile the relationship between the county and the Guard units stationed there, even convincing the military to supply 30 percent (40 percent, according to another record) of the labor and expenses.[83]

Yu's success was not pure luck; he was handpicked and well supported by high officials from Nanjing. In fact, his very appointment appears to have resulted from consideration of his talents in tactical mediation. The construction of the Jiangpu wall, in this sense, should be considered a collective effort of Nanjing high officials. Indeed, the long list of acknowledgments in a local gazetteer, including the grand coordinator, minister of war, river controller (a concurrent assignment with vice-censor-in-chief or assistant censor-in-chief of Nanjing), Censorate regional inspectors, military commandant, and ward-inspecting censor, bears clear witness to the deep involvement of Nanjing offices and their critical role in the successful completion of the Jiangpu city wall.[84]

Gaochun Vs. Jiangpu: The Role of Political Negotiation

Despite the shared obstacles to wall building, the trajectory of wall politics in Gaochun and Jiangpu could not be more different: in Gaochun the building of city walls was embedded in a matrix of local initiatives, whereas in Jiangpu it proceeded under close supervision of the Nanjing government. In the end, Gaochun remained unwalled, and in Jiangpu, two walls were built. The sharp contrast in outcome reflects above all the relative positions of Jiangpu and Gaochun in regional geopolitics: one was a satellite city across the river from Nanjing, and the other was an orphan town half-destroyed for the benefit of the empire at large. As newly designated county seats, both exhibited unstable identities. But because they were differently situated vis-à-vis the political geography of the Nanjing Metropolitan Area, identity took on different, if not opposite, forms. Gaochun clung to its past and longed to rejoin the "mother county" from which it had been split and to resume its old status of market town. Jiangpu, on the other hand, shielded by its patron Nanjing, welcomed its new status. In fact, Jiangpu was so empowered by its new position and identity that it immediately initiated a campaign against its mother county, Luhe 六合.

This rivalry between Jiangpu and Luhe over the construction of a river dam began in the Ming era and continued until the nineteenth century. It was triggered by the drastic reshaping of political geography in the Luhe area. Before the separation, the main transportation route to the Yangzi River for Jiangpu locals was along a river that passed through Luhe. When Jiangpu became a county, the route was seen as a detour and an annoyance. Jiangpu would want to create a waterway of its own that would be a shortcut to the Yangzi River. In the eyes of Luhe residents, however, the new canal would significantly undermine the geographical advantage of their town and thus they strongly opposed its construction. Both sides lobbied hard for their cause at the prefectural and provincial levels. Ironically, both sides made similar arguments. Both highlighted the possible costs and benefits to farmlands in each county in terms of irrigation and flood control, and both accused the other side of seeking to benefit not peasants but merchants.[85]

Here again, the regulation of lived space through such things as canals, walls, or dams fundamentally shaped and defined people's lives, and the high stakes naturally triggered strong reactions. What is particularly striking are the ways in which people negotiated these issues. Indeed, the long-term and persistent negotiations in Gaochun are consistent with the momentous, late sixteenth-century trend demonstrated in Chapter 1, in which reform plans were often initiated at the bottom and locals succeeded in forcing the state into negotiations. The examples in this chapter shed further light on the growing number of collective actions in late imperial China. This phenomenon first drew the close attention of historians because it indicated a shifting balance between the state and society at a time of enormous economic development. For example, the surge in the number of urban popular protests in the sixteenth and seventeenth centuries was considered a clear sign that urbanization had transformed the role of Chinese cities from sites for state authority to battlegrounds of political strife. Earlier works took a Marxist view and maintained that such incidents of political disobedience exemplified class conflict and a burgeoning class-consciousness induced by the market economy. The emergence of a distinctive "urban ethos" (*shimin sixiang* 市民思想) appeared to be at odds with the agrarian values of Confucian orthodoxy and thus substantially undermined traditional ("feudalistic") political authority.[86] Peasant rebellions, endemic in Chinese history and often marking the end of dynastic cycles, now were joined by popular movements led by the urban lower classes.

This line of scholarship, however, was dictated by specific teleological agendas (such as the search for evidence of class struggle facilitated by economic development), sometimes at the cost of blatant oversimplification of historical developments. As Harriet Zurndorfer rightly points out, "What is relevant [to these historians] is the general idea of opposition, not understanding the specific conditions which generated violence and political protest."[87] To rectify this problem, scholars began to pay closer attention to the specific social-political environments that bred popular movements. For example, Kobayashi Kazumi examined the ideological dimension of popular movements and argued that, contrary to previous belief, not all popular protests challenged existing authority.[88] In the same vein, James W. Tong conducted a statistical analysis of 630 cases of collective action throughout the Ming era and concluded that the statistical pattern correlated less with theories of class conflict or social change than with ideas concerning a survival mentality and the regime's capacity to contain collective action.[89] In terms of popular protests (about 150 out of the sample of 630), Tong found that proportionately more cases occurred when extreme hardship was not ameliorated by government relief or local public works and when the state capacity to contain and prevent internal disturbances diminished. Overall, few of the 630 events involved antagonistic class conflict, and more urbanized and commercialized counties did not have significantly higher levels of collective action.[90]

Since empirical studies do not support traditional paradigms of popular protests such as dynastic decline or class struggle, Harriet Zurndorfer has called on the field to move "toward a typology of violence and political protest in China." In a review essay, she categorized popular movements as urban riots, peasant rebellions, feuds, and millenarian uprisings.[91] Subsequent scholarship has further nuanced the typology of popular protests, thereby giving us more insight into the power struggles underlying political confrontation. For example, Wu Jen-shu's works provide a systematic and comprehensive survey of urban collective actions between the sixteenth and the eighteenth centuries, including food riots, strikes, anti-official activities, protests against royal family members and eunuchs, tax-resistance movements, and bond-servant uprisings. He analyzes the correlation between collective action and fluctuations in rice prices, fiscal policies, governmental responses, and law enforcement regarding popular protests. In order to achieve a general understanding of the nature of collective action, Wu also surveys the geographic distribution and social backgrounds of leaders and participants, the means and organization of social mobilization, and motivations for participation (as discerned by analyzing posters and dramas).[92]

In brief, the academic approach to popular protests has progressed from treating them as symbols of grassroots opposition to understanding them as context-specific and historicized products of a capricious power-dynamic between state and society. However, most studies still focus largely on the act of protest itself and consider violence and antagonism the intrinsic elements of protest. The nonconfrontational collective actions of Gaochun locals and the conciliatory responses by the government bring to light a new aspect of collective action that has not yet received adequate attention in the field. Indeed, nonviolent collective action is not as exceptional in late imperial China as might appear in modern scholarship. Although expressions of dissatisfaction easily led to violence, violence did not constitute a defining element of popular protest. James W. Tong acknowledges that in the hundreds of cases of collection action that he reviewed, some were of a nonviolent nature.[93] Through his study of organized merchant groups and guilds, Tong finds that organized political action often took the form of political contributions to influence government decision-making. Since joint petitions were not unusual, a political action initiated by an organized group might involve people from multiple counties or provinces as well as different trades. Most significantly, "many of these collective actions were not just spontaneous expressions of grievances but sophisticated and well-informed lobbying efforts."[94] Petitioners would cite pertinent articles from *Da Ming huidian* 大明會典 (Collected statues of the Ming dynasty), the ultimate authority in imperial administrative regulation, as legal grounds to justify their complaints, and the petitions were addressed to specific officials.

In this sense, the Gaochun city-wall protest extended nonviolent political action from guild members to general taxpayers. After all, whatever triggered it, popular protest was, in essence, about unmet popular expectations and perceived social injustices. People voiced discontent in hopes of official redress. Violence erupted only when the situation provoked open confrontation. Yet the focus on violence and confrontations in historiography often overshadows the calculated and well-strategized aspects of popular protests. Fully explicating this dimension of popular action requires a somewhat different perspective. That is, when we view collective action as a form of rational political negotiation, the center of analysis shifts from challenges to and struggles against state authority to the process by which agreement and compromise are reached between locals and state agents. This approach allows us to transcend the tug-of-war view of the state-society relation and, in its stead, focus on the interactive process in which both sides bargained according to their own perceptions of the issues of contention. The final section of this chapter, therefore, analyzes the two main factors that informed and shaped the negotiations over wall construction in the Nanjing Metropolitan Area:

(1) the shifts in political geography, particularly those arising from the move of the capital from Nanjing to Beijing; and (2) the rise of commercial towns in the sixteenth and seventeenth centuries, which problematized the meaning of "city" for urban residents.

THE NEGOTIATION OVER
THE METROPOLITAN CITYSCAPE

The Geographic Factor

So far, the story told in this chapter has taken a few turns. We started with a popular protest against a city wall in the Nanjing area and the perception and presentation of this local crisis by Gaochun elites. As the story unfolded, we found that the protest itself, the seemingly decisive factor in the success of the Gaochun anti-wall campaign, was simply one segment in an ongoing history of local activism in response to a defeat in a major water dispute. This development was not surprising in light of the absence of stable sources of funding or prescribed procedures for implementing the Ming court's wall-building mandate. Thus, the order to build a wall was an added fiscal burden on an already overstretched budget and local offices forced to scramble for funding from all possible venues. The ad hoc nature of wall construction lent itself to embroilment in local politics, and as a result, local objections to these projects could take a wide variety of forms—protest was sometimes voiced as a distrust of the gentry, sometimes as defiance of unpopular magistrates. In Gaochun's case, the ultimate source of the local objection lay with the East Dam and the decision to change the status of Gaochun from a trading town to that of an administrative city, a change that required, among other things, a city wall.

Our understanding of the successful outcome of the Gaochun wall protest is further nuanced by consideration of another metropolitan county, Jiangpu, which encountered similar obstacles to its wall construction plan. Although the two situations were analogous, they provoked very different government responses, the dynamic of which was largely dictated by geographical factors. The physical proximity of Jiangpu and Nanjing translated into unusually tight political ties between the two cities. This political intimacy increased when Nanjing became the southern capital and its main function shifted from political center to military stronghold overseeing south China for Beijing.[95] This change fortified the importance of Jiangpu since it was located at a strategic point across the Yangzi River from Nanjing. In order to gain full command over southern China's defense line, Nanjing had to extend itself across the river into Jiangpu county.

By the same token, geographical placement also plays a key role in the catastrophic development of Gaochun and the subsequent local activism that eventually defeated the city-wall mandate. Located along a transportation route to Nanjing, Gaochun prospered when that city served as the capital of the Ming empire. Its importance was greatly enhanced after the Yangzi River became too dangerous to be used for tribute grain transportation. Since the best alternative was a water route across the southern Three Lakes area, the Nanjing court invested tremendous amounts of money and labor to carve a canal, the Yanzhi River, out of hostile terrain. Centrally located along the new route, Gaochun became a key point connecting the imperial capital and the Lake Tai region, otherwise known as the "empire's granary."[96] However, when the court moved to Beijing, the Grand Canal became the main transportation route for tribute grain and the lifeline of the empire. Having lost this main source of income, Gaochun was already heading into decline. Conditions only worsened when Gaochun lost the battle over the East Dam.

The greatest irony of the story is that Gaochun was not promoted to the level of county seat until after the court had moved to Beijing and tribute transportation rerouted via the Grand Canal. Why was this promotion belated? The only document that discusses the reasons for this change of status attributes the change to fiscal factors: the vast size of Lishui county made tax collection, already in arrears, difficult, a rationale commonly cited in adjustments (either annexation or separation of territorial units) of field administration.[97] In addition to fiscal considerations, the state may have believed that its location at a crossroads for traffic to Nanjing had made Gaochun prosperous enough to stand as a county on its own. One thing is clear, however: having lost its major sources of income, Gaochun was being promoted to a position it could no longer afford. This may have compelled Gaochun residents to reflect on their place in the area and conclude that Gaochun was essentially a "town" being made to shoulder undeservingly heavy responsibilities. What Gaochun locals did not recognize is that their predicament was not merely an unfortunate product of poor timing. It was also symptomatic of a greater issue, one that concerns the institutional management of two urban systems, which had deeply penetrated each other by the early seventeenth century.

G. William Skinner's theorization of urban hierarchy is useful here. In his seminal essays in *The City in Late Imperial China*, Skinner presents two urban hierarchies: one created and regulated by the imperial bureaucracy for the purpose of field administration; the other shaped by commercial transactions. The first represents, in Skinner's words, "official China," a world of yamens and ranked officials in a graded bureaucratic system, whereas the second reflects the "natural" structure of Chinese society, a world dominated by trade and informal politics. The two worlds were brought into close interaction by the long-standing institutional practice of converting prominent trading towns into administrative sites.[98] As Kawakatsu Mamoru's research indicates, the institutional transformation of market towns into capital cities continued from the Song through the Qing dynasties.[99] As he also points out, however, the criteria for such changes in status were rarely, if ever, specified. He suggests that the change in status should be understood within the particular context of each region, especially in relation to the dominant city. In the case of Gaochun, the influence of the central city, Nanjing, extended into the issue of city walls, a symbol that marks the boundary between official cities and commercial towns.

To wall or not to wall, as revealed in the clash between Gaochun and the state, presented different challenges and problems for both sides. The Ming state's responses to local dissent regarding wall construction appear to be rather disparate. The inconsistency proves to be less a function of local opposition (voiced in both Gaochun and Jiangpu) and more a result of the relative weight of each city in the political geography of the Nanjing Metropolitan Area, one that was radically reoriented in the transition from primary to secondary capital. For Nanjing's "core counties," which had been part of the Nanjing area for centuries and were more tightly integrated into the region, the impact was weaker. For new counties like Gaochun and Jiangpu, however, the impact of Nanjing's change in status was momentous: no longer the center of imperial administration, Nanjing was repositioned as a regional

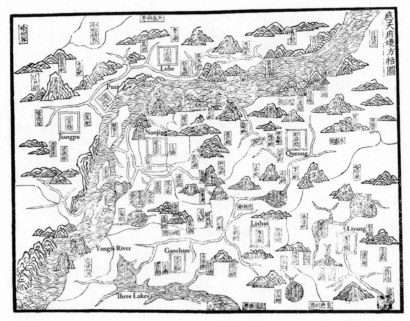

Map 2.2 The Nanjing Metropolitan Area (SOURCE: Chen Yi, *Jinling gujin tukao*, 1516. (The counties of the Nanjing Metropolitan Area are marked by double squares.)

military stronghold. Jiangpu, the city right across the Yangzi River, came to be perceived as a vital component of defense, to which city walls were essential. To achieve this goal, financial and political resources at higher levels were pooled to overcome local resistance. In Gaochun, the transfer of the capital led to a decline in importance. The Yanzhi River soon became dilapidated, and the resulting impairment of the water connection between Gaochun and Nanjing stripped Gaochun of its military relevance. As a result, the debates over the need to wall Gaochun became a financial issue, one that soon became enmeshed in the fiscal overhaul of Gaochun following the disastrous result of the East Dam dispute.

The uneven geopolitical structure that resulted from the move of the capital stands in sharp contrast to the idealized political geography portrayed in contemporary maps. Typically, these maps envision political space as centered on the highest government office with each subordinate unit situated in a homogeneous political space equal in both pictorial size and distance from neighboring units. In Ming maps of the Nanjing Metropolitan Area (see Map 2.2), the geographical proximity of

Nanjing and Jiangpu is significantly masked in cartographical representation (for a comparison with a modern map, see Map 2.3, p. 122). The idealized cartographical space belies the harsh political reality by impressing on viewers that, from the perspective of the central office in Nanjing, all counties are evenly viewed and treated in the political space.[100]

The Rise of Market Towns

From the perspective of Gaochun residents, the city-wall proposal was another step in the long-term blight locals had suffered since their defeat in the fight over East Dam. The symbolic meaning of walls led Gaochun residents to question the decision to promote Gaochun. In their words, Gaochun was no more than a market town "the size of a village."[101] In view of the proliferation of market towns, which is often considered the main characteristic of late imperial urbanization, the conflict over Gaochun's appropriate status is indicative of the increasingly complicated boundary between the official and the commercial city systems. Indeed, the transformation of market towns into administrative cities (or vice versa) had been a regular institutional practice since the Song dynasty, when the mushrooming of market towns signaled the promise of great revenue growth. When the state wanted to create new territorial units in the field administration, market towns were usually considered natural candidates for administrative seats. Such changes were often embraced by locals with enthusiasm since they brought closer ties to the power center and more political resources, including increased quotas for the civil service examinations.[102] Gaochun's unusual resistance was undoubtedly the product of the misfortunes following the water dispute after Gaochun was divided from Lishui. At the same time, the locals' heightened self-awareness of being "town dwellers" reflected a growing sense of identity and was shared by contemporary market town residents.

One clear indication of this newfound local pride is the emergence of *xiangzhen zhi* 鄉鎮志 (gazetteers of villages and towns), an offshoot of local gazetteers.[103] The appearance of this genre is particularly striking in the late Ming, when the compilation of local gazetteers had become routine governmental business. As early as the fifteenth century, the court issued edicts mandating the compilation of gazetteers corresponding to the different levels of the bureaucratic hierarchy (province, prefecture, county) and using a specified organizational scheme.[104] In contrast to these state-sponsored publications, town gazetteers were produced through local initiatives, and the content of these works expressed the specific concerns of each town. The voluntary and spontaneous production of *xiangzhen zhi* clearly distinguishes them from official gazetteers following a standardized format. Most interesting of all, since market towns were not formal territorial units, the editors had to demarcate the boundaries of their towns according to the actual reach of their lived experiences. With no ready archives to draw on, the editors of town gazetteers had nothing but their personal observations and experiences. This intimate vantage point not only lent unusual originality to their accounts of town life but also facilitated a sense of community. Common in the prefaces of town gazetteers are remarks distancing these works from official gazetteers. To the editors, the difference between town gazetteers and official gazetteers was more than apparent: town gazetteers were produced through communal effort, not bureaucratic routine. Official gazetteers were mandated from above, whereas town gazetteers were initiated from below.[105]

This burgeoning communal identity might have been provoked by the fact that market towns, regardless of their economic significance, were often underrepresented in official gazetteers because of their lack of formal status in the administrative hierarchy.[106] The sense of neglect was sometimes expressed through implicit hostility toward administrative cities. For example, the editor of the gazetteer of Hengtang 橫塘, a market town outside Suzhou, bitterly remarked on the lack of attention in the official gazetteer: "Seen from the viewpoint of the prefectural seat [Suzhou], Hengtang is nothing but a grain of tare; however, in the minds of Hengtang residents, how could our town still be as trivial as a tiny speck of grain?"[107] In an important sense, the compilation of town gazetteers defied the official definition of "city." Similar challenges and transgressions can also be found in the realm of popular religions. For example, the Ming code stipulated that only capital cities could house city god temples (*chenghuangmiao* 城隍廟). However, in the late sixteenth century many market towns in Jiangnan built their own.[108]

The lack of institutional support for market towns meant that the rise and fall of these places was subject to the caprices of the market.

Despite their critical importance in mediating between official administrative cities and the countryside, during economic downturns some
market towns quickly dwindled back to villages. For example, Wuqing
zhen 烏青鎮, a renowned market town in Zhejiang, first claimed its
name during the Chunxi era (1174–89) of the Southern Song; however,
after half a century's boom, in 1275 it abruptly went into decline. By 1276
all the shops and wine houses of the town had disappeared or been converted into residences. Only in the mid-Ming did Wuqing again experience economic prosperity. Perhaps this very instability prompted town
dwellers to compile gazetteers, not only as a testament to their affluence
but also in the hope that an articulated sense of cultural identity would
sustain the town through future economic downturns.[109]

Not surprisingly, this elevated self-consciousness was undergirded by
the extraordinary economic performance of market towns in the sixteenth century. As Skinner has noted, one unique trait of Chinese urban
history lies in the "limited proliferation of capital cities."[110] In the millennium between the first urban revolution in the Song dynasty and the
end of the imperial era, the number of administrative cities remained
relatively constant despite drastic population growth. In other words,
the impressive economic growth of late imperial China, one that in
many historians' estimation is on a par with that of western Europe
prior to the industrial revolution, might be due in great part to the proliferation of commercial towns. However, despite the vital importance
of market towns in late imperial China, little attention has been paid to
the institutional response to the flourishing of market towns. This curious omission may have resulted from the fact that the academic interest
in the rise of market towns has focused on the alternative urban model
they posed in opposition to traditional official cities. Indeed, supported
by commercial wealth and immune from the heavy-handed governmental control experienced by administrative cities, many market towns exhibited a high degree of autonomy deemed inherently lacking in Chinese cities by Max Weber.[111] This tendency was further exacerbated by
the imperial state's cap on the number of administrative cities. Therefore, although efforts were made to convert some market towns into
administrative cities, many established towns, such as the famous Four
Great Towns, which boasted populations of over a million in the high
Qing, remained outside the official urban hierarchy and functioned

primarily as commercial centers. In the absence of the institutional resources that administrative cities enjoyed, these powerful market towns instituted their own systems of social welfare, defense work, and social service. In many cases, these measures amounted to de facto self-governance. However, scholars have cautioned us of the danger of assuming that the unique niche of liberty enjoyed by market towns, despite their seemingly progressive profiles, naturally gave rise to a class of elites resembling the European urban bourgeoisie. David Faure, in his research on Foshan, one of the Four Great Towns, found just the opposite: as the town grew increasingly prosperous, leadership was gradually assumed by a group of degree-holding literati whose social attributes and practices were similar to those of the traditional rural gentry.[112]

In other words, the unofficial status of market towns should not automatically be taken as a sign of independence from the imperial state. Although many powerful market towns were never converted into administrative cities, the state was still able to extend its authority into these towns. In the Song, market towns mediated between administrative cities and the countryside not only economically but also administratively by assisting the field administration below the county level. Under appointed town-supervising officials (*jianzhen guan* 監鎮官), major market towns were administered and taxed in the same fashion as regular administrative cities.[113] Initially, the Ming regime continued the administrative practice of setting up police stations (*xunjian si* 巡檢司) and tax bureaus (*shuike siju* 稅課司局) in market towns in order to maintain social order and extract commercial taxes.[114] However, during the late Ming fiscal reform, this kind of administrative oversight was decreased in the hope of stimulating economic activity.[115] In place of police stations and tax bureaus, less permanent assistant-level officials from county or prefectural offices were stationed in major market towns. The withdrawal of an official presence was intended not to undercut state authority but to provide for greater flexibility in accommodating the swift rise and fall of market forces.[116] This withdrawal was not, however, universally welcomed by town residents; many took great pains to petition *for*, not *against*, an additional state presence in their towns or sought to attain official approval of their de facto self-governance.[117] Indeed, such institutional connections could have benefited both sides. The wealth of market towns and the opportunities found in them drew people from all walks of life, including criminals and greedy "wicked" yamen clerks. As a result, as evidenced in the petitions collected in town gazetteers, requests for governmental intervention were not uncommon.[118] In other words, the relationship between the state and cities may not have been perceived by contemporaries as being as antagonistic as modern scholars tend to believe.[119]

All in all, the emergence of a potent commercial city system indeed marks a watershed in Chinese history. However, rather than treating this phenomenon as an antithesis to the official city system in the belief that the rivalry between the two impacted heavily on the nature of Chinese modernity, we may find it more productive to examine the interaction between the two city systems; namely, the institutional practices that mediated the two systems as well as the social ramifications of the relevant adjustments, such as the phenomena we have observed in Gaochun and Jiangpu. After all, both sides had plenty to offer to each other: the state coveted the rich revenues that market towns generated, and despite their economic sway, markets towns could not sustain their prosperity without the political and cultural resources monopolized by the state. When circumstances allowed, such mutual reliance might result in a basis for negotiations.

CONCLUSION

To wall or not to wall, in the final analysis, was a negotiation between the official and the commercial city systems. Walls are about boundaries, and boundary making is always a product of power and negotiation. More important, the boundary between the two systems grew sharper in the Ming, which saw city walls as the ultimate marker of civilization fundamental to its Mandate of Heaven.[120] This development is particularly noteworthy, since city walls had long been considered a defining mark not only of Chinese urbanism but of Chinese civilization at large:

Chinese civilization was identified with the growth and spread of walled urban centers up to the end of the imperial era. Walled cities, with their carefully selected sites, their close association with local drainage systems and waterways, their cosmologically significant designs, their ideologically informed patterns of land use, and their role as functional nodes of largely self-sufficient regions, were perhaps the major landmarks of traditional China. Their morphology was determined above all by the layout of the city wall and the patterning of its

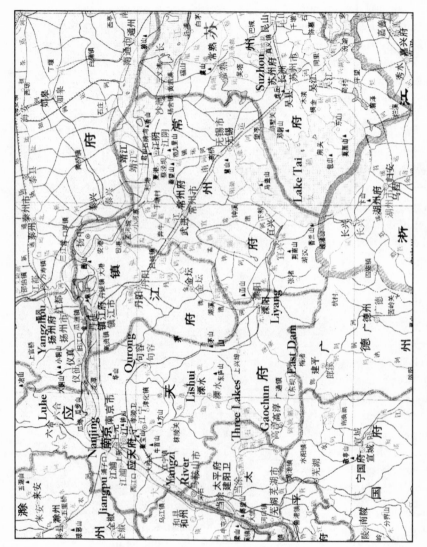

Map 2.3 Nanjing Metropolitan Area in the Ming dynasty (Tan Qixiang, *Zhongguo lishi ditu ji*, p. 49).

gates. The result was a family of urban forms distinctively Chinese, and despite gradual evolution, remarkably stable in worldwide perspective.[121]

As exemplified in this widely cited characterization by Sen-dou Chang, since the spatial reach of Chinese civilization was marked by walled cities, it is only natural that the physical manifestation of this cultural symbol remained relatively stable over the past two millennia. However, this generalization may in fact be more a reflection of a cultural ideal and less a description of reality.[122] The Ming's aggressive position on the necessity of city walls to all official administrative sites, therefore, is an anomaly rather than the norm.[123] Not only were city walls elevated to ideological centrality, but also construction was persistently enforced through imperial proclamations. City walls in the Ming were not just the most visible urban architecture but an embodiment of state presence.

Viewed from this perspective, the contrasting cases of Gaochun and Jiangpu reveal a dynamic picture of the intersection of the two city systems. Formerly a market town, Jiangpu smoothly took on its role as a military stronghold for Nanjing while continuing to expand its commercial reach through its water dispute with Luhe. In contrast, Gaochun, another market town at the southern end of the Nanjing Metropolitan Area, failed to sustain itself on either the political or commercial front. This failure prompted locals to question its promotion to the status of a county seat and to oppose the construction of a city wall. In view of the insistent enforcement of the city-wall policy in sixteenth-century China, Gaochun's triumph is indeed striking. The order to build a city wall was rescinded, and Gaochun remained an unwalled county seat, as the activism of local residents led to negotiation and amendment of a critical element of imperial spatial ideology.

CHAPTER 3

Imaging Nanjing: A Genealogy

Published in the early seventeenth century, the urban guidebook *Jinling tuyong* 金陵圖詠 (Illustrated odes on Nanjing) consists of a selection of pictures, each of a different scenic spot, accompanied by texts and cartouches identifying and describing their special attractions. *Jinling tuyong* also provides brief directions telling visitors how to get to the sites, along with specific instructions to guide the viewing experience. Yet despite these instructions for actual tourists, the book was created for a much broader audience. Its author, the famous native Nanjing official Zhu Zhifan 朱之蕃 (1564–?), claimed in his preface that he commissioned the book out of a desire to see the sights and document a tour of them, a plan long hindered by illness. With its detailed directions for seeing Nanjing, the book purported to be a *substitute* for an actual touring experience and was intended to facilitate "armchair travel" (*woyou* 臥遊)[1]—a celebrated cultural practice among literati.[2] Obscuring the boundary between actual and imaginary travels, the idea of *woyou* brings to light the multifaceted functions of *Jinling tuyong*, which aimed not only at directing physical spatial experiences but also at presenting the imagined space of Nanjing to the reading public.

What the preface does not address, however, is that this "imagined Nanjing" was envisioned through the eyes of a particular social group. Immediately after its well-received first publication, Zhu published a revised and enlarged edition with an addendum containing dozens of poems on Nanjing as well as a historical atlas of the city.[3] However curious at first glance, the assembling of three seemingly disparate works in the second edition proves to be not a random choice but a statement to the literary world—a visualization of Nanjing authored by a group of prominent native families.[4] As demonstrated in this chapter, by including two other works in the second edition, Zhu was able to point his readers at a genealogy of Nanjing images created for different needs to allow them to "see" the city through imaginary eyes: through the eyes of an emperor who wanted his subjects to be awed by the glamour of his new capital, which most of them would never see; through the eyes of a native Nanjing scholar who yearned to uncover the long-vanished past of his city; and, finally, through the eyes of Zhu Zhifan himself, who created a virtual tour of the scenic sites of Nanjing to commemorate the enduring friendship among four prominent Nanjing families. Provoked by particular desires and agendas, these efforts to "see" inspired a series of unique renderings of Nanjing as an imagined space.

Specifically, as the story of *Jinling tuyong* unfolds, Nanjing, with its expansive reconstruction at the beginning of the Ming dynasty, is first presented as a monument to the founding of the Ming empire. This imperial vision is gradually countered by images marked by the increasing presence of native elites as well as urban prosperity, a process that coincides with the changing urban character of Nanjing. That is, as the city was transformed from an imperial capital to a metropolis where cultural and economic activities, rather than political functions, dominated and defined urban life, so too its images changed from depictions of sacred space that epitomized imperial power and glory into those of a lived space crowded by locals and their daily activities. These distinct efforts to visualize Nanjing do not operate in isolation. The following analysis of *Tuyong*'s images demonstrates that the visual cues in each set of Nanjing images are closely related and contingent on one another to a degree that makes the spatial imagining of Nanjing an ongoing dialogue. In this sense, *Jinling tuyong* was not just a book but an active force in shaping the imagined space of Nanjing through its own vision of the city.

Finally, the shifting ways of looking are not unique to Nanjing but a variation of greater cultural trends during the Ming era. The images collected in the expanded 1624 edition of the Nanjing guidebook resulted from two separate projects: Nanjing atlases and Nanjing tours, each of which represented a popular mode of spatial imagination with very different visual interpretations of urban space. The analysis of *Jinling tuyong*, therefore, can also serve as a guide to look into the creation, social use, and cultural influence of city images during the Ming. With this goal in mind, this chapter begins with an investigation of the social biography of the 1624 reprint of *Jinling tuyong*, followed by an analysis of the visual projections of Nanjing included in this collection. Together, the social biography and visual analysis elucidate the particular purpose and intended audience for each of the different "imagined Nanjings" while bringing into focus the changing vision of urban space during the course of the Ming dynasty.

SOCIAL BIOGRAPHY OF THE EXPANDED VERSION OF *JINLING TUYONG*

The Two Editions

Following its first publication in 1623, *Jinling tuyong* was expanded in 1624 to a three-volume set: a historical atlas, a compilation of collaborative poems, and the original illustrated tour guide (see Fig. 3.1):

Chen Yi 陳沂 (1469–1538), *Jinling gujin tukao* 金陵古今圖考 (Historical and contemporary *tu* of Jinling; hereafter *Historical Atlas of Nanjing*).

Yu Menglin 余孟麟, Gu Qiyuan 顧起元 (1565–1628), Zhu Zhifan 朱之蕃, and Jiao Hong 焦竑 (1541–1620), *Jinling yayou bian* 金陵雅遊編 (The elegant tour of Nanjing).

Zhu Zhifan 朱之蕃, ed., illustrated by Lu Shoubo 陸壽柏, *Jinling tuyong* 金陵圖詠 (Illustrated odes on Nanjing).

Zhu Zhifan offered some clues as to how the three works came together. The connection between the tour guide, *Jinling tuyong*, and the poetry collection, *Jinling yayou bian*, is explained in the preface. The poems in *Jinling yayou bian* were written by four famous native Nanjing literati, including Zhu Zhifan himself, for twenty sights in the Nanjing suburbs. Each author made a poem using the same rhyme for each sight, resulting in a set of four poems for each of the twenty scenic spots. The initiator of this project published the poems under the title *Jinling yayou bian* at the turn of seventeenth century.[5] Two decades later, Zhu extracted his twenty poems, added another twenty, and commissioned illustrations for each scene; these were published as *Jinling tuyong* in 1623. Thus, the *tuyong* continued and expanded the lyrical elaboration on how to look at Nanjing found in *Jinling yayou bian*.

Compared to the direct connection between the poems and guide, the reason for including Chen Yi's *Historical Atlas*, published a century

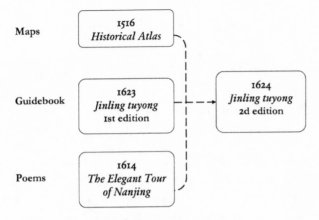

Fig. 3.1   Components of the 1624
edition of *Jinling tuyong*

earlier in 1516, is less straightforward.* Zhu's preface to the 1624 edition
points out that, despite its high intellectual value, this atlas was on the
verge of disappearing. He hoped that including it in the guidebook
would enhance its circulation. Zhu commended Chen's atlas for its excellence in presenting Nanjing both textually and visually, praise that
applies equally to Zhu's work. Chen's atlas accounts for the geographical features and evolution of Nanjing since its inception as an urban
center and documents changes in the city by pairing each map with a
textual account. Similarly, Zhu Zhifan's *Jinling tuyong* is organized as a
dialogue between textual and visual accounts of 40 scenic sites in and
around Nanjing. Taken together, whether the imaging of Nanjing is
mediated by poems, maps, or pictures in *Jinling tuyong*, the three volumes invariably concern the physical appearance of Nanjing and ways
of looking at it.

---

*For analytical convenience, the *tu* in *Jinling gujin tukao* and *Hongwu jingcheng tuzhi* are
referred to here as "atlases" since they do exhibit qualities similar to those of modern
maps. It is important to keep in mind, however, that contemporaries thought of these
images, as they did those in *Jinling tuyong*, as *tu*. For a detailed discussion of the cultural
connotations of *tu* 圖 (a broadly construed visual tradition that includes almost every
kind of graphic representation ranging from textual charts, diagrams, and maps to illustrations in general) vs. *hua* 畫 (paintings) in the Ming era, see Clunas, *Pictures and Visuality*, 104–9.

Through Native Eyes: Nanjing Atlases and Tours

A shared concern with the visualization of Nanjing only partially explains Zhu's production of the set. Chen Yi's *Historical Atlas*, according to his preface, was not an isolated creation but a sequel to *Hongwu jingcheng tuzhi* 洪武京城圖志 (Illustrated gazetteer of the Hongwu capital, 1395; hereafter *Hongwu Atlas*), compiled under the name of the founding emperor of the Ming dynasty. Since the Ming dynasty was only a small part of his atlas, Chen referred readers interested in Ming Nanjing to the earlier work. The deference was not simply a matter of paying homage to the emperor; as discussed in the next section, the internal continuity between the two atlases was so strong that they were intended to be viewed together.

When examined against this background, the collection of maps, poems, and guides in the second edition of *Jinling tuyong* in fact contains two separate projects, both of which visualized the urban space of Nanjing through varied literary and artistic formats: atlases (*Hongwu jingcheng tuzhi* and *Jinling gujin tukao*) and tours (*Jinling yayou bian*, a poetry collection; and *Jinling tuyong*, a guidebook) as illustrated in Fig. 3.2. By putting the three volumes together, Zhu responded to a contemporary trend of trying to establish a genealogy of texts and images about Nanjing by Nanjing natives separate from those by nonnatives. For example, Gu Qiyuan, one of the coauthors of *Yayou bian*, distinguished between Nanjing gazetteers created by Nanjing natives and those that were not. Gu also compiled lists of literary works in various genres authored by Nanjing natives.[6]

Indeed Zhu's publication was not an isolated act but part of a group of publications about Nanjing by a close circle of native literati:[7]

Chen Yi, *Jinling gujin tukao*, 1516.

Chen Yi, *Xianhuayan zhi* 獻花岩志 (Gazetteer of Xianhua Grotto), author's preface dated 1576; reprinted and prefaced by Jiao Hong, dated 1603.

Yu Menglin, Gu Qiyuan, Zhu Zhifan, and Jiao Hung, *Jinling yayou bian*, ca. 1600.

Zhu Zhifan, *Jinlin tuyong*, 1623.

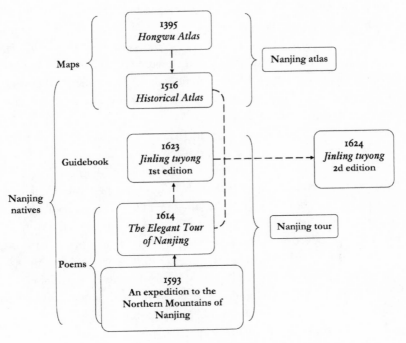

Fig. 3.2   Sources of the 1624 edition of *Jinling tuyong*

Gu Qiyuan, *Kezuo zhuiyu* 客座贅語 (Superfluous chats from the guests' seat), 1617.

Zhou Hui 周暉, *Jinling suoshi* 金陵瑣事 (Trivia about Nanjing), preface by Jiao Hong dated 1610.

Jiao Hong, *Jinling jiushi* 金陵舊事 (Past events in Nanjing) and *Jing-xue zhi* 京學志 (Gazetteer of the prefectural school in the [Southern] Capital), preface dated 1603.

Sheng Shitai 盛時泰 (fl. 1552–60), *Qixia xiaozhi* 棲霞小志 (Short record of Qixia Monastery) and *Niushou shan zhi* 牛首山志 (Gazetteer of Mount Niushou, 1577), both published by Jiao Hung; and *Jinling quanpin* 金陵泉品 (Springs in Nanjing). According to *Jinling suoshi*, this last book was produced at Zhou Hui's urging.

The close connections among this group of Nanjing natives ties their individual works into a collective and deliberate effort to narrate Nanjing from a "native perspective."[8] Of these works, the three volumes in the second edition of *Jinling tuyong* appear to be the most visually oriented, which may be part of the reason why Zhu Zhifan chose to publish them together. More important, the omission of *Hongwu jingcheng tuzhi* in the second edition highlights the change of authorship from the imperial court to Nanjing's native literati. By breaking the ties between the two atlases, Zhu reclaimed representational Nanjing from the emperor for Nanjing natives.

While highly original, Zhu's rendition was also a product of its time. The two projects—atlas and tours—that gave rise to *Jinling tuyong* epitomize two modes of city images popular in the Ming era. The first type, as discussed in the next section, highlights a state-centered view of urban space, which continued to resonate with those produced in local gazetteers. The second type, as we will see, grew out of a new cultural trend in the sixteenth century—a rising interest in the "particularity of places."[9] This trend presented great metropolises such as Nanjing as a space for leisurely touring and cultural performance. By examining the expanded edition of *Jinling tuyong* against the two modes of spatial imagination, we will find that what became open to negotiation was not only the authorship of Nanjing images but also the perspectives through which urban space was to be viewed.

MAPPING NANJING

The Imperial Vision of the Hongwu Atlas

The Representations of Imperial Capitals.   According to the preface of the *Hongwu Atlas*, the founding emperor of the Ming dynasty commissioned the work when he decided to establish the empire's capital in Nanjing. Laden with political messages, representations of imperial capitals often extend beyond the city itself to symbolize the empire at large. Rhapsodies on the capitals of the Western and Eastern Han composed in the Eastern Han, for example, present a strong critique of the Western Han regime through the seemingly innocent description and comparison of the two capital cities.[10] Anthologies such as the Southern Song *Dongjing meng Hua lu* 東京夢華錄 (A record of Dreaming of Hua [Xu] in the Eastern Capital) serve as nostalgic laments over a fallen dynasty. Politics of capital representation can also be found in visual productions. The famous *Qingming shanghe tu* 清明上河圖 (Spring festival on the river) handscroll, for example, portrays a festival in the Northern Song capital city, Kaifeng. All the details of urban life, such as the busy streets overflowing with commodities, flaunt the empire's wealth and prosperity to its audience in the most immediate form of visual display.[11] By the same token, ideological concerns also affected, and often dictated, the production of city maps, especially those of imperial capitals.[12] Indeed, due to their symbolic importance, both visual and textual representations of the capital were rarely, if ever, only about the capital city itself.

What, then, was the agenda behind the *Hongwu Atlas*? Its compilation at the beginning of the dynasty and the absence of representations of other capital cities seem to exclude the possibility that the atlas functioned as political nostalgia or critique. In addition, since the maps are rather schematic and, unlike Tang images of the capital Chang'an, show few urban street or architectural details, the maps were probably not of great practical use for administrative or military purposes.[13] Why, then, did Hongwu commission this atlas? The preface by one of his court officials offers a few clues:

Even though the emperor has created a capital city as grand as possible, people from afar are still unable to see its glory themselves. Therefore, the emperor has ordered the Ministry of Rites to portray the city in minute detail. This way the magnitude of a united empire can be grasped at a glance. Further, the emperor has also produced wood-block prints based on the picture of the capital so that the image of the imperial capital can be circulated to the four corners under heaven and someone who has never set foot in the capital can *see* its grandeur.[14]   (Italics added)

This preface indicates that the *Hongwu Atlas* was produced to present the new imperial capital to *tianxia*, the realm under heaven, as a symbol of the greatness of the newly founded Ming empire, which had just successfully united China after centuries of alien rule and interdynastic wars. Although the original handscroll is no longer extant, judging from the wood-block prints modeled after it, what was on display was not the urban civilization and commercial prosperity of an agricultural empire as shown in *Qingming shanghe tu* but the urban structure and establishments of the capital city. However, the goal was the same: to display the empire's power and wealth through representations of its capital city and overwhelm the world "at one glance." Apparently the illustrations—a series of capital portraits—measured up to Hongwu's expectations and were converted into wood-block prints for even wider circulation, most likely through official channels.[15] What is the "Nanjing" that Hongwu desired his subjects to "see" with their imaginations? The answer to this question lies in the particular site that the Hongwu emperor chose for the display of imperial grandeur.

Negotiating with Nanjing's Past: A Topographically Defined City.   In 1378, after prolonged debate, Hongwu finally settled on Nanjing as the primary capital.[16] The court's task now became to present Nanjing, a city with a long history as an imperial capital, as a unique "Ming" capital city, a task significantly compounded by the city's past. Since first established as a major city in approximately 333 BCE, Nanjing had accumulated an unfortunate record of being the capital for regimes that had failed to unite the Middle Kingdom. In fact, before Hongwu's time, Nanjing had served as the capital seven times.[17] Given its long and inauspicious history, it is not surprising that the Hongwu emperor had to strive to distinguish Nanjing as the capital of his newly united empire from the many other historical cities built on the same site.[18]

This agenda is clearly visible in a literary campaign initiated by the Hongwu emperor. The emperor solicited writings from high officials for a pavilion named Yuejiang lou 閱江樓 (River-viewing pavilion), which was situated on a hilltop in Nanjing's northwest corner, overlooking the Yangzi River and the city. The Hongwu emperor was so dissatisfied with the essays submitted by his officials that he wrote an essay himself (assuming the role of a fictitious official) pleading with the emperor to suspend the construction plans in the name of frugality. Naturally, the request was granted. Although the pavilion was never built, the essays of the emperor-official and one of his closest advisors, Song Lian 宋濂, betray crucial insights into the regime's vision of the capital. "Nanjing," Hongwu claimed, although it shares the same location, "is not the Jinling of antiquity, nor is it the Jianye of the Six Dynasties."[19] Why? According to Song Lian, since none of those regimes had succeeded in unifying the realm, Jinling in the past had failed to embody the royal aura of its surrounding mountains and rivers.[20] But this was certainly not the case now. With the newly established Ming empire, Nanjing was the capital of a new, "revolutionary enterprise" that had successfully united China.[21]

The difference between historical and Ming Nanjing was more than mere rhetoric. Under Zhu Yuanzhang's supervision, Nanjing was expanded in a way that defied the traditional ideal form of imperial capitals. The ideal Chinese city, imperial capitals in particular, had always been square in shape with the throne facing south, the royal position. The earlier cities built on the site of Nanjing had generally conformed to this norm.[22] However, the Hongwu emperor made an unusual decision to prioritize military function over tradition.[23] He expanded the city to its natural limits so that Nanjing could "take full advantage of the surrounding mountains and rivers" (*jin ju shanchuan zhi sheng* 盡據 山川之勝).[24] As a result, the shape of the city was significantly dictated by the peculiarities of the surrounding landscape. To the west it was bordered by the Yangzi and low marshlands and hills and to the north by hills and Xuanwu lake. Only on the southern and eastern sides did the contours of the city wall display any regularity. There the city projected south and east in two square sections like the bottom and right arms of a Greek cross. The southern section was based on the old Yuan city of Jiqing with additions to the northern side of the square. The square arm of the cross extending to the east contained the Ming imperial city and the highest government offices.

Zhu Yuanzhang's decision to deviate from the ideal form of imperial capital, though unusual, was not exceptional in the history of capital planning. Despite the symbolic value placed on the ideal form of capitals, owing to different natural constraints and pragmatic concerns, deviations and modifications were hard to avoid. However, even when topographical reality forced a deviation from the classical norm, the court still tried to maintain symbolic integrity at the representational level. For example, the Southern Song capital of Lin'an faced east, but images of the capital were turned 90 degrees "west-up" (as opposed to the usual north-up) so that on paper the throne still faced south, with the emperor presiding over his subjects in the correct orientation.[25] Indeed, imperial city planning not only was intended to align people and the universe according to the traditional cosmology but was also part of a representational program that affirmed and asserted a new regime's ideological legitimacy. As Nancy Steinhardt has pointed out, "In China the imperial city is more than the ruler's capital. It is an institution. It is an articulated concept for which a design is drawn and about which ideology—namely purpose and meaning—has been written, accepted, and transmitted through the ages."[26] As a result, the reality of a city was often masked by officially promoted representations. Since these plans deliberately highlighted the new capital's continuity with traditional designs, many innovations to the physical capitals on the ground went unpictured.[27]

In light of the perpetual struggle between ideal and reality in city planning, the Hongwu maps are indeed striking for their candid acknowledgment, if not highlighting, of the irregular shape of the city as defined by the surrounding terrain. Since ancient times this terrain had been known for its "royal air." Its commanding position was characterized by the phrase "coiling dragon, crouching tiger" (*longpan huju* 龍盤虎踞), implying that the surrounding hills made it impregnable. Yet despite this ancient belief, the cities built on this site had for the most part been presented as square in shape, and the natural terrain had never featured as prominently as it did in the planning of Ming Nanjing. Breaking with the tradition, the idiosyncratic presentation of Nanjing in the *Hongwu Atlas* visually confirmed the insistent claim of the Hongwu emperor that Nanjing was the capital of the only regime to accomplish the unification enterprise and that separated it from other "Nanjings" of the past.

Indeed, different from all its predecessors, Ming Nanjing was clearly defined topographically and, more significantly, represented as such in the *Hongwu Atlas*.[28] Although the map was still not scaled proportionally, unlike later Qing maps (see, e.g., Fig. 3.13, p. 148),[29] the contours portrayed on the map recognized the natural outline of the city. This naturalism became a unique signature of images of Ming Nanjing and was widely adopted in later popular guidebooks and encyclopedias, such as the tourist map in the early seventeenth-century *Hainei qiguan* 海内奇觀 (Fantastic spectacles within the realm; see Fig. 3.12, p. 148).[30]

Viewing Nanjing as Layered Spaces.   With a topographically defined base map, the *Hongwu Atlas* was able to claim a special place for Ming Nanjing in this city's long and complex history. Yet built on this base map, what was the "imagined capital" intended for the imperial subjects to "see" with their imaginary eyes?[31] Maps, like any kind of spatial representation, are inevitably a reductive representation of actual space. Often the choice of what is to be depicted is not random but carefully calibrated to highlight the underlying message. We can discover the intended vision behind this set of Nanjing images by closely examining the aspects of the city that were chosen as emblematic tokens of the "imagined capital."

In brief, the *Hongwu Atlas* consists of thirteen topoi: palaces, city gates, mountains and rivers, shrines, temples, schools, government offices, bridges, streets and markets, entertainment quarters, warehouses, pasturelands, and gardens. To better illustrate these themes, two types of images were made: architectural diagrams (palaces, shrines, and schools) and city maps (landscapes, temples, entertainment quarters, streets, bridges, and government offices). The themes of the *Hongwu Atlas* were by no means randomly chosen but spoke directly to Hongwu's vision and urban policies in Nanjing. The atlas thus personifies the imperial presence and dominance in the re-creation of Nanjing, an ancient city that for first time became the capital of a united empire. For example, in contrast to traditional imperial city planning, Taizu moved the palace city (*huangcheng* 皇城) from the central axis to the eastern side of Nanjing. This placement was intended to avoid the old palace site of the Six Dynasties states because their failure to unite China was considered an ill omen for the newly established Ming empire.[32] By the same token, the congregation of temples in the suburbs, as clearly shown on the temple map, resulted from Hongwu's policy of separating temples and marketplaces so that the spiritual and secular realms would not mix spatially.[33] Even the natural landscape was partially confiscated by the state. The two most prominent landmarks, Bell Mountain and Lake Hou, were converted into an imperial cemetery and a bureau and storehouse for census archives, which were off limits to Nanjing residents. The mountain and river map demonstrates clearly how Hongwu pushed the city to its natural limits and had the capital defined by the surrounding terrain. The entertainment quarter was also Hongwu's invention, but this did not mean he tolerated licentious pleasures. He was widely known for throwing street idlers into prison for their lack of "productivity."[34] To confine the entertainment quarters to a group of state-controlled buildings was merely another means of social regulation.[35] Finally, amid the welter of streets and bridges lie a number of city wards, created under Hongwu's policy of forced migration of craftsmen and service workers into the capital to support court and government

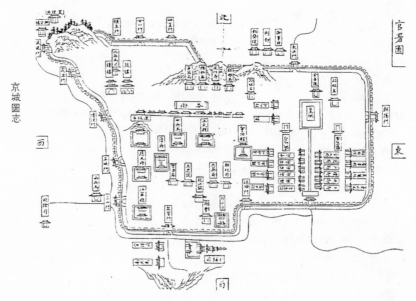

Fig. 3.3 *Hongwu Atlas* (1395): government offices

operations. In the end, the atlas bears the distinct signature of urban planning and policies during the Hongwu reign. Hence this atlas not only symbolizes the dominant presence of the state in recreating Nanjing as imperial capital, its selective representation of Nanjing also closely associates the city with Taizu as an embodiment of his "revolutionary enterprise" of a newly unified empire.

Furthermore, on the foundation of the topographically defined base map, the *Hongwu Atlas* creates a set of extraordinary city maps by differentiating Nanjing into multiple layers, each with a different function. Using the same base map, this series presents Nanjing as a city of multiple spaces overlaying one another, adding up to the one city of Nanjing. Although the contemporary cartographic convention provided templates for cities, these city maps tended to lump all urban institutions and streets together in one layout. Never before had there been a series of superimposable maps, each with the same contours, portraying various aspects of the same city. For example, the map of the government offices (Fig. 3.3, *guanshu* 官署) details all the major civil and military institutions located in the capital, thus highlighting the political aspect of Nanjing as a capital city.[36] The map of temples and shrines (Fig. 3.4, *siguan*

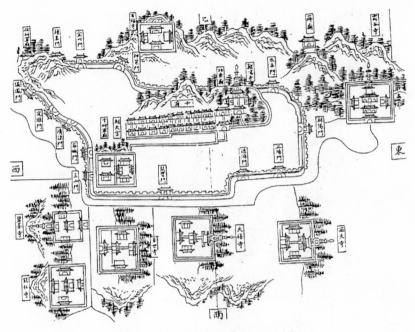

Fig. 3.4 *Hongwu Atlas* (1395): temples and shrines

寺觀) marks not only Buddhist and Daoist temples but also the state shrines for legendary officials, presenting Nanjing as a space for religious dedication and state worship.[37] The map of markets, streets, and bridges (Fig. 3.5, *jieshi qiaoliang* 街市橋樑) specifies traffic routes and connections, central marketplaces, and residential wards, signifying Nanjing as a space for transportation, transaction, and human residence;[38] while the maps of the entertainment quarters (Fig. 3.6, *louguan* 樓館) and mountains and rivers (Fig. 3.7, *shanchuan* 山川) demonstrate Nanjing as a space for social entertainment and natural landscape, respectively.[39]

The innovative format of *Hongwu Atlas* presents an intriguing interpretation of urban space. The city is not just about many individual establishments placed next to one another within a single walled space, as in conventional city maps. Instead, the serial aspect of the atlas layers one space over first one and then another space. Again, differentiating the multiple functions of a city, just like the making of maps itself, is inherently selective and subjective. It highlights certain aspects of urban

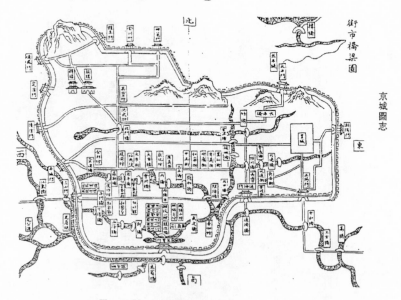

Fig. 3.5 *Hongwu Atlas* (1395): streets, markets, and bridges

space while suppressing others. Taken together, the subjects chosen by *Hongwu Atlas* point to Taizu's unique vision of Nanjing as a capital fit for a united empire. The innovative cartographic design further created an effective medium for conveying the imperial vision: the topographically defined base map fashioned a unique "Ming perspective" from which to view the capital city of Nanjing; the selectively crafted superimposable images pay tribute to its patron emperor, Hongwu, and present Nanjing as a monument to the revolutionary enterprise he created.

Standardized Production of City Images in the Ming Era.   The explicit emphasis on the underlying political authority in picturing the space of the Hongwu capital resonated in the subsequent projection of Ming cities, albeit in a very different form. Most representative of this trend are *difang zhi*, local gazetteers, in which the greatest number of city images could be found. As the compilation of *difang zhi* became routine government business in the early Ming and the format was standardized, the supplementary maps became increasingly schematic.[40] Compared to the maps in Song and Yuan gazetteers, the Ming maps simplified spatial details to focus on two central institutions: the gov-

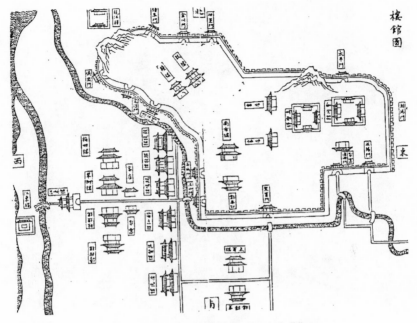

Fig. 3.6 *Hongwu Atlas* (1395): entertainment buildings

ernment offices in charge of field administration and official schools to train future bureaucrats. Often the gazetteers included individual architectural plans for these structures. To visually highlight their importance, these core institutions would be placed in the center of a map of the capital city. By the same token, being the locus of imperial state power, the capital city would be pictured at the center of the map of the territory. In actual presentation, the reader would find his gaze gradually focusing on the power center: typical *difang zhi* begin with a bird's-eye overview of an idealized political territory with a city representing state authority positioned in the center. The map of the city then focuses on its political and cultural centers—government offices and schools—whose inner structures are further illustrated with architectural maps.[41] Together, the architectural, the city, and the territorial maps create a visual scheme that views the imperium through the trappings of political power.

This visual scheme is underwritten by a cultured perspective on lived space. After surveying hundreds of extant Ming gazetteers, Chang Che-

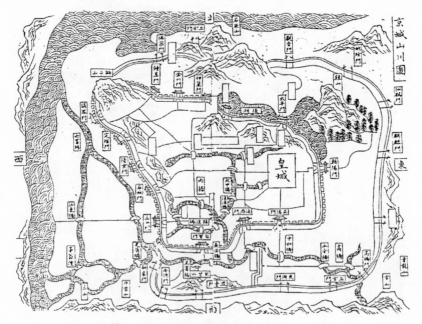

Fig. 3.7 *Hongwu Atlas* (1395): mountains and rivers

jia concluded that the cartographic conventions in gazetteers did not reflect contemporary techniques, which were sufficiently advanced to produce more accurately scaled grid maps. Yet although grid maps do appear in some gazetteers, this cartographic tradition occupies only a marginal place in the production of Ming maps. In other words, what gazetteers sought was not physical accuracy but the proper interpretation of space. The cartographic idiosyncrasy also manifested itself in the projection of urban forms. Edward Farmer, for example, points out the insistence on representing (or, rather, misrepresenting) city walls in the ideal rectangular shape even where the site would not allow this.[42]

Thus, the *Hongwu Atlas*, in spite of its originality, is still a product of its time and observes many of the same conventions of portraying cities found in Ming gazetteers. Crafted under a deliberate choice of cartographic format, these images present a culturally unique perspective that looked at lived space from a state-centered vantage point and reduced urban space to a collection of government offices and facilities.[43]

The Historical Vision in Chen Yi's
Historical Atlas of Nanjing

The dominant presence of the state in images of the city did not prevent other innovative approaches to spatial representations, such as Chen Yi's *Historical Atlas of Nanjing*. A self-proclaimed sequel to the *Hongwu Atlas*, Chen's work was later incorporated by Zhu Zhifan into the expanded edition of *Jinling tuyong*. First published in 1516, the atlas consists of a series of city maps dating from the inception of Nanjing as a city until Chen Yi's time. Zhu's effort to give the work wider circulation was successful. Chen's atlas was frequently adapted and reprinted in later gazetteers. Even the plagiarized versions achieved wide popularity, as observed by an esteemed scholar of the early twentieth century, Liu Yizheng 柳詒徵. A devoted collector and preservationist of rare books, Liu republished Chen Yi's work and noted in his preface that it had been incorporated in the most popular book on Nanjing, *Moling ji* 秣陵集 (Moling was also an ancient name of Nanjing), without acknowledgment.[44]

Chen Yi belonged to a prominent group, the *Jinling sanjun* 金陵三俊 (three prodigies of Nanjing), active in the early sixteenth century during Nanjing's first renaissance.[45] In his preface to the atlas, Chen stated his motivation for creating such an unusual work: "My family has lived in Nanjing for three generations. Even though we have enjoyed all the grandeur of palaces and magnificent sights in the city, still little is known about how the city looked before."[46] Despite the numerous poems written on the subject of Nanjing's grand history, Chen implied that there was "little known" about its physical layout. Inspired by his own curiosity and desire to "see" the historical Nanjing, Chen took advantage of his access to a rich array of sources as a compiler of the prefectural gazetteer to produce this atlas.

The atlas consists of sixteen maps of Nanjing city. Beginning from Nanjing's earliest recorded history, each map represents a point of significant spatial reorganization and is accompanied by a textual description of the main physical changes during the time in question. The atlas includes four maps for the Ming period (one for the city itself, one for the Nanjing Metropolitan Area, one for the mountains, and one for the

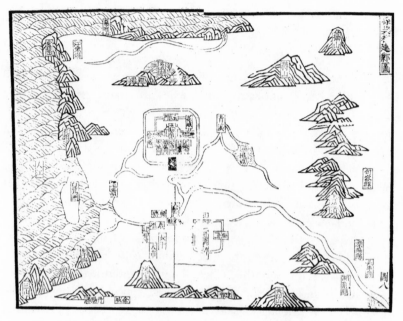

Fig. 3.8 Map of Nanjing in Three Kingdoms era, when the city, then named Jianye,
was the capital of the state of Wu (220–80 CE); Chen Yi, *Jinling gujin tukao* (1624)

rivers going through the area). However, even though maps of Ming
Nanjing consume a quarter of the space in an atlas covering 1,600 years
of Nanjing's history, Chen still felt they did not do justice to his city
and cautioned readers that "as to Nanjing city of our time, there already
is *Hongwu jingcheng tuzhi* [for your reference]."[47] Chen's deference to the
Hongwu Atlas was not mere modesty but a gesture toward a link between the two atlases: the same cartographic formulation of the space
of Nanjing city.

Chen Yi's production, however, projects the contours of the Ming
city back into earlier times. Instead of differentiating the functions of the
contemporary city as in the *Hongwu Atlas*, Chen's atlas shows how the
city evolved through time, against the terrain of Ming Nanjing. For example, the maps of Jianye during the Three Kingdoms period (220–80
CE) and Jiankang during the Southern Dynasties (420–589 CE) (Figs. 3.8–
9) show Nanjing when it served as the capital during periods of division.[48] Even though located on the same site, Jianye and Jiankang were
built on a much smaller scale than Ming Nanjing. Nevertheless, Chen Yi

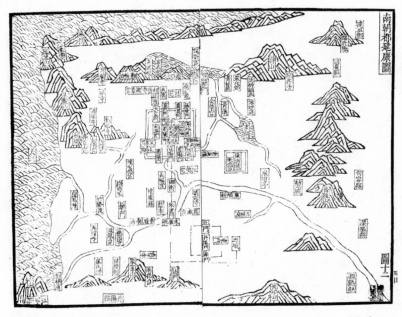

Fig. 3.9 Map of Nanjing during the Southern Dynasties, when the city, then named Jiankang, was the capital of several states from 420 until 589; Chen Yi, *Jinling gujin tukao* (1624)

still used the same cartographic formulation—the base map created for the *Hongwu Atlas*—to frame these historical cities. By doing so, he facilitated comparison of Ming Nanjing with the historical Nanjings. Such an agenda is best exemplified when the series of historical maps concludes with a map in which all the historical Nanjings are juxtaposed on the Ming terrain (Fig. 3.10).[49] In doing so, he recast the urban history of Nanjing cartographically—and measured it against Ming Nanjing.

By employing the Ming perspective established by the *Hongwu Atlas*, Chen Yi effectively confirmed the Hongwu emperor's vision of Ming Nanjing as heir to the "royal air" this area was famous for, since only Ming Nanjing, among all the cities, was actually contoured by the natural terrain and formally integrated the idea of "coiling dragon and crouching tiger" into city planning. From this perspective, Chen Yi's work is, in fact, an extensive exegesis of the *Hongwu Atlas*. Outfitted with similar visual techniques (superimposable maps), it visually details the path by which Nanjing evolved to the city it became in the late fourteenth century. True to Hongwu's words, "Nanjing was not the

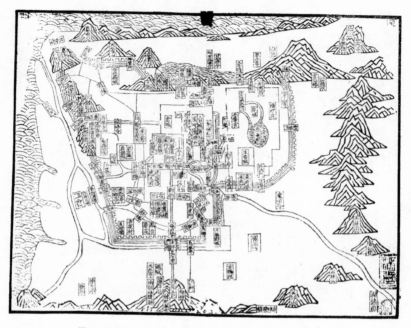

Fig. 3.10 Map superimposing all historical sites of Nanjing on a
map of Ming Nanjing; Chen Yi, *Jinling gujing tukao* (1624)

Jinling of ancient times nor the Jianye of the Six Dynasties." Chen Yi
completed Hongwu's cultural enterprise in re-envisioning an ancient
city into a capital bearing a distinct Ming signature. Even though former names for Nanjing—Jinling, Jianye, Moling—were still current
during Ming times, the city now was shown to be visibly distinct from
its predecessors.

However, even as he confirmed Hongwu's vision of his ideal capital,
Chen Yi also modified and compounded the imperial vision with a historical perspective. Ironically, in applying the base map in the *Hongwu
Atlas* to historical sites, Chen Yi undermined Hongwu's personal claim
on Ming Nanjing's creation and design. Instead, the cartographic rumi-
nation of Nanjing's past highlights the evolving form of the city as part
and parcel of the historical process. Nanjing was detached from the
shadow of the Hongwu emperor and placed back in the purview of history, an agenda more to the liking of traditional literati. The transition,
albeit ambiguous and subtle, paved the way for works by Nanjing's native literati in the following century, when Hongwu's vision ceased to
hold sway over the imagination of Nanjing.

A Nostalgic Quest for Lost Time:
The Revival of the Nanjing Atlases

For the Hongwu emperor and Chen Yi, the endeavor to visual-ize Nanjing involved far more than the simple physical act of seeing. The intent was to prescribe a perspective to see from—a vantage point particular to the Ming. Both atlases project the space of Nanjing onto a topographically defined terrain explicitly marked by the urban planning of the Ming state. This particular vision, however, took on a different meaning after the court moved to Beijing in 1421.

Following the transfer of the capital, Hongwu's grand vision of Nan-jing was gradually obscured. Even though the stated purpose of the *Hongwu Atlas* was to make the world be "in awe of Nanjing as if they were standing in front of the capital," by the end of the fifteenth cen-tury the atlas had become difficult to access. In the 1490s, when Wang Hongru 王鴻儒 (?–1519) arrived in Nanjing to work at the Ministry of Revenue, he found to his surprise that not much information about the city that was once the imperial capital was available: "When I was an of-ficial in the Southern Capital, I was really interested in knowing more about the city's past, especially the great battles and achievements of the Hongwu emperor." Wang quickly realized that it had been almost a century since the *Hongwu Atlas* was made, and the people who fought with Hongwu to establish the dynasty were long gone. Even the stories about the splendor of Nanjing had become unreliable tales.[50]

In 1492, Wang Hongru saw a copy of the *Hongwu Atlas* held in a pri-vate collection and became fascinated by it: "Although the atlas alone could not fully satisfy my lifelong quest [for knowledge about Nanjing], most of the great establishments of Nanjing were there to be viewed. Such a pleasure!" He was excited by this discovery, and the news spread fast. Later the county magistrate heard about the manuscript and pro-posed to "reprint the set and increase its circulation."[51] The attenuation of memories of the former capital was not solely a matter of time. The nostalgic quest for old Nanjing, as testified by contemporary accounts, was augmented by the political milieu at the time, which deliberately obliterated Nanjing's past as the imperial capital.

Indeed, after the primary capital was moved to Beijing in 1421, the Beijing court endeavored to establish its primacy by downplaying the significance of Nanjing in the earlier life of the Ming dynasty.[52] This strategy provoked adverse reactions among some literati, such as the noted essayist Gui Youguang 歸有光 (1507–71). Gui first encountered the *Hongwu Atlas* in 1531 when he traveled to take the civil service examination, and a *jinshi* from his hometown showed Gui his personal copy. It must have made a strong impression on him. Twenty-nine years later, as he was viewing the maps in the Yuan Nanjing gazetteer, it struck him how the differences between the divided regimes (the Six Dynasties) and a united empire (the Ming) were reflected in the appearance of Nanjing. This led him to question the widespread notion that the Hongwu emperor had not planned to stay in Nanjing permanently and that the Yongle emperor had fulfilled Hongwu's plan of moving the capital to Beijing.[53] Gui argued that anyone who looked at the atlas would know that the Hongwu emperor envisioned Nanjing as the permanent capital and built the city accordingly. Nanjing under Hongwu was, and here Gui quoted the emperor's "Yuejiang lou ji," "no longer the Nanjing of antiquity, no longer the Jianye of the Six Dynasties."[54]

Gui tapped into the dual-capital politics of his time by re-enacting the visual effect intended by the Hongwu emperor. Reiterating the founding emperor's statement when he looked at Nanjing from the imaginary Yuejiang Pavilion, Gui maintained that "what should be seen" in Hongwu's plan was the greatness of a capital in a unified empire that rescued the city from its inauspicious past. Political undertones aside, the late Ming curiosity about early Ming Nanjing played an important role in reviving and recirculating early Ming images of Nanjing in the late Ming period. This interest was underwritten by a deep sense of nostalgia—people like Gui were clearly aware that the Nanjing portrayed in the *Hongwu Atlas* was long gone—which is exactly what made this atlas precious. It enabled them to visualize a Nanjing that no longer existed.

The recovering of Nanjing's lost glory as former capital was of interest not only to the elites. The section on "palaces" in the late Ming popular encyclopedia *Sancai tuhui* 三才圖會 (Comprehensive illustrated encyclopedia) adapted images from the *Hongwu Atlas* to illustrate "palaces" and "capitals," even though Beijing had been the primary capital for more than two centuries (Fig. 3.11).[55] The popular tour guide *Hainei qiguan* had only one city map—that of Nanjing—and that was framed in

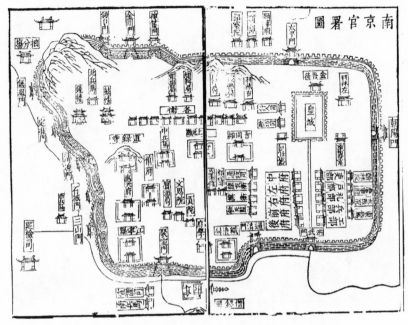

Fig. 3.11 Adaptation of the *Hongwu Atlas* in *Sancai tuhui* (late Ming)

accord with the terrain contour devised for the *Hongwu Atlas* (Fig. 3.12).[56] Through various iterations by commercial presses, the founding emperor's effort to visualize his capital also satisfied the popular desire to view and remember the "capital city" at a time long after its glory days. Not only did the images from the *Hongwu Atlas* circulate widely in popular publications, but Chen Yi's map also appeared repeatedly in Qing gazetteers.[57] Only in the nineteenth century was this set of maps replaced by the new standard of scaled cartography (Fig. 3.13).[58]

Aside from their extraordinary visual innovations and lasting appeal, both the *Hongwu Atlas* and Chen Yi's project a panoramic view and a highly politicized urban space, one detached from actual lived experiences. After the court moved to Beijing, urban life gradually gravitated toward cultural and economic activities, making the gap between representation and reality even more apparent. Indeed, awareness of the irrevocable changes was clearly registered in the nostalgia for Nanjing's days as the imperial capital. On one hand, this sentiment prompted the enthusiastic pursuit and reproduction of the early Ming images of

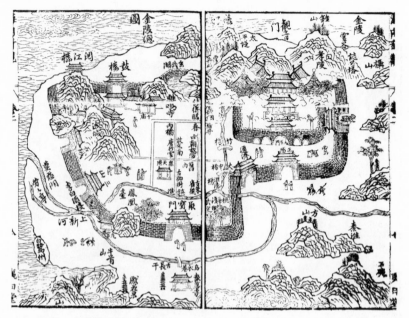

Fig. 3.12 Tour map of Nanjing city in *Hainei qiguan* (early seventeenth century)

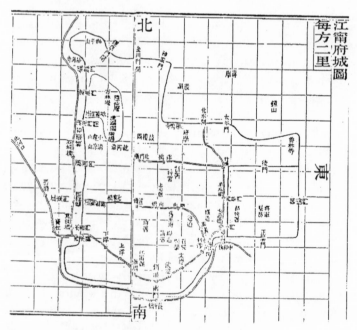

Fig. 3.13 Late Qing map of Nanjing; *Jiangning fuzhi* (1736)

Nanjing. On the other hand, as the imperial gaze ceased to hold immediate relevance for later Ming visitors, a new vision of Nanjing was in order. As discussed in the following sections, for people "near and far" who wanted to see Nanjing with either actual or imaginary eyes, a new mode of viewing gradually prevailed over the course of the sixteenth century, one that was rooted in the cultural practices of landscape appreciation.

TOURING AND TOUR GUIDES: THE EMERGING MODE OF GEOGRAPHIC IMAGINATION

Cultured Touring and Social Distinction

The Proliferation of Scenic Sites in Sixteenth-Century China. The two projects of the Nanjing atlases and the Nanjing tours occurred roughly a century apart. During this period a new mode of geographic imagination that envisioned a place—be it a county, a mountain, or a city—through its representative sights, *jing* 景, began to gain ground. *Jing,* an elusive and difficult term, is variously rendered as "scenes," "sights," "scenic spots," or "vistas" in English. The ascendance of *jing* provoked a different mode of viewing urban space in sharp contrast to the panoramic, politicized views of cities in official gazetteers. Instead, the format of *jing* broke a place down into a host of snapshots resonating with previous aesthetic experiences.[59] Through a series of images, *jing* molded spatial experiences into a cumulative process of reaching full knowledge of a place through a tour of its parts. The sequential nature of *jing* lent itself to conventional formats of Chinese art such as handscrolls or albums. Whereas the scroll emphasizes spatial and temporal continuity, the album highlights a series of discrete moments of observation.[60] In addition, the visual representation of *jing* is often accompanied with lyrical elaboration that presents literary responses in appreciation of a particular fraction of a place in the form of inscriptions or colophons.

The popularity of *jing* grew out of new cultural trends in the sixteenth century, when China witnessed an unprecedented surge in the production of tour guides, topographical gazetteers, and works describing specific geographical locations such as towns, mountains, temples, lakes, and rivers,[61] all eagerly consumed by an emerging reading public.[62] The intensifying attention to the "particularity of places," suggested by Timothy Brook, was a product of an empire-wide cultural movement motivated by an elevated sense of place, local pride, practical purpose, and historical consciousness.[63] It embodied a new cultural attitude, an emerging awareness among late Ming people that they could articulate their lived experiences through the representations of places.

This view is particularly true in the development of *jing*, which came to be the linchpin of local pride during this period. Although accounts of *jing* can be found as early as the Song, this practice became so popular in the Ming that by the late seventeenth century literati complained about the excessive number of *jing*. Zhao Jishi 趙吉士 (1628–1706), for example, attributed this abuse of *jing* to the Yongle reign, when the court was moved from Nanjing. Poetry and paintings on the "eight scenes of Beijing" were actively solicited from high officials to endow the area in and around the city with a heritage worthy of an imperial capital.[64] Most representative of all is the renowned painting by Wang Fu 王紱 (1362–1416) titled *Eight Scenes of Beijing* (*Beijing bajing* 北京八景). Indeed, a close reading of the inscriptions indicates that Wang's exquisite rendering of the landscape around Beijing was much more than a regular art production. Highly politically charged, this painting was part of a publicity campaign to mold public attitudes toward Beijing in order to ease the transition of the capital from Nanjing to Beijing.[65]

Ever since, as Zhao Jishi lamented, the "eight scenes" model acquired ever-greater momentum and was widely imitated all over the country. By his time, similar collections of *jing* poetry had been composed not only for major cities but also for small villages, towns, temples, and gardens—virtually every nameable place. Given this trend, it is not surprising to find that the Hongwu base map of Nanjing underwent yet another metamorphosis in the early seventeenth century as most of the government buildings were supplanted by tourist attractions (Fig. 3.12). In a sense, the surging number of topographic artworks, gazetteers, and tour guides at the time directed viewers' gazes away from the symbols of political authority and toward *mingsheng* 名勝, famous sites known for their natural beauty or historical associations.

With the proliferation of *mingsheng* came a rich array of late Ming publications surveying famous sites within the imperial realm, such as

Yang Erzeng's 楊爾增 *Hainei qiguan* 海内奇觀 (Fantastic spectacles within the realm, 1609), He Tang's 何鏜 *Mingshan shenggai ji* 名山勝概記 (Records of famous mountains and magnificent scenery, 1633), and Cao Xuequan's 曹學佺 *Da Ming yitong mingsheng zhi* 大明一統名勝志 (Compendium of famous sites within the united realm of the Great Ming, preface dated 1630). Interestingly enough, among them we find no definitive version of the best sights of the empire; instead each selection reflected the editor's personal opinion.[66] The lack of consensus might be a deliberate marketing strategy to make each publication a unique commodity. Yet it might also reflect the intensive competition among famous sites in an age of frenetic *jing*-making. Generally speaking, in addition to these famous visual compendiums featuring the most celebrated sites, most guides were organized around a particular theme (such as famous mountains or temples) or a place (such as Nanjing or West Lake). Since the central subject of this chapter, *Jinling tuyong*, is one such cultural product, a brief survey of the nature and social function of this genre will place this book in a proper contemporary context and shed light on its significance to the Nanjing community.

The rapid growth of guidebooks was closely related to the increase in physical mobility in the sixteenth and seventeenth centuries. As more people traveled, tourism became a popular leisure activity with a broad appeal across late Ming society.[67] One salient feature of late Ming tour guides lies in the unusual value placed on readers' imagination. Indeed, at a time of unprecedented access to travel, it is interesting to find editors like Zhu Zhifan presenting their guidebooks specifically as intended for armchair travelers. In fact, some authors even argued that *woyou* surpassed physical travel as long as proper ways of viewing were performed. That is, for a cultured reader, tour guides were a superior substitute for actual visits. This curious notion brings to the fore the peculiar nature of "tour" and "tourism" in late Ming culture. As Tobie Meyer-Fong points out, the authors of late Ming guidebooks, like their contemporaries, deliberately distinguished between travel as a process involving movement between places, *xinglü* 行旅, and "touring," *you* 游, a destination-oriented aesthetic activity associated with the literati elite and their social imitators. Thus late Ming guidebooks should be further divided into two groups. One group aimed at facilitating physical movement. Typical of works in this group are route books proffering practical geographic information or pamphlets alerting travelers to common scams and tricks. The other group was devoted to the proper performance of cultured sightseeing, marking the places to visit with instructions on how to look.[68] The different emphases—the practicalities of travel versus cultured sightseeing—are clearly reflected in their approaches to the target audience. The titles of practical travel guides such as *Shishang yaolan* 士商要覽 (Essential reading for gentry and merchants) suggest efforts to reach an audience of diverse social statuses. In contrast, the prefaces of tour guides are often at pains to identify and eulogize the "true sightseer."

The growth of the two types of guidebooks is intrinsically related. The large number of practical travel guides reflects the fact that in an increasingly mobile society the appeal of and opportunities for tourism were no longer reserved for the privileged few but shared across a wide social spectrum. As itinerant merchants and common sightseers enthusiastically pursued the pleasure and prestige of touring, a further nuanced cultural distinction for an elevated form of tourism was in order.[69] The rising demand for guidebooks such as *Jinling tuyong* reflects the equally, if not more, important concerns of contemporary readers for guidance to a culturally appropriate manner of experiencing landscape, a knowledge of which was considered essential to the repertoire of status performance. In the words of Meyer-Fong, these publications are in effect vehicles for "cultural mapping" because "they defined the practice of sightseeing as they were used to define the sightseer as subject."[70]

This characterization is crucial. Although compendia for famous sites were written in earlier periods, such as Wang Xiangzhi's 王象之 *Yudi jisheng* 輿地紀勝 (Records of famous sites in the realm, 1227) and Zhu Mu's 祝穆 *Fangyu shenglan* 方輿勝覽 (Topography book for visiting places of scenic beauty, 1239), late Ming authors exhibit a much higher degree of self-consciousness about the very meaning of sightseeing: Who is the entitled sightseer? What is worth seeing? And what constitutes respectable touring behavior? With the cultural valence ascribed to landscape appreciation on the rise, an increasing number of literati began to describe themselves as someone fond of *you* (*hao you* 好游). By the late Ming, *you* 游 (touring) had developed into a highly sophisticated practice in elite circles. Elaborate treatises on *you dao* 遊道 (the way of *you*) distinguish every nuanced type of *you* and have strong opinions on what makes one's travel culturally desirable, such as the means of travel, the proper age for travel, choice of companions, and worthy destinations.[71] For devoted practitioners, *you* was not just a simple act of sightseeing but a deliberate display of style and talent. The aura of a successfully performed *you* was said to be especially coveted by the class of *shengyuan*, the majority of whom, owing to the extremely competitive nature of the civil service examinations, were bound to spend an extended period of their life trying to pass the next higher-level examination with no certain career prospects in sight. For this group of lettered men, status anxiety was a fact of life, and the promise of alternative routes to establish a name could not have been more alluring.[72] Thus the emergence of a repertoire of elite status performance in which the elevated form of *you* occupied a central place is not surprising. Nevertheless, *shengyuan* were not the only ones bedazzled by cultured touring. The surging numbers of literati tourists led contemporary observers to suspect a self-serving motivation behind the popularity of touring. Xie Zhaozhi 謝肇淛 (1567–1624), for example, was cynical about *you*: "People are into touring simply because they crave the lofty fame that comes with it."[73]

As cultured touring came to be seen as a crucial benchmark for taste and status, social rivalry over its proper performance intensified. Particular groups such as merchants and *shanren*[74] became common targets in contemporary criticism for the vulgarity of their touring.[75] Yet the battle lines appear to be much more complicated than just a distinction between elites and the aspiring nouveaux riches who emulated them. For example, many criticisms pointed to officials using the government courier service to enjoy personal sightseeing activities. The late Ming cultural arbiter Qian Qianyi singled out one notorious official of his time, Feng Yuancheng 馮元成, as the epitome of touring misconduct.[76] Feng was said to be a zealous practitioner of touring culture. Every area he visited was packed by his entourage. Dressed in his official robes and stationed at a monastery, Feng would command his staff to scout the surrounding scenic spots and produce poetry as stridently as if he was holding court at his office. Feng and his many peers, Qian Qianyi complained, were to be blamed for the voluminous run-of-the-mill poetry on Hangzhou.[77]

Within this line of criticism there emerged the notion that the meaning of *you* was not dictated by the physical act of sightseeing. Tang

Xianzu 湯顯祖, the great Ming playwright renowned for his emphasis on the infinite capacity of human emotions, extended this position into spatial practice. In his preface to He Tang's *Mingshan shenggai ji*, Tang Xianzu employed the concept of *yi* 意 (mindset) to evaluate different attitudes toward landscape appreciation.[78] In his search for the ideal true sightseer, Tang first looked at two groups: the rich and the powerful. Although both had the necessary means to travel extensively and enjoy the magnificent sights listed in He Tang's collection, Tang found that they often fail to possess the right mindset to truly appreciate the landscape. The economically affluent (i.e., merchants) surround their residences with landscaped gardens but end up entertaining themselves with fake mountains and streams. As for the eminent and the powerful, they are so burdened with worldly concerns that the beauties of nature inspire in them only feelings of their weighty responsibilities for the people's welfare. On the other hand, those who do possess the required inner qualities to truly engage with the landscape often cannot afford to travel. They have to resort to imaginary traveling, *woyou*. This seeming compromise by no means indicates the cultural valence of *woyou* since according to Tang, the truth of nature lies in the eyes of the beholder—no matter whether he is looking at a real landscape or a represented one. Willpower conquers all. "With *yi*, a place more than a thousand miles away can be conjured up right before one's eyes. Otherwise, even if the scene is just a few feet away, it is still beyond the reach of those who do not possess *yi*." In Tang's opinion, true engagement with scenery ultimately hinges on the power of one's mind.

Having established the value of *woyou* in cultural sightseeing, Tang lauded He's contribution: with publications such as He's, even those without means could pursue the pleasures that only extraordinary (and often remote) landscapes could bring. In a sense, the dispute over "authentic sightseeing" precipitated a reinterpretation of *you*, one that prioritized mental, instead of physical, engagement with landscape. To buttress this point, Tang Xianzu even ventured as far as to attack the qualifications of those who could afford to travel all over the empire and actually did so to be authentic sightseers. As someone excluded from circles of power, Tang particularly singled out bureaucrats for criticism:

For those who have achieved success and wealth and embark on long-distance travels. . . . They are most likely too occupied with business to conduct sightseeing. Even if they could make time and detour to visit these sites, the trip is often rushed between tight schedules and [they are so] surrounded by retinues and entourages that they can could spend only seconds on the site, barely enough to applaud its beauty before leaving.

In contrast to Tang's support for non-officeholding literati in the competitive world of cultured touring, Ye Xianggao's 葉向高 (1559–1627) preface to *Jinling yayou bian* expresses a different, if not opposing, sentiment. According to Ye, despite the grand scenery around Nanjing, most high officials were so trapped in the pursuit of fame and success that they had lost interest in nature. As a result, the enterprise of landscape appreciation had come to be monopolized by the so-called *saoren moke* 騷人墨客 (men of letters), in this context referring to literati who had failed to attain official titles and indulged in literary pursuits. The distinct appeal of *Jinling tuyong* in comparison with similar publications, argued Ye, resides precisely in the fact that it was produced by eminent Nanjing officials who also pursued the lofty matter of scenic appreciation.

The disagreement between Tang and Ye over who among the elite class (those with or without high official titles) were truly entitled to claim the cultural prestige of landscape appreciation exposes the complicated nature of social distinction in the late Ming world. Contrary to what some scholars have argued, the battle over taste was not only about the threat to elite identity. In fact, tensions within elite ranks appear to be just as strong, if not more intense, as those between elites and aspiring nouveaux riches.[79] The need for such a nuanced form of social distinction stems from the fact that many late Ming literati circles had already overstepped prescribed social boundaries to include officials, *saoren moke*, and oftentimes merchants. This social promiscuity provoked reactionary as well as progressive responses. The reactionaries vowed to restore the blurred social boundaries; the progressives began to contemplate new perceptions of social distinction—such as *yi*—that were so subjective as to escape any status label.

The amount of rivalry and hostility provoked by the contested notion of "true sightseer" is indeed revealing. The argument itself attests to the fact that touring and sightseeing had developed into well-recognized forms of cultural performance coveted by a wide array of social groups. The resultant anxiety and tension explain why *woyou* was so enthusiastically advocated: those who lacked the means (money, time, health) could under this rubric engage in truly inspired sightseeing. Indeed, many late Ming literati echoed Tang's argument that physical experiences should not dominate the cultural aura associated with *you*. To satisfy the growing demand for the imaginary tourism of *woyou*, the market was flooded with topographic artworks and illustrated travelogues, for, as many contemporaries suggested, images provided a much more accessible venue for geographic imagination.[80] Even official gazetteers intended to document governmental operations were enlisted to satisfy the needs of armchair travelers. A county magistrate in Henan in 1660, for example, stated that gazetteers were his favorite casual reading, "transporting me as though I were myself seeing it with my own eyes."[81] The existence of such readers was not lost on contemporary gazetteer editors. A good example is *Jinling fancha zhi* 金陵梵刹志 (Gazetteer of Buddhist monasteries in Nanjing),[82] complied by Ge Yinliang 葛寅亮 in 1627 when he served at the Bureau of Sacrifices under the Ministry of Rites, the government agency overseeing the operation of Buddhist establishments. Monasteries at the time performed multiple functions; they were simultaneously integrated and centralized religious institutions, economic entities, and publishers.[83] All these activities fell under the government's purview. Although Ge's explanatory notes at the beginning of his book indicate that his intent in compiling this gazetteer was to facilitate religious administration, he nevertheless made it clear that he was accommodating the interests of armchair travelers as well. In addition to detailed accounts of geographic sites, the main buildings of the temple complex, temple properties (i.e., farmland), relevant government regulations on clerks, and the publication of Buddhist sutras, he also included travel literature in the entry for each temple. To further aid visitors, Ge Yinliang even produced images with famous travel destinations specifically marked.[84]

Social Tourism and the Formation of "Touring Communities"

The social contention and anxiety over the proper performance of landscape appreciation bear clear witness to the fact that *you* had become part of a greater cultural repertoire for elite status performance. Indeed, by providing a platform for cultural performance, cultured touring contributed to the rising demand for social distinction at a time when prescribed boundaries were often trespassed. Since this increasing social promiscuity also prompted new ties and communities, not surprisingly, the practice of landscape appreciation was again utilized in the development of social networks.

The popularity of *you* gave rise to two new subtypes of tourism. The first featured wild adventures in seldom-explored exotic sites. Among this group of travelers, Xu Xiake 徐霞客 (1587–1641), probably the best known, ventured to the furthest corners of the empire. Wang Shixing 王士性 (1547–98) was also well known for his series of *zhuangyou* 壯遊 (grand tours), each documented in detail in poetry, essays, and even paintings.[85] The second subtype was more in the nature of leisured excursions, which, in the minds of late Ming literati, was often associated with the goal of "seeking friends," or, as we might say, social networking. Yuan Zhongdao 袁中道 (1570–1623), one of the famed Three Yuan brothers known for their vignette-style writings (*xiaopin* 小品), described his deep passion for *you* in terms of its socializing function: "I took a liking to *you* when very young. Since then, wherever I visited, I have always sought out local luminaries to befriend." And with much pride, he declared that, thanks to his long-term passion, he now enjoyed an extensive social network that extended to virtually every corner of the empire.[86] With similar purposes in mind, literati planned trips in accordance with the celebrities they wanted to associate with. Active in late Ming literary circles, Qin Gao 秦鎬 abandoned his pursuit of success in the civil service examinations after a few failures and devoted himself to literature. In lieu of studying for the examinations, Qin traveled extensively, visiting numerous famous sites. After a visit to Qian Qianyi at his home in Yushan 虞山 (modern Changshou), he recounted his extended journey along with the wonderful authors he came to know, maintaining that his tour was not only about his passion for natural landscape but also about the desire to "seek friends."[87] Indeed, Qin's journey was organized around visits to major literary figures of the time. Qian Qianyi, an extremely influential literary critic whose verdict could determine one's place in the literary world, was naturally the highlight of Qin's social tour.

Given their explicit purpose of social networking, many such tours focused on major metropolises with easy access to prestigious elite circles. In fact, Kong Shangren 孔尚任 (1648–1718), the famous early

Qing playwright, named five "must-visit" metropolises for his peers: Beijing, Nanjing, Yangzhou, Suzhou, and Hangzhou.[88] Best known for his intimate portrait of late Ming Nanjing in *Peach-Blossom Fan*, Kong Shangren had a sharp eye for the inner workings of literati society. He efficiently dissected the mechanism of urban tourism in an essay written for a new volume of collected poetry compiled by his friend Guo Gaoxu 郭臬旭. Guo had just returned from a trip to Yangzhou, where he had been showered with banquets and poetry because an earlier visit by Guo had resulted in his famous volume of touring poetry on the city. An anthology of these exchanges was assembled, and Kong Shangren was asked to write a preface. Guo's warm and enthusiastic reception in Yangzhou, as Kong Shangren observed, was not an accident but part of contemporary culture. According to Kong, by the end of the seventeenth century, urban touring had developed into an established realm of competition analogous to that of the civil service examinations. In this universe, one's achievement was measured by the quality of one's poetry elaborating on the sights or commemorating the social occasion. A triumph in such literary ventures brought the author literary acclaim, just as passing the metropolitan examinations would entitle one to enter the ranks of officialdom. As described by Kong, major cities, with their rich endowment of celebrated luminaries as an influential audience, became the perfect stages to display one's talents. This development is not surprising—unlike ordinary scenic spots that garnered attention only from locals, great cities enjoyed empire-wide fame and prestige. Therefore, recognition of an author's literary treatments of urban sights led to fame and publicity at the national level. As a result, visiting and lyricizing renowned sights in a major city became the most effective way to make a debut in the literati world.

The analogy between urban tourism and the examination culture further extended into the social ties and communities both generated. Just as the candidates who passed the examination in the same year were called *tongnian* 同年 and seen as reliable political allies in their future official careers, Kong Shangren elaborated, similar bonds of *tongyou* 同游 developed among fellow tourers who visited the same site. Guo's fame from his previous visit to Yangzhou earned him an esteemed place in the city's *tongyou* community; these bonds were manifested in the outpouring of poetry celebrating his visit. The ties developed from touring could also be bequeathed. According to Kong, if a son of a deceased *tongyou* visited the old site in his place, the fellowship would be renewed and extended into the next generation. The strong bonds among tourers mandated the best efforts of the older generation to assist the members of the next generation in establishing their names in the elite circle. The formation of touring communities, in this sense, became ritualized. Granted, Kong conceded, the bonds created by leisure touring may not seem to carry sufficient moral weight to be a suitable foundation for literati communities. Still, he insisted, such a relationship was much more respectable than those formed for self-serving reasons.

Kong Shangren's remarks, albeit reserved in tone, are indeed revealing. The social rituals developed around touring had created a culturally elevated venue for elites to establish and celebrate their special bonds in a very public manner. Since such allegiances were tied to a particular site or place, they appeared less politically provocative than other forms of literati associations. Yet even without the self-righteous moral conviction typical of late Ming literati societies, the elegant façade of *you* offered an adequate cultural space that was sufficiently ambiguous for elite social networking. The act of sightseeing thus transcended the mere interaction between space and people and came to be laden with significant indications of social distinction and affiliation.

Indeed, the rich late Ming culture of sightseeing led to the creation of many communities around shared experiences with specific sites. The forming and sustaining of communal ties drew heavily on the production and exchange of literary and artistic works on touring. In this sense, leisured urban excursions were in effect a variation of elite gatherings. The ritual surrounding such gatherings required the production of group poetry, sometimes even paintings, to conclude and commemorate the occasion and materialize the newly created social ties. To take full advantage of social tourism, Kong Shangren urged that, just as a seasoned examination candidate would familiarize himself with the most current style of examination essays, an ambitious tourer should be well versed in the genealogy of touring poetry associated with a particular site as well as the development of its literary styles.[89] This knowledge would assist him in properly positioning his work in relation to the relevant literature and thus facilitate entrance into the touring community. In some cases, these cultural products were not only souvenirs but even substitutes for the actual act of touring. For instance, when Zhong Xing 鍾惺 (1574–1624), a renowned late Ming vignette writer, mapped out his touring community, he did so according to participation not in an actual trip but, rather, in the representation of it. That is, it was the sharing of the paintings and poetry about the tour that brought a group of literati together. Zhong Xing described this particular touring community in his inscription on Hu Pengju's 胡彭舉 painting about Ling-gusi 靈谷寺, a monastery near Nanjing known for its beautiful pine grove. Hu's painting was created to commemorate a tour made by Hu Pengju and his friends, some of whom visited the same site with Zhong Xing on two other separate occasions. Since all three trips were documented with poetry and painting exchanges even though Zhong Xing never went on a trip with Hu Pengju, he believed that reading the touring poetry and viewing the paintings made them in effect members of the same cohort of *tongyou*.[90]

Once formed, touring communities could be rather resilient in surviving gaps in time and space. In the extremely ritualized form of social tourism, such ties could be passed down to the next generation. Kong Shangren drew an analogy between the crucial role of the scenic poetry exchanged every generation and the function of *nianyi pu* 年誼譜 (genealogy of the friendship between persons of the same graduation class in the civil service examinations), which cemented and bore witness to the newborn alliance. As discussed in the next section, the story of *Jinling tuyong* is one of a cross-generational touring community that eventually extended across the dynastic divide. In fact, in many cases, we find that such literary and artistic exchanges not only enabled the touring communities to endure across generations but also allowed them to overcome geographic separations. Suzhou, the cultural capital of the Ming empire, is a case in point.

During the sixteenth century, Suzhou witnessed an upsurge in topographical images, many of which were produced to commemorate social gatherings at specific sites and served to further cement the participants' social ties. The earliest pioneer of this trend was Shen Zhou 沈周 (1427–1509), a key founder of the Wu school of painting, who is often credited as the first to develop the topographical genre in Suzhou. Shen belonged to a close-knit circle of local literati, some of whom had long before reached high positions elsewhere. Shen produced multiple topographical images portraying the sites where many social gatherings were held and memories were attached. As members of this community later dispersed throughout the empire, his works served as means of sustaining the social ties through times of separation. Art historian Mette Siggstedt observes that "Shen's painting of the Wu sceneries represented a link between the literati who stayed back in Suzhou and the ranking officials serving in Peking. His landscapes depicting the famous sites of Wu [Suzhou area] with their historical and cultural connotations were testimonies of the cultural heritage of the region and must have strengthened the local identity."[91] By preserving the sentiments associated with a particular site and occasion, commemorative touring artworks enabled literati communities to overcome actual spatial barriers and sustain personal bonds. Over time, however, owing to the prominence of such Suzhou painting masters as Shen Zhou and Wen Zhengming 文徵明 (1470–1559), famous local sites such as Tiger Hill 虎丘 or Stone Lake 石湖 soon became popular subjects for paintings. Mass production, either via emulation or outright forgery, made these images increasingly conventionalized. As these famous sights were stereotyped through the voluminous production of topographical pictures, the intimate relation among the pictures, artists, and recipients was lost. In the end, impersonalized images of Suzhou came to be shared by the general public as the most recognizable visual icons of the area (expressed in the style of the Wu school of painting), and the spatial connotation of Suzhou was redefined.[92]

To sum up, the rise of tourism in the sixteenth century resulted in a chain of linkages among landmarks, literati communities, and the popular geographic imagination. As opportunities for travel gradually opened to the general population in the late Ming, the practice of tourism was further differentiated. Literati came to adapt social tourism into a prized venue for literati networking. Under this trend, sightseeing ceased being simply an engagement with the natural landscape and became a public display of talent and status. The poetry and paintings that commemorated tours were vital to this culture. They enhanced the public visibility of the author's cultural performance and materialized the alliance formed during the group outing. Thus, the surging output of topographic literature and art in the late Ming should be considered not just another change of style but a representation of a new relationship between space and people—even for non-elites.[93] Featuring celebrated authors, these site-specific publications elevated the fame and prestige of local landmarks for the general public. As these sites gained popularity, the intimacy implied in the original art or literature was gradually diluted, and eventually the sites were transformed from lived space into symbols of the popular geographic imagination.

The display and exchange of literary sentiments not only consolidated existing communities but also facilitated new ones. Indeed, one unique feature of the late Ming touring culture lies in its deliberate creation and aggressive promotion of tourist destinations. New sites were constantly developed, bringing new groups of people together in the process. The rise of Mount Huang 黄山 (Anhui) as a prestigious site in the late sixteenth century serves as a prime example. Considered a national emblem in modern China for its supreme scenery, Mount Huang is in fact a relative latecomer to the pantheon of Chinese famous sites. Most scholars agree that the opening of Mount Huang and its rise in importance are due largely to the efforts of the Buddhist monk Pumen 普門. A poor migrant from Shaanxi, Pumen made the promotion of Mount Huang his life goal. He started by soliciting support from local elites and powerful families in exploring remote sites and improving access to the mountain. In the competitive world of late Ming famous sites, imperial patronage was considered crucial in enhancing visibility. With this in mind, Pumen decided to expand his lobbying efforts to the capital. To achieve this goal, he tried to buttress his credentials by acquiring an endorsement from his teacher, a renowned abbot. When this effort failed, Pumen took a more secular approach. He carried paintings of Mount Huang to the capital and fraternized with prominent elites and powerful eunuchs. All these activities and connections eventually helped Pumen gain the support of the empress dowager, a much-needed boost for the rise to eminence of Mount Huang.[94]

As the status of Mount Huang grew, so did the fame of Pumen and the affiliated literati groups in Anhui. This in turn drew more visitors to the area. Poetry and literary societies were formed in the process of exploring and writing about the mountain's remote sites; lecture series were even held about the mountain. Active among those associated with these literary societies were merchant-literati such as Pan Zhiheng 潘之恆 (1556–1622), highlighting the complicated social composition of such communities. In view of the intense social activities surrounding Mount Huang, a mid-seventeenth-century monk lamented "the departure of Buddhist monks from the mountain and the appearance in their stead of secular literati."[95] Along with this development came the proliferation of images about Mount Huang, which gave rise to the signature visual style of the Anhui school of painting inspired by the unique topographical features of the mountain.[96]

Nanjing witnessed a similar scenario in the rise of Xianhua Grotto 獻花岩 south of the city. Its rise to fame began in the Tang dynasty when the renowned *chan* master Farong 法融 (594–667) chose this place as his residence and meditation site. It was said that Farong's superior spiritual power attracted birds carrying floral offerings—hence the name of the grotto, Xianhua, "offering flowers." Located near another famous site, Mount Niushou, Xianhua Grotto was long overshadowed by its more established neighbor. The situation changed when, during the Chenghua reign (1464–87), a monk from Shandong named Master Gudao 古道師 (Master of the ancient Way) engaged in a prolonged meditation retreat, sitting still for a few years beneath the grotto. According to legend, a high official who happened to be visiting a neighboring mountain (most likely Niushou) saw splendid glowing clouds looming to the north. He headed for the clouds and found them to be shooting out of the grotto where the monk was meditating. The official was amazed and attempted to talk to the monk, who remained silent and refused to break his meditation. Moved by his piety, the official donated funds to build a temple on the site and petitioned the emperor to name the temple Xianhua. The site was further developed in the hands of the monk Deda 德達, a second-generation disciple of Master Gudao. Deda was said to excel in preaching and apparently was quite an entrepreneur in developing and promoting Xianhua Grotto. He devoted great efforts to exploring remote sites and improving their accessibility. Because of his hard work, staircases and walkways were built, sightseeing terraces and resting pavilions were constructed along the touring routes, and viewing instructions were inscribed on stones or posted on boards along the way.

When Chen Yi, the author of the Nanjing historical atlas, visited this place in the mid-sixteenth century, the fame of Xianhua Grotto had surpassed that of Mount Niushou. Accompanied by his prominent elite friends, Chen Yi visited the grotto and produced a gazetteer to commemorate this trip. His celebrity status in Nanjing lent even more charm to the site. Despite its word-of-mouth reputation, however, Chen Yi's gazetteer was not widely circulated and became a highly sought-after treasure among connoisseurs. Half a century later, in 1602, on an occasion of a literati gathering, Chen Yi's grandson showed the original manuscript to one disciple, who was so overwhelmed by Chen Yi's work that he determined to have the gazetteer republished. Another member of the same literary circle was Jiao Hong. Using the gazetteer as a guide, Jiao retraced Chen Yi's footsteps along the path to Xianhua Grotto and searched for the poems that Chen Yi and his friends had inscribed on the sites. These poems were then recovered and included in the republication of Chen Yi's gazetteer. Thus, in resurrecting a legendary mountain gazetteer, late Ming Nanjing elites reenacted a group outing of mid-Ming Nanjing icons. Separated by time and human mortality, the two generations forged a connection through the inscribed landscape.

This section has demonstrated that under the sway of social tourism, the appreciation of landscape was transformed into a ritual of status performance as well as a venue for social networking. A variety of examples illustrate the geographic reach of social tourism and its many elements. The story of Mount Huang, for example, lends a social dimension to the rapid growth of *jing* in the late Ming, in which the birth of new scenic sites was intrinsically related to the creation of new touring communities. The formation of touring communities could be achieved through actual shared experiences or, by extension, the exchange of literary works and visual images. These exchanges materialized the intangible social ties, and even allowed the touring community to survive physical separation. In fact, touring communities were so resilient that they could even bridge generational gaps. The revisiting of old touring itineraries was no longer a matter of reminiscence but a well-recognized cultural gesture to evoke old social ties and extend touring communities into new generations. All in all, in the context of social tourism, the production of poetry and artwork was in itself a potent act of alliance and solidarity. In this light, the surging volume of touring literature in the late Ming not only was a product of changing aesthetics but also reflects the ascendance of a new form of community building. This background allows us to read the following social biography of *Jinling tuyong* in terms of the communities it facilitated and further explicate its significance to the Nanjing society. Through the adaptations of touring literature into tour guides and local gazetteers, the touring community was no longer confined to a closed literati circle, and the cultural meaning of that form of community was renegotiated.

A SENSE OF PLACE, A SENSE OF CULTURAL CONTINUITY: TOURING AND TOUR GUIDES IN NANJING

The Story of Three Nanjing Tours

True to the contemporary practice of social tourism, the making of *Jinling tuyong* was intrinsically related to a series of group outings across two generations of prominent Nanjing families. Driven by the desire to commemorate the enduring ties among these elite families, the production of sightseeing literature ultimately led to the creation of an illustrated guidebook to Nanjing's most famed scenic sites.

The first tour took place in 1593. Six literati, all natives of Nanjing, took a trip to the northern mountain area of Nanjing and recorded their expedition in a set of collaborative poems. A preface to the poems by Yao Ruxun 姚汝循 (1535–97) details the itinerary of this three-day trip as well as various encounters en route.[97] For each of the six *jing* (main scenic points) on the trip, each of the authors wrote a scenic poem. The poems for the same site used the same rhyme (*heyun* 和韻). Composing such collaborative poems was a popular intellectual game at the time. The exchange of and collaboration on poetry served as a statement to the literary world, a pledge essentially, publicly demonstrating social ties among the authors. At that time, Zhu Zhifan was studying at the Imperial University in Beijing. When he returned to Nanjing, his father showed him this set of collaborative poems. His father's passion impressed Zhu Zhifan so much that Zhu exerted himself to collect poems from each author written in their personal calligraphy and to publish the set. He was racing against time. Two years after Zhu Zhifan's return to Nanjing, two of the original authors passed away, and five years later yet another two died. This collection became a final memorial for Zhu's father.[98]

One decade later, another set of collaborative poems came into being, as the result of a second tour. Three of this new group of authors came from the same families—Gu, Jiao, and Zhu—who had taken part in the "northern expedition." Jiao Hong outlived all his travel companions and participated in the second tour. Gu Qiyuan and Zhu Zhifan took their fathers' places and continued to honor the family tradition by touring Nanjing and making scenic poems using matching rhymes. The product of this tour was published as *Jinling yayou bian*, in which the number of sites commemorated in and around Nanjing more than tripled to twenty. There was no preface detailing the overall itinerary; rather, short descriptions of the sites served as prefaces for individual poems. According to Zhu Zhifan, one of the coauthors, the original manuscript of *Jinling yayou bian* was kept at the house of Yu Mengling (another coauthor) for more than two decades and was finally published by Zhu in 1624, as part of the second edition of Zhu's *Jinling tuyong*, an imaginary tour in which twice as many sights were appreciated as in *Jinling yayou bian*. In addition to the poem, each *jing* was illustrated by a wood-block printed image.

Different from its predecessors, which were intended to commemorate the group making the tour, the tour created by Zhu Zhifan in *Jinling tuyong* was a virtual one, whose goal was to fulfill Zhu's desire to "visit" all the sights of his native city. This virtual *woyou* tour, Zhu claimed, presented a long-overdue, full view of Nanjing to the reading world. Indeed, the expanded collection of scenic sites in *Jinling tuyong* clearly owed much to the growing competition over *jing* as emblems of local pride. Since every gazetteer now featured a list of famous sites, highlighting the beauty of the area and preserving records of historic sites, Zhu stated in his preface, he had grown dissatisfied with the current convention of listing only eight or sixteen *jing* for Nanjing, a city with a long history and an important role in the Ming dynasty. As a Nanjing native, Zhu felt a sense of duty to produce the most comprehensive list of *jing* to showcase the grandeur of his hometown.[99]

In the end, over the course of the three tours, the geographic coverage of the Nanjing tour expanded from the mountains north of Nanjing to the entirety of the immediate city environs; the documentation of the tour also evolved from private exchanges (collaborative poems) into a guidebook for the general public—from an exercise cementing the social ties of a small group of Nanjing elites into a book instructing the public on how to view Nanjing, a development clearly reflected in the texts and images of *Jinling tuyong*.

From Commemoration to Guidebook:
The Birth of a Native Paradigm

In comparison to *Jinling yayou bian*, *Jinling tuyong* not only introduces more scenic spots, with illustrations, but even prescribes very different ways to look at Nanjing. This development is closely related to a change in function. Over the course of three tours, the nature of the publications moved from lyric commemoration of a group outing to an elaborate vehicle for *woyou*. In *Yayou bian*, the preface for each *jing* serves mainly as an explanatory note of the destination to provide a geographic context for the group poetry. In *Tuyong*, however, the texts present explicit instructions on viewing each site. Together with the individual illustrations of each location, they create a more visually and textually composite experience for virtual sightseeing. For example, *Jinling yayou bian* relates of the famous Qixia Temple 棲霞寺:

Forty *li* northeast of the city wall is a mountain producing *she sheng* 攝生 (life-nourishing) grass called Mount She. In the Southern Dynasties, the eminent monk Shao who lived here made his residence in the Qixia Monastery. In the Qi dynasty, over a thousand Buddha statues were carved on the rock surface, thus giving the area the name "Thousand Buddhas Hill." To date, it still looks majestic, and its variegated colors immediately catch people's eyes. To the right is the "Heaven Open Grotto" with the poems by Xu Xuan 徐鉉 [917–92], Shen Chuanshi 沈傳師 [769–827], and Zhang Zhigui 張稚圭 [dates unknown], inscribed on it. On the side of the hill is a stone stele erected by Emperor Gaozong of the Tang dynasty. The rock opens up like a window to reveal a view of the sky. Together, the temples, cracked rocks, and running streams constitute a calm and pure scene that has always been considered spectacular.[100]

The same site was rendered differently in *Jinling tuyong*. In its entry *Qixia shenggai* 棲霞勝概 (Famous sights of Qixia), the prospect changes:

[Mount Qixia] is located fifty *li* northeast of the prefectural city. Since many medical herbs that help nourish life grow there, it is named Mount She [the nourishing mountain]. With its multiple ridges and isolated peaks, its form resembles a canopy, hence it is also called Mount Canopy. In the Southern

Dynasties, the eminent monk Shao lived here and made his residence at a temple. There are scenes like Thousand Buddhas Hill and Heaven Open Grotto. The farther you get into the mountain, the quieter and more open it becomes. When you reach the top and look out over the Yangzi River, the sunshine reflected on clouds looks like a long belt surrounding the mountain. It truly deserves the name Qixia, "Perched amid the Rosy Clouds."[101]

What the two texts share in common are the historical allusion to monk Shao and the folklore about a life-nourishing herb associated with the site, which lend literary allure to the viewing experience. However, the instructions for appreciating the site changed significantly between the two versions. The same scene is framed with different facts (such as its distance from the city and the name of special indigenous herbs) and accorded different visual cues: *Jinling yayou bian*'s description focuses readers' attention on the Thousand Buddhas Hill and the Heaven Open Grotto; *Jinyong tuyong* encourages readers to take a more panoramic view of the Yangzi River. Although the basic scenic cues remain the same (the Thousand Buddhas Hill, the Heaven Open Grotto, and the temple), the suggested touring routes vary, as does the expected visual pleasure and enjoyment. The earlier work keeps its tourists in the area of the temple and statues, the later one encourages them to explore farther, until they arrive at the peak overlooking the Yangzi River in rosy sunlight, where they can finally grasp the riddle in Qixia's name.

The descriptions of Mount Niushou are another example. Both *Yayou bian* and *Tuyong* highlight its main topographic feature, a twin peak, as well as an anecdote from the fourth century about Jin Yuandi's (r. 317–22) plan to build a palace on the mountain. To counter objections that the hilly topography would prevent the construction of palace gates, Yuandi's prime minister, Wang Dao 王導—also a famed Nanjing native son—pointed to the twin peak and said, "These can serve as heavenly gates." Yet similarities aside, whereas *Yayou bian* lists the main historic relics in the area, *Tuyong* alerts readers to nearby scenic sites such as Mount Zutang 祖堂山 and the Xianhua Grotto that can easily be incorporated in the itinerary. *Tuyong* also details the splendid view awaiting the prospective visitor: as he looks back on the mountain, the placement of the monastery and palace on the mountain's slope resemble the composition of a painted screen. The description also boasts that the misty clouds at dawn and dusk are such an extraordinary spectacle that a visitor would forget his exhaustion from climbing up to the mountain top. The entry even notes that a visit to Mount Niushou does not have to be confined by seasons since the site attracts visitors all year long regardless of cold and heat. As illustrated by these two examples, a simple note in *Jinling yayou bian* on a particular *jing* is expanded in *Jinling tuyong* into elaborate instructions for viewing the site.

Changes aside, the shared focus on background information in both texts is noteworthy. Indeed, the seeming obsession with historical details and literary allusions is not just a matter of stylistic embellishment; a central element of cultured sightseeing was the infusion of cultural or historical references into immediate visual perceptions. On rare occasions, *Tuyong* even alerts viewers of recent changes that might upset anticipations based on literary allusions. A site entitled "Asking for Wine at the Apricot Village" is a case in point. The title derives from a poem by the medieval poet Du Mu 杜牧 (803–52?) portraying celebrants at the mid-spring festival seeking shelter from a sudden rain. Someone asks a herd boy where to find a tavern, and he points to a village hidden in a cloud of apricot blossoms. Inspired by this poetic image, *Tuyong* located the site just outside Nanjing's city wall next to the Phoenix Terrace. An old apricot grove conveniently provided a site for the story. However, according to *Jinling tuyong*, the fame of the site almost brought its own ruin: because of the story of the apricot blossoms, the site was often crowded with visitors in springtime who bustled around, trampling, climbing, and breaking branches off the trees. Tired of dealing with these ill-behaved tourists, the gardeners cut down the trees for fuel. Since only a tenth of the previous thousands of apricot trees survived, there was no "apricot blossom" village tavern for herd boys to point to. Even though the area was still a pleasant destination, the dissociation from the ancient poetic allusion had clearly compromised its appeal. Fortunately, *Tuyong* points out, in recent years fragrant gardens had mushroomed and spread out as numerous as squares on a chessboard in the area in place of the old apricot grove. *Tuyong* concludes with a sense of relief that "as another wave of flourishing comes after decline, the ancient trace is finally preserved."[102] Here the "ancient trace" refers not to an actual historical site but to a well-established lyric image essential to *Tuyong*'s composite touring experience.

Despite the shared emphasis on cultured sightseeing, in general *Tuyong* takes a more aggressive and instructive approach to the consumption of scenic sights. To further enhance its function as a medium for virtual touring, *Tuyong* also includes illustrations for each *jing*, with notable sights identified by cartouches. These images not only allow for a more immediate consumption of space but, most significantly, mark the arrival of a native paradigm in the imagining of Nanjing. To be sure, long before the Ming era, a well-established literary tradition of *jing* was already in place. Its regulatory forces were so strong that, Stephen Owen argues, it is nearly impossible to imagine Nanjing without invoking its long history of poetic imagery. In Owen's words, "To confront Nanjing was to recall the past, but one in which a historical past and a literary past were inextricably woven together."[103] Until the early Ming, the act of scenery appreciation was still very much embedded in the city's received poetic past. Most scenic paintings present views of Nanjing that draw heavily on the established poetic tradition. Moreover, probably because the artists were mainly based in Suzhou, the *jing* portrayed in these paintings were concentrated along the Yangzi River and were visible without having to enter the city. True to Zhu Zhifan's complaint, these images were dictated by an "outsider's perspective" and somewhat myopic in their representation of Nanjing's scenery.[104] Determining to present a complete view of his hometown, Zhu produced *Jinling tuyong*, which, in time, significantly subverted the sway of "poetic Nanjing" and grounded subsequent art and literary production in a native perspective.

The currency of *Tuyong*'s images might come from the fact that during the process of the three Nanjing tours, a string of prominent names came to be associated with *Jinling tuyong*. Such associations were easily translated into public acceptance and commercial success. Of particular prominence were the two coauthors Jiao Hong and Zhu Zhifan. Both men were high-profile local icons holding the highest title that could be achieved in the civil service examinations, *zhuangyuan* 狀元 (optimus). One street in Nanjing was even named after Zhu and his title. In the extremely competitive publishing environment of the late Ming, attributing the authorship of a book to a famous person was a common marketing tool. Because of their prestigious titles, Jiao's and Zhu's names were more than once "borrowed" for collections of sample essays for the civil service examinations.[105] It is no wonder, then, that a guidebook such as the *Tuyong* with so many celebrated names would make a strong impression on readers.

Most significantly, the stardom of the authors—all Nanjing natives—had a significant impact on locals' attachment to the landmarks described in the book. This sentiment grew particularly strong in the wake of the dynastic transition when the images of *Jinling tuyong* were intensively copied by Nanjing school painters.[106] In light of late Ming social tourism, it is clear that the adaptation of *Tuyong*'s images in effect re-enacted the tour taken at the peak of late Ming prosperity and precipitated a continued sense of community across the dynastic divide. At a time when the ownership of the landscape changed hands and established visions were imperiled, the "ways of looking" supplied in *Jinling tuyong* came to play an important role in facilitating the re-imaging of the city.

This sense of cultural continuity reached a new height in the hands of Zhou Lianggong 周亮工 (1612–72), a powerful Nanjing cultural luminary and art patron. In the 1660s, Zhou assumed the task of compiling the prefectural gazetteer, *Jiangning fuzhi*, and commissioned one of the Nanjing Eight Masters, Gao Cen 高岑, to produce images of Nanjing with exactly the same perspective and compositional framework as those found in the *Jinling tuyong*.[107] This gesture had a profound cultural significance since local gazetteers had developed into an essential vehicle for articulating local identity by the late Ming.[108] The adaptation of *Tuyong*'s images in the local gazetteer drastically expanded the touring community associated with *Tuyong* from a group of native literati to the Nanjing community at large. It transformed the scenic images, originally produced to commemorate an elite confederation, into the official face of Nanjing at a time when the cultural identity of the land was called into question by the Manchu invasion. However, the effort to reconnect with late Ming prosperity did not imply complete oblivion to the reality of life under a new regime. The tumultuous dynastic transition indeed left its own mark on the public vision of Nanjing—a point further illuminated below by a comparison of *Tuyong*'s images with their early Qing adaptations.

The Transformation of Tuyong *Images During the Dynastic Transition*

A Vernacular Rendering of Nanjing in Jinling tuyong.   Produced at the height of late Ming tourism, the images of *Jinling tuyong* are rather idiosyncratic in their rendition of *jing*. The innovation of *Tuyong* is most apparent if measured against its time, when scenic painting had developed into an established genre named *shengjing tu* 勝景圖. The visualization of *jing* in general exhibits stylistic affinities with landscape paintings. Yet, unlike literati paintings that tend to represent natural terrain in abstract terms, *shengjing tu* often center on specific geographical sites. However, topographical artists in late imperial China exhibited little concern with replicating the physical appearance of scenic sites.[109] Instead, they worked to develop "a schema, a configuration that supplies the relative location of scenic materials, the characterizing shapes of the peaks, and so forth."[110] The images are schematic and, more important, culturally laden, since it is often the literary associations and historical allusions, instead of reality, that dominate the composition. The unveristic approach is hardly surprising; as Timothy Brook argues, to portray a *jing* in visual terms is to materialize a received prospect, projecting "an established and well-defined view onto a known landscape."[111] In this sense, the visualization of *jing* is in fact not too different from mapping, both of which entail a particular interpretation of space by reducing natural landscape or built environment into a chosen set of recognizable icons.[112] The schematic nature of scenic images, therefore, should not be considered a reduction of topographical representation; rather, scenic painting was about creating vocabularies for a shared spatial imagination.[113]

Nanjing as Lived Space.   What kind of visual vernacular, then, does *Jinling tuyong* create? Its 40 images, one for each scenic attraction, present a series of prospects in and around Nanjing. Following the convention inherent in the sequential character of *jing*, *Jinling tuyong* provides a cumulative spatial experience leading to a comprehensive knowledge of the place for the reader. However, *Tuyong's* composition of each *jing* differs from a conventional *shengjing tu*, which tend to center on one particular item in the scenery and usually do not depict people, except as generic figures directing viewers' attention to specific highlights of the landscape. In contrast, the images in *Tuyong* demonstrate unusual interest in visual details by creating numerous "secondary spaces" within a scene and directing the viewer's attention to a host of subordinate scenes marked by people engaging in a wide variety of activities. Granted, these scenes are derivative and auxiliary to the primary sight—many of them are not even mentioned in the corresponding textual descriptions. Yet the crowds of small figures and their intensive interactions are so prevalent that they often distract from, if not eclipse, the focus on the central scene. As a result, in *Tuyong*'s images, the represented space is no longer dominated by the splendor of landscape but subjected to the particularities of social activities.

For example, *Tuyong*'s rendition (Fig. 3.14) of the scene around the Qinhuai River, where the famous pleasure quarters of Nanjing were located, shows the river in three curves, which divides the space into six segments.[114] With the city wall indicated at the upper left corner, one more layer is added to the scene. From the top, viewers first see a pagoda before a mountain. Then entering the walls and following the flow of the river, they encounter to the left of the first curve a cluster of buildings marked as *jiuyuan* 舊院, the old pleasure quarters of Nanjing, which had seriously declined by that time—accordingly no tourists are shown in this illustration. Across the bridge is the Confucian temple and school, where people wander about the streets and bridges. To the left is Chaoku jie 鈔庫街, Treasury Street, also populated by either tourists or residents. To the right of the next curve is the Examination Hall, surrounded by a river that is thronged with people in boats. It is indeed a crowded image, fully populated by secondary spaces around the primary landmark, the Qinhuai River.

A similar composition was employed to depict many other sights, such as Changgan li 長干里 (Fig. 3.15).[115] The scene is structured around a neighborhood. The viewer first enters a city gate, crosses a bridge, and then passes through an arch inscribed with the characters for Changgan li. From there, viewers, just like the little figures in the image, would wander about the neighborhood. To the right are the Bao'en Temple and its famous encaustic tiled pagoda; to the left is a

Fig. 3.14　Qingxi youfang, *Jinling tuyong* (1624), 31a

Money God temple. To the south is another temple and bridge. The figures found throughout the image not only create many secondary spaces within the temple area but also serve to indicate the diverse possible uses of the space. As we see in the picture, some seem to be enjoying the sights, others work, still others chat. A few are just out for a stroll.

What is being conveyed in *Jinling tuyong* is that the appreciation of *jing* is not only a matter of having one's gaze directed and consuming the space at one glance; it is also about living and experiencing the space in a variety of ways. *Jing* might be deployed as a theme by poets or paint-

Fig. 3.15 Changgan li; *Jinling tuyong* (1624), 11a

ers, but, for most people, a *jing* signified a lived space where people played, worked, or just passed by in their daily life. The images in *Tuyong* are full of details in which figures kick balls, practice swordfighting, work in the field, carry goods, or simply walk around chatting with neighbors (Figs. 3.16–20).[116] Indeed, the renditions of Nanjing throughout *Jinling tuyong* consistently exhibit a heightened interest in demonstrating the many ways people inhabit a scene as a lived space. To achieve this goal, *Tuyong*'s images tend to highlight topographical partitions and crowd the derivative spaces with figures and activities of

Fig. 3.16 A kick ball game; *Jinling tuyong* (1624), 17a

all sorts, including both leisure and work. Since these inhabited spaces are derived from the central landmark and not specifically mentioned in the accompanying texts, their meaning can be attained only through the activities performed there. Thus in comparison with the Nanjing atlases discussed earlier, these images no longer visualize the space of Nanjing through a grand scheme such as empire or history; rather, they are organized around the particularities of daily life and social interaction.

Visualizing the Urban Prosperity of the Southern Metropolis. The proliferation of secondary spaces in *Jinling tuyong* clearly deviates from mainstream scenic images structured around a central focal scene. The attention to visual details allows *Tuyong* to develop a unique way of

Fig. 3.17 Sword practice; *Jinling tuyong* (1624), 39a (detail)

looking at and looking into the lived space of Nanjing through the performance of a wide array of social activities. The idiosyncratic representation of Nanjing may have been inspired by *Tuyong*'s function as a guidebook; that is, by cataloging the possible uses of each area, *Tuyong* enables viewers to explore the possibilities of space to the fullest extent. Yet at the same time, the emphasis on the social uses of space also evokes a sense of urban prosperity for viewers. Indeed, the extraordinary visual approach in *Tuyong* is not an isolated invention but reminiscent of the conventions of cityscape paintings, where social activities, instead of the natural landscape, inform and differentiate the representational space.[117]

A good case in point is the contemporary cityscape painting of Nanjing titled *Nandu fanhui tu* 南都繁會圖 (The prosperity of the Southern

Fig. 3.18 People carrying goods outside the city gate;
Jinling tuyong (1624), 16a

Capital)—a handscroll portraying the energetic urban life in late Ming Nanjing.[118] Following the tradition of the cityscape handscroll set by *Qingming shanghe tu*, Nanjing is presented as a generic urban streetscape that wends from the countryside and culminates in the imperial palace, an established mode for presenting the glamour of urban prosperity. Moving from beginning to end, the viewer walks through an urban space marked not by its physical structure but by an array of spectacles vividly portrayed. Yet, interestingly, this seemingly realistic city portrait is interlaced with unrealistic details. For example, a lantern mountain in the middle of the central street scene implies that the time is Lunar New Year's; however, the dragon boat competitions portrayed on the

Fig. 3.19 Working in the fields; *Jinling tuyong* (1624), 15a

upper portion would take place in the fifth month of the year (Fig. 3.21).[119] Nevertheless, if this image is viewed as a demonstration of the performativity of urban space, in line with what has been observed in *Tuyong*'s images, then the core message of this painting lies in cataloging a wide variety of possible use of urban space, not in capturing an actual moment in Nanjing. Urban space, fully inscribed with social activities, is no longer monopolized by a single, culturally approved prospect but divided and subdivided by the people who inhabit the space. It is people and their interactions, above all else, that animate urban space and furnish it with particular connotations, much in the style of *Jinling tuyong*.

Fig. 3.20 Archery practice; *Jinling tuyong* (1624), 14a

The Re-imagining of Nanjing in the Early Qing Dynasty. The unique visual details and attention to urban sociality in *Jinling tuyong* disappeared in the early Qing adaptation. The painter kept the original viewing perspective and composition but significantly simplified the secondary spaces created in the late Ming version. In the case of the Qinhuai River (Fig. 3.22; cf. Fig. 3.14, p. 174), the three curves are condensed to a single curve, and the people who appear in *Tuyong*'s images, who are granted an actual function signifying the possibilities of space, are now reduced to minor details serving only an aesthetic function as pointers to the central scene.[120] The whole image is centered on and dominated by the landmark the painter intended to highlight. No secondary space is allowed to distract the viewers' attention.

Fig. 3.21 *Nandu fanhui tu*, early seventeenth-century handscroll, detail

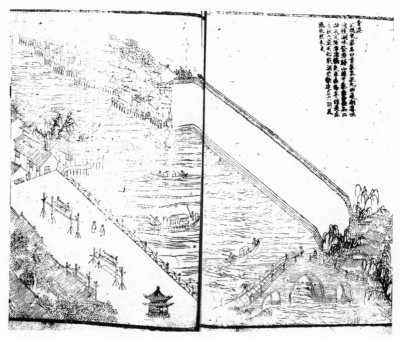

Fig. 3.22 Qingxi; *Jiangning fuzhi* (1668), 2.28b–29a

The same editing process can also be observed in the scene of Changgan li, in which the picture is refocused on the central area. The rest of the winding streets and back alleys are left out, and the temples detailed in *Tuyong*'s image obscured (Fig. 3.23; cf. Fig. 3.15, p. 175).[121] The arch, the pagoda, and three pairs of figures are there to show the scene as specified in the textual description, instead of the many other possibilities of the space displayed in *Tuyong*'s images. Above all, the "people" shown in the images are no longer active interpreters of space but passive "scene pointers" at the command of the painter. Similar changes can be identified throughout the set. Out of 40 scenes, more than 30 exhibit the same simplification process.

The removal of visual details with their undertones of urbanity in the early Qing adaptation of *Jinling tuyong* appears to be a development inextricably related to its time: two decades after the publication of *Jinling tuyong*, wars broke out, and eventually the Ming regime ceded power to the Manchus. As the military combat over territory wound down, the battle over the cultural landscape began. Nanjing, as the first and final

Fig. 3.23 Changgan li; *Jiangning fuzhi* (1668), 2.7b–8a

capital of the Ming regime, became a critical battlefield in the fight over political symbolism, particularly the former Ming palace and the Xiaoling mausoleum.[122] This puts the prevalent adaptations of *Jinling tuyong*'s images in late seventeenth-century Nanjing in a very different light. In the works of prominent Nanjing artists such as Gao Cen (for the prefectural gazetteer), Zou She 鄒喆, Hu Yukun 胡玉昆, and other of the Eight Masters, the same motifs from *Jinling tuyong* are repeatedly employed. Yet, despite similar compositions and inscriptions, the early Qing pictures returned to the conventional format focused on a centralized scenery. Evoking the rituals developed from the late Ming social tourism, the persistent adaptation of *Jinling tuyong* motifs clearly signifies the effort to extend the touring community of Nanjing elites across the dynastic divide. Yet, how do we explain the removal of urban scenes from these works? It is possible that, being the professional artists that most early Qing painters were, they considered the conventional format for scenic painting a more apt choice. After all, the creation of secondary spaces in *Jinling tuyong* is rather idiosyncratic and might well be inspired by its function as a guidebook. Still, in light of the highly sensitive political atmosphere in the early Qing, it is even more likely that these Nanjing painters deliberately omitted all visual cues of urban sociality, the signature of the late Ming imagination of Nanjing, to distance themselves from the past, from the late Ming landscape marked by urban glamour.[123] The re-creation of late Ming images but with the urban sociality removed gestured a deliberately ambiguous acknowledgment of the change in regimes: on one hand, the sharing of visual vocabulary with *Jinling tuyong* conveys a sense of cultural continuity during a time of political disruption. On the other hand, the conspicuous modification also allows a necessary distance for adjusting to a new political environment. In doing so, *Tuyong*'s early Qing reincarnation is able to articulate a new identity that reconciles past and present.

The negotiation of identity through landscape appreciation during the dynastic transition was not unique to Nanjing. An interesting comparison is Yangzhou, a port city along the Grand Canal. Lacking an established repertoire of famous sites inherited from the late Ming, the urban elite in Yangzhou had to reinvent a late Ming cultural milieu to provide the city with a sense of cultural continuity as it recovered from the traumatic war and regime change.[124] Tobie Meyer-Fong, in her intriguing study of early Qing Yangzhou, presents a city struggling between the political transition and the ensuing cultural confusion:

In post-conquest Yangzhou, the reconstruction and visiting of famous sites became a vehicle through which the literati elite could present themselves as members of a single class through a celebration of shared cultural values, manifested in conventions for the appreciation of place. Thus through leisure touring and gatherings, early Qing elites gestured toward a culturally constituted Yangzhou. Moreover, by highlighting widely recognized literary icons from the past, they claimed a place for the city alongside more famous places in the empire, and Jiangnan in particular. In so doing, they created a new Yangzhou, filled with references to a Ming past in which, paradoxically, Yangzhou itself had enjoyed little prestige.[125]

In an effort to bridge the cultural gap resulting from the dynastic transition, post-Ming Yangzhou reinvented its historicity in Ming Jiangnan; the key for this was cultured sightseeing.

These events bear clear witness to the importance of landscape appreciation in the working of cultural identity and social solidarity. Such place-specific sensibility is by no means permanent but intrinsically shaped by its time, to which the dynastic division appears to be critical. In Yangzhou, the loss and confusion during the regime change prompted the re-imagination of the city in the early Qing through the celebration of a past it had never had. In the case of Nanjing, although the re-creation of *Tuyong's jing* provided a sense of communal continuity across the dynastic transition, the rendition of urban space was subtly altered to register a distinct sense of changed times. The impact of dynastic change on the sense of place was not transitional, but continued to gain momentum. Thus, entering the eighteenth century, late-Ming-style social tourism would be formally challenged by imperial tours and their accompanying cultural production, a development briefly discussed in the epilogue.

EPILOGUE:
THE POLITICS OF PLACE-MAKING
AND REMAKING

The story presented so far is one of a continuous negotiation over city images. Created at the beginning of the dynasty, the *Hongwu Atlas* epitomized Taizu's vision of Nanjing. Its multilayered projection of the city creatively visualized the complicated nature of urban space. The shared topographically defined base map further rescued Nanjing from its own ill-fated history as a capital of only part of a divided empire. This mission was completed in Chen Yi's *Historical Atlas*, which overlaid Ming Nanjing on top of all the preceding cities and cartographically marked the uniqueness of Ming Nanjing. At the same time, it also removed the strong personal presence of Hongwu and recast Nanjing as a product of history, an approach more akin to the disposition of literati-scholars.

The omnipresence of the state or history was countered, and gradually overshadowed, by the proliferation of touring literature and topographic artworks that highlighted the particularity of places. Under the sway of social tourism, the appreciation of landscape was integrated

into the repertoire of identity performance, and the production of famous sites in the late Ming became deeply enmeshed with the workings
of local communities.[126] With this trend, public place-making was increasingly intertwined with private agendas. Personal, even familial, history was inscribed on the local images, as in the case of *Jinling tuyong*.

In many ways, the publication of *Jinling tuyong* concluded the place-
making process of Nanjing in the Ming era, but it by no means finalized
it. As the dynastic transition significantly politicized late Ming social
tourism, the images of *Jinling tuyong* underwent a subtle transformation
in the new dynasty: the strong undertone of urban sociability disappeared in its early Qing adaptation. The metamorphosis of *Tuyong* images, in a sense, symbolizes the end of an age of localized city images in
anticipation of strong recentralization under a new (Qing) dynasty of
conquest. Indeed, two decades after the publication of *Jinling tuyong*, the
Manchus took over the empire and would soon come to realize that although they controlled the physical land, the cultural landscape had
been deeply woven into the fabric of local society. As the unification of
physical territory was accomplished, the highly localized and fragmented representational landscape compelled the court to embark on
another cultural enterprise. By the eighteenth century, Manchu emperors were making tours of their realm and producing illustrated guides
listing the places they visited, imposing an imperial gaze onto the highly
particularized local landscape via the emperor's footsteps. Indeed, the
numerous Southern Tours undertaken during the late seventeenth and
eighteenth century not only passively marked the territory of this newly
acquired land but also reimposed a centralized perspective on the realm
of representation. Because of these efforts, the localized landscapes developed in the late Ming were reunited by the imperial itinerary. New
landmarks, graced by the imperial gaze and footprints, soon proliferated. As such, cultured touring turned from a venue of social networking and status performance into a battleground between state power
and the local community.

In the case of Nanjing, most notable are the numerous scenic sites
marked by the Qianlong emperor with 156 poems during his imperial
tour of Nanjing. This set of imperial images and poems interfered powerfully with the local tradition. They sometimes took the place of the 40
Tuyong scenes in official gazetteers as well as in private writings. For ex-

ample, the early nineteenth-century prefectural gazetteer dismissed all previous cartographical traditions as "ludicrous" and eliminated all scenic images. In their place are voluminous accounts taken from the record of the Southern Tour.[127] Even private gazetteers such as *Sheshan zhi* 攝山志 (Gazetteer of Mount She) submitted to the imperial taste and produced a new set of Qixia Temple images from the vantage point of the emperor's throne.[128] Although the imposition was indeed overwhelming, the imperial vision was by no means absolute. There was resistance. Among the Qing gazetteers, some never mentioned the Southern Tour,[129] and others simply acknowledged all image-making efforts in both eras and documented them as such.[130] The imagining of Nanjing, in a sense, ceased to reflect a process of community building and became one fraught with contention.

Finally, the growing publication of tour guides in late imperial China has been often interpreted as a sign of intensified popular travel and consumption, part of the cultural development prompted by economic prosperity.[131] Nevertheless, despite the apparent similarity to a modern guidebook, a seventeenth-century guidebook like *Jinling tuyong* offers no information on shopping, dining, or lodging, information that modern tourists look for in a guidebook. *Jinling tuyong* concerns nothing but space and the experience of space, both physical and imaginary. With its concentrated focus on space and spatial experiences, *Tuyong* not only provides a guided tour of the scenery but also marks a series of critical moments in the changing perceptions of urban space. As shown in this chapter, the expanded edition of *Jinling tuyong*, in fact, resulted from two separate projects: the atlas (including the *Hongwu Atlas* and Chen Yi's *Historical Atlas*) and the tour of Nanjing (in three stages). Produced under distinct agendas, they represent two distinct popular modes of city images in the Ming, with very different interpretations of urban space. Zhu Zhifan's publication bridges and reorganizes the two projects, turning them into a pair of contrasting views of Nanjing, one presenting the centralized vision of the Hongwu emperor and the other the vision of Nanjing native elites. Through his revision of *Jinling tuyong*, Zhu completed the process of transforming Nanjing as an imagined space from an emperor's capital to a southern metropolis.

Nanjing Through Contemporary
Mouths and Ears

NARRATING THE CITY

We have explored Nanjing as an urban community, a metropolitan area, and an imagined space. This chapter examines how the city was construed as a discursive subject by looking at two Nanjing *ketan* 客談 (conversations with guests). Compiled in the early seventeenth century, Gu Qiyuan's 顧起元 *Kezuo zhuiyu* 客座贅語 (Superfluous chats from the guests' seat) and Zhou Hui's 周暉 *Jinling suoshi* 金陵瑣事 (Trivia about Nanjing)[1] assembled a rich array of conversations about Nanjing among urban elites. In their prefaces, Gu and Zhou attributed their works to lively conversations with their guests. Indeed, Zhou's original title, *Shangbaizhai ketan* 尚白齋客談 (Chats with guests at the Shangbai Studio), explicitly acknowledged the origin of the contents. To preserve these prized exchanges, Gu Qiyuan instructed his servants to transcribe the conversations. The less affluent Zhou Hui most likely did so himself. As Zhou noted in his preface to *Suoshi*, "Even though these entries are as different from one another as the scent of orchids from that of chrysanthemums, all of them originated from what I heard from my guests." He then excerpted the specific parts related to Nanjing and published them.[2] In this sense, it may be more accurate, or at least historically empathetic, to consider Gu Qiyuan and Zhou Hui curators who put their collected conversations on display, even though they might have in fact authored or even elaborated on some of the entries themselves. Both works appear to have been well received at the time. Zhou Hui's *Jinling suoshi* was soon followed by two sequels, and their popularity may have inspired Gu Qiyuan to publish his *Kezuo zhuiyu*, a text that was also mentioned frequently by his contemporaries.[3]

The *ketan* was not invented during the Ming or unique to the city of Nanjing. The eighteenth-century *Siku quanshu* 四庫全書 annotated bibliography lists quite a few examples dating to the Song dynasty, for example, *Chaoshi keyu* 晁氏客語 (Dialogues with the guests of Mr. Chao), authored by Chao Yue 晁説. This work is considered a variation of the *yulu* 語錄 (recorded dialogues), which is usually a record of dialogues between a Confucian or Buddhist master and his disciples. Chao collected conversations of his guests regarding court politics and current events.[4] Each entry notes the name of the guest who offered the information.[5] Since many of these anecdotes are personal eyewitness accounts, Chao's *ketan* provides precious semi-oral accounts of contemporary politics and society.[6]

Although the genre of *ketan* was not new, the explicit focus on Nanjing in *Kezuo zhuiyu* and *Jinling suoshi* gave contemporary readers a view of life in Nanjing very different from that found in political and literary narratives in circulation at the time. A Ming reader looking for information about a particular city would typically turn to *difang zhi* 地方志 (local gazetteers). Especially in the Ming, the compilation of *difang zhi* had become routine government business.[7] As early as 1412, the government began to mandate specific guidelines for their production.[8] Although the requirements were not strictly enforced, Ming local gazetteers commonly follow a generic textual matrix: astronomy and topography are documented and mapped, as is the evolution of the place as a political unit. The land, local products, taxes, and corvée labor are surveyed and documented. The names of local officials and of those who achieved success in the civil service examinations are also charted. Officials and gentry who made an impact on local society are celebrated in a biographical section, as are locals noted for their virtue, particularly loyalty, filiality, or chastity, and those with special spiritual or technical skills. Public buildings and private gardens are celebrated in poems and lyrical essays, and local history and government works are recorded.

The state-imposed format allowed the government to build a systematic and comprehensive archive of its territory. Especially for local officials, who were by law non-natives, gazetteers were invaluable references for field administration.[9] In view of the weighty administrative concerns behind the compilation of local gazetteers, it is not surprising to find that cities, which were not independent administrative units, were embedded within a greater territorial unit (county, prefecture). The only exception was the imperial capital, which did constitute an administrative unit on its own and was documented as such in *duyi bu* 都邑簿 (capital manuals).[10] For other cities, since their physical structures and residents were documented in different sections of the local gazetteer, readers had to piece together many separate discussions to gain a full picture of a city.

Contrary to the political narration, which views cities through the lens of a larger administrative unit, the literary narration of the city is completely urban-centered, organized around space and time as experienced in the city. This literary tradition can be traced to *Dongjing meng Hua lu* (see Chapter 3). As a nostalgic recollection of life in Kaifeng before its loss to the Jurchens, its narrative sought to recover the vanished urban glamour and street life textually. The abundance of palpable details tinged with nostalgic sentiments leaves one with the impression that the author believed the act of writing could restore the past. Written at a time when China first witnessed the development of megalopolises driven by commerce and with populations of over a million, *Dongjing meng Hua lu* is notable for the author's unapologetic relish and vivid portrayal of the glamour and allure of urban life.

Compared with capital manuals (*duyi bu*), which approach urban space as a locus of imperial ritual and propriety, *Dongjing meng Hua lu* projects the capital city as an arena of personal experiences and lived space. With no official mandate behind its production, the entries in *Dongjing meng Hua lu* are organized along specific spatial and temporal templates in order to capture the transient nature of urban life. Indeed, the elaborate descriptions of urban landmarks and the annual festivals present a richly woven tapestry of urban experiences. Although the literary value of *Dongjing meng Hua lu* was debated among traditional critics, its innovative approach to the city and city life inspired other urban surveys in the Ming era, such as *Dijing jingwu lue* 帝京景物略 (A brief account of sights in the imperial capital), *Chang'an kehua* 長安客話 (Remarks from a guest in Chang'an), *Ru meng lu* 如夢錄 (Record of dreamlike things).[11] Although, in this particular literary tradition, the emphasis on personal recollections might not be as strong as in *Dongjing meng Hua lu*, the format of the earlier work continued: urban space and time were reified into textual parameters around which the city was narrated.

In contrast, this concrete sense of time and space dissolves in the seemingly random choice of subjects in the two Nanjing *ketan*. Indeed, readers of the two *ketan* would first be impressed with the casual, serendipitous manner in which Gu and Zhou presented their colorful entries. Opening the pages of *Jinling suoshi*, for example, readers are greeted with an account of two Nanjing families graced by a visit of Zhu Yuanzhang, a list of calligraphers responsible for steles in the major palaces and temples in Nanjing, a legend relating that two members of the royal family in Nanjing are reincarnations of the famous historical heroes Guan Yu 關羽 and Yue Fei 岳飛, and a discussion of the best spring waters in the city. Unlike gazetteers or typical city literature, the *ketan* is structured neither by state-mandated schemes nor by temporal/spatial parameters. The juxtaposition of one story against another seemingly unrelated one mimics the ebb and flow of casual conversation. This allows for a much more inclusive and tolerant collection of entries—ghost stories, passages from memorials and imperial edicts, urban tall tales and street gossip, wise words uttered by luminaries as well as street vendors. To be sure, the random and eclectic outlook of *ketan* makes it a fitting medium for expressing the amorphous lived experience of a highly mixed and mobile urban population. More important, the *ketan* itself was a product of the increased fluidity and fast-paced exchanges of urban life, namely, the elite salon. Gu Qiyuan's preface to *Kezuo zhuiyu* attributes the origin of his collection to such gatherings:

I have often been moody and ill lately, and so my regular guests familiar with my lifelong pursuit of stories about my hometown of Nanjing compete with one another to entertain me with anecdotes of old and new. Occasionally, during our conversations, one or two stories are so amazing and strange that they bring laughter. Yet more frequent are stories that would benefit local society and verify local records.[12]

These stories ultimately led to the creation of *Kezuo zhuiyu*. Gu Qiyuan, a coauthor of Zhu Zhifan's *Jinling tuyong* and of *Jinling yayou bian*, came from one of the most prominent families in Nanjing. Gu's father, Gu

Guofu 顧國甫, became a *jinshi* in 1574. Gu Qiyuan had an even more stellar record: he earned first place in the provincial examination in 1598 and became a *jinshi* immediately the year after. Ranked third highest in the palace examination, he was appointed a compiler at the Hanlin Academy. After serving as an assistant supervisor to the heir apparent and vice minister of personnel in Beijing, he retired to his home in Nanjing and built a famous garden, Dun yuan 遯園 (Garden of escape), where he hosted regular literati gatherings.[13] Given his official statue and local connections, Gu's salon was famed as one of the central sites for Nanjing literati to build social networks and exchange information—including the stories in *Kezuo zhuiyu*. Zhou Hui's official career was much less impressive than that of Gu, but his *Jinling suoshi* is also a product of urban salon culture.[14]

What kind of information was exchanged during these gatherings? Although *ketan* literally means "conversations with guests," not all the recorded conversations took place in the author's salon; in fact, a great number of exchanges happened elsewhere but were deemed worth repeating. Serving as a receiving station for hearsay and rumors, a *ketan* was virtually the print extension of an active oral network through which news and rumors circulated in late Ming society. This seeming idiosyncrasy of *ketan*, in fact, was part of a prominent trend in the late Ming cultural scene. Authors of novels and dramas drew heavily on social events, treading a thin line between news, rumors, and hearsay.[15] These news-based publications were so popular and influential that in a sense they elevated informal and private exchanges of petty gossip and tall tales into a shared social imagination. The next section of this chapter first surveys the circulation of news and gossip in the late Ming print world and then examines how the idea of Nanjing was negotiated through the popular tales that traveled into the elite salons on which *Kezuo zhuiyu* and *Jinling suoshi* were based.

Although such entertaining anecdotes fill most of the pages of *ketan* publications, they do not fully describe the rich array of entries collected in these two particular Nanjing *ketan*. Gu maintained that his "conversations with guests," while assembling interesting and sensational anecdotes, also contain discussions of the public welfare and scholarly exchanges on Nanjing-related issues. Indeed, Gu's *Kezuo zhui-*

yu, as does Zhou Hui's *Jinling suoshi*, delves extensively into issues of particular interest to contemporary urban elites. After the migration of rural gentry to cities, urban elites began to enjoy a much more commanding presence in the late Ming. Yet curiously, the urbanization of rural gentry received little attention from contemporary critics. Most social commentators focused on the destructive effects of commerce and consumption on the prescribed social hierarchy and cultural propriety. The absence of urban elites from public discourse makes the window of *ketan* all the more precious. Above all, the growing density of urban elites had turned cities into fertile grounds for socializing and networking, significantly altering the relationship between elites and their lived space. Chapter 3 looks at how the viewing of urban sights facilitated ties and allegiance among urban elites; this chapter explores how the changing residence patterns affected the literati's political engagement and cultural practice.

Finally, having explored the intensified flows of information and population intrinsic to the production of *ketan*, this chapter looks at an entry in *Kezuo zhuiyu* that formally theorizes such fluidity: a *fengsu* 風俗 (social customs) treatise that divides Nanjing into five neighborhoods based on the dynamics between *zhu* 主 "hosts" (locals) and *ke* 客 "guests" (sojourners). The treatise reinvents the paired concept of "guest" and "host" with reference to a wide range of ideas, such as "identity," "economic power," "social status," and "cultural capital," contingent on the particular context of each neighborhood.[16] This unique framework allows the author to exploit the transient flow of people and resources in and out of the city to characterize the fluid nature of urban life. At the same time, although using "host and guest" as a *modus operandi* in theorizing urban space is indeed revolutionary in the tradition of *fengsu* discourses, it was by no means a concoction of the author's creative mind. In fact, the opposition between hosts and guests proves to be a much-invoked metaphor at the time to express the growing tensions between natives and sojourners because of a dated migration control policy. In a peculiar turn of history, the clash between the early Ming rural ideal and late Ming urban society came to dictate the ways by which urban space was conceived.

PRINTED GOSSIP AND
STREET NEWS IN 'KETAN'

The Development of Ketan *in the Late Ming*

Ketan's collection of salon conversations drew heavily on an oral network that had come to be particularly active in the late Ming. Indeed, scholars see this period as an age of intensive socializing when people of different classes enthusiastically formed clubs and societies of all sorts (*she* 社 and *hui* 會).[17] The literati salon so central to the making of Nanjing *ketan*, as it turns out, was just one of the many contemporary forms of social networking. This trend, not surprisingly, led to an unusually high volume of information exchange. Yet, in contrast to the focus on court politics in earlier *ketan*, most of the works published in the Ming favored street gossip and local scandals. As such, entertaining tales constitute the main contents of most Ming *ketan*. A good example is Lu Cai's 陸采 *Yecheng kelun* 冶城客論 (Conversations of friends in Nanjing).[18] It consists of a wide array of news and hearsay-based fantastic tales that Lu collected from his friends when he left his hometown and studied at the imperial university at Nanjing.[19] Lu began every entry with the name of the source—mostly just surnames—although occasionally he indicated the person's occupation as well. A rough picture of the busy social life of a university student (*jiansheng* 監生) emerges from the pages of this *ketan*. Lu's contacts ranged from family friends who happened to be in town to fellow students from all over China (who shared fascinating stories from their respective hometowns) to military officers to Daoist priests. Yet although Lu mined his acquaintances for stories, many of the anecdotes do not directly relate to his informants but are merely reiterations of hearsay from a much broader circle of sources.

Judging from the great number of news accounts in Nanjing *ketan*, Gu Qiyuan's and Zhou Hui's social circles were equally enthusiastic about passing along street gossip and urban tales about Nanjing. Their informants' interest in curiosities allowed Nanjing *ketan* to present a much more vernacular view of urban life than that often found in gazetteers or literati essays. For example, an entry in *Kezuo zhuiyu* on *chan'guai* 產怪 (bizarre births) describes all the inhuman births in Nanjing—one woman gave birth to a dozen eggs, another to a turtle-shaped baby, and yet another to a *yaksha*-like baby.[20] Of these "amazing and strange stories," as Gu Qiyuan called them, some are so sensational that they were probably quite well known among Nanjing residents. One entry in *Kezuo zhuiyu* relates a famous thief of the Wanli era. His legendary skills allowed him to make a "flying jump" to the roof of a building and steal precious objects without making a sound or leaving a trace. Only after a servant betrayed his identify did people discover that this notorious thief was in fact a respected member of elite circles in Nanjing.[21]

Oral networks played a critical role in extending the life of such community memory. Another interesting piece of social news in Zhou Hui's *Xu Jinling suoshi* tells the story of a local bully named Wang Xiu'er 王繡二, who practiced black magic with newborn babies.[22] This crime was soon uncovered, and Wang was sentenced to death despite his money and connections. This story was so popular among Nanjing residents that it was made into a play. Although the script was no longer available by Zhou Hui's time, he still learned of the event, most likely because the tale had been passed on by word of mouth. In fact, many Nanjing *ketan* entries seem to have drawn on such an oral network that preserved tales from as early as the late fourteenth century, the golden age of Nanjing as the capital of a newly founded dynasty.[23] The loosely defined temporal frame is indicative of the particular connotations of "news" at the time. The Chinese term for news, *xinwen* 新聞, contains a twofold meaning: *xin* "new" not only refers to the contemporariness of information circulating within various media such as novels, *biji*, and dramas but also suggests a sense of novelty that further enhanced the public appeal of such stories.

The fascination with novelty was part of the aesthetics of *qi* 奇, a prominent feature of the late Ming cultural scene. The popularity of *qi* is well attested by its recurring appearance in the titles of late Ming publications: *Pai'an jingqi* 拍案驚奇 (Slapping the table in amazement), *Jin'gu qiguan* 今古奇觀 (Novel spectacles in the past and present), *Hainei qiguan* 海內奇觀 (Fantastic spectacles within the realm), *Mingwen xuanqi* 明文選奇 (Amazing selection of Ming essays), *Xinke Mao gong Chen xiansheng bianji zhushu beicai wanjuan shouqi quanshu* 新刻眉公陳先生編輯諸書備採萬卷搜奇全書 (Complete collection of amazing stories), *Yuanxi qiqi tushuo luzui* 遠西奇器圖説錄最 (Collected diagrams and explanations of wonderful machines from the far west), and *Gaoqi wangshi* 高奇往事 (Amazing tall tales from the past). Gu Qiyuan himself observed of the competition for *qi* at his time: "In the last ten years or so, official canons have loosened, and since then people have been free to present their *qi*. Everyone tries something new, and the styles in writing are dramatically changing. Novelty! Novelty! It never ends. There is always more and more *qi*." Although Gu was criticizing the style of examination essays, he also captured the general popular taste at the time.[24] The ever-changing nature of *qi* called for ceaseless competition that drove itself forward. Once the quest for *qi* began, it took on a life of its own: the more sensational, the better.

The enthusiastic search for novelty and thrill in the mundanities of everyday life not only increased the popularity of *ketan* but also prompted a new publishing trend: news mixed with rumors was circulated widely into various genres, such as *shishi xi* 時事戲 (current events plays)[25] and *xiaoshuo* 小說 (vernacular stories). Writers of these works recounted, commented on, and criticized contemporary events and the world they lived in. This newfound cultural interest significantly expanded the circulation of street news and gossip about local events, which used to spread informally through local oral networks. Through print publications, contemporaries gained a much broader view of their society beyond immediate everyday interactions. The intersection of an active oral network and a flourishing publishing industry made *ketan*, a format long predating the Ming, a unique late Ming cultural product. A closer look at the late Ming publishing industry will help us to gauge the social impact and cultural significance of Nanjing *ketan*, especially given the lack of sources relating to readers' responses.

The Expanding Social Horizons

The increasing exposure to news-based publications allowed late Ming society to be increasingly connected. Spreading news was said to have become part of people's daily routine. Chen Jiru 陳繼儒 (1558–1639), a well-known cultural celebrity, remarked that *Wu ren* 吳人 (people in the Lake Tai area around Suzhou) were so invested in other people's business that they would ask for the news the minute they sat down (*wusu zuoding zhewen xinwen* 吳俗坐定輒問新聞).[26] The popular curiosity about current events was not confined to the political realm but extended into petty social affairs. The new profession, *mai xinwen* 賣新文 (news sellers), for example, specialized in collecting and publishing social events. The late Ming novel *Huanxi yuanjia* 歡喜冤家 (The happy foes) records a story about two couples who become mixed up in a dark bedroom. One of the husbands becomes furious when he finds out what happened. He is, however, advised not to tell because:

Should you make this scandal known to anyone, all the people in the street will chat about this. One person passes it to another two; the two persons again each pass it to another three. When the story starts to circulate, it would soon catch the attention of those news sellers—such a sensational affair is exactly something they dream about. Before you know it, your story would be published and put out on market, and the whole world will know what happened to you.[27]

In addition to the most immediate form of printed news, stories with high entertainment value sometimes were collected in publications such as *ketan*, or even further elaborated into dramas and novels. Adapting real life stories into print or live theater had become a common practice by the late Ming. For example, Kong Shangren, whose *Peach Blossom Fan* was based on real events in the Qinhuai pleasure quarters of Nanjing, once mentioned that it was a common practice for theaters to produce fresh scores on learning the recent news.[28] In the wake of major political scandals, the market would be flooded with dozens of dramas to satisfy the curious crowd.[29] Vernacular stories also drew heavily on contemporary society. For example, a prominent writer of late Ming vernacular fiction, Ling Mengchu 凌濛初, in his brief introduction to *Er ke pai'an jingqi* 二刻拍案驚奇 (Slapping the table in amazement, second collection, 1632), recalled how he came to write his stories: when he was taking the examinations in Nanjing, he just "idly picked out one or two remarkable situations [he] heard of from the past and present—items worth recording—and elaborated them into stories."[30] Ling Mengchu's account of the origins of *Er ke* represents more than his own story. Another popular series of vernacular novels, *Sanyan* 三言 (Three words), authored by Feng Menglong 馮夢龍, also contains many stories that originated in contemporary news events.[31]

In view of the increasing popular appeal of news stories, it is not surprising to find that *ketan*, with their recorded conversations, stand out for their unique sense of immediacy. The frequent citation of realistic details such as names and locations further enhanced *ketan*'s implicit claim of truth and authenticity.[32] Yet, the popularity of *ketan* also made publication such a competitive business that authors were driven to take full advantage of the limited sources, sometimes at the cost of credibility. The fierce competition is vividly conveyed in the story of Lu Cai, who criticized Shen Zhou 沈周, a Suzhou cultural luminary, for being gullible in recording in his *Kezuo xinwen* 客座新聞 (News from guests' seats) whatever stories his guests brought to him, no matter how incredible. Lu, however, soon fell victim to his own criticism when he heard an intriguing story from Zhu Yunming 祝允明 (1460–1526), another Suzhou celebrity.[33] Lu was convinced that Zhu must have already included this fascinating anecdote in his own collection; later, to his great delight, he learned that this particular piece of news had not appeared in Zhu's *biji* or its two sequels—most likely because of its lack of credibility. Fully aware of the problematic nature of the source, Lu seized on the chance and added it to the end of his *Yecheng kelun*. The competitive quest for *qi* thus to a great extent obscured the boundaries separating news, hearsay, and rumor.

The surging flow of news and hearsay was perceived in different lights by contemporary critics. Some believed that this cultural phenomenon presented new opportunities for moral inculcation. The late Ming scholar Chen Liangmo 陳良謨 (1482–1572) argued that, from the viewpoint of popular moral education, news-based stories were far more convincing and effective than the classics and histories, which were too esoteric and obscure to be appreciated by anyone but scholars. Despite the prevalence of the Four Books in mass education, their moral lessons simply passed through the eyes and ears of common folks without being absorbed. However, such was not the case with street talk and news. Once heard, it immediately grabbed the attention of people and stayed in their minds for a long time. Why? Chen believed that the explanation lay in the fact that the ancient classics were simply so remote that they lacked the persuasive power of current events. "It is human nature to be moved by concrete events that are close to us in time and space."[34] Drawing on their immediate relevance to everyday life, news events held such impressive sway over the public mind that even news-based vernacular novels began to enjoy the same level of social influence as established religions such as Confucianism, Daoism, and Buddhism and had emerged as the fourth "teaching."[35]

However, the same power of persuasion, when applied inappropriately, could also have just the opposite effect. Most problematic was the practice of authors sensationalizing their "real life" stories in order to profit from readers' voyeuristic interests. In some extreme cases, publishers simply fabricated lascivious plots in order to prevail in the fierce market competition. The popularity of such publications was believed to have seriously compromised the moral integrity of the general public. The seventeenth-century author Lu Wenheng 陸文衡, for example, singled out a group of novel writers in Suzhou who fabricated bawdy stories to entice readers to buy their books.[36] He denounced them for damaging social morality; they deserved to suffer cruel karmic retribution either in this life or in the afterworld.[37]

Moreover, the immediacy of news stories also lent themselves to serving as ready instruments for personal vendettas or political agendas. Such phenomena could be observed not only in the cultural capital of Suzhou, where it was said that literati would make up songs or dramas to slander an enemy's reputation,[38] but also in remote areas, such as Ningling 寧陵 (in Henan), the hometown of Lü Kun, where sharp social commentary circulated through local theaters. As discussed in Chapter 2, Lü Kun's proposition for wall construction brought vehement attacks and criticisms, many of them expressed through posters or local plays specifically produced to attack Lü. The effects of these cultural products were rather striking: not only did they immediately thwart the wall-construction proposal but they also forced Lü Kun to publish an open letter to appease the angry public.[39] These media enjoyed such a broad social and geographic reach that not only Confucian scholars but also Buddhist masters found their deep infiltration into everyday life alarming. Zhu Hong 袾宏 (1535–1615), a leading Buddhist abbot, in his *Zizhi lu* 自知錄 (A record of self-knowledge), which is essentially a ledger of merit and demerit for disciples to practice a moral bookkeeping of their daily conduct, took particular note of the use of novels, dramas, and songs to defame the innocent, a sin that calls for twenty negative points. Considering that the maximum penalty for defying one's parents was ten points, the offence was deemed rather severe.[40]

Taken together, publications with a strong interest in street news and contemporary social events were not new and can be found as early as the twelfth century in Hong Mai's 洪邁 (1123–1202) *Yijian zhi* 夷堅志 (The record of the listener). Nevertheless, the late Ming controversy and debate surrounding this genre indicates a profound change of scale. Simply put, voyeuristic interest in contemporary society had developed into a lucrative cultural industry and the sharing of local news and scandals became a conspicuous element of social life. Despite its pervasive influence, there appears to have been little government control over the literary adaptation of news stories through drama, vernacular stories, or *ketan*. As a result, these works became subject to a wide range of agendas. Confucian scholars strove to take advantage of this growing popular interest in news stories by giving it a place in the Confucian scheme of mass moral education. Others used it to advance political agendas and mobilize the crowd. Still others saw the increase in sensationally embellished news stories as a threat to the moral integrity of the reading public. The anxiety over the appropriate social use of news stories exposes the potentially subversive nature of this emerging cultural industry. Historians have noted the catalytic role of novels and dramas in collective actions and political protests. In extreme examples such as the riot against the famed artist Dong Qichang 董其昌 (1555–1636), a satire criticizing the bullying of locals by Dong's servants set off massive violence against him and his family.[41] Although most of these cultural products were not as politically charged, they still provided a vernacular social imagination much different from the prescribed narratives in local gazetteers and official accounts.

Nanjing, a City of Anecdotes

The contention over the social function of news events bears clear witness to the much-increased access of late Ming people to their society. The expanding social horizon sheds new light on the impressive grassroots solidarity and enthusiastic political participation of the Nanjing community during the corvée reform discussed in Chapter 1: the connectedness of the urban community was not just confined to political issues but extended into daily exchanges of news and hearsay. Even mundane scandals became topics worth probing. With the flourishing of publishing and the growth of information flows, lives and events outside immediate daily experiences were no longer beyond reach. In some cases, such as the story of Wang Xiu'er, the circulation of news stories through oral networks or formal media such as dramas even served as an alternative form of social justice. How, then, was the idea of Nanjing negotiated through these exchanges?

To begin with, the entries in *ketan* present a view of the Nanjing community that is much more tolerant and inclusive. Readers of these works encounter a jumble of celebrated officials and their humble neighbors, who were, for example, accidentally poisoned by mushrooms, watermelons, and taros.[42] In the pages of these works, the urban community materialized in real flesh and blood. The stories of lofty local figures, whose biographies in the local gazetteers were decorated with lengthy honorary titles and venerable deeds, reveal a side of their lives rarely seen by the public. Readers learn that Gu Qiyuan, troubled by toothache, was advised by a friend: "When it comes to sore eyes, you should keep them still; but for teeth, you should keep them in constant motion."[43] Gu apparently went to great lengths to uncover similar opinions in ancient texts to support this folk remedy. Readers also discover that he shared the folk belief in the efficacious divination sticks at the temple of the Black Emperor. The statue of the Black Emperor is said to have originated from a gate in the city wall of the Southern Tang dynasty (923–36). "Whatever I prayed, the message I drew always gave me the exactly accurate response," Gu observed. The divination sticks responded to people's prayers as if the deity was speaking to them in person. Once Gu asked about a daughter's illness, and the stick answered with an image of a skeleton on a deserted hill. Surely enough, his daughter passed away soon afterward. Later Gu himself became ill, and every time he prayed, the stick would predict his prognosis accurately.[44]

These recorded conversations also kept alive stories of ordinary people, ones that because of the insignificance of the protagonists would normally have vanished into historical obscurity. For example, Zhou Hui's *Jinling suoshi* recounts a story of a late Ming fortuneteller in Nanjing whose son passed the provincial examinations. The fortuneteller's family and friends urged him to quit his less than respectable calling, but he refused. It was not until later, when his son died before he could receive an official appointment, that the father revealed the ominous prediction he had divined for his son. Another story concerns a merchant named Wu from Suzhou who opened an incense shop in Nanjing. Wu had a black dog that suddenly turned violently aggressive. He had no choice but to sell the dog to a local butcher who offered 75 copper coins. Wu asked for 100. However, that night he had a dream in which a man dressed in a blue gown told him that he owed Wu 75 coins in his previous life and had returned as a dog to clear the debt. The next day, Wu accepted the butcher's offer.[45]

In addition to the urban working class, minority groups in Nanjing such as the *huihui*, Muslims, also receive considerable attention as an exotic novelty. This group was known for excelling at the jewelry trade, and a few anecdotes portray them cleverly spotting valuable stones in the most unlikely places as well as their cunning ploys to attain the gems.[46] At the same time, mainstream achievements of *huihui* are also noted in a list of the Muslims who passed the civil service examinations, revealing a certain degree of integration of *huihui* into Nanjing elite society.

Owing to their origins in casual conversation, the majority of the entries in the Nanjing *ketan* are anecdotes, essentially miniature dramas taking place on the stage of everyday urban life. This familiar narrative mode must have commanded the attention of late Ming readers who had grown accustomed to perceiving their world as mediated through sensational stories and intriguing dramas.[47] Compared with the pantheon enshrined in local gazetteers, membership in the city as defined by these anecdotes is more inclusive of people from a wide range of social strata and geographic origins, so long as their life involved a human interest story. These humble urbanites came to be remembered through word of mouth and, because of the publications of *ketan*, in print as well.

These casual anecdotes also present the city's landmarks in a very different light. Take, for example, the warehouse at Lake Hou that stored the census data of the Ming empire. Established at the beginning of the dynasty, this institute provided the foundation for the fiscal operations of the Ming empire; the area around the lake was subject to the highest security, and access was strictly regulated. Yet *Kezuo zhuiyu*'s interest in this institution focuses on a key with a yellow string attached, which, as the legend had it, was crafted by the empress of the founding emperor Zhu Yuanzhang herself. Once, while serving on duty, a university student (*jiansheng*) took the key home. His wife, not knowing the sacred

Fig. 4.1 Nanjing imperial observatory; Ge Yinliang,
Jinling fancha zhi (1627)

origin of the worn and tattered string, replaced it with a new one. The
poor fellow did not notice the substitution until he returned the key. The
absence of the old string put the whole crew in terror of severe punishment. Although the crisis was averted by a successful recovery of the
original string, the accident, along with the legendary yellow string,
attained a central place in the popular imagination of the census warehouse. Through this urban tale, the intangible sense of Lake Hou's sanc-
tity is translated into palpable intimidation of state law and authority.

Another story involves the famous copper armillary sphere (*tong hun
yi* 銅渾儀) at the Nanjing Imperial Observatory (Qintianshan guan
xiang tai 欽天山觀象台, Fig. 4.1), an instrument used to set the calendar that confirmed cosmic approval of the dynasty. The readers' attention, however, is directed to the ornamental dragons at the feet of the
sphere, which were said to have once flown away on a stormy night.

Following their flight to freedom, two pairs of silver locks were added to secure these dragons in place. The fascination with the untamable dragons probably reflects popular uneasiness toward the observatory's intervention in the sacred interactions between humans and the celestial realm, *tian*.

The less than orthodox nature of their narratives of the city was not lost on Gu Qiyuan and Zhou Hui, which might explain why both chose to feature in the titles of their collections words such as "trivial" (*suoshi* 瑣事) and "supernumerary" (*zhuiyu* 贅語). For us, however, these trivial conversations prove to be invaluable for the popular outlooks they betray: Nanjing, as it emerges from these urban tales and street gossip, is a city of anecdotes about the wisdom and folly of the elite as well as humble folk—anecdotes that create a vernacular imagining of urban society by casting the city in a light more familiar to contemporary readers than that presented in other urban accounts.

'KETAN' AND URBAN ELITES' ENGAGEMENT WITH URBAN SOCIETY

The Urbanization of the Gentry Class

As mentioned above, the entries in Nanjing *ketan* are two-tiered in terms of their sources: some anecdotes were widely known among the general public, others expressed the informants' concern regarding the urban public itself—such as city welfare and municipal operations, even the very notion of "Nanjing" itself. For these urban elites—native or sojourning alike—what mattered was not only the fascinating events said to have happened in Nanjing but also the "city" in and of itself: how the city operated in the administrative system as well as how it was construed in the literary world. At a time when the influx of rural gentry into cities was greatly complicating the established ethos of the elite class, the exhaustive attention to the idea of the city in these conversations reflected the efforts of urban literati to redefine their newfound place in urban society. How, then, did urban residence affect elite practice and self-perception?

Two anecdotes from the Nanjing *ketan* offer some clues. One entry in *Kezuo zhuiyu* praises the virtue of a highly regarded Nanjing official,

Wang Yiqi 王以旂 (*jinshi* 1511), who apparently lived in a less privileged neighborhood next to the marketplace. Every time he returned home, he deliberately avoided passing through the marketplace, so that "all my neighbors and local folks would not be disturbed by my presence."[48] In contrast, an anecdote by Zhou Hui tells the story of a Censor Li, who had to pass by a ward mainly occupied by blacksmiths who never stood to show respect. Their behavior angered Li, who then asked the police to arrest the whole ward for punishment. The residents of the ward explained that former minister Ni Yue 倪岳 (1444–1501), who lived in the same ward, had asked them to remain seated whenever he himself passed. The police officer, moved by the high spirit of fraternity of Ni, later told Censor Li, "Even I felt ashamed [for arresting them] after hearing what they said."[49] Li's embarrassing insistence on status distinction, however, was highly praised by others as the "ancient way." The editor of the Qingjiang 清江 (Jiangxi) gazetteer lamented the lost golden age: when "*shiren* 士人 [scholar-officials] entered the marketplace in their formal attire, people would stand up to show respect."[50]

The conflicting viewpoints reveal the challenges and confusions that the urban environment presented to traditional social ethics. The Chinese term for "city," *chengshi* 城市, literally "walls and markets," highlights the city's two primary functions of political administration and economic transaction, each of which, in its own right, generates a social hierarchy that may conflict with the other (e.g., the clout of high officials vs. the influence of powerful merchants). In the classic urban plan, such as that of Tang Chang'an, the markets were enclosed in separate wards and thus the political and economic realms operated independently in the same city. However, after the urban revolution of the tenth and eleventh centuries, such zoning divisions collapsed, and urban communities of various sorts—officials, merchants, craftsmen—blended together.[51] The flow of people from all walks of life into and out of the city created a mixed social fabric that did not conform easily to the communal ideal of the countryside, where the Ming government instituted routine communal gatherings and rituals such as *xiang yinjiu li* 鄉飲酒禮 (village libation ceremony) to inculcate and uphold the ideal social order. When this system declined in the latter part of the Ming, private efforts (such as *xiangyue* 鄉約, "community compact") were initiated by the elites to take its place.[52] However, similar initiatives were entirely lacking in cities, where frequent shifts in status and identity further complicated the translation of the communal ideal into an urban setting.

The absence of prescriptive measures opened room for diverging, if not contradictory, interpretations of urban ethics. In the case of Qingjiang, we find a prospering market town coping with an increasingly urbanized environment. The gazetteer editor found the changes problematic and blamed the deteriorating social decorum on the weighty presence of newcomers in town, who had no knowledge of or respect for the local gentry residing in the countryside. As a result, a once tightly knit community was split by the commerce-driven flow of population into the urban area. In this booming market town, when confronted with an increasingly commercialized local society, locals took a conservative position reasserting the importance of the prescribed social hierarchy originally conceived for rural communities. However, in a more established metropolis such as Nanjing, we find the same situation was viewed with a more liberal attitude—official etiquette should not be insisted on at the cost of intruding on urban daily activities. It is worth noting that both of the officials applauded in the anecdotes, Ni Yue and Wang Yiqi, happen to be Nanjing natives. Growing up in a humble neighborhood, they developed a more organic relationship with the urban community, whereas Censor Li was most likely a temporary resident brought to Nanjing by his posting.

Such sympathy for Nanjing residents is explicitly expressed throughout the *ketan* compiled by Gu Qiyuan and Zhou Hui, perhaps because both men's families had resided in Nanjing for generations and had developed a deeply rooted and organic affiliation with the city and its residents. It is important to note that urban elites such as Gu and Zhou had become a unique breed in late imperial China. Their families had moved to the cities generations earlier, with many becoming absentee landlords in the countryside. On one hand, by being close to the political centers located in cities, the urbanized gentry was now able to form a firm alliance with local officials and consolidate control over the countryside, creating a hegemony scholars refer to as *xiangshen zhipei* 鄉紳支配 (gentry dominance).[53] On the other hand, the physical distance from their rural estates also alienated these gentry from rural production, sometimes to the point of disastrous obliviousness—as in the case of the irrigation system in the Jiangnan delta. Once removed from the countryside, many landlords exempted themselves from the communal responsibility of maintaining the local irrigation system and indirectly contributed to the deterioration of the local economy.[54] The flip side to this phenomenon, however, was that these urbanized elites also became enthusiastic participants in urban politics. Indeed, the influence of Nanjing elites in support of Ding's reform discussed in Chapter 1 is a case in point.[55] Here the range and scope of urban matters recorded in *ketan* allow us to view these elites' engagement in a much fuller perspective. The attention paid by Nanjing elites to corvée reform was not just an isolated phenomenon but part of their extensive concerns for municipal operations, ranging from small details such as how the keys to the city gates were handled to more important matters such as urban tax reform, management of military households, and transportation of tributary rice. Although most *ketan* entries deal with nondivisive issues such as a survey of waterways and bridges in Nanjing and subsequent discussions on how to improve Nanjing's water transportation, some do reflect active involvement in controversial urban political issues.[56]

For example, one anecdote relates a scandalous political clash over city land use.[57] The conflict was triggered by the mansion owned by Xu Tiansi 徐天賜, the Prince of Wei's brother. Located in Dagong ward, Xu's house was next to the Nanjing prefectural school. The two buildings were so close to each other that there was little space for the Xu family to expand their residence. To solve the problem, Xu conspired with the Yingtian prefect and school inspector to bribe a few students to initiate a proposal to trade a parcel of private land for the school property next to the Xu residence. However, this plot was exposed by a righteous student, Zhou Gao 周皋, after he posted an article titled "Fei fei zi" 非非子[58] on the school walls. Zhao's poster insinuated foul play in the school land deal by referring to a fictitious story in which Confucius is so poor that his students have to sell his land. The public opinion and sanction—*gonglun* 公論—provoked by this article was such that the conspiring supervisor withdrew from the agreement and forfeited the whole deal. Naturally Zhou won much applause among Nanjing residents.

The deepening engagement of urban elites with the urban community was not lost on contemporary minds. Some attributed it to the close daily interactions with urban residents. For example, the primary author of *Jinling tuyong* and prominent Nanjing native official, Zhu Zhi-fan, took note of the political advantages of urbanites over peasants when he joined friends and colleagues for an excursion into villages near Nanjing. During their trip, they traveled in the mountains, sight-seeing and having *chan* dialogues with monks. At night, the tour group sat together, with incense burning and tea boiling, discussing the recent urban corvée reform in Nanjing. As he engaged in heated conversations about Nanjing with friends in this nearby village, Zhu came to realize just how easily urban residents could convey their problems to the au-thorities or influential figures because of physical proximity, a privilege denied rural residents. In fact, distance from the urban administrative center made official intervention that much more difficult, leaving peasants vulnerable to the predation of crooked officials and with little recourse to the law.[59]

Although daily interactions in a densely populated urban environ-ment might play an important role in drawing elites into urban politics, equally important, if not more essential, to such political activism was the constant exchange of opinions among urbanites as well as among elites in their salons. Short of the concepts and practices akin to mod-ern democracy, either *xiangshen gongyi* 鄉紳公議 (gentry advocacy) or the broadly construed *shimin gongyi* 市民公議 (urban public opinion) had to grow from these noninstitutional and private conversations. Al-though most daily exchanges might not be politically charged, they did help establish an important communication venue for the urban com-munity to form a consensus and take action, as we observed in Nanjing *huojia* reform. In fact, some contemporary observers even asserted that active information exchange and discussion had distinguished urban elites from their rural counterparts and forced them to be more atten-tive and responsive to public opinion. For example, the 1579 gazetteer of Hangzhou explicitly addressed urban elites (*shengcheng shifu* 省城士夫) and the rural gentry (*shidaifu ju xiang zhe* 士大夫居鄉者) in separate categories and accorded each group different roles and held them to disparate moral expectations.[60] The basis for this distinction, the editor held, lay in the stronger binding force of public censure in cities. He observed that the abuse of power and privileges by rural gentry had sig-nificantly damaged social relations in the countryside but not in cities.

Hangzhou's urban elites took a good name much more seriously, exercised stronger self-discipline, and kept their distance from illicit interference in local governance. The editor believed that part of the reason urban elites behaved better than their rural peers resided in the strong sanctioning power of urban *qing yi* 清議 (pure opinion). This observation confirms what we find in Nanjing, where the active information network enhanced the influence of "public censure," as attested in the story "Fei fei zi."[61]

The de facto urban-rural divide in elite identity is indeed intriguing, since it defies the institutional setup of the Ming administration system, under which cities were embedded in greater territorial units composed mostly of villages. The urbanization of the gentry not only altered the dynamic between the state and its rural and urban subjects but also brought differentiations among the governing elites, a distinction that appears to have registered on contemporary minds. In fact, the self-identity of urban elites was so entangled with the urban realm that after the fall of the Ming dynasty, cities became the fundamental symbol of these elites' commitment to the Ming regime, and the act of denouncing city life, *bu rucheng* 不入城 (never set foot in cities), was considered by some as the ultimate gesture of loyalty to the fallen Ming empire.[62] Although this gesture might in part be related to the fact that cities were the administrative sites of the conquering Qing regime, the absence of similar expressions during any previous dynastic transition indicates that elites' identity had become more intertwined with urban life by the late Ming.

The Idea of Nanjing

As urban welfare began to weigh heavily on the minds of urban elites, not surprisingly the idea of the city started to feature prominently in their performance of scholarly research or connoisseurship. Considering themselves curators of Nanjing in the realm of cultural knowledge, the contributors to the Nanjing *ketan* meticulously collected and studied written accounts about Nanjing. Because of the city's long history, many of these accounts included myths and misinformation that called for further clarification and correction; or, in Gu's term, *kaoding zaiji* 考訂載籍 (investigating and settling problems in written archives). These micro–evidential research notes investigate the ancient sites around Nanjing as well as the names of the city gates, rivers, mountains, and ancient tomb sites. Some aim to clarify rumors and settle controversial records, such as the entry about Shishi Terrace 施食臺 (Terrace of food offerings) at Jiming Temple 雞鳴寺. The temple was built at the beginning of the Ming when Zhu Yuanzhang finished the construction of the imperial university and built a terrace for his mother to overlook the school. However, the site of the terrace was an ancient battlefield and execution ground and was believed to be haunted. According to a local legend, Zhu asked a few Tibetan priests to hold a sacrifice to appease and exorcise the wandering ghosts. The story was recited again by a mid-sixteenth-century monk, Daoguo 道果, in an account of this site. Nevertheless, an entry in *Kezuo zhuiyu* cited the well-known strict policy under Hongwu reign against religious patronage by the inner court to prove that this story could not have been true.[63]

The intellectual endeavors of Nanjing elites also extended into efforts to leave accounts of their contemporary city, such as the dresses women wore or the story of a legendary monk that was on everyone's lips. The exhaustive notes on Nanjing's past and present constitute a fascinating collection of "Nanjing trivia," where list after list was compiled in order to characterize the ephemeral city life: local slang served as secret codes that only Nanjing natives were able to crack; unique species of birds and flowers native to Nanjing were registered in the *ketan*; excellent poems, paintings, calligraphies, and music produced by Nanjing natives were catalogued; and so forth. Some of these lists strike readers as serving no purpose other than pure trivia. For example, one of Zhou Hui's lists details the names of Nanjing native sons who passed the provincial examination in Beijing, Nanjing, or other provinces; Nanjing natives who passed the provincial examination and were originally Vietnamese or Muslim; Nanjing native fathers and sons who passed the examination the same year or who held the same official titles such as minister or censor; Nanjing natives who passed the civil service examinations as *chuanlu* 傳臚 (list leaders, those who headed the lists of the second and third tiers of passers in the palace examination), *jieyuan* 解元 (prefectural/provincial graduates with highest honors), *jinshi* 進士 (metropolitan graduates), *jinshi weiguan* 進士未官 (*jinshi* who did not receive official appointments), *juren weiguan* 舉人未官 (*juren* who did not receive official appointments), and *gongshi* 貢士 (tribute students who passed the metropolitan examinations); brothers from Nanjing who were metropolitan graduates or passed the examination the same year; Nanjing natives who headed the Ministry of Revenue for three terms or who were education intendant for three times; or the military officers and civil officials who were awarded residences by the court.

Despite the tediousness, behind the tireless inventorying of Nanjing trivia is an inquiry into the connotations of "Nanjing." What, after all, was Nanjing? Other than being a varied space for hosting natives and sojourners, what made Nanjing Nanjing? To answer this question with trifling "cultural knowledge" might appear pointless from our perspective, and certainly it was so from the point of view of Qing evidential scholars. However, the seemingly idiosyncratic collecting and ranking of local trivia was an activity familiar to late Ming literati, who considered connoisseurship the most fashionable intellectual pastime and a means of constructing social identity.[64] In light of the dense cultural valence ascribed to the act of collection, the curating of Nanjing trivia worked to facilitate a shared sense of "Nanjing-ness" for late Ming literati. In their assiduous efforts, Zhou Hui and Gu Qiyuan, along with all their guests, negotiated and defined the discursive boundaries of Nanjing. Eventually, all the "trivia" collected in the two Nanjing *ketan* contributed to a rendition of Nanjing that bears a unique late Ming signature.

In all, despite their eclectic appearance, the collection of conversations recorded in Nanjing *ketan* should be considered not random exchanges between salon hosts and their guests but an index of the increasing engagement of urban elites with city life. As demonstrated in this reading of Nanjing *ketan*, the persistent effort to improve the administration and documentation of Nanjing indicates that the urbanization of the gentry class had lent remarkable weight to the idea of the city in elites' political practice and cultural interest. The multifaceted contemplation of the city ultimately led to an inquiry into the meaning of Nanjing-ness addressed in a manner in line with the intellectual fashions of the late Ming: a series of seemingly trivial notes. In the process of collecting and connoisseur exchange, the conceptual boundaries of Nanjing are confronted and construed. Yet, the quest for Nanjing-ness does not stop at the connoisseur level. The final section of this chapter will examine a treatise by Gu Qiyuan that looks further into the internal differentiation within the city. If all these connoisseurial inquiries into Nanjing-ness establish a conceptual profile for the city, Gu's treatise further exposes how political and economic forces unique to Nanjing shaped various urban neighborhoods. To this end, Gu Qiyuan re-defined an established binary of host and guest into a key concept for theorizing urban spatiality.

HOST AND GUEST: THE THEORIZATION
OF URBAN SPATIALITY

The conversations in *Kezou zhuiyu* and *Jinling suoshi* present the city of Nanjing as a space marked by frequent exchanges of information and an influx of new members. Although the genre of *ketan* long predates Gu and Zhou, the *ke* (guest) in the name of the genre matches the texts' focus on the transient nature of urban life. This fruitful coinci-dence may have, in part, inspired one of the authors, Gu Qiquan, to exploit the genre designation—"guest"—as an analytical concept. In a highly experimental treatise entitled "Nanjing *fengsu*" 風俗 (literally "wind-like customs," often translated "social customs") in *Kezuo zhui-yu*,[65] Gu employed the binary "host" (natives) and "guest" (sojourners) to divide Nanjing into five neighborhoods. As demonstrated in the fol-lowing discussion, the treatise turns the active public life revealed in Nanjing *ketan* into a subject of analysis, contemplating how such social, cultural, and political fluidity should be understood and conceptualized. In this sense, the *fengsu* treatise is not just another entry in Nanjing *ketan* but caps and concludes the seemingly random collection of urban con-versations.

Yet the significance of the *fengsu* treatise extends further. The exposi-tion of the ever-shifting social composition of urban neighborhoods al-lows Gu to venture into a conceptual frontier, formally theorizing so-ciological ties between urban space and the people who inhabited it. Crystallizing amorphous urban experiences into cogent philosophical abstraction, the treatise marks a watershed in the conceptualization of Chinese urban space. Its originality notwithstanding, Gu's contempla-tion of urban spatiality was not conceived in a social vacuum; rather, it was intrinsically related to the tensions between native urban residents and sojourners at his time. The rest of the chapter is devoted to a close study of the treatise as well as the social issues it invokes.

Gu Qiyuan's Treatise on Nanjing Social Customs

Gu's particular interest in space made the established discourse on *fengsu* an apt choice on which to base his analysis. The concept of *fengsu* dates to the Warring States period and Han dynasty. It defines the nature and disposition of the inhabitants of a locality through the environmental characteristics of the place.[66] The most representative view can be found in the "Geography Treatise" of *Hanshu* (History of the Han): "All people share a constant nature, but the influence of the wind/environment leads to variations in character, speed of action, and characteristic sounds such as language and music."[67] According to this formulation, differences in people's preferences and inclinations are not accidental but contingent on the space they inhabit. Through the mediation of *feng* 風, universal human nature is converted into the localized practices and dispositions generally termed *su* 俗.

By the Ming era, discourses on *fengsu* had gradually become institutionalized. Since a section on *fengsu* was mandated as standard in local gazetteers, every prefecture or county began to document and evaluate its own local customs. Although many *fengsu* sections in Ming gazetteers delivered a rich picture of the lives of local residents by summarizing their livelihoods, annual calendar of festivals, and ritual activities, in general the thick description of local life was often eclipsed by a state-centered classification scheme that encapsulated the lived experiences of each locale into a set of qualitative terms to rank their level of governability, ranging from the positive ones like *chun* 醇 (pure), *mei* 美 (beautiful), *hou* 厚 (generous and honest), and *pu* 樸 (simple and plain) to the negative ones such as *bo* 薄 (superficial), *e* 惡 (mean), *lou* 陋 (vulgar), *cu* 粗 (coarse), *bi* 鄙 (stingy), *ye* 野 (wild), *yin* 淫 (excessive), *she* 奢 (extravagant), and *xia* 黠 (cunning). In contrast to modern statistical techniques, which translate social character into numbers and diagrams, these qualitative terms allowed for a basic classification of territory in order to maintain enormous bureaucratic operations while retaining enough flexibility to encompass the huge local variation in the Chinese empire.[68]

Despite the emphasis on social custom as an outgrowth of natural environment, the discourse of *fengsu* also had strong political implications since the medium connecting space and people, the "wind," could be either naturally derived from the environment or artificially imposed by political authority. The natural phenomenon was often termed *fengsu*, and the political one was called *fengjiao* 風教 (literally, "wind-like education," i.e., popular education).[69] *Fengjiao* not only justifies the cultural intervention of political authority but in fact prescribes such interference—*yifeng yisu* 移風易俗 (turn the wind and change customs)—as the social responsibility of governing elites. Therefore, it is not surprising that toward the latter part of the Ming, *fengsu* discourses developed from plain social description into a forum of social criticism against the prevailing influence of commerce. In this renewed format, time and change figured prominently in the making of social customs. Writers lamented the deterioration in *fengsu* and attributed the decline to the allure of commerce. Consumption of luxuries and transgression of the prescribed social hierarchy were among the most often cited offenses.[70]

Indeed, *Kezuo zhuiyu* contains a number of entries commenting on corrupt social customs in late Ming Nanjing, such as constant overspending on funerals.[71] However, in his treatise on *fengsu*, Gu was more observant than critical, focusing on the different manifestations of *fengsu* in Nanjing. He found that even within the city itself the temperament and behavior of locals varied by area, and he wanted to explore the factors behind this differentiation. Gu's urban focus is particularly significant given the ingrained rural bias of contemporary *fengsu* discourse. The rural-centered view is best illustrated in an often-invoked proclamation in the *fengsu* sections of Ming gazetteers: "The different social customs between Qi and Lu, or the varied local cultures between Wu and Yue, are based on the land. If the land is rich, then so is the local culture. If the land is impoverished, then so are social customs."[72] The reasoning here is clearly premised on a rural economy in which the nature of the land determines the locals' way of life. In an urban area, where the livelihood of residents does not rely on the nature of the soil, the land does not hold the same sway over local culture. Instead, given the principal functions of Chinese cities as centers for political administration and economic transactions, it was not the quality of the land but the quantity of political and economic resources that dictated the livelihood of locals. This distinct dynamic was conceptualized by Gu as *renwen* 人文 (social relations) and *wuli* 物力 (material forces), a paired concept whose specific attributes were further determined by the social composition of each neighborhood, particularly the proportion between *zhu* 主 (hosts = Nanjing natives) and *ke* 客 (guests = sojourners).

Table 4.1 presents Gu's conceptualization of urban spatiality. Gu first characterized each spatial division by the main social, political, or economic institutions located within it. He saw these as attracting different types of natives and sojourners and bringing varied political and economic resources to an area; these qualities in turn determine each neighborhood's *renwen* and *wuli*. In other words, the varied manifestations of *renwen* and *wuli* constitute the link mediating between space (the first column on the left) and local residents, or to use Gu's word, *xiaoren* 小人 (humble folk, the column on the far right). In the convention of *fengsu* discourses, *xiaoren* is an imagined general public, neutral in moral inclinations and thus easily swayed by what its members witnessed and experienced in daily life. For *xiaoren* in an urban environment, the combined effect of *renwen* and *wuli* shapes their temperament and behavior. Most interestingly, in Gu's formulation, *renwen* and *wuli* are not abstract forces but concrete phenomena determined by the interactions between natives and sojourners in each area.

Based on the scheme of *renwen* and *wuli*, Gu's treatise conceptualizes the urban space of Nanjing as five neighborhoods, each delineated by geographical landmarks and analyzed with the same formula. The division of Nanjing into five neighborhoods might have to do with the fact that both Beijing and Nanjing were officially divided into five boroughs (eastern, western, south, north, and central; see Map 4.1)[73] under the jurisdiction of the *wucheng bingmasi* 五城兵馬司 (warden's offices).[74] The five-borough capital administrative system was inaugurated in Nanjing and then was replicated in Beijing when the court moved there. The five warden's offices were in charge of policing, firefighting, and borough-tax collection. They were supervised by a borough-inspecting censor and worked in coordination with the county and prefectural offices. Yet, Gu's five neighborhoods did not correspond exactly to the five boroughs (Map 4.2), since Gu's division was based on social

Table 4.1

Gu Qiyuan's Conception of Nanjing Neighborhoods in Terms of *Fengsu*

Political institutions and social landscape	*Renwen* 人文 (social relations)	*Wuli* 物力 (material forces)	Cultural landscape as seen in *xiaoren* 小人 (humble folk)
1. Eastern District			
Where all the imperial institutions are scattered about	[Embodied as political power.] Rich with guests and poor with hosts (with high officials and their powerful clerks running around day and night exerting their influence).		The humble folk in this area look awkward, peculiar, and churlish.
2. Central District			
Where the prefecture and county government are located and all the merchandise is gathered.		[Embodied as financial power.] Greater among guests and less among hosts. Every day this area is crowded with thousands of noisy market clerks and brokers.	The humble folk in the area are unsettled, superficial, and competitive.
3. Southern District			
Where all the high officials and aristocratic families reside.	[Embodied as the social status of the residents.] Favors the hosts. All the sojourning literati and wealthy guests compete with one another in styles of spending.	[Embodied as consumption pattern.] Tends to be showy and extravagant. Furthermore, deeply saturated in the allure of the entertainment quarter, common people are strongly affected, with their women imitating courtesans' dress all the time.	The humble folk, especially those in the east and west Wuding Bridge area, tend to indulge in entertainments and are idle.

Table 4.1, cont.

Political institutions and social landscape	*Renwen* 人文 (social relations)	*Wuli* 物力 (material forces)	Cultural landscape as seen in *xiaoren* 小人 (humble folk)
4. Northern District			
Where the army and National University students congregate.	[Embodied in social composition.] Equal between guests and hosts.	Overall wealth is negligible; anyone looking for pleasure and sensual indulgence would have moved south.	The remaining residents are withdrawn and destitute.
5. Western District			
Mostly open space.	Scarce among both hosts and guests. The social composition is roughly three tenths commoners and seven tenths army.	The *wuli* [embodied as consumption] is very conservative. Their poor diet and clothing consist primarily of coarse food and unrefined cloth rather than delicacies and lavish silks.	The humble folk here appear depressed and destitute and are often ridiculed by the wealthy residents of southern Nanjing.
Shangyuan county (rural)			
Outside the walls, mostly located near rivers and mountains, rocky and barren.			The folk here look wearied and worn, easily agitated and litigious.
Jiangning county (rural)			
Fertile and productive.			People are honest, pure, and willing to be at the disposal of the government.

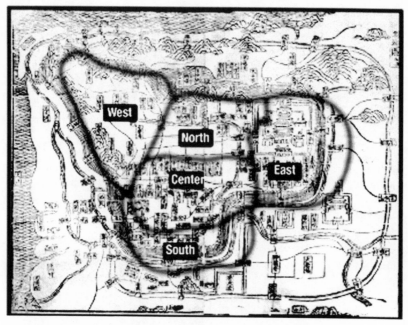

Map 4.1 Official demarcation of five Nanjing boroughs (SOURCE: *Jinling gujin tukao*)

and cultural dynamics instead of administrative convenience. The following section describes each of Gu's neighborhoods and observes how Gu saw *renwen* and *wuli* at work in each. (See the Appendix for a complete translation.)

The Fengsu of the Southern Metropolis

Eastern.   In Gu's scheme, the first district (see Map 4.2) is located in the eastern part of the city, where the old palace and numerous institutions of the secondary court were located. The people acted in a manner described by Gu as "awkward, limp, intimidated, and churlish." The local culture was not immediately affected by the strong presence of the state; rather, it was mediated through *renwen*, a broad concept of social relations, here largely shaped by the power dynamics between local residents. Local residents were composed of two groups, hosts and guests. "Guests," as Gu used the term, refers to officials, who under the rule of avoidance were natives of other places; "hosts" are natives of Nanjing. Based on this division, the distribution of power in the Eastern

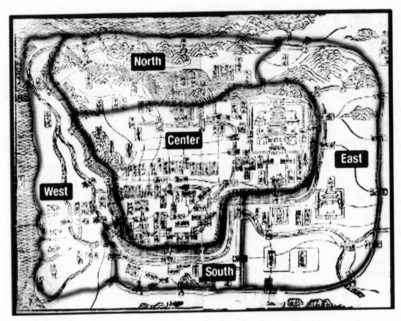

Map 4.2 Gu Qiyuan's neighborhoods (SOURCE: Gu Qiyuan, *Kezuo zhuiyu*, 1617)

District appeared to favor guests over hosts. Such unbalanced power relations materialized in daily life as "high officials and their powerful
clerks running around day and night exerting their dynamic influence."
Under the everyday flaunting of power, common people were accustomed to being slighted and overwhelmed by a sense of vulnerability,
which translated into being "awkward, limp, intimidated, and churlish."

    Central. The second district served as the administrative and
trading center of the city. Within it were the prefectural and county
governments, which oversaw all transactions conducted in the markets.
Trade was concentrated in this area, and a tremendous amount of material wealth was on display every day, with "myriad goods gathered" in
front of residents' eyes. The *wuli* (material forces) were embodied as the
financial power possessed by local hosts. In Gu's estimate, "The *wuli* is
richer at the guest part and less so at the host part," which expresses an
imbalance of influence between the sojourning merchants and the native Nanjing folk. In particular, as *wuli* materialized in daily life as a
scene crowded with thousands of noisy market clerks and brokers, it

created an environment so stirring and chaotic that the humble folk in this area appeared unsettled, superficial and competitive, constantly fighting over limited resources.

Southern.   The third district was the most ostentatious part of town. Here all the high officials and long-established prominent families resided. With all these powerful families present, the *renwen* here, shaped by the social status of the residents, favored the hosts, namely, the Nanjing natives. Rather than symbolizing the financial power people possessed (as in the previous neighborhood), the *wuli* here was manifested in public as consumption patterns. As such, people in this area tended to be more showy and extravagant. Under the strong influence of hosts, all the guests, including sojourning literati and wealthy visitors, competed in spending styles. This lifestyle extended into the inner quarters. Given the area's close proximity to the famous Qinhuai 秦淮 entertainment quarters, women were greatly affected by the allure of Qinhuai and imitated the styles of dress and makeup popular among courtesans. This situation was most extreme in the east and west Wuding bridge area, where humble folk indulged themselves and become idle.

Northern.   The fourth district was a residential area occupied mainly by students, military officers, and eunuchs. There was an equal balance of *renwen* between guests and hosts, whereas the *wuli*, the overall wealth on display, was negligible. Essentially all residential, this area continued to lose pleasure seekers to the southern part of the town. As a result, the remaining residents, those who were unwilling or financially unable to move, tended to be conservative and destitute.

Western.   The last district, in the northwest part of Nanjing, was mostly open space and sparsely inhabited. The ratio of civilians to military personnel was three to seven. The *renwen* here is described as "thin," reflecting the sparse population of both guests and hosts. The *wuli* was manifested in a tight local economy. With the local population roughly 30 percent commoners and 70 percent military personnel, the area's poverty was strikingly visible in the meager local diet—vegetables and coarse rice instead of meat—and rough clothing. Given the difficult circumstances, the humble folk here appeared depressed and destitute and were often ridiculed by the wealthy residents of southern Nanjing.

Urban Vs. Rural: The Spatialized Social Customs. The innovation of Gu's treatise resides not only in his nuanced analysis of urban neighborhoods but also in the deliberate distinction between urban and rural space in the Nanjing area. After examining social customs in the five urban neighborhoods of Nanjing, Gu described the city's rural hinterland, the quarters outside the city walls in the two urban counties of Shangyuan and Jiangning. According to Gu, half of the rural land of Shangyuan was located near the river and mountains and was rocky and barren. Accordingly, the folk there looked wearied and worn and were easily agitated and litigious. In contrast, rural land in Jiangning was fertile and productive. The soil bred people who were honest, pure, and willing to be at the disposal of the government. Echoing the conventional formulation of local customs, Gu's connection between people and space in the rural area was rather straightforward: rich lands produce model citizens who contribute labor and taxes whenever they are called on, whereas wastelands force people to compete for limited resources, leading to conflicts and litigation. True to the conventional view of social customs, Gu saw a direct correlation between the nature of land and the local culture.

However, unlike his peers, Gu did not find the same formula appropriate for the complicated urban society of Nanjing. To be sure, for agricultural settlements, the nature of the land largely determines the lifestyle of local dwellers. Yet how is this space-people conceptualization translated into urban settings? What equivalent of soil breeds and shapes the manner and behavior of city residents? Gu's great innovation, as we have demonstrated, lies in his use of *renwen* and *wuli* to articulate a conceptual link between the urban environment and urbanites. In this view, the nature of urban space is characterized not by fertility but by the political, social, or financial capital that people in all walks of life bring to the lived space. In Gu's scheme, *renwen* serves as a comprehensive conceptual tool that characterizes social dynamics in urban settings. It could be shaped by political power and authority, as in the vicinity of the Nanjing palace (district 1) or by social status (district 3);

even its absence could significantly affect the formation of local culture (district 5). Along the same lines, *wuli* could represent either the financial power of sojourning merchants (district 2) or the conspicuous consumption displayed by native upper classes (districts 3 and 4). Using this analytical framework, Gu was able to demarcate urban neighborhoods according to their resident institutions (government offices, universities, military practice grounds), which drew different groups of people (officials, students, merchants, outsiders), who in turn gave rise to a varied mix of *renwen* and *wuli*, which then shapes the behavior of commoners. In this formulation, the differentiation of urban space was ultimately determined jointly by *renwen* and *wuli*, whose formation was, in turn, intrinsically intertwined with two forms of identities: native place (the interaction between Nanjing natives as hosts and non-natives as guests) and social class (the affect of the behavior of the rich and powerful on commoners).

Gu's sociological interest extended to the issue of gender, and his conceptualization of urban spatiality took domestic space into account. Since the influence of *renwen* and *wuli* stems largely from the very public display of political or economic capital in everyday life, one might assume that women, who were not permitted in the public realm, would be immune to it. However, in Gu's observation, the power of *fengsu* was so penetrating that it was able to reach into the excluded inner quarters. This was most evident in the case of the women who lived near the courtesans in the renowned Qinhuai pleasure quarters. These courtesans were put in the public eye not only by the attention they drew from male suitors but also through publications such as *Jinling baimei* 金陵百媚 (Hundred beauties in Jinling) and *Qinhuai shinübiao* 秦淮仕女表 (A list of Qinhuai ladies), in which their beauty and charm were appreciated and ranked. In fact, the public exposure of courtesans was such that even gentry women in the inner quarters copied their styles and fashions. This reverse social imitation had become so apparent in Gu Qiyuan's time that it became a recurring theme in Gu's biographical writings, in which he judged the virtue of gentry women by their ability to resist the temptations of courtesan fashion.[75]

Discursive Roots: The Cultural and
Social Contexts of Gu's Treatise

Spatial Differentiation in Contemporary Fengsu *Discourse.*   Granted, Gu's treatise embodies a drastic departure from the rural-centered focus of conventional *fengsu* description; yet Gu was not totally out of joint with his time. The key concepts in the Nanjing *fengsu* treatise—the spatialization of social customs and the host/guest dynamics—also appear in contemporary *fengsu* discussions, albeit with a much lesser degree of conceptual sophistication. The shared interest in these concepts shows that Gu's treatise is not just an exercise in abstract thinking but speaks to larger social developments at the time. A contextualized reading of Gu's key ideas, therefore, exposes the social references embedded in Gu Qiyuan's analysis.

The internal differentiation of urban space, for example, was also noted in some contemporary gazetteers. In general the *fengsu* sections of Ming gazetteers tend to characterize the genius of a place in qualitative terms (such as "hardworking" or "decadent"), but some editors did expand the formulistic account into a quasi ethnography of local society, detailing people's livelihoods (the major and minor local occupations), local products, rites of passage (rituals for marriage, death, or adulthood), and social activities (annual festivals). When this ethnographic approach was applied to highly commercialized cities such as Suzhou in the Lake Tai area, the effect of spatial division—as in Gu Qiyuan's characterization of Nanjing—becomes apparent. One *fengsu* section in the 1642 gazetteer *Wuxian zhi*, for example, depicts the urban space of Suzhou as differentiated by residents' occupations. Since the city of Suzhou was divided between the jurisdictions of two counties, Wuxian on the west and Changzhou on the east, the description in *Wuxian zhi* focuses on the western part of the city. According to editor Wang Huanru 王煥如, since most of the residents were craftsmen, this part of the town was much more lively and noisy. Wang further provided a detailed sociological map of the city's population: the areas near Gold Gate and Chang Gate were crowded with tradesmen, whereas brokers resided mostly near the city walls. Between Xu Gate and Pan Gate were government offices full of clerks and civil servants. The educated gentry families dwelt largely in the area near Chang Gate. In the inner quarters were women who have long been known as excelling in embroidery. Most significantly, with rapid commercialization, city residents and handicraft industries spilled into areas outside city walls, expanding the de facto reach of urban space. The extra-mural area was dotted with small pieces of poor land cornered by mountains and lakes, and people toiled in every possible way to survive. Other than farming and fishing, both men and women worked all sorts of side jobs such as weaving, rock collecting, and producing vessels, tiles, houses, and other goods. Most of the residents spent the year working elsewhere as contract laborers.[76] Highlighting the concentration of similar professions in different parts inside and outside the city walls of western Suzhou, the *fengsu* section of this edition of *Wuxian zhi* presents a sociological map similar to Gu Qi-yuan's map of Nanjing. In both cases, the differentiation of urban space was based on the varied social activities resulting from a highly commercialized economy and attests to the influence of *wuli* on urban ecology.

In a similar vein, some editors of *fengsu* essays found that commercial forces not only diversified the livelihood of urban residents but also gave rise to different economic environments between cities and the countryside. The editor of the 1579 Hangzhou gazetteer, Chen Shan 陳善, took note of a de facto urban-rural division in locals' economic practices. Since the urban economy was growing at a swift pace, the city was crowded with people from all over the country, and the resultant tight competition diminished everyone's profit share. Most urbanites, despite their glamorous public façade, were deeply in debt. In Chen's estimation, half the urban population was just scraping along from day to day with absolutely no savings to spare. Rural areas were also experiencing cash flow problems, only for a different reason. Peasants used to count on local wealthy families for emergency loans. However, since the government cracked down on such practices three decades earlier, peasants were left with little recourse but to go to the loan sharks, who then prospered in a bankrupt peasant economy.[77]

Granted, the sway of material force (*wuli*) over social life is a common theme in late Ming *fengsu* discourse. Writers commonly characterized the increase in extravagance as an unfortunate byproduct of the flourishing of commerce. The polemic against the influence of commerce was heightened by the tight regulation of material consumption in the Ming empire: the government promulgated extensive stipulations on the clothing, housing, even means of transportation, permitted each social status. Under the elaborate sumptuary laws, any form of conspicuous consumption that overstepped the prescribed lines was considered an offense and deemed degenerate. Although aware of the conventional rhetoric, however, Gu Qiyuan and gazetteer editors such as Wang Huanru and Chen Shan resisted a simplistic view on *wuli*. Instead, they expanded the lopsided criticism of extravagant consumption into an ethnographic survey of the varying effects of commercial forces on the social landscape.

Faulting Outsiders for Deteriorating Social Customs.   In addition to presenting a more diversified and differentiated social landscape, some contemporary *fengsu* sections also took full notice of the importance of host/guest interactions in shaping local customs. For example, the editor of the 1642 *Qingjiang xianzhi* captured the different social dynamics between cities and countryside arising from the strong presence of urban sojourners. According to the editor, rural Qingjiang was dominated by large lineages, each with tens of thousands of members. Despite this seemingly ideal social organization (super-sized family-cum-community), judging from the high number of suits brought to the local court, the villages were still suffering from internal conflicts and disputes. In the urban area, which had much less social coherence, the concern was the overwhelming impact of the guest population:

The fact that the urban population is composed largely of people from different places mixing together leads to the grave concern of guests overwhelming the hosts. We hear that in the past social customs in the city were quite plain and simple. . . . Now all these city folk revel in their wealth and [indulge in] luxurious spending inappropriate to their social standing [i.e., in violation of the sumptuary regulations], and scholars slip into a new career as merchants. The ancient way is thus irrecoverably lost, alas![78]

Obviously, the commercial lifestyle introduced by sojourners worried the local elites.

In fact, this anxiety over the negative impact of sojourners on locals appears not to have been confined to urban areas but was widely shared across the empire. A telling example can be found in Funing subprefecture, an area on the southeast coastline that experienced a high flow of immigrants in the sixteenth century. Unlike the typical view of late Ming *fengsu* discourse, which attributes the decline of local culture to commercial power or a failure of government, the *fengsu* section in an early seventeenth-century Funing gazetteer held *kemin* 客民 (guest people) responsible for everything that went wrong in the area.[79] In the 1538 edition of the Funing gazetteer, which predates the influx of migrants, the author of the *fengsu* section appears to have been content with the local culture.[80] Because of Funing's remote location, commerce had not been able to affect locals' way of life in the first half of the sixteenth century. The editor reported that no one wore flashy clothes or worked in "low" professions such as of merchants, craftsmen, or servants. Local folk valued their hometown and never abandoned it for other places. In fact, there was no travel or migration to big cities. The craftsmen and tradesmen in the market, the tenant farmers in the field, and the civil servants were all non-natives.

However, toward the beginning of the seventeenth century, locals begin to voice discontent.[81] As non-natives flooded into the region, native residents began to blame the outsiders for the escalating social unrest. The hostility toward newcomers appears to have grown out of incessant waves of migration: the first waves consisted of new military units, and then came the overflow of floating population from nearby crowded counties (Zhangzhou 漳州 and Tingzhou 汀州). These settlers populated the valleys and mountains, significantly altering the old lifestyle in Funing. As the gazetteer editor poignantly stated, "Since the number of guests is double that of hosts, the price of rice has skyrocketed, and theft and robbery have become increasingly more menacing. Lawsuits and local disputes have increased both in complexity and number. Among the commoners, the thrifty ones are more and more extravagant. Local customs have abated."[82]

The plight of Funing natives was replicated in many other areas, such as Lianghu and Sichuan, that had become major destinations for *liumin* 流民 (floating population) in the late Ming.[83] In Yinshan (Sichuan), social customs were said to have deteriorated significantly "since the number of sojourners rose as high as half of the native population. As locals began to lose their sense of propriety, more and more people turned litigious."[84] Typical of similar complaints lodged against outsiders, the editor attributed the decline in local morals to the failing relationship between hosts (natives) and guests (immigrants). In some extreme cases, such antagonism even escalated into a major cause for social conflicts.[85]

The Heterogeneity of Urban Space.   In brief, when placed in the context of late Ming *fengsu* discourses, most of the innovative elements in Gu Qiyuan's treatise prove not to be isolated inventions but sentiments prevalent at the time. The flourishing of commerce not only loosened the sense of social propriety but also brought greater differentiation between the city and countryside as well as within the city itself. The increasing physical mobility also led to an intensification of the host-guest relation; as a result, sojourners and immigrants were often blamed for the deterioration of social customs in areas most affected by domestic migration. While referring to similar social phenomena, Gu Qiyuan's treatise on Nanjing nonetheless exhibits a much stronger analytical power than any of the contemporary *fengsu* discourses; it expands and systematizes ideas already developed at the time. To be sure, the sway of commercial power was well recognized by contemporary observers and was believed to be the culprit behind the changes in (or rather, deterioration of) social behavior; nevertheless, Gu held that commercial forces, even in a major metropolis such as Nanjing, had no monopoly over the formation of social custom. Political clout and social prestige—or *renwen*—played an equally important role in shaping the minds and behaviors of the common folk. At the same time, although fully aware of the rising tension between sojourners and natives, Gu viewed guests not as intruders but as active contributors of *renwen* and *wuli* and thus provided a more balanced and fuller view of sojourners' influence over urban life. In doing so, Gu convincingly demonstrated that the collective effect of *renwen* and *wuli* shape the disposition of local denizens in a way very different from the immediate correlation between land and peasants. This conceptual sophistication distinguished Gu from other *fengsu* discourses and allowed him to make an explicit argument that the heterogeneity of urban space, unlike its rural counterpart, did not result from natural topography but was a function of the movement of people. It was the diverse and fluid composition of the urban population, above all, that determined the differentiation of urban space.

Ultimately, the theorization of urban space boiled down to the dynamic between hosts and guests. Yet although this paired concept exhibited impressive analytic force in dissecting urban spatiality, it was also fraught with political and social tensions that resonated strongly with Gu's contemporary readers. Indeed, with population and spatial mobility on the rise, guests and hosts vied for the limited amount of fertile land to feed their families as well as auspicious lots to bury their dead.[86] In cities, they also competed for the same markets and resources. Therefore, the prevailing resentment toward "guests" was not just xenophobia against outsiders but also a symptom of the underlying conflict of interests between old and new populations. That said, the tension between hosts and guests in the late Ming was not just a product of commercialization but stemmed from an obsolete migration control policy premised on the ideal of a homogeneous peasantry rooted in its home soil. The clash between a thriving commercial economy and an antiquated institutional framework, as discussed in the following section, rendered an unusual sense of urgency to the core notion of "host and guest" in Gu Qiyuan's treatise.

Zhu 主 *(Natives) Vs.* Ke 客 *(Sojourners):* *A Key Concept in Late Ming Society*

Immigration Vs. Population Control. The central trope of "host and guest" in Gu Qiyuan's treatise not only accurately captures the transient nature of urban life but also invokes the rising tension surrounding migration. The sharpened distinction between hosts and guests was in part institutionalized in the Ming through a rigid household registration system. In principle, once a household was registered, any voluntary migration of its members was deemed illegal. Such a strict policy of migration control was necessary because registered residents provided conscripted labor vital to the operations of local government, and their number needed to be kept constant. Although exceptions were made on a case-by-case basis, the Ming state in general was firm about enforcing the nonmigration policy through relentless deportation of illegal immigrants, sometimes at grave social costs.[87] The rigorous regulation of geographic mobility, however, created an un-expected loophole in the fiscal system for illegal immigrants: the ab-sence of any official venue and statutory grounds for registering the floating population in effect allowed these migrants to be exempt from tax or labor conscription. This systemic advantage for sojourners had grave consequences after the middle of the Ming dynasty, especially in areas that bore the brunt of the overflowing population.[88]

In Mianyang prefecture 沔陽州 (Hubei), for example, guests were observed to be "regularly in excess of the hosts." Yet despite being newcomers, these migrants soon outperformed the natives in the local economy. First, their main source of income, the newly reclaimed *hutian* 湖田 (lake polders), was not subject to taxation. Moreover, with no standing in the household registration system, the immigrants were not liable for labor services. As a result, these well-off migrants possessed vast stretches of land and enormous fortunes yet bore no obligation, whereas natives of lesser means had to shoulder all the corvée and tax burdens. In the eyes of the locals, the guests enjoyed an undeserved af-fluence beyond the reach of the state and, worst of all, at their ex-pense.[89] In Ganzhou 贛州 (Jiangxi), it was estimated that more than three-fourths of the land was owned by "guest households." Although the migrants were liable for land taxes, they were in effect exempted from corvée service because of the lack of formal registration.[90]

Not surprisingly, this loophole encouraged further illegal migration. As locals fled their native places to evade taxes and labor service, the remaining population had to shoulder greater burdens, causing more people to flee the official registry. Although officials were aware of this vicious cycle, not until the latter half of the sixteenth century did the court realize the gravity of the problem and begin to gradually lift the ban on migration.[91] This policy change was made possible in part by implementation of the Single Whip method, which converted most la-bor service obligations into a unified silver payment. With state reve-nues increasingly based on land instead of corvée labor, it became pos-sible for the government to loosen its grip on household registration without debilitating the operations of local government offices. Al-though this new policy greatly expanded the freedom of physical mo-bility within the empire, its primary goal was to tax the unregistered population. Not surprisingly, this reform did not receive enthusiastic

cooperation from the floating population, who had fled their home villages to escape poverty in the first place.[92]

The lack of means to tax migrants and sojourners posed different
challenges to urban administration. For example, in the 1590s in Beijing,
according to one magistrate of Wanping county, Shen Bang 沈榜
(1540–97), who oversaw half the capital's jurisdiction, the root cause of
the shortage of corvée labor lay in the high proportion of guest households. The large number of government offices in Beijing generated an
extremely high demand for conscripted services, but the county office
had very limited numbers of eligible *ding* 丁 (adult males) on the roster
since the majority of inhabitants were classified as "guests" and were
exempt from labor conscription.[93] However, the nature of "guests" in
cities was so different from that in the countryside that placing more
weight on land taxes would not fully solve the problem. Above all, the
guest issue in cities was greatly complicated by the strong presence of
sojourning merchants, who, compared with rural migrants, were more
transient and difficult to hold liable for taxes or corvée services. Although by the late Ming many merchants were increasingly domiciled in
one particular city as a base for their operations, since they possessed
no land, even the post–Single Whip tax code could not touch them.[94]

The problematic situation in cities was well articulated by Lin Lian
林燫, minister of works during the Wanli reign. Lin pointed out that in
the countryside the government clerks were able to register land with
little resistance, but in cities there existed no equivalent measures to tax
sojourning merchants. As a result, although guest merchants took full
advantage of their urban residence to build close ties with high officials
in the host city and to profit from the poor by charging high interest
rates, "the magistrate can never levy a speck of grain or an inch of cloth
on them."[95] The loophole enjoyed by urban merchants was indeed
troubling since a tax plan that favored merchants at the cost of farmers
fundamentally violated the long-standing Confucian doctrine that
ranked farming as the livelihood most essential to Chinese civilization
and commerce as the least. Whereas the Single Whip reform was able
to hold landlords liable for taxes on the land they possessed regardless
of their primary residence, the same measure did not extend to merchants who floated between cities, and whose primary means of wealth
did not lie in land.

The Issue of Migration in Nanjing.   Nanjing was no exception to troubled host-guest relations. The influx of population not only reconfigured its physical cityscape but also challenged the existing administrative system, especially on issues regarding corvée conscription. After the court moved to Beijing, the cityscape of Nanjing gradually deviated from the grand plan of the Hongwu capital.[96] The increase in urban commerce attracted massive numbers of street vendors who infringed on the wide streets, significantly altering Nanjing's urban landscape. Boosted by the influx of sojourners, a flourishing real estate market disrupted the integrity of Hongwu's design of occupation-based residential wards.[97] The impact of migration extended beyond the level of the built environment. According to Gu Qiyuan, the influx of sojourners seriously eroded the livelihoods of Nanjing natives. For example, before the Zhengde reign (1506–21), most pawnshops were run by Nanjing natives. By Gu's time, however, native shopowners had been driven out of business by outside traders. The same trend was also observable in the silk and salt trades. "Guests," in Gu's opinion, were the ultimate culprits for the increasing impoverishment of Nanjing natives.[98] The problem arose because sojourners took full advantage of Nanjing's economy but were not subject to labor service. The unjust fiscal burden and its social consequences gravely concerned Gu Qiyuan, who believed that the problem went deeper than just a simple loophole. "There is something extremely unfair about the corvée conscription in Nanjing," Gu observed. Military households were liable for numerous kinds of labor levies to the extent that there was always one family member serving at any given time. Commoner households, in contrast, were subject to labor conscriptions only when they owned land. Even millionaire households did not have to serve a day of labor as long as they owned no land. Granted, corvée was levied on urban/suburban households, but only those who registered as Nanjing natives were liable to serve, in effect exempting countless transients who resided in the city but were not registered with the local office. As a result, Gu found that land taxation was on the whole fair and just, but labor levies discriminated against military households, landowners, and native residents.[99]

Gu's insight exposes the bias inherent in the Ming corvée system. Although military households are beyond the scope of this book, the other two are critical to our inquiry into the challenges facing late Ming cities. For Nanjing civilians, the fiscal injustice ultimately came down to the unwarranted break given non-native and non-landowning rich residents. Rectification of this problem depended on a revision of the premises of urban administration: How should urban wealth be measured and urban residence be determined? Although several possible criteria for taxing urban wealth (such as real estate, see Chapter 1) were suggested to balance the burden between landowning and landless urbanites, the problem regarding urban sojourners was never fully solved.

In order to ensure that urban sojourners bore a fair share of the fiscal burden, Nanjing officials worked to expand their legal options. They found a ready precedent in the primary capital of Beijing. Also plagued by an uneven tax burden between the registered natives and nonregistered sojourners, as early as 1527 Beijing initiated a series of census surveys of the floating population (*chaliuyi* 查流移) and demanded that all merchants who had purchased estates in the city after a significant length of local residence should be subject to labor conscription.[100] Following this precedent, many local offices, including the one in Nanjing, conducted similar surveys to level the fiscal burden between natives and sojourners.[101] However, another major obstacle soon emerged: the line between guests and hosts was, in fact, hard to draw. The general understanding was that, after a certain length of local residence (*nianjiu* 年久), a person's status should be changed from "guest" to "host," thus making him liable to all local taxation. However, how long was long enough? In addition, since there was no registration record for sojourners, how could the government know if a sojourner had stayed over the time limit and should be registered as a local? To solve this problem, Gu Qiyuan suggested that more concrete criteria for residence be established, such as using family burial grounds or urban properties as evidence that these outsiders had indeed put down roots in Nanjing.

To be sure, with the rising tide of fiscal reform and the pressing demand for fiscal justice, more specific rules were created to manage the guest population. In 1602, an edict prescribed the line to be drawn at the thirtieth year of residence; after that sojourners could apply for a new registration status and relieve themselves of the "guest" status.[102] Moreover, as some cities moved to tax urban real estate as an equivalent to rural landownership, they also worked to register the properties owned by sojourning merchants as the basis for the new urban tax. Not surprisingly, the measure met with resistance. In Linqing 臨清, a major entrepôt along the Grand Canal, all the rich merchants apparently managed to keep their status as sojourners for the purpose of evading urban estate taxes.[103] Even with increasingly concrete measures for converting migrants into legal residents, efforts to tax sojourners still fell short. Seeing the repeated failures to register Nanjing's floating traders, Zhou Hui concluded that the reliance on population registration inevitably doomed any reform because it was just too expensive to keep registration current.[104] Instead, Zhou proposed a more radical procedure, one that followed the precedent set by Jingzhou 荊州, where the local government had decided to tax rich merchants that conducted business along the Yangzi River on a seasonal basis. That way taxes were not levied through the residential registration system but were directly imposed on sojourning merchants present on site. It was more in the nature of a commercial tax: no matter where a merchant was officially registered, as long as he conducted business within the Jingzhou jurisdiction, he had to pay taxes to the local government. Although such an aggressive measure might indeed have improved the situation, the Ming government never went that far.

Hosts and Guests in the Southern Metropolis.   In light of the heated tension between natives and sojourners in the late Ming—Nanjing not excluded—the balanced view of guest/host interactions in Gu's *fengsu* treatise appears all the more significant. After all, the primary target of attack—landless rich merchants—accounted for only a segment of the guest population in a great metropolis such as Nanjing. Literati, men of letters with or without official appointments, figured as prominently in the stream of transients passing throughout the city. Wu Yingji 吳應箕, a cofounder of the Fushe, a major late Ming political society, commented on the fluid nature of Nanjing sojourners in his memoirs: "The Southern Capital is supposed to be a place where people from all directions converge. But altogether the arrivals are mostly sojourning merchants and imperial university students. There are in the end very few people really taking their families and migrating to Nanjing."[105] In addition to the students, who were selected from all over China to study at the imperial university, the provincial examination held every three years in Nanjing also attracted a constant flow of people. The traffic of examination candidates grew heavier as the examinations became more competitive. Wu Yingji, a well-known and active literatus, sat for the provincial examination eight times, which translated into constant travels to Nanjing for at least twenty-four years. Wu indeed became a regular sojourner in the city of Nanjing, and his experience was certainly not exceptional at the time.

In addition to the institutional setting that drew the educated to Nanjing, literati at times flocked to Nanjing at the call of luminaries, a trendy social practice in the late Ming.[106] The Fushe is an example: when a general convention was called at Tiger Hill in 1632, a scenic site outside Suzhou, thousands of members from Shandong, Jiangxi, Shanxi, Hunan, Fujian, and Zhejiang poured into the meeting place, a spectacle that deeply impressed contemporaries who witnessed the scene. In fact, Fushe was an association of many individual *she* (literati societies) whose main activity was to hold such social gatherings in or around major cities. One such famous gathering in Nanjing took place during the Mid-Autumn festival in 1605, with over a hundred literati invited to meet. Adding to the festivities was the attendance of more than forty courtesans from the Qinhuai pleasure quarters, who put on fake mustaches and masqueraded as exam candidates. It was such a spectacular sight to behold and to remember that "decades later Nanjing people still talked about it with great eagerness."[107]

Interestingly, the influx of literati and their relationship to the city were also filtered through the prism of the host-guest analogy, as seen in Qian Qianyi's portrayal of the cultural scene of Nanjing in the Jiajing period: "In the middle of the Jiajing reign, [a circle formed in which] Zhu Yuanjie and He Yuanlang are *yugong* 寓公 (sojourners); Jin Zaiheng and Sheng Zhongjiao serve as *dizhu* 地主 (native hosts); others like Huangfu Zixun and Huang Chunfu are *lüren* 旅人 (travelers). . . . This was the first time the Nanjing literary circle became prominent."[108]

Here the host-guest trope was further elaborated into sojourners, native hosts, and travelers. The gathering of a wide spectrum of native and non-native literati in Nanjing not only enriched its *renwen* but also made the city a leading cultural center that constantly drew visitors from all over the empire. The dense presence of literati made Nanjing an ideal socializing ground and a prime site for social tourism (Chapter

3). It also had significant political ramifications for ordinary city folks. As discussed above, the close interaction with elites allowed urban residents to communicate their plight and discontent to authorities with much greater ease and efficacy than was possible for villagers.

While touring literati crowned the city with cultural prestige and intellectual vitality, the influx of affluent merchants brought constant displays of material splendor. Despite the negative opinions of commercial power routinely registered in local gazetteers, some contemporary observers had come to recognize that the social effect of *wuli* was a complicated matter to assess, especially in an urban environment. For Nanjing residents, although unregistered sojourning merchants took advantage of a flawed fiscal system and depleted the natives' livelihood with aggressive business practices and abundant capital, they also created employment opportunities and stimulated the urban economy. Radical discourses such as *chongshe lun* 崇奢論 (A proposition to value extravagance) developed in the late Ming advocated the social benefits of a flourishing monetary economy with conviction and enthusiasm. *Wuli*, though seen as corrupting the social fabric of farming communities, were also recognized as an indispensable foundation of urban society.[109]

At the elite level, the sway of *wuli* manifested itself in a somewhat different manner. The influx of material power supported a lively cultural market, on which many literati came to rely for their elegant lifestyle. The mingling of the merchants and literati, sometimes to the point of forming a symbiotic relationship, was frequently noted by contemporary observers.[110] Zhou Hui's *Jinling suoshi* cites a famous conversation in a renowned Nanjing temple, Waguan si, 瓦官寺, in which Wang Shizhen 王世貞 (1526–90), a late Ming cultural icon, remarked that Huizhou merchants crawled toward Suzhou literati just as flies flocked to a stinky lamb. And Zhan Dongtu 詹東圖, a native of Huizhou, immediately countered: "Suzhou literati also swarm to Huizhou merchants just as flies buzz around smelly meat." As if implicitly agreeing to the pointed sarcasm, Wang Shizhen responded with nothing but a smile.[111]

The popularity of this dialogue shows that it struck a strong chord with its contemporary audience, probably because of the sharp satire on the complicit relationship between merchants and literati in late Ming society. On one hand, merchants were eager to insinuate themselves into prestigious elite circles to elevate their social standing; on the other hand, the impoverished literati class, owing to the competitive civil service examinations, became increasingly receptive to the overtures of merchants. Like Wu Yingji, many literati spent an extended period of time preparing for and repeatedly sitting the examinations. Many unfortunate ones, such as the great fiction writer Feng Menglong, never passed. With their official careers in limbo, the livelihood of these men of letters came to be closely intertwined with either wealthy patrons or the active publishing market, both of which were brought to the city by the *wuli* of "guests."

All in all, in a large city such as Nanjing, the constant high demand for labor and capital greatly compounded the dynamics between hosts and guests, who competed but also relied on one another. Despite the heated controversies surrounding the guest population, this fact of urban life was not completely lost on late Ming observers, as has been well demonstrated in Gu's thesis that grounds urban spatiality in the interaction between hosts and guests. Compared with the generally hostile attitude toward immigrants in rural areas, the sentiment in a great city like Nanjing was much more mixed and ambivalent. In some cases, the presence of guests was even perceived with sympathy and characterized with a willingness to accommodate. For example, luminaries such as Qian Qianyi considered the broad geographical base of urban elites as the foundation for Nanjing's cultural prestige and allure. By the same token, having spent most of his life in Nanjing where sojourners from all walks of life crossed paths every day, Gu had the vantage point of observing both the bright and dark sides of the guest-host dynamics. Such intimate knowledge may have been behind Gu's unique treatise in which moral judgment gave way to an analytical conceptualization of the Southern Metropolis. It is thus only fitting that at the very core of Gu's conception, everyday interactions and demographic movements define urban space.

CONCLUSION

This chapter explores the changing perceptions of the city at a time of extensive urbanization. Instead of the conventional political or literary narrations of the city, it approaches this issue by looking at a collection of recorded conversations among literati about Nanjing. This view

allows us to explore the ways in which the city was registered in contemporary daily conversations, which in turn proved to be closely related to the cultural and social changes facing cities at the time.

The publication of conversations was part of an important late Ming
cultural phenomenon: a strong interest in street news and current
events. Greatly enhancing the visibility and influence of the news anecdotes, which had previously circulated only through oral networks, this
development broadened the access of late Ming people to their society.
Through publications of novels and dramas, not only major events
such as court politics but even urban legends and local scandals became
widely shared knowledge. Given this trend, it was not surprising that
many such anecdotes found their way into literati salons, and ultimately,
ketan collections. With a clear focus on Nanjing, these stories presented
to the reading public a much more inclusive and experiential image of
urban society than the official accounts and hagiographies commemorated in local gazetteers. Instead of celebrating prominent native sons
and chaste daughters, *ketan* highlighted the wisdom of fortunetellers
and the adventures of local shopkeepers. In this parallel universe, au-
gust court institutions became the props in someone's folly. In an important sense, the intensive information flow in cities elevated the informal and private exchanges of petty gossip and tall tales into a shared
vernacular imagination of Nanjing.

Furthermore, the growth of physical mobility also affected the inner
working of urban community. Especially significant was the continuous
exodus of rural gentry into cities, which turned major metropolises such
as Nanjing into busy social grounds. Historians have found that an
increasing number of literati flocked to cities for careers outside officialdom or just to expand their social networks. Although this social development received little attention from contemporary critics, the conversations recorded in *ketan* offer us a wealth of sources for examining the
ways by which lived experiences in cities affected the literati's political
and cultural engagements, even their identities. In the case of Nanjing,
urban residence not only brought urban elites into close contact with issues in urban administration but also lent additional weight to the idea of
Nanjing as a subject of intellectual scrutiny and cultural connoisseurship.

In many ways, Nanjing, as it emerges from the rich array of recorded conversations, was a city marked by intensive information flows

and the shifting composition of its members. The fluidity of the urban environment was elevated into a powerful analytical tool by Gu Qiyuan, who exploited the dynamics between "host" (native) and "guest" (sojourner) to divide the city into five urban neighborhoods. In doing so, Gu formalized the transient nature of urban life in a fascinating contemplation of urban spatiality. The binary of "host and guest" also evoked the rising social tensions around migrants owing to an outdated migration control policy. Drawing on this concept, Gu's treatise reinvented the long-established *fengsu* discourse into a formal analysis of urban spatiality. Whereas in the countryside it was the nature of land that determined the lifestyles of peasants, in cities it was the combination of varying economic and political resources brought by hosts and guests that accounted for the unique culture and behavior found in different parts of the city. Just as Nanjing was administratively divided into five boroughs, Gu also divided Nanjing into five districts based on his host-guest scheme. In doing so, Gu transformed the administrative geography into one marked by social practices and interactions, a formulation that clearly distinguishes cities from the rural area.

This urban-rural division was not institutionally imposed but grounded in the daily experiences of urban life marked by the influx of political, economic, and cultural resources. This particular interpretation of urban space is reminiscent of the illustrations of *Jinling tuyong*, in which urban space is defined and differentiated by urban sociability. Ultimately, with no institutional basis, urban space in Ming China was marked not by formal legal autonomy but by the inflowing population and new social activities. At the same time, although cities did not enjoy independent political status, emerging urban reality still posed substantial challenges to the official prescriptions for cities. As demonstrated in the first half of the book, the institutional boundary of urban space, whether marked by a new city tax or city walls, had become the subject of political negotiation and lobbying. Social contention over the idea of the city was not exclusive to the city of Nanjing. Rather, it arose in response to a host of urban questions as the Ming empire underwent extensive urbanization, a development analyzed in the Conclusion.

Toward a New Perspective on
Late Imperial Urbanization

URBANIZATION IN THE MING EMPIRE

Through the lens of Nanjing, this book has embarked on a journey in search of the meaning and consequences of urbanization in the Ming empire. The Introduction begins with a close examination of the discrepancies between the multifaceted spatial developments of late Ming Nanjing and the current narratives of late Ming prosperity. This analysis brings into focus the need to further distinguish the effects of urbanization from those of commercialization when studying late imperial China. That is, although the mid-Ming commercial boom was closely related to the simultaneous expansion of urban sectors, it should not be conflated with urbanization. Studying urbanization on its own terms, the Introduction further argues, requires a more concentrated focus on space as an analytical category, an examination of how the very constitution of urban space changed in response to urbanization. Here the idea of "urban space" is more broadly construed—not the physical construction of streets and walls but how such space is defined and functions in economic, political, and cultural orders. As G. William Skinner's inspiring model demonstrates, urbanization not only increases the number of cities or the scale of urban population but also expands and reshapes the spatial configuration of the city system in late imperial China. This approach, above all, allows us to consider space not as passive historical background but as part of an ongoing historical process. How, then, this book asks, did urbanization affect the ways in which urban space was institutionally regulated and culturally rendered? Divided into two pairs, the four Nanjing case studies serve as useful departure points for addressing these questions.

Negotiating Urban Space Through Political Action

Chapters 1 and 2 examine a corvée reform and a city wall protest that challenged the institutional prescriptions of urban space: how urban space was to be taxed and how its boundary was to be marked. Both cases feature aggressive local initiatives and a high level of social mobilization: town hall meetings were convened to poll public opinion; pamphlets and tracts were produced to shape local consensus. Although both sets of collective actions exemplified the agency and solidarity of local communities, the agendas of both events—to reinvent a taxable city and to contest the walled urban boundary—were in fact driven by deeper structural causes.

In contrast to the well-defined urban administration in the preceding Song or Yuan dynasties, cities occupied a much more ambiguous place in the Ming system, which was constructed around the Hongwu ideal of self-supervising village communities. Not only was urban space not governed separately from the countryside, but the meticulously crafted urban tax scheme was replaced with ad-hoc labor conscription. Although comparable ambiguity can be found in the Ming court's policy toward commerce, historians believe that the "benevolent neglect" of commerce may in fact have inadvertently bolstered an unprecedented level of economic growth.[1] Similar inattention to cities, however, led to a more problematic situation. Beginning in the middle of the fifteenth century, persistent fiscal reform efforts began to convert labor service obligations into regular tax payments based on rural landownership. This move threw into sharp relief the implicit urban-rural divide embedded in the early Ming tax scheme, raising questions such as: How were taxes on urban residents levied when farmland could not be used as the basis for taxation? How did the government assess the more fluid wealth possessed by urban residents, and how did it acquire information from always reluctant taxpayers? Curiously, despite its enthusiastic endorsement of the Single Whip reform, the court never formally addressed issues of urban taxation but instead left them to be dealt with locally. As a result, the ingrained rural bias of the Ming regime ironically brought urban residents together to negotiate a reform on their own terms. In their efforts to transplant the fiscal reform to urban settings, many cities eventually resorted to imposing urban property taxes on city dwellers as the equivalent of rural landownership, placing urban space under the purview of the imperial state for the first time in the Ming dynasty.

Urbanization not only forced an institutional recognition of the urban-rural distinction in fiscal practice but also significantly affected the management of city systems. Chapter 2 examines another official prescription for urban space that came under attack in the early seventeenth century: city walls. Although city walls had always been an essential element in Chinese urban morphology, the particularly persistent enforcement of wall policy in the Ming dynasty rendered city walls a marker of state power. As unwalled market towns proliferated in the wake of the sixteenth-century commercial boom, city walls came to symbolize the dividing line between the official and the commercial city systems. Nevertheless, what seemed to be a well-defined boundary was in fact a fluid one subject to governmental interference and local contestation: since the Song era the state had been promoting towns into administrative seats (or vice versa, demoting capital cities in decline back to towns) to meet the changing needs of the field administration. The anti-wall protest in one of the Nanjing metropolitan counties, Gaochun, further brought to light the role of local initiatives and lobbying in the making of the walled boundary.

In this context, it is not surprising that, to make their case against wall construction, Gaochun locals argued that their city was better served by remaining a trading town than by being promoted to a county seat. However striking, Gaochun's contention was no mere rhetoric but was deeply grounded in town dwellers' newfound identity in the wake of the rapid growth of market towns during the sixteenth century. Frustrated by the lack of a formal administrative status for market towns, residents began privately publishing gazetteers of "our town" celebrating local traditions and thus challenging the state-imposed definition of urban space. Similar transgressions can also be found in the realm of popular religion such as the worship of *zhen cheng-huang* 鎮城隍 (town gods) in clear violation of state rituals. The expressed tension between towns and cities lent an additional layer of social strife to the issue of wall building. To wall or not to wall, therefore, was not just a conundrum in local construction but a public negotiation between administrative and commercial city systems that had grown increasingly alienated.

Negotiating Urban Space Through Spatial Representation

Although imperial cities were in general not formal administrative units, as urbanization swept through the Ming empire, we find new social needs and demands pressing on the state to adjust existing institutional practices to accommodate the growing presence of urban society. The second half of the book further studies how the emerging urban reality registered in contemporary minds by examining visual and textual representations of Nanjing. Again, the deep political engagement of Nanjing residents seems to have found expression in the representation of Nanjing as a city defined by its people. Together, the two chapters illustrate the imagining and conceiving of Nanjing's space via the daily practices of urbanites: either through the illustrations in *Jinling tuyong*, in which urban space was defined by the activities of locals and visitors, or through Gu Qiyuan's *fengsu* treatise, which mapped out urban neighborhoods through everyday interactions between natives (*zhu*) and sojourners (*ke*). The emphasis on urban sociability in these works also reflected the fact that their own creation was a product of the intensifying social life in cities at the time. Neither work was an isolated production. Rather, they were parts of larger projects: *Jinling tuyong* continued a series of collaborative poems that commemorated the long-lasting fellowship among a group of prominent Nanjing native families; Gu's treatise belonged to a *ketan* collection that recorded conversations between the salon host/author and his guests/visitors. Although their making embodied two primary social bonds among Nanjing elites—family coalitions and literati networks—*tuyong* and *ketan* also drew on larger cultural trends at the time in their unique rendition of Nanjing.

The visual imagination of Nanjing in *Jinling tuyong* exemplified an emerging mode of popular tourist images that conceived of urban space as sites for leisured touring and socializing. It formed a sharp contrast to the city atlases massively produced in local gazetteers that presented an official rendition of urban space as the center of state power and a civilizing influence on backwater hinterlands. This development is closely associated with the practice of cultured sightseeing. In the lofty name of landscape appreciation, the rituals of social tourism provided a culturally prized venue for literati to form and materialize their social ties and allegiance. Major metropolises, with their abundance of worthy inhabitants, were considered the most productive ground for aspiring literati to "see" as well as to "be seen" in. The production of commemorative scenic paintings, poetry, and even illustrated guidebooks such as *Jinling tuyong* was not just a matter of sentimentality; more important, they bore witness to and publicized existing or newly formed social ties.

Having explored the shifting ways of viewing urban space, the book turns in its final chapter to the narration of the city. Published in the format of *ketan*, both texts under survey—*Kezuo zhuiyu* and *Jinling suoshi*—were collections of casual conversations about Nanjing, many of which drew on street news and gossip. The focus on tall tales was typical for the late Ming publishing industry, which was highly news-sensitive, weaving current events and "real stories" into novels or drama performances to cater to an increasingly inquisitive audience. This cultural practice rendered "Nanjing," the city along with its people, a discursive subject shared by an ever-broadening reading public. Amid the numerous ruminations—many of them tedious trivia—over the idea of Nanjing emerged a formal theorization of urban space that translated the daily experiences of urbanites into a sociological map of urban neighborhoods. Similar to *Jinling tuyong*, Gu Qiyuan's *fengsu* treatise also placed the urban spatiality of Nanjing in dialogue with a specific state-mandated vision for the city. Based on a host/guest scheme, Nanjing was divided into five neighborhoods, much like the administrative division of the city into five boroughs. The close interplay between administrative and social geographies allowed Gu to demonstrate that it was the social and economic interactions among city residents, rather than state power wielded by the five borough offices, that dictated the formation of Nanjing's inner boundaries.

The ingenious deployment of a host/guest matrix, this chapter further argues, was a product of its own time, conceived against a generally heightened sensitivity to the floating population. The rising tension between "host" and "guest" was not mere xenophobia; it had institutional roots in Hongwu's population mobility control policy, which aimed to secure his ideal of village communities. Essentially prohibiting internal migration in any form, these regulations made it impossible for the state to register and tax the floating population, a failing that became a major source of tension between the native and the migrant populations. This finding brings the search for the shifting place of cities in the Ming empire full circle: in an ironic twist of history, the Hongwu vision, one that frustrated formal recognition of cities, eventually defined the ways through which urban space was conceived in the late Ming.

The Early Ming Legacy and Eclipsed Urban Issues

Taken together, what emerges from these chapters is that the concept of the city was rediscovered, disputed, and reconceived as the Ming empire underwent the long sixteenth-century urbanization. In many ways, the central subjects of the four chapters bear the signature of Nanjing's particularity: the striking grassroots collaboration appears to have resulted from Ding Bin's ingenious synthesis of contemporary populist reform measures; Gaochun's persistent objection to the city-wall construction was intrinsically related to the shifting political geography of the Nanjing Metropolitan Area. Yet the underlying causes of these political actions were also widely shared across the empire as cities came to figure prominently on the Ming landscape: How to incorporate cities into the new taxation scheme? How to balance the official and commercial city systems? By the same token, although not every late Ming city produced its own version of *Jinling tuyong* or *ketan*, many did draw on the same cultural practices (social tourism) and vocabularies (*zhu* vs. *ke*) to communicate the changing nature of urban space.

These findings further bring to the fore the importance of the early Ming legacy, since the impetus for these developments appears to have resided in a host of institutional and cultural premises that took shape at the beginning of the Ming dynasty. The enduring early Ming influences expose an unlikely connection between two phases of the Ming dynasty generally perceived as disjunctive, if not opposing extremes, separated by the mid-dynastic boom. Among them, the Hongwu ideal of self-supervising, immobile rural communities appears to be of most

<u>importance</u>. Under this rural-centered vision, cities were conservatively defined as administrative sites instead of expansive commercial grounds that could be actively exploited by the state. This stance not only later became the source of a host of urban questions of central concern to this book, but it also significantly marginalized such urban issues, leading to disparate and uncoordinated official responses to the tides of urbanization.

The rural bias and its urban consequences in the Ming system are most apparent in the prolonged fiscal reform spanning two-thirds of the dynasty's existence. As the growing market economy gradually encroached on the solidarity of rural communities, village-level self-management began to fray and soon became the source of systematic fiscal oppression and impoverishment of the rural middle class. After battling to sustain the collapsing rural communities for over a century, the Ming state finally abandoned its original social vision and succumbed to a realistic course of action that gradually made landownership the sole basis for state revenue. The resultant Single Whip reform also enabled the government to reduce its dependence on the gradually diminishing owner-cultivator stratum in rural society as primary collectors and transporters of tax revenues. Although this move did substantially curb corvée abuses in the countryside, its effects in cities, as demonstrated in this book, were far more ambivalent. Even for its target beneficiaries—rural residents—the result was regrettable; it allowed the state to withdraw its commitment from the village to the county level. The retreat of state power created a vacuum at the grassroots level and prompted a series of late Ming activist movements such as *xiangyue* (village compacts), *baojia* (mutual security system), and campaigns to restore village schools and public granaries, all aiming to revive the earlier ideal of rural communities through local volunteerism.[2] However, similar to the state-sanctioned fiscal reforms, private initiatives also centered their efforts on salvaging the destitute rural society. Thus, at a time of extensive urban development, curiously little attention was paid to the construction and expansion of urban infrastructure as well as the need for a new ethos to cope with the increasingly complicated urban society. The rural-centered bias of the early Ming system, in a sense, dictated the efforts that aimed to repair it.

The same predisposition can also be seen at the discursive level. As the rise of a long-distance domestic trade in daily staples such as rice and cotton necessitated the extensive participation of average peasants in an active market economy, cities came to penetrate deeply into rural life. Economically, the operation and expansion of these commercial networks became heavily dependent on the growing number of towns and cities serving as exchange nodes; socially, the resultant exodus of landed elites from villages to cities deprived villages of much-needed capital investments and further alienated peasants in the countryside. Although in reality the disappearance of self-sustaining villages and the expansion of the urban sector were intrinsically related, the "urban factor" was conspicuously missing from contemporary discourses. Late Ming commentators recognized that the disintegration of rural communities not only threatened the survival of the empire but also provoked a deep moral crisis. Yet for them, the archenemy of the early Ming rural ideal was "the lord of silver and god of copper cash,"[3] not the rise of urban society— that is, the clash was primarily construed as one between prescribed ritual propriety and extravagant commercial consumption. As late Ming officials and activists preoccupied themselves with the looming rural crisis, the issue of cities simply slipped from view.

The persistent rural bias to a great extent obscured the multifaceted ramifications of late Ming urbanization for contemporaries and, in turn, modern scholars. Nevertheless, the inattention to cities should be considered less a product of indifference than a matter of priority. That is, the preponderant focus on reconstructing rural society relegated urban issues to a secondary concern for policymakers and public forums. As a result, discussions and reactions regarding urban issues tended to be presented in an indirect and fragmented manner. The understated nature of urban issues in the Ming era, consequently, makes it imperative for us to trace this previously obscured aspect of history through specific cases. The choice of Nanjing as a central case study is based not only on the abundant materials available during this time period but also on its special place in the Ming empire. Serving as the primary capital, Nanjing was extensively rebuilt to embody the imperial vision of the peasant empire-builder Zhu Yuanzhang. Yet because of the move of the capital in 1421 to Beijing, Nanjing gradually transformed from a political capital into a commercial metropolis during the second half of the Ming dynasty. The drastic shift in Nanjing's urban character rendered the reconfiguration of urban space—be it at the institutional or conceptual level—more acutely felt and expressively articulated.

Indeed, the close attention to Nanjing as well as the constant comparison of Nanjing to other cities throughout the four chapters has proved rewarding. Taken together, they point to an important fact that, local variations aside, the overall trajectory of changes in response to urbanization was not aimed at setting up separate urban administrations or cultural traditions; rather, the intent was to innovate and modify existing institutional and cultural practices. This insight explains why historians have consistently failed to uncover novel developments in late imperial cities such as political autonomy or city-specific cultural expression. More important, as discussed in the following section, this finding also brings to light a particular set of parameters for us to measure the terms and nature of late imperial urbanism, one rooted in the dynastic history of China rather than the historical experiences of western Europe.

NEGOTIATING THE BOUNDARIES OF LATE IMPERIAL CHINESE URBANISM

As demonstrated in the Introduction, the problems of the Weberian paradigm lie not only in its Eurocentrism but also in the reified concept of "the city" it imposes on China, where the boundaries of the "urban" were in constant flux and open to negotiation. Moving beyond the shadow of the Weberian ideal city requires us to further historicize the definition of "city" in China and examine how such economic entities were registered in political and cultural realms. In view of the reticence of contemporary officials and literati on urban issues, we have to resort to less obvious sources such as the varied institutional and cultural practices that fundamentally shaped the infrastructure and experiences of everyday life for the urbanites. The central inquiry of this book—how urbanization affected the very constitution of cities in institutional and cultural terms—has given rise to such an analytical framework. As shown below, it allows for an understanding of Chinese urbanism that is properly attuned to the predominantly rural nature of Chinese empires as well as their unique conceptions of power and space. Altogether, the analysis culminates in a conclusion that highlights the dynastic influence on *longue durée* market-driven urbanization.

Institutional Practices: The Administration and Management of Urban Space

The first half of this book focuses on two institutional definitions of urban space at work during the Ming era: how cities should be taxed, and how urban settlements were made into official cities. Since the social ramifications for local society of these institutional practices varied widely, this analytical framework effectively prevents us from viewing the administration of urban space as a tug-of-war between state and society. For example, whereas Nanjing embraced the implementation of urban taxes with great enthusiasm, such taxes could also be viewed as unnecessary exactions in cities where most wealth was invested in land (see Chapter 1). Even within more commercialized areas such as Hangzhou, the same tax proposal initiated an enormous controversy and eventually led to a violent riot. By the same token, locals responded to the management of city systems in diverse ways. The residents of Gaochun harbored deep resentments about the promotion of their town into an administrative seat, but the residents of Wuqing 烏青, a market town in Zhejiang, petitioned numerous times asking to be made into a county seat.

Furthermore, by highlighting the diversity in local receptions of specific policies, this approach allows us to unpack the idea of a homogeneous state and, in its stead, substitute different agencies staffed with bureaucrats holding wide-ranging policy positions and of varied levels of competency. For instance, despite officially proclaiming the Single Whip reform or city-wall construction to be empire-wide policy, the Ming state left specific courses of action to the discretion of local officials, who theoretically consulted constantly with the locals. What eventually materialized at the local level, as the first two chapters show, was a mix of varied interpretations of the general policy. First, not every official deemed the implementation of urban taxes essential to fiscal justice. In many cases, including Nanjing, the initiative for taxation came from locals. The conversion of market towns to seats of local government was more disorganized, given the lack of apparent standards or guidelines for such adjustments. Some officials were attentive to such issues and took pains to ensure that the adjustment met the needs of local residents,[4] but there were also cases such as Gaochun, in which the decision to promote it to a county seat was apparently made by bureaucrats out of touch with local reality.

The disparate policy positions within state agencies bring to light the open-ended nature of imperial governance. The implication of this finding is profound: since implementation of these loosely prescribed institutional practices required collaboration from locals, this opened a space for political negotiation subject to local initiative and interests. The political activism seen in the late Ming fiscal reform is a case in point. In lieu of centrally stipulated local applications of the Single Whip method, officials instead sought local consensus and popular participation to justify and facilitate the implementation of the reform. Contrary to conventional wisdom, the resultant local activism was not shaped by antagonism between state and society. Instead, it was driven by the need for state agents and local residents to collaborate to reach shared goals. In this sense, despite the apparent similarity to the practices of modern democracy, the aggressive polling of public opinion and public hearings during the late Ming reform in fact arose from a very different matrix of power dynamics.

This insight allows us to revisit the thorny issue of autonomy in China, where the state and society were so intertwined that it is nearly impossible to distinguish a clear-cut autonomous public sphere. For example, the proliferation of market towns in late imperial China has drawn great attention from historians for their autonomous place outside the official urban administration. However, these towns frequently petitioned for, not against, a state presence in their towns. In some cases locals even sought to attain official approval of their de facto self-governance. However, if we do not privilege the idea of political autonomy and its core emphasis on formal independence from state power, we find that, in the intertwined world of state and society in China, what stand out are the enormous flexibility and political advantages to be gained *within* the system, not outside it. This flexibility was not necessarily forced through manipulation and contestation; rather, it was a built-in mechanism essential to governing a vast and diverse country such as China.

Cultural Practices: The Imagination and
Conceptualization of Urban Space

Late Ming urbanization not only prompted institutional adjustments but also led to new ways of viewing and comprehending
urban space. As discussed in the Introduction, although the emerging
urban culture did not give rise to distinct architectural styles or urban
aesthetics challenging the perpetual rural ideal, the lack of a well-
defined urban theme in literary and art traditions should not be mistaken as a sign of cultural inertia toward cities. On the contrary, as
shown in the second half of the book, the late Ming witnessed a new
perception and conceptualization of urban space that captured the vitality of urban life at the time. Instead of creating separate urban genres
and motifs, however, these conceptual innovations were folded into existing cultural practices in service of specific functions in contemporary
society. This unique feature allowed urban sentiments to be expressed
through many readymade media. More important, it transformed the
cultural formulation of urban space from an abstract intellectual exercise into an active force shaping and critiquing the operation of urban
society.

For example, the appreciation of scenic sites was a time-honored
literati pursuit, but the urbanization of the gentry class and the resultant
intensification of social life in cities transformed this established practice into a venue for celebrating social ties among urban elites. Just as
the publication of *Jinling tuyong* paid tribute to the enduring friendship
of several prominent native Nanjing families, the production of poetry
or artwork depicting scenic sites in other cities such as Suzhou or
Yangzhou also embodied social alliances. The changing character of
urban sightseeing was clearly reflected in the rendition of urban space.
As the curating of scenic sites became embrocated with the making of
the literati community, the visualization of urban space was expanded
from a display of state authority to one animated by social interaction
and daily experience.

Indeed, late Ming elites recognized that urbanity and spatial differentiation were marked less by physical appearance than by social practice:
Chapter 4 offers a close examination of a *fengsu* treatise that conceptual-

izes urban-rural and intra-urban differences according to the behaviors and attitudes of inhabitants. The treatise was a clever reinvention of ancient *fengsu* discourse, which had evolved into a favored forum for social criticism in the late Ming. Seeking to establish links between the natural environment and locals, who, within this metaphor, grew on it, this discursive format posed an interesting question of space: In cities, where it was not the land that fed and nourished its people, what were the mediating forces between space and its inhabitants? Gu Qiyuan, a native Nanjing luminary, proposed that the equivalents were *renwen* (social forces) and *wuli* (material forces), themselves products of the interaction between natives (*zhu*, hosts) and sojourners (*ke*, guests). The employment of a host/guest binary not only exhibited remarkable analytical force but also invoked the widely felt hostility between natives and outsiders in newly developed internal frontiers or in urban environments, where the influx of sojourners and immigrants, along with the political, economic, and cultural capital they brought, transformed the realities of everyday life. The currency of this analogy lent additional poignancy to Gu Qiyuan's penetrating comments on social relations within the city of Nanjing.

Viewed from this perspective, the rarity of new cultural trends specifically labeled "urban" in late imperial China is indeed deceiving. The absence of an explicitly marked urban ideology does not by default imply the dominance of rural culture, since the expression of urban sensibilities was conducted by renegotiating existing genres or discourses rather than carving out a separate cultural territory. This finding not only helps us better appreciate elite cultural products such as *Jinling tuyong* or *Kezuo zhuiyu* but also sheds new light on other forms of cultural practice, such as folk religions, an important source of cultural influence that falls outside this book's scope. Although there does not appear to be an articulated urban/rural distinction in folk beliefs and customs, this by no means suggests that they were insulated from the impact of urbanization. The intriguing story of the Zongguan cult 總管 uncovered by Hamashima Atsutoshi is a telling example in which changes in the legends associated with a local deity reflected shifts in rural-urban relations in the late Ming. A popular folk deity originating in the late Yuan and early Ming, Zongguan served as the protector for the grain-tax transportation, a corvée duty assumed by rural landlords. However, with the urbanization of the sixteenth century came the growth of absentee urban landlords. The migration of landlords along with their social and financial resources substantially disrupted the coherence of rural communities as well as the integrity of agricultural production. As the rural economy deteriorated, peasants ceased to be self-sufficient and had to supplement their livelihood by exchanging handicrafts for rice in local markets. Thus the price and availability of rice became crucial to the survival of peasants. Around this time the tales associated with Zongguan shifted from protection of tribute rice transportation to the succor of the rice-hungry peasants. In his new form, Zongguan, no longer a protector of landlords, was a low-ranking officer so anguished by the peasants' plight that he violated his orders and released tax rice to them. To take responsibility for his action, Zongguan committed suicide and became a patron deity of the newly impoverished small peasants in the countryside.[5] This finding again confirms the view that the cultural response to urbanization might involve a reinterpretation of existing cultural practices and that only by focusing on this process can we fully grasp the perception of rural-urban distinctions in China on their own terms.

The Continuity and Discontinuity of Dynastic Urbanism

Finally, as we move beyond the Occidental-Oriental dichotomy, the importance of dynastic traditions in dictating the terms of Chinese urbanism becomes increasingly apparent. As we have seen, the institutional and cultural practices that arose in response to late Ming urbanization invariably bear a distinct dynastic signature. The story traced throughout this book, in a sense, is one of how late Ming society outgrew the early Ming vision of an empire of villages in which cities were primarily administrative sites marked by city walls symbolizing the imperial presence. The collapse of the outdated fiscal scheme and migration policy in turn prompted a renewed appreciation of cities, both institutionally and culturally. This finding restores the importance of dynastic frameworks, which have grown increasingly obsolete since the primary focus of the China field shifted from court politics to the cultural and social changes brought by commercial forces, the scope of which inevitably spans dynastic boundaries. When examined from this perspective, the dynastic disjunction, especially with regard to the administration of urban space, is indeed striking. Within the last millennium of imperial China, which spanned four dynasties, Song (960–1279), Mongol-Yuan (1271–1368), Ming (1368–1644), and Qing (1644–1912), urban governance was subjected to a series of different visions. The Song regime, arising in a time "when China was among equals," constantly faced great fiscal pressures either to maintain its military force or to pay off the invading nomadic neighbors; in response, it developed an aggressive form of state economic activism. Its exploitive exactions of urban space range from a sophisticated scheme for levying taxes on urban real estate to the expansion of urban taxation from administrative centers to market towns. The fiscal reliance on cities may have contributed to the court's neglect of wall construction since the walls would have obstructed the commercial flows and undermined state revenue. During the Song, the state demanded the morphological signature of Chinese urban space—city walls—only in areas needing military protection.[6]

The preoccupation with the fiscal capacity of cities changed in the following conquest dynasty, the Mongol-Yuan empire, which considered cities the bases for colonial rule. To further extend its control into the countryside, the Yuan ordered that city walls—especially in the territory of the old Southern Song—be torn down, and it set up separate administrative agencies in major cities; this was the only time in Chinese history when cities were governed separately from the countryside. The Yuan's unique institution of municipal governance, the Lushi si, was first developed by the northern dynasties and was perhaps an administrative tradition passed down to the succeeding nomadic regimes, including the Yuan. The centrality of cities in imperial governance was revoked in the Ming, since the founding emperor envisioned his territory as first and foremost an empire of villages. Created around an ideal rural empire, the early Ming system proved incapable of sustaining itself during the mid-dynastic commercial boom. In the stream of ensuing fiscal reforms, cities gained a new salience and were gradually reincorporated into the tax system to satisfy the pressing demand for fiscal justice.

Although for the most part the institutional framework created by the Single Whip reform was continued by the subsequent and also the last dynasty, the Qing, this conquest regime held a very different view of cities. Unlike the Mongols, who used cities as sites of exaction, the Manchu rulers treated cities as sites of ethnic segregation and coexistence. The administration of urban space was thus further complicated by ethnic divisions and the enclosure of land for the Banner garrisons. Given the new vision, it is not surprising that urban taxation was discontinued, regardless of the changes initiated by late Ming urban residents.[7] This "Manchu apartheid" in major cities gradually fell apart over the course of the eighteenth century, as China confronted an unprecedented challenge from the sea.[8]

This line of investigation illuminates not only the disjuncture among different visions of the role cities played in a vast agrarian empire but also the internal dialectic among them. For example, the unique vision of Zhu Yuanzhang is widely considered a native reaction reclaiming the Han Chinese world order from the alien rule of the Mongol-Yuan empire. Similarly, the practice of social tourism and the resultant proliferation of scenic sites in the late Ming weighed heavily on the following regime. The Manchus realized that although they controlled the physical land, the cultural landscape had been deeply woven into the fabric of local society. As the physical territory was unified, the highly localized representational landscape compelled the court to embark on another cultural enterprise: by the eighteenth century, Manchu emperors were making tours of their realm and producing illustrated guides listing the places they visited, imposing an imperial gaze on the highly particularized local landscape via the emperor's footsteps. They were also producing a physical presence through inscriptions on steles, name boards for temples and schools with their calligraphy, and local palaces, which in turn became local sights.

The host-guest dynamic in cities central to Gu Qiyuan's conception of urban spatiality also exhibited significant fluctuation from dynasty to dynasty. Guided by its economic activism, the Song required only one year of residence before granting local registration to sojourners.[9] Population mobility was further enhanced during the Mongol rule when trade routes across the Eurasian continent became much more accessible. After the fall of the Yuan, the return to a native ideal empire led to a rigorous migration control policy with only minimum mobility allowed. The limit on physical mobility became an encumbrance to the fiscal system, leading to escalating conflicts between the native and the migrant populations. Toward the end of the Ming dynasty, the court relaxed the limits on migration. The Qing continued this lenient policy. In the meantime, the guest-host interaction in cities was gradually institutionalized through guildhalls for merchants and literati.[10] With their enthusiastic participation in urban welfare measures, long-term guests became increasingly integrated into urban society, as William Rowe's research on Hankou has established.

Having begun with Nanjing, this book concludes with some reflections on urbanism and urbanization. Urbanization not only created more and larger cities on the Chinese landscape but also prompted both the state and the society to reconsider and reformulate the place of the city in a centralized rural empire. This finding not only brings to light the previously overlooked spatial dimension of late Ming development but also complements and nuances the *longue durée* view of late imperial Chinese urbanization. The medieval urban revolution marked the beginning of market-driven urbanization in China, which spanned the four dynasties of late imperial China. All these regimes confronted the challenges and opportunities arising from an urbanizing rural empire. In the case of the Ming, the impetus of change lay in the inherent tension between the institutionalized rural ideal and economic development, which eventually necessitated adjustments in the administration and conceptualization of the expanding urban realm. However, it is clear that the Ming example represents merely one such scenario. Throughout the last millennium, each reigning dynasty had a distinct vision of the place of the city in the imperial structure, which in turn conditioned its social and cultural response to urbanization. Yet, despite the diversity, there also appears to be a distinct inter-dynastic dialogue over the terms of urbanism throughout the last millennium, a fascinating phenomenon that will require more research to trace its particular trajectory and internal dynamics. This book's approach readily lends itself to comparative studies between China and other premodern rural regimes with regard to their encounters with urbanization, a topic that has attracted less attention than it deserves. Urbanization plays such a central role in our lives that its modern characteristics may have inadvertently eclipsed our view of its premodern, precapitalist past. In this sense, this book serves as an invitation for more studies on the meaning and consequences of urbanization in preindustrial, agrarian environments such as China as well as other parts of the world.

Appendix

Gu Qiyuan's Fengsu *Treatise*

南都一城之內民生，其間風尚頓異。自大中橋而東歷正陽朝陽
二門，迤北至太平門復折而南，至玄津百川二橋，大內百司庶
府之所蟠互也。其人文客豐而主嗇。達官健吏，日夜馳騖於其
間，廣參其氣，故其小人多尷尬而傲僻。

People's lifestyles, especially their customs and fashions, differ greatly
in the Southern Metropolis. The area from Dazhong Bridge to Zheng-
yang Gate and Chaoyang Gate, then north to Taiping Gate and then
back south to Xuanjin Bridge and Baichuan Bridge is where all the imperial institutions are scattered. Therefore, *renwen* [social relations, embodied as political power] is rich among the guests and poor among the
hosts. With high officials and their powerful clerks running around day
and night exerting their dynamic influence, the humble folk in this area
look awkward, peculiar, and churlish.

自大中橋而西，緣淮清橋達於三山街斗門橋以西，至三山門又
北，自倉巷至冶城轉而東至內橋中正街而止，京兆赤縣之所彈
壓也，百貨聚焉，其物力客多而主少；市魁駔儈千百嘈喋其
中，故其小人多攪攘而浮競。

The area starting west of the Dazhong Bridge up to Huaiqing Bridge
and Sanshan Street and west of Doumen Bridge, and then north from
Sanshan Gate to Cang Avenue and Yecheng and turning east to Nei
Bridge till Zhongzheng Street is where the prefecture and county governments are located and all the merchandise is gathered. The guests
possess more *wuli* [material forces, embodied as financial power], and
the hosts, less. Every day this area is crowded with thousands of noisy
market clerks and brokers. Therefore the humble folk in the area are
unsettled, superficial, and competitive.

自東水關西達武定橋轉南門而西至飲虹、上浮二橋，復東折而
江寧縣至三坊巷、貢院，世胄官族之所都居也，而人文之在主
者多，其物力之在外者侈，遊士豪客，競千金裘馬之風，而六
院之油檀裙屐浸淫染於閭閻，膏脣耀首，仿而傚之。至武定橋
之東西，嘻甚矣，故其小人多嬉靡而淫惰。

The area with boundaries starting at Dongshui Customs House, going
west to Wuding Bridge, turning to South Gate, and west to Yinhong
Bridge and Shangfu Bridge, and then east into Jiangning county to the
Sanfang Avenue and the Examination Hall is where all the high officials
and aristocratic families reside. The *renwen* here [embodied as the social
status of the residents] favors the hosts. The *wuli* [embodied as consumption patterns] tends to be showy and extravagant. All the sojourning literati and wealthy guests compete with one another in the styles of
spending. Furthermore, deeply saturated in the allure of the entertainment quarters, the common people are strongly affected, with their
women imitating courtesans' dress all the time. This situation goes to its
extreme in the east and west Wuding bridge area. As a result, the humble
folk here tend to indulge themselves in entertainments and become idle.

由笪橋而北，自冶城轉北門橋鼓樓以東，包成賢街而南，至西
華門而止，是武弁中涓之所群萃，太學生之徒所州處也。其人
文主客頗相捋而物力嗇，可以娛樂耳目羶慕之者，必徒而圖
南，非是，則株守而處，故其小人多拘狃而劬瘠。

The area starting north of Da Bridge to Yecheng and turning to the
east of the North Gate Bridge and the Drum Tower, up to the south of
Chengxian Street and Xihua Gate is where the army and imperial university students congregate. The *renwen* here [embodied in social com-
position] is equal between the guests and hosts, but the overall wealth is
negligible. Since anyone looking for pleasure and sensational indulgence would have moved south, the remaining ones are withdrawn and
destitute.

北出鼓樓達三牌樓、絡金川、儀鳳、定淮三門而南，至石城，
其地多曠土，而人文主與客並少，物力之在外者嗇，民什三而
軍什七，服食之供，糲與疏者倍蓰於梁肉紈綺，言貌僕僿，南
人常舉以相啁哳，故其小人多悴欷瑟而蹇陋。

The area north of the Drum Tower and the Sanpai Tower, passing the
three gates of Jinchuan, Yifeng, and Dinghuai, and south to the Stone
City is mostly open space. The *renwen* here [embodied as population] is
scarce among both guests and hosts. The *wuli* [embodied as consump-
tion] is very conservative. The social composition is roughly three-
tenths commoners and seven-tenths army. Their poor diet and clothing
consist primarily of coarse foods and unrefined cloth rather than feasting delicacies and lavish silks. As a result, the humble folk here appear
depressed and destitute and are often ridiculed by the wealthy residents
of southern Nanjing.

Reference Matter

Notes

For complete bibliographic data on works cited here by short forms, see the Works Cited, pp. 319–50.

INTRODUCTION

1. See Hsu Hong, "Mingchu Nanjing huangcheng"; and idem, "Mingchu Nanjing de dushi guihua."

2. State housing such as *tafang* 塌房 was created to provide dwellings for the forcibly moved population and officials at the beginning of the Ming; see Fuma Susumu, "Mindai Nankin no toshi gyōsei."

3. Indeed, as von Glahn (*Fountain of Fortune*, 2–3) observes, in the field of late imperial Chinese history, "Few studies of intellectuals, the arts, literature, and popular culture in this period fail to include a prefatory invocation of the social consequences of the growth of the market economy."

4. For a thorough analysis of the cultural changes stimulated by the flourishing of commerce in the late Ming, see Brook, *Confusions of Pleasure.*

5. Spence, "Energies of Ming Life."

6. Ko, *Teachers of the Inner Chambers*, 31.

7. Critiques of corrupt social customs appear to have been an empire-wide discourse, and their prevalence has been established by comprehensive surveys of late Ming gazetteers; see, e.g., Hsu Hong's "Mingmo shehui fengqi" and "Mingdai houqi huabei shangpin jingji." Studies of late Ming social customs have become a major enterprise in the past two decades.

8. See Mori Masao's "Minmatsu no shakai kankei" and "Minmatsu ni okeru chitsujo." In these articles, Mori compares discourse on social customs in the Song, Ming, and Qing dynasties and argues that late Ming discourse exhibited a much deeper sense of anxiety over social disorder and cultural crisis than that of the Song or the Qing.

9. Elvin, "'Female Virtue.'"

10. See Clunas, *Superfluous Things.*

11. Wang Ji, "Shu Taiping Jiulong huiji" 書太平九龍會籍 (On the membership of the Jiulong Association in Taiping), in idem, *Longxi Wang xiansheng*

quanji, 7.37a–38b; Wang Gen, "Yulu," 語錄 (Recorded dialogues), in idem, *Wang Xinzhai xiansheng quanji*, 3.9a.

12. Qian Daxin, "Zazhu yi: zheng su" 雜著一正俗 (Miscellaneous writings no. 1, rectifying customs), in idem, *Qianyantang wenji*, 17.282.

13. See the review essay by Zurndorfer, "Old and New Visions."

14. The study of the "sprouts of capitalism," pioneered by Fu Yiling (see, e.g., *Mingdai Jiangnan*), dates the indigenous Chinese commercial revolution to the sixteenth century. For a review of this approach, see Feuerwerker, "From 'Feudalism' to 'Capitalism.'"

15. For the strongest argument of an early date for Chinese modernity, see Rowe's preface to *Hankow: Commerce and Society* and his "Approaches to Modern Chinese Social History."

16. Luo Xiaoxiang's dissertation on late Ming Nanjing (*From Imperial City to Cosmopolitan Metropolis*) also points out the importance of noncommercial factors in urban development. Nanjing's capital status, she agues, did not stifle its thriving urban society; on the contrary, the presence of central government and trans-regional elites served to sever ties to local interests and elevated Nanjing to a truly cosmopolitan city. In particular, compared to other provincial cities or market towns, Nanjing exhibited more openness to incorporating new political or social trends into urban life (230). Luo's view certainly complicates and complements the silver-driven narrative of late imperial urbanization. However, the lively political and cultural life in late Ming Nanjing was not just a product of the city's special status in the administrative hierarchy and the Jiangnan regional network. As shown in this book, dynamic events such as the *huojia* reform (Luo, chap. 1) were in fact driven by a set of urban questions facing many late Ming cities.

17. The author thanks one of the anonymous reviewers of the book manuscript for the Harvard University Asia Center publications program for making this point.

18. To be sure, many excellent urban biographies focus on a particular city in a specific dynasty. Yet, few works have actively explored the connection between urbanization and infrastructure in different dynasties. Nevertheless, recently more studies have begun paying attention to the close connection between dynastic politics and urban development. For example, Susan Naquin, in her preface to *Peking: Temples and City Life*, suggests that city life in the Ming and Qing dynasties might have exhibited more differences than the continuity thesis allows. Michael Marmé (*Suzhou*) also pays close attention to the influences of Ming policies on the urban development of Suzhou. Following this trend, this book intends to take this trend a step further, using Nanjing as a

central case to explore the particular form and nature of urbanization in the Ming dynasty.

19. The comparison between forms of urban taxation is further addressed in Chapter 1.

20. The influence of Weber's analysis of Chinese cities, published in the early twentieth century, was still strong among urban historians until the 1980s. Despite the size, economic centrality, and social complexity of traditional Chinese cities, as William Rowe (*Hankow: Commerce and Society*, 1) poignantly commented, "an influential school of Western historiography came to identify the inadequate development of urban institutions as the principal cause of China's 'backwardness.' According to this view, urban places in China had failed to perform the catalytic function necessary to bring about the sorts of social, economic, and political changes that had transformed the West since the medieval times and provided the basis of its superior material civilization in the nineteenth and early twentieth centuries."

21. Driven to determine the position of Chinese cities in relation to European ideal types, China historians have investigated topics ranging from market networks, merchant guilds, and native-place associations to autonomous non-state institutions and civil society, in order to underscore the similarities and dissimilarities between Chinese and European cities and to position Chinese cities within a global spectrum of urban forms. The influence of the Weberian thesis is further amplified by the fact that Weber's emphasis on an autonomous urban community vis-à-vis an omnipotent state resonates strongly with the field of Chinese history in general. In studies ranging from arguments for oriental hydraulic despotism to the theory of capitalist sprouts, sinologists from different intellectual traditions invariably view the imperial state as a detrimental force inhibiting the development of social autonomy as well as economic development. See Wittfogel, *Oriental Despotism*; Feuerwerker, "From 'Feudalism' to 'Capitalism'"; Brook, ed., *Asiatic Mode of Production*; and Kamachi, "Feudalism or Absolute Monarchism."

22. A comparable trajectory of historiography can also be found in the field of Chinese religion and early thought, where efforts to refute Weber also inadvertently perpetuate the central Weberian premises; see Puett, "Introduction," in *To Become a God*. The author thanks one of the anonymous reviewers of this manuscript for this reference.

23. Emphasizing the primacy of economic (instead of administrative) functions of Chinese cities, Skinner's model constitutes the most critical watershed in the development of Chinese urban history. This model reconceives the spatial constitution of traditional China by employing a highly quantitative central-place model. Skinner begins with marketplaces where peasants regularly

conducted minimal trading activities. He then proceeds to construct a hierarchy of marketing centers, each with hexagonal-shaped commercial hinterlands. Villages clustered around a standard market, several standard markets clustered around an intermediate market, which was further clustered with other intermediate markets around a central market. Moving up the scale of marketing centrality, one observes a higher level of integration and concentration of regional resources and population. By introducing a continuum of gradually increasing spatial centrality, Skinner replaces the oversimplified assumption of an urban-rural gap that had previously prevailed in studies of Chinese peasants. That is, by breaking China into eight geographically defined macro-regions, Skinner's spatial analysis disposes of the oversimplified notion that, on one hand, portrayed villages as isolated and self-contained entities, while, on the other hand, further characterized the rural-urban continuum as an inherently connected trading network. This paradigm not only inspired research on regional urbanization but also informed studies of individual cities. The thesis is articulated in Skinner's chapter in a book he edited, *The City in Late Imperial China*. Nevertheless, a model of this vast temporal and spatial coverage inevitably requires more empirical confirmation and modification. With the publication of an increasing number of studies using Skinner's paradigm, there seems to have emerged a consensus regarding the limits of economic geography in shaping urban space in China. Take, for example, Wang Qincheng's study on northern Chinese market networks, "Wan Qing Huabei." Having garnered data from numerous local gazetteers, Wang not only concludes that many market networks do not comply with the optimal hexagonal model, the core of Skinner's thesis, but also that the number of local markets is not proportional to population or level of commercialization. These findings lead the author to suggest that there might be other forces at work in shaping the geographical distribution of urban hierarchies. Along similar lines, William Rowe, in synthesizing the findings of a volume edited by Linda Cooke Johnson, *Cities of Jiangnan in Late Imperial China* (see esp. 1–16), finds that the evidence indicates that it is not just the market economy but also political power that ultimately determines the fate of a city, even for a predominately commercial entrepôt such as Yangzhou. Contrary to Skinner's prediction, these new case studies invariably find that regional primacy is based on a wide mix of factors in addition to the economic one. In the absence of more comprehensive surveys, no definitive conclusion can be made at this point about the role of commercialization in the fate of cities, but these new works do point to a more inclusive view of the dynamics of late imperial Chinese urbanization. For a comprehensive review of the Skinner paradigm, see Carolyn Cartier, "Origins and Evolution of a Geographical Idea."

24. In a provocative essay entitled "What Weber Did Not Know: Towns and Economic Development in Ming and Qing China," David Faure rightly cautions the field that "comparative research is inherently refreshing, but it is only too easy for the comparative researcher to be trapped within the framework that is set up for comparison" (Faure and Liu, *Town and Country in China*, p. 79). Indeed, China historians have constantly found themselves trapped by the proposition of the "great divergence" and the like; despite the comparable economic and urban development in late imperial China, we can resort only to historical contingencies to explain why China still evolved along a trajectory of modernity much different from that of Europe. For example, the "sprouts of capitalism" school holds that if indigenous development had not been disrupted by the invasion of Western imperialism, China would have modernized on its own terms. The key to this dilemma, I believe, lies not in the thriving late imperial cities but in the society in which urbanization was embedded. That is, only by studying the particular ways the expanding urban realm—one that is by all measures parallel to that of the west—have registered in Chinese culture and society can we get a full understanding of late imperial urbanism.

25. Zurndorfer, "Not Bound to China."

26. Mote, "A Millennium of Chinese Urban History"; idem, "City in Traditional Chinese Civilization." Mote also elaborated on this thesis in "A Millennium of Chinese Urban History" and in "Transformation of Nanking." In sum, the urban-rural continuum thesis is an all-encompassing concept characterizing the rural foundation of Chinese life at institutional, physical, and psychological levels. Administratively, cities were not recognized as independent units but embedded in a county-prefecture-province hierarchy. The institutional integrity of cities was further undermined in the Ming and Qing eras, when cities tended to be divided administratively into the jurisdictions of multiple counties. As a result, Chinese cities, despite being physically demarcated by city walls, were subordinated to political units that were predominantly rural. As for the psychological aspect, Mote points to elite aesthetic preferences for the bucolic life as seen in landscape paintings, poetic compositions, and urban garden designs. Finally, the physical aspect is manifest in indistinguishable city and countryside architecture in terms of designs, building materials, styles, and ornaments. Both featured flat profiles with one-story structures or one- and two-story components forming single units "arranged to enclose, and include the use of, open ground." No civic monuments could be found in Chinese cities that attested to the presence of a distinct urban society. This argument also reacts against the strong emphasis on an urban-rural dichotomy in Chinese village studies. For a review of three branches of the study of local communities and rural villages that invariably perpetuate the idea of urban-

rural dichotomy, see Rowe, "Approaches to Modern Chinese Social History," 255–59.

27. Mote's general formulation later gained a more specific economic dimension under Mark Elvin's modifications. Dividing post-medieval urban development into two stages—the rapid growth of major conurbations during the Song (960–1279) and the proliferation of middle-level market towns in the Ming and Qing eras—Elvin ("Chinese City") elaborates on the different urban-rural landscapes thereby created. In the first stage, the expansion of metropolises broke down the earlier urban plan of tightly controlled marketplaces and segregated quarters, resulting in a landscape in which "the differences between the great cities and the countryside and the lesser centers must have been very marked." In contrast, he refers to the second wave of urbanization as "urban devolution," since during this period, the top cities remained at the same magnitude while lower-level market towns multiplied at a remarkable pace. This development to a degree further obscures the urban-rural division since many market towns were no different from villages except in size and social composition. He observes that for these "Chinese town-like villages," the differences between villages and cities are more in size than in character. Supplying a specific economic foundation for the urban-rural continuum, Elvin also confines its applicability to the Ming and Qing periods.

28. Mote, "Transformation of Nanking," 103–5.

29. Mote, "A Millennium of Chinese Urban History," 54.

30. Arnade et al., "Fertile Spaces"; Reynolds, *Kingdoms and Communities*. For the relationship between the urban and the rural economy, see, e.g., Britnell, *Commercialization of English Society*; Stabel, *Dwarfs Among Giants*; and Nicholas, *Town and Countryside*. For the relationship between urban and rural religion, see Rubin, "Religious Culture." For relations between cities and territorial sovereigns, both Chevalier's *Les bonnes villes* and Mundy and Riesenberg's *Medieval Town* discuss the gap between the appearance and reality of city life.

31. Norimatsu, "Shindai chūki ni okeru shashi, hayari, shōhi"; Lin Liyue, "*Jianjiatang* yu Lu Ji 'fan jinshe' sixiang"; idem, "Wan Ming 'chongshe' sixiang"; Wu Jen-shu, "Mingdai pingmin fushi de liuxing"; idem, "Ming Qing xiaofei wenhua"; Chen Guodong, "You guan Lu Ji 'Jin she bian' zhi yanjiu"; Chao Xiaohong, "Jin ershi nian lai you guan 'shemi' zhi feng yanjiu."

32. The most original and systematic survey of the formation and operation of this urban society can be found in Wang Hongtai, "Liudong yu hudong." The first chapter looks at gardens, temples, teahouses, and courtesan houses as public spaces for an increasingly fluid urban society. The second and third chapters examine the social life of urban-based literati and their relationship with courtesans. The final two chapters deal with the information flow and the

consumption of objects in Ming and Qing cities. Highlighting new developments in all these different aspects, Wang's work offers an in-depth look into trans-local urban society in late imperial China.

33. *Minben* 民变 (popular protest) is an important issue for Japanese scholars, and many of their main arguments are addressed in the following chapters of the book. For a comprehensive overview of urban collective actions in the Ming-Qing era, see Wu Jen-shu, "Ming Qing chengshi minbian de jiti xingdong"; idem, "Jieqing, xinyang yu kangzheng"; and idem, "Ming mo Qing chu chenshi shougong ye gongren."

34. See the chapters by Paolo Santangelo on eighteenth-century Suzhou ("Urban Society in Late Imperial Suzhou") and Fuma Susumu on seventeenth-century Hangzhou ("Late Ming Urban Reform") in *Cities of Jiangnan*. The Introduction to this volume by William Rowe (13–14) points out that "most striking in the studies of Fuma and Santangelo is the specific preoccupation of both urban elites and urban administrators with *urban* problems, both groups being completely accustomed to assuming the discreteness of the municipal unit as a locus of managerial responsibilities."

35. Faure and Liu, eds., *Town and Country in China*, 1–3, 13–15.

36. Harrison, "Village Identity in Rural North China," 86.

37. Faure, "What Weber Did Not Know."

38. Harrison, "Village Identity in Rural North China," 104.

39. Ibid.

40. Citation from Faure and Liu, *Town and Country in China*, 14. In this introduction, the editors hold that, despite the apparent urban growth, the similarity of cultural performance in both cities and countryside is clear evidence of a prevailing rural-centered worldview in late imperial China. The power of this cultural paradigm is such that "not that Chinese people would have failed to recognize the concentration of population in the town or city, its prosperity, or its administrative or commercial function," but that despite such recognition, "not only villagers but also town and city residents would have seen the town and city from the vantage point of the village" (ibid., 5). However, the chapter in this collected volume by Zhao Shiyu ("Town and Country Representation as Seen in Temple Fairs") demonstrates that even with the same religious practice, when village temple fairs invaded the cities or city temple fairs descended upon the villages, the power and economic differences between town and city could still be clearly expressed. I take this a step further, arguing that the different social practice in cities indeed allows for the articulation of new views and perceptions about urban life through old cultural forms.

41. Gu Qiyuan, *Lanzhen caotang ji*, 14.15b. See also Clunas, *Fruitful Sites*, for late Ming garden culture.

42. Berg, "Marveling at the Wonders of the Metropolis."

43. One telling example is Suzhou, the leading art center of the Ming, where no cityscape paintings are known to have been produced before the eighteenth century. Even though a contemporary writer such as Zhang Dai 張岱 in his *Taoan mengyi* 陶庵夢憶 attests to the popular appeal of urban spectacles in late Ming leisure culture, still this commercial metropolis and fashion center was consistently presented in scroll painting after scroll painting of bucolic scenes such as Shen Zhou (authenticity debated), *Collection of Views of Suzhou* (National Palace Museum, Taipei, Taiwan). For more on the development of Suzhou images, see Ma Yachen's "Picturing Suzhou," which also points out the same phenomenon.

44. See Wang Hongtai, "Liudong yu hudong," chap. 2. This point is further developed in Chapter 3 of this book.

45. Indeed, even Mote ("Transformation of Nanking," 117) concedes that "it would be a mistake to exaggerate urban-rural uniformities, to be sure." Yet he was very ambiguous about how to qualify the urban-rural distinction.

46. Yinong Xu, *Chinese City in Space and Time*.

47. Rowe, *Hankow: Commerce and Society*; idem, *Hankow: Conflict and Community*.

48. See Rowe, *Hankow: Conflict and Community*, 342. Rowe's thesis, although appealing to many historians, has been criticized. As Frederic Wakeman ("Civil Society and Public Sphere Debate") rightly cautions, this newly formed urban identity appears to be somewhat fragile and does not fully replace particularistic native-place identity. For example, most of the merchant organizations in Hankow were composed of sojourners and were run from their headquarters in Shanghai. Wakeman holds that since the city affairs were managed by sojourners with strong ties to their native places, Hankow could not be a city of solid self-consciousness. Moreover, Wakeman contends that the existence of an urban community identified by Rowe was in fact rife with conflicts among groups from different native places. One prominent example is the dispute between Anhui guildsmen and Hunan guildsmen over the use of the latter's pier in 1888. In the end, conflicts between native-place groups at the annual Dragon Boat races escalated to the point that the government had to ban the races altogether. Many similar cases show that the city was fragmented along native-place, occupational, and even neighborhood lines. Rowe is aware of this problem and devotes a whole section of his book to social conflicts in order to show that these conflicts actually enhanced citywide solidarity. He addresses this seeming contradiction through references to social theorists in maintaining that "conflict is the necessary complement to cooperation, providing a safety valve for norms and rules of behavior by system participants" (Rowe, *Hankow:*

Conflict and Community, 216). Rowe believes that it is indifference, rather than passionate conflict, that is detrimental to community formation.

49. Of course, Rowe does not imply that Chinese and European cities are identical in early modern times. The major difference, in Rowe's view, lies in the lower level of social protest in Chinese cities. Social stability was not the result of a strong repressive state power; rather, it was a function of effective social mediation and containment, and "a highly institutionalized sense of urban community . . . accomplished on the initiatives of the local society itself, especially but not exclusively that of the urban elite." In other words, the unusually low frequency of urban popular protests suggests an even higher level of urban solidarity in traditional Chinese cities. See Rowe, *Hankow: Conflict and Community*, 344–46.

50. Ibid., 3–5.

51. The public sphere and civil society originated in European history when in the eighteenth century the rising bourgeoisies began to demand a voice in state affairs, resulting in a new space negotiated between the state and the closed realms of business and family. In essence, this model posits an idealized public sphere that allows open discussion and rational decisions among individuals for the common good, an autonomous space that mediates between state and society. However, scholars have also cautioned that such a historical phenomenon, once theorized, became an "ideal type" never fully realized in any historical or contemporary society and hence should not be used as a norm to measure any polity; see Brook and Frolic, eds., *Civil Society in China*, 8–9.

52. Rowe, "Public Sphere in Modern China."

53. For example, one major journal in the field, *Modern China*, convened a symposium, which was later published as a special issue (vol. 19, no. 2, 1993) dedicated to the question of the public sphere and civil society in China. Another symposium on civil society was held in Toronto in 1995, published later as *Civil Society in China*. Other scholars such as Philip Kuhn, David Strand, and R. Bin Wong have published separately on the issue.

54. Specifically, Rowe finds the emergence of urban autonomy in Hankow when the management of salt trade, tea brokerage, and *lijin* 厘金 (a "customs" tax) collection was gradually transferred from officials to elites. However, Frederic Wakeman ("Civil Society and Public Sphere Debate") disagrees, arguing that these seemingly merchant-run organizations were in fact subject to strong state control. Even the coordination of citywide guild confederations, Wakeman contends, was in fact achieved by imperial mandate and closely administered from the top down by two expectant circuit intendants. In other words, far from being autonomous, the power of merchants was essentially dependent on official patronage and hence subject to state control.

55. Wong, "Great Expectations." His views on the relationship between state and society in China, especially in comparison with early modern Europe, are further developed in *China Transformed*.

56. Wong, "Great Expectations."

57. On the factual level, Bin Wong (ibid.) argues that to brand the trajectory of late imperial China with one overarching category such as civil society suffers from the risk of misleading oversimplification. In fact, elite activism in late imperial China should be seen as occurring in at least two stages. Eighteenth-century social management was achieved through vertically integrated bureaucratic control of the empire, whereas in the late nineteenth century the supervision of local affairs was a combined official and elite initiative. In other words, society-state dynamics changed too substantially between the sixteenth and twentieth centuries to be subsumed under the same conceptual label.

58. See Philip Huang, "'Public Sphere' / 'Civil Society,'" 232. Huang's "third realm" thesis effectively exposes the intertwining state-society relationship in China and sheds new light on the Wakeman-Rowe debate. However, the primary example Huang cites to illustrate the nature of the third realm, the Qing judicial system, especially his treatment of "civil law," is criticized by Jérôme Bourgon in "Uncivil Dialogue" and "Rights, Customs, and Civil Law."

59. Philip Huang, "'Public Sphere' / 'Civil Society,'" 168.

60. Wakeman, "Boundaries of the Public Sphere."

61. For example, despite his skepticism on the appearance of a formal public sphere, Wakeman (ibid.) acknowledges that "there is ample evidence to support the contention that the late Qing saw the expansion of a public sphere in the sense of an arena of non-state activity at the local level that contributed to the supply of services and resources to the public good." What is at issue here is the conceptualization of this development.

62. Kuhn, Review of *Peking: Temples and City Life*.

63. Naquin, *Peking*, 170.

64. Ibid., Preface, xxxi.

65. Most telling are the examples about *huiguan* and their informal political influences; see Susan Naquin, *Peking*, 598–621.

66. In his review of Naquin's book, Philip Kuhn also remarks on the distinction between theory and practice when evaluating the state's influence on urban public spaces: "Only hazily and episodically did anyone perceive a religious 'space' beyond the regulatory grasp of the state, and any such perception was embedded in practice rather than theory. . . . Although temple life had its own distinctive effects on society, nobody assumed it to be part of a realm immune to state authority."

67. Naquin, *Peking*, 248.

68. Belsky, *Localities at the Center.*

69. See Farmer, *Zhu Yuanzhang and Early Ming Legislation*; and also Schnee-wind, "Visions and Revisions."

CHAPTER I

1. The main document about Nanjing's *huojia* reform was written by the presiding official, Ding Bin 丁賓, "Zhengqian gumu zongjia yisu junmin zhongkun" 徵錢顧募總甲以甦軍民重困 (On levying money to hire out corvée labor of *zongjia* in order to relieve the burden on the residents and army) in *Ding Qinghui gong yiji*, 2.3a–11a.

2. *Huojia* was the urban form of a general local defense corvée known as *baojia* 保甲, which became popular during the mid-Ming. As Lü Kun 呂坤 (1536–1618), the renowned scholar-official, explained: "Regarding the burden of firemen (火夫 *huofu*) and spearmen (槍夫 *qiangfu*): firemen patrol throughout the gates and wards in cities at night for the purpose of fire watching and theft prevention; the spearmen in the countryside were structured as *baojia*, originally for the purpose of providing local surveillance and protection"; see Lü Kun, "Shang xun'an tiaochen libi" 上巡按條陳利弊 (A proposal to the circuit intendant listing local problems and possible solutions), in *Quweizhai ji*, 5.63b–64a. Shen Bang 沈榜 ("Jiedao" 街道 [Streets], in *Wanshu zaji*, 42), the magistrate of Wanping county (one of the two counties responsible for the local administration of Beijing), also described *huojia* 火甲 and *baojia* 保甲 as representing the same system but located inside and outside the city walls, respectively. The function of these two groups was similar to that of local police today.

3. According to the statistics compiled for the corvée reform, there were some 670 *pu* in Nanjing, each with about a hundred households in its jurisdiction; see *Nanjing duchayuan zhi* (1623), *juan* 20–21. Although *pu* literally refers to the small shed in which people on duty could rest and suspects were confined, not every *pu* actually had a shed, and thus we should consider *pu* more an administrative unit rather than an actual building. Since Beijing operated according to an urban administrative system similar to that of Nanjing, a description of neighborhood organization in Ming Beijing provides useful background; see Wakeland, "Metropolitan Administration in Ming China," pp. 245–60.

4. The quote is from Zhou Hui's *Xu Jinling suoshi*, which gives a comprehensive description of the system consistent with other contemporary records. It succinctly summarizes the function, organization, and problems associated with the *huojia* system. It defines the duties of *huojia* as night patrol and fire watch:

The neighborhood [fire-]captain system put into practice by Taizu was a good system. Every day [the roles of] one neighborhood captain and five firewatchers were rotated among residents door by door. The wealthy hired people [to fulfill these duties], whereas the poor had to serve the rounds themselves. They were equipped with gongs, drums, watchmen's rattles, bells, and lanterns, as well as torches. Each person [on rotation] held one of the implements and was on duty for one *geng* 更 [two-hour period] of night watch. From the third point of the first watch to the third point of the fifth watch, no one was allowed to be out. Shelters were set as patrol stations during periods of rain and snow and could also be used to detain criminals. When anything happened, first one shelter, then another, would light its lantern and strike gongs and drums to alert the others. Whenever equipment like swords, spears, military weapons, or firefighting apparatus was damaged, the shelter-repair household would be summoned to offer repair service. However, the head of *huojia* was held liable for cases like *feichai* 飛差 [extraordinary official duties, lit. "flying conscription"] and homicide, and all kinds of corrupt or fraudulent practices, which might go for years without resolution. This was the most injurious part of the system and urgently needed to be changed.

See Zhou Hui, "Huojia" 火甲, in *Xu Jinling suoshi, juan xia,* 135, preface dated 1610, one year after the Nanjing tax reform. The English translation is adapted from Wakeland, "Metropolitan Administration in Ming China," 252–53.

5. *Huojia* aimed at local security and was separate from regular corvée such as *lijia* 里甲 or its urban form *fangjia* 坊甲, which were based on residential registration. See elsewhere in this chapter for more on *lijia* and *fangjia*.

6. Gu Yanwu, *Tianxia junguo libing shu, juan* 6, lists many cases of this nature. Sojourning merchants, especially those registered in other localities, were often able to evade corvée labor. See Chapter 4 for more details on the Ming regulation of sojourners.

7. For a general introduction to the Single Whip method and its historical significance, see Liang Fangzhong, *Single Whip Method.*

8. Luo Xiaoxiang's "Mingdai Nanjing de fangxiang yu zipu," for example, considers Nanjing's *huojia* reform as clear evidence of urban identity and autonomy. She argues that the fact that the strong bond among Nanjing residents was fostered by administrative needs instead of commercial activities defies Weber's thesis that premised urban identity on the appearance of guild associations. I agree that commercial forces played only a partial role in shaping Nanjing's reform activism. However, as this chapter shows, despite the role of administrative organizations (*pu*) as catalysts, the extensive grassroots participation in Nanjing was not an exclusive urban phenomenon and should not be cited as evidence of "urban consciousness" (ibid., p. 55).

9. Wang Yunhai and Zhang Dezong, "Songdai fangguo hudeng"; Umehara Kaoru, "Sōdai toshi no zeifu"; Yanagida Setsuko, "Sōdai toshi no kotōsei"; Kumamoto Takashi, "Sōsei 'jōkaku shi hu'"; Kusano Yasushi, "Sōdai no okuzei to chizei."

10. For more about the Yuan political system, see Farquhar, *Government of China Under Mongolian Rule.*

11. Skinner, "Cities and the Hierarchy of Local Systems," in idem, ed., *City in Late Imperial China*, 307–44. Skinner argues that it was a common practice in late imperial China to split major cities between at least two counties in order to strengthen the state's control of cities by dividing the political focus of the urban middle class.

12. According to Otagi Matsuo ("Gendai toshi seido to sono kegen"), *lushi si* has a strong flavor of the city council in Europe, which was only natural considering the Euro-Asian empire context in which it was situated. Recent researches further trace this institution to Liao and Jin, both nomadic regimes with an emphasis on urban control; see Han Guanghui, "Yuan dai Zhongguo de jianzhi chengshi"; and idem, "Jin dai zhu fu jie zhen chengshi lushisi yanjiu."

13. This explains why Nanjing's reform had to rely on residents' volunteering their tax information—there were no records of the property of urban residents. As a matter of fact, there were even no clearly set rules for assessing taxes on affluent urban merchants who did not own land. For more information, see below.

14. For a comprehensive survey of this topic, see Heijdra, "Socio-Economic Development of Rural China."

15. To be sure, there are excellent studies on late Ming urban tax reform such as Fuma Susumu, "Minmatsu no toshi kaikaku"; and von Glahn, "Municipal Reform and Urban Social Conflict." Based on these pioneering works, this chapter further explores how the institutional setup affected the course of urban tax reform in the late Ming.

16. In prescribing the basic administrative unit, the Ming court mandated the compilation of the Yellow Register (*huang ce* 黄册). Under this design, a uniform grassroots organization, *lijia*, was implemented throughout the country to facilitate the formation of self-supervising rural communities. Both taxes and corvée were levied through *lijia*. *Lijia* was extended into cities, under different names (坊 *fang* within the cities and *xiang* 厢 in the suburbs). For a detailed survey of the Ming field administration, see Brook, "Spatial Structure of Ming Local Administration."

17. Here I adopt the term "civil governance" as used by Peter Bol. In his essay "Society," the institutionalization of "self-supervising rural communities" is seen as the result of early Ming legislation based on the historical experience of southeastern literati elites rather than an expression of a presumed natural village community, the *kyōdotai* 共同體, which has been the subject of much debate among historians in Japan. Bol seeks to explain why in contrast to the Song ideal of civil order (*wenzhi* 文治) to be achieved through state bureaucracy, Zhu Yuanzhang chose to put his faith in local communities. In this sense, although the reliance on local self-governance had been a long-established

practice prior to the Ming, Taizu's ideal still stands out for its alienation from local officials.

18. See ibid.; and Farmer, *Zhu Yuanzhang and Early Ming Legislation.*

19. Bol, "Society"; Nakajima Yoshiaki, *Mindai gōson no funsō.*

20. Zhu Yuanzhang, *Da Gao* 大誥 (The great pronouncement), 3.34; cited in Schneewind, "Visions and Revisions," 41–43. Original translation from Dardess, *Confucianism and Autocracy,* 245–46.

21. For a more detailed discussion of this process, see Heijdra, "Socio-Economic Development of Rural China."

22. Scholars have pointed out that such wide-ranging conscriptions for corvée duties were not part of Zhu Yuanzhang's legislation but grew out of the subsequent expansion of the bureaucratic system and rapid population growth. As such, the practice of local conscription was often conducted on an ad hoc basis and was therefore difficult to regulate. See Iwami Hiroshi, *Mindai yōeki seido,* 1–86; Taniguchi Kikuo, *Mindai yōeki seidoshi,* 3–34; and Iwai Shigeki, "Yōeki to zaisei no aida." This argument is also confirmed by Liu Zhiwei in his study of the Guangdong area, *Zai guojia yu shehui zhi jian,* 71–92.

23. Other reforms were implemented only regionally. For example, *shiduanjin fa* 十段錦法 was practiced only in the Jiangnan area between the late fifteenth and mid-sixteenth centuries. This method also converted the corvée into taxes based on landownership and number of able-bodied adults. But instead of rotating among the administrative communities, it used the prefecture or county as the basic accounting unit. For a comprehensive survey of the Ming fiscal reform in English, see Heijdra, "Socio-economic Development of Rural China"; or Liang Fangzhong, *Single Whip Method.*

24. Liang Fangzhong summarizes the general guidelines of the Single Whip Method as (1) the conversion of labor service into land tax; (2) the deprivatization of collection and transportation of tax revenues; and (3) annual silver payment in place of rotating labor service. Even so, not all these features appeared in every local incarnation. Even the chronology of adoption of the method varied greatly. See Liang Fangzhong, "Mingdai yitiaobian fa nianbiao" 明代一條鞭法年表 (A chronology of the Ming Single Whip reform), in *Liang Fangchong jingjishi lunwenji,* 485–576.

25. See Liang Fangzhong 梁方仲, *Mingdai liangzhang zhidu;* and Heijdra, "Socio-Economic Development of Rural China."

26. Liang Fangzhong, *Single Whip Method.*

27. Liang Fangzhong, "Yizhiyoudan de yanjiu" 易知由單的研究 (Study of easy-to-understand slips), in *Liang Fangchong jingjishi lunwenji,* 368–484.

28. See Qi Biaojia, *An Wu xi gao.*

29. *Guangdong tong zhi* (1602), 10.53b–54a.

30. Heijdra, "Socio-economic Development of Rural China," 480–82. Iwai Shigeki ("Yōeki to zaisei no aida," pt. 4, 30–33) also argues that in the process of nationalization, the publication of local budgets became an increasingly common practice. See also Liang Fangzhong, "Yitiaobian fa" (Single Whip method), in *Liang Fangchong jingjishi lunwenji*, 87–89.

31. *Nanning fuzhi* (1637), 3.14a–14b.

32. Ibid., 3.15a–15b.

33. The problems in the Ming financial system lay mostly in the conscription and apportionment of labor service, which heavily depended on the discretion of local authorities; see Liang Fangzhong, *Single Whip Method*, 15–19.

34. *Ming Shenzong shilu, juan* 367 (1612), 9238–41.

35. Zhu Guozhen, "Zi shu xinglue" 自述行略 (Self-narrated résumé), in *Zhu Wensu gong ji*, 334.

36. *Haiyan xian tujing* (1624), 6.6a–b, "令該里區甲人戶公議, 照田認役."

37. *Shaoxing fuzhi* (1683), 15.9b, excerpts from *Liangzhe junping lu* 兩浙均平錄 (Account of equalizing the tax levies in the Zhejiang area), issued in 1566.

38. *Ming Shenzong shilu, juan* 58 (1577), 1337–40.

39. The emergence of *gonglun* 公論 (public opinion) in late Ming society is well established by Japanese scholarship, see Kishimoto Mio, "Minmatsu shinsho no chihō shakai to seron"; Fuma Susumu, "Chūgoku kinsei toshi"; idem, "Minmatsu no toshi kaikaku"; idem, "Minmatsu minpen to seiin"; idem, "Minmatsu han chihōkan shihen"; and idem, "Minmatsu han chihōkan shihen horon."

40. Qian Qianyi, "Yu Yang Mingfu lun bianshen" 與楊明府論編審, in *Muzhai chu xue ji*, 87.17a–21a. Yang was magistrate of Changshu 常熟 county between 1628 and 1635.

41. Indeed, in most cases cited in the above studies (see note 39 to this chapter), we find the terms *difang gongyi* 地方公議 (local public opinion) and *shiren gongyi* 士人公議 (gentry advocacy) used almost interchangeably. For example, Fuma, in his "Minmatsu minpen to seiin," a survey of a series of protests and petitions, demonstrates that the direction of *gongyi* was so shaped by such spontaneously convened local councils that "public opinion" virtually amounted to political advocacy articulated by the governing elites.

42. On this point, Hamashima Atsushi (*Mindai Kōnan nōson shakai*, 215–642) offers prime examples of this type of social conflict in Jiangnan rural areas; Richard von Glahn's "Municipal Reform and Urban Social Conflict" focuses on similar class conflicts in Jiangnan cities.

43. For a structural and historical analysis of the formation of the gentry class, see Shigeta, "The Origin and Structure of Gentry Rule."

44. See Hamashima Atsushi, "Minbō kara gōshin e." Granted that the stark contrast between the two could also be attributed to an overly romanticized view of the past, its appearance nevertheless reveals a rising antagonism in late Ming society toward the abuse of privileges by the landed gentry.

45. Both Fuma and Kishimoto point out the diversity of positions and the power struggles underlying the practice of *gongyi*. See also Hamashima Atsushi, *Mindai Kōnan nōson shakai*, 215–642, on the different positions of local gentry regarding their waiving of privileges.

46. *Shaoxing fuzhi* (1683), 14.42b–43a. The document is dated 1547.

47. Jin Zhijun, *Fu Wu xi lue, juan* 3. Jin's directive was issued in 1642.

48. Gu Yanwu, *Tianxia junguo libing shu*, 23.46–47.

49. *Xingning zhi* (1637), 2.72b–73a.

50. Some scholars view the late Ming fiscal reform as symbolizing the "sprouts of capitalism" or as reflecting an indigenous early modernity in China. Ongoing debates over such denominations notwithstanding, there is general agreement that the Single Whip reform was an outgrowth of the advancement of a monetized economy supported by the influx of silver from Japan and the New World. For a more detailed discussion on this issue, see the Introduction.

51. See Liu Zhiwei, *Zai guojia yu shehui zhi jian*, 186–275.

52. This unique development is made especially clear when compared with Song fiscal reform. At first glance, the late Ming fiscal reform that converted labor services into silver payments is rather similar to the *guyi fa* 雇役法 (hire-out corvée) in the Northern Song New Policies reform (1069–1073). However, the New Policies reform was based on strong faith in civic government in combating powerful local families (*jianbing zhijia* 兼并之家). The early Ming social vision, in contrast, put much less trust in government than in local communities and endeavored to strengthen the latter, an emphasis that continued to influence the late Ming fiscal reform. See Bol, "Society."

53. According to the *Mingshi* 明史 (Official history of the Ming dynasty), Ding's long-term appointment in Nanjing resulted from his defying the powerful chief councilor Zhang Juzheng 張居正 in Beijing; see *Mingshi, juan* 221.

54. See *Jiangning fuzhi* (1668), 30.31b–32a. The account (記 *ji*) of this shrine, authored by Li Changgeng 李長庚 and with a preface by Jiao Hong 焦竑, was dated 1630, three years before Ding's death at the age of 91. Building shrines in honor of outstanding living officials (*shengci* 生祠) violated ritual propriety but was a popular practice in the late Ming.

55. Even though Beijing pioneered the professionalization of *huojia*, this early 1421 precedent did not really prevent bureaucratic exploitation. Soon after the Yongle reign (1402–24), for example, a memorial in 1436 proposed to divide Beijing residents into three levels to serve the neighborhood corvée. A

1488 edict in *Huangming tiaofashi leizuan* asked Beijing propertied households to serve as *huojia* once a year. Other cases were recorded in Wang Qi, "Lidai yifa" 歷代役法 (The levy systems in every dynasty), in *Xu Wenxian tongkao, juan* 16, 2913.3–15.1. These records indicate that in practice mandatory labor service was continually imposed on Beijing residents.

56. In fact, it was not uncommon for the two capitals to cite each other's practices in order to justify proposed policy changes. For example, an 1579 edict shortened the interval for shops in Beijing to be inspected and ranked for corvée service from ten years to five. The edict indicated that this decision followed the new system recently implemented in Nanjing. This document is cited in Shen Bang, "Puhang" 鋪行, *Wanshu zaji*, 93–94. However, twenty years later, the tables were turned. This time a 1599 memorial by Li Tingji 李廷機 proposed to reform Nanjing's *puhang* 鋪行 based on Beijing's precedent; see *Ming Shenzong shilu, juan* 342 (1599), 6337–39.

57. Ding Bin, "Zhengqian gumu zongjia yisu junmin zhongkun" in *Ding Qinghui gong yiji*, 2.3a–11a.

58. Officials and gentry were entitled to a waiver of part of their duty to serve, but how much could be waived depended on a complicated set of rules. To establish the ground rules for waiver privileges, Hai Rui 海瑞 even edited a book entitled *Jianke zhaofan ce* 簡可照繁冊 (Simplified corvée manual); cited in *Nanjing duchayuan zhi* (1623), *juan* 20–21.

59. *Nanjing duchayuan zhi* (1623), 20.81b–82a.

60. Indeed, the *huojia* reform in Nanjing was a prolonged process. As early as 1586, when Hai Rui served as Nanjing censor-in-chief, he already converted part of the government conscription into a fixed payment and compiled levy books such as *Jianke zhaofan ce* and *Difang fuchai ce* 地方夫差冊 (Register of corvée) to document the standardized service charges; see Hai Rui, *Hairui ji*, 290–306. Hai Rui's reform is discussed below.

61. Jiao Hong, "Paimen tiaobian bianmince xu," in *Nanjing duchayuan zhi* (1623), 36.69b–71b; Gu Qiyuan, "Difang fuchaice xu" in *Lanzhen caotang ji*, 16.29a–30b. In addition, Zhou Hui 周暉 also wrote an essay on *huojia* included in his best-seller *Jinling suoshi* 金陵瑣事 (Trivia about Nanjing) (*juan xia*, 135). The rich documentation on Nanjing's *huojia* reform indicates that this event not only is important in historical hindsight but also drew intensive attention from contemporary Nanjing luminaries. Ding Bin's memorial on the subject naturally supplied the official version of this story and was adapted and included in several important collections such as *Nanjing duchayuan zhi* and Gu Yanwu's *Tianxia junguo libing shu*. At the same time, unofficial accounts proliferated such as the ones written by Gu Qiyuan, Jiao Hong, and Zhou Hui's, all key members of a native elite group active in the public life of late Ming

Nanjing (more about them in Chapters 3 and 4). The public and private accounts are consistent at the factual level but differ in their emphases: Ding's memorial focuses on the bureaucratic process with a special emphasis on the populist support for his reform, whereas the elite accounts present the same process in terms of institutional precedents. Essays by Jiao, Gu, and Zhou highlight the fact that since the *huojia* system in Beijing had already been transformed from labor service into cash payment, it was only natural for Nanjing to follow suit. Jiao argued that the Nanjing reform was successful because at long last the laws of the two capitals had finally come together (or rather, that the secondary capital had finally caught up with Beijing). Gu went even further to argue for the superiority of the new Nanjing system to Beijing's. One reason why this Beijing precedent was emphasized in these elite accounts might have to do with their intention to certify the reform by establishing its statutory status.

62. See "Wucheng zhizhang" 五城職掌 (The jurisdictions of the Five Wards), in *Nanjing duchayuan zhi* (1623), *juan* 20–21.

63. It is curious that Ding Bin's official report focused exclusively on the building of public consensus from the bottom up with no mention of the contribution of local elites. Yet not only did Jiao Hong and Gu Qiyuan write to sustain the new system, but both also actively participated in the reform process as Ding's personal consultants. In celebrating the success of the reform, Jiao Hong particularly emphasized the difficulty involved in launching a reform in which so many powerful people's interests were at stake. The key, Jiao pointed out, lay in a public consensus. To achieve this goal, Ding consulted officials, local gentry, elders, the wealthy, and poor and deprived households in order to arrive at a collective consensus. Note here that Jiao presented an idealized order of public consultation, one that embodied the inner hierarchy of the local community. Although different from Ding's populist version, Jiao's representation still corroborates Ding's account of his pursuit of public consensus in the most literal manner. The discrepancies between Ding's report and elites' accounts might also reflect their different views. Despite the many stages of local consultation, Ding Bin decided that the ones involving the general public were most crucial to the success of the reform.

64. The only exception was Hangzhou, former capital of the Southern Song dynasty, where the Song urban taxation outlived two dynastic transitions and was still in effect in the Ming. Contemporary comments make it clear that it was the only exception in the Ming dynasty; see *Hangzhou fuzhi* (1579), 7.34a–b.

65. Urban corvée, or the so-called *fangxiang yi* 坊廂役 (ward corvée), was not specifically distinguished from the general *lijia* corvée organization, except for certain duties designated specifically for urban residents such as serving in

commercial tax offices (*shuike si* 稅課司) or police bureaus (*xunlan* 巡欄); see *Wanli Da Ming huidian*, 20.10b.

66. "Fangzhang" 坊長 (ward heads), in *Taiping fuzhi* (1577), 4.12b–15a.

67. "Tianfu" 田賦 (Land tax), in *Jianchang fuzhi* (1613), 2.7b, 2.10a.

68. Shi Jian, "Lun jun zheng li bi" 論郡政利弊 (A discussion about the pros and cons of the current policies in Suzhou prefecture), in *Xicun ji, juan* 5. For a more contextual analysis of this text, see Hamashima Atsushi, *Mindai Kōnan nōson shakai*, 241.

69. *Nanchang fuzhi* (1574), 8.33a–b.

70. *Qiongzhou fuzhi* (1617), 5.51b–52a.

71. *Yongjia xianzhi* (1566), 3.45a–47a.

72. See "Hufuyi" 户賦議 (Discussion on household tax), *She zhi* (1609), *juan* 3.

73. This explains why in some places the tax rate favored urban residents. For example, in Yiwu county, the new urban poll tax following the Single Whip reform was less than a third of the rural poll tax; see *Yiwu xianzhi* (1640), 7.15a.

74. Gu Yanwu, *Tianxia junguo libing shu*, 25.441a–b.

75. Liu Guangji, "Chaiyi shu" 差役疏 (A memorial on corvée), in *Xinxiu Nanchang fuzhi* (1588), 25.18a–19b.

76. These cases are researched in more details in Hamashima Atsushi, *Mindai Kōnan nōson shakai*, 284–328.

77. "Juntian shiyi" 均田十議 (Ten propositions about equalizing the corvée share to be distributed according to landownership), in *Jiaxing xianzhi* (1637), 10.38a–39a.

78. Zhu Guozhen, "Fu shihu yi" 附市户議 (A proposition regarding urban households), in *Zhu Wensu gong ji*, 329–30.

79. The main target of Ding Yuanjian's objection was a local proposition that substituted reductions of gentry privilege with a tax on urban households. Although Ding conceded that in principle the reform should place more weight on exploiting the wealth of merchants in order to further relieve the burden on peasants, the either-or option of gentry versus the urban rich, however, was used as an excuse to fend off attacks on the gentry's privileges. See Ding Yuanjian, *Zunzhuotang wenji*, 2.33a–34b; for a fuller discussion on Ding's position in the reform, see Hamashima Atsushi, *Mindai Kōnan nōson shakai*, 322–24.

80. *Quanzhou fuzhi* (1612), 6.76a–b. The editor's opinion is in line with Hamashima's argument in *Mindai Kōnan nōson shakai* (449–522) that one reason progressive gentry went against their class interests and supported the corvée reform movement was the imminent threat of peasant uprisings in the late Ming

and early Qing. They believed that only by abolishing the much-resented gentry privilege could class tension be relieved.

81. *Wuxian zhi* (1642), 9.9b–12a.

82. *Songjiang fuzhi* (1630), 11.22a–24a.

83. Iwai Shigeki, "Yōeki to zaisei no aida"; idem, "Chō Kyosei zaisei no kadai to hōhō."

84. Sun Chengze, *Chunming mengyu lu*, 35.36b–38a.

85. See Wang Yuming, "Mingdai zongjia zhezhi kaoshu"; and Chen Baoliang, "Mingdai de baojia yu huojia."

86. Yang Xichun 楊希淳, "Yishi Zhao Baishi Shanji zhuan" 義士趙白石善繼傳 (The biography of Zhao Shanji), in Jiao Hong, *Guochao xiancheng lu*, 113.43a–46b.

87. Gu Qiyuan, "Fangxiang shimo" 坊廂始末 (A survey of urban ward corvée), in *Kezuo zhuiyu*, 2.64–66.

88. Zhao Shanji's campaign aimed at reforming the so-called *fangxiang yi* 坊廂役 (ward corvée), which was separate from *huojia*. However, toward the end of the Ming era, both were overburdened by the excessive government requisitions.

89. Yang Xichun, "Yishi Zhao Baishi Shanji zhuan," in Jiao Hong, *Guochao xiancheng lu*, 113.43a–46b.

90. This development is described in detail by Gu Qiyuan, "Fangxiang shimo," in *Kezuo zhuiyu*, 2.64–66. However, he did not specify when all of this was finally settled, but, from what we read in Ding Bin's biography, ward corvée reform was still a problem and became one of his major accomplishments in Nanjing; see *Jiangning fuzhi* (1668), 19.18a.

91. See Fuma Susumu, "Mindai Nankin no toshi gyōsei," 245–47.

92. Part of the budget deficit might have been absorbed by appropriating funds for rural corvée since both the city and the countryside fell under the jurisdiction of the same county office. Such fiscal remedies were short-term and doomed to fail, since they merely filled one hole by digging another. For example, in the case of Nanjing, in the early fifteenth century, county officials used the surplus from ward taxes to subsidize the *lijia* in the countryside; in the final quarter of the sixteenth century, they channeled other funds of the local government to supplement the low budget of the wards in order to pacify the outcry of ward households. No matter which direction the subsidy went, the deficits remained. See Gu Qiyuan, "Fangxiang shimo," in *Kezuo zhuiyu*, 2.64–66.

93. Hai Rui, "Fuchai ce" 夫差冊 (Register of corvée), in *Hai Rui ji*, 290–306.

94. For a biography of Hai Rui and contemporary perceptions of his idiosyncratic career, see Ray Huang, *1587, A Year of No Significance.*

95. See Iwai Shigeki, "Yōeki to zaisei no aida," pt. 4, 62–79; and Ray Huang, *Taxation and Governmental Finance in Sixteenth-Century Ming China*. For a study of the Guangdong area, see Liu Zhiwei, *Zai guojia yu shehui zhi jian.*

96. Hai Rui, "Fuchai ce," in *Hai Rui ji*, 290–306. This development mirrored that in Beijing, whose overbureaucratized infrastructure might have first compelled the government to levy labor services through *huojia*. As a result, although established mainly for local security and patrolling, *huojia* was in effect systematically exploited by resident offices to conscript local residents into serving as clerks and runners; see Shen Bang, "Li yi" 力役, *Wanshu zaji*, 50–52.

97. Iwai Shigeki, "Yōeki to zaisei no aida." In fact, shortfalls in local funding became even more severe during the Qing dynasty, according to Iwai's research.

98. *Ming Shenzong shilu, juan* 383 (1603), 7210–11.

99. Despite being a reincarnation of the nominally abolished ward corvée, *huojia*, because of the egalitarian nature of its residence-to-residence assignment (*paimen*), was considered by some as a form of levy that served social justice better. For one thing, it took account of sojourners. Gu Qiyuan, a prominent Nanjing elite, suggested that Nanjing should adopt this form for labor conscription, since one of the problems facing the commutation of ward corvée into monetary payments was that the official registry failed to keep up with the constantly changing urban population. And indeed, no law stipulated the registration of the sojourning population in Ming cities. See Gu Qiyuan, "Lizheng" 力征 (Labor levies), in *Kezuo zhuiyu, juan* 2.

100. For more discussion regarding the tension between native and sojourning populations, see Chapter 4.

101. "Ge paimen zachai" 革排門雜差 (Forbidding all door-to-door miscellaneous corvée), in *Jianchang fuzhi* (1613), 2.40b.

102. "Zayi" 雜役 (Miscellaneous corvée), in *Qiongzhou fuzhi* (1617), 5.65a–67a. It listed several nonstatutory corvée services that later became formal conscriptions, including *zongjia*. The various denominations for *huojia* could be attributed to the highly diverse nature of the Ming local defense system. See Chen Baoliang, "Mingdai de baojia yu huojia."

103. Lü Kun, *Xinwu Lü xiansheng shizhen lu*, 465–67.

104. For studies of the late Ming *huojia* reform, see Fuma Susumu, "Minmatsu no toshi kaikaku"; and von Glahn, "Municipal Reform and Urban Social Conflict."

105. Ding Bin, "Zhengqian gumu zongjia yisu junmin zhongkun," in *Ding Qinghui gong yiji*, 2.3a–3b. The volunteering of tax registration is reminiscent of an earlier precedent during the *junyao* 均徭 reform that converted part of the labor service obligations into cash payments. Since there were never clearly set rules for assessing taxes on affluent urban residents who did not own land, the inspecting officials had no choice but to let urban residents voluntarily report their wealth in order to determine the rank of corvée in which they should serve (called *zizhan* 自占, "self-reporting"); see Wang Qi, "Lidai yifa," in *Xu Wenxian tongkao*.

106. Ding Bin, "Zhengqian gumu zongjia yisu junmin zhongkun," in *Ding Qinghui gong yiji*, 2.3a–b.

107. Among the various proposals for urban taxation, the revival of the urban housing tax in Hangzhou was the most radical and triggered a violent uprising. The new tax in question, *jianjia* 間架, was based on the exact size of the architectural framework, and the rate was unprecedentedly high. It stirred a vehement conflict between the rich, who would be largely responsible for financing the hiring of labor service under the new system, and the poor, who had nothing more to lose under the old system. See Fuma Susumu, "Minmatsu no toshi kaikaku."

108. These examples are discussed in more details in ibid.

109. Although a thorough discussion of this issue is beyond the scope of this book, it would be interesting to investigate whether there was a link between the historical context of each city and the urban tax base adopted. For example, in Songjiang, a tradition of establishing *yitian* (corvée fields) as a solution to fiscal deficits could be traced to the Song era; see *Songjiang fuzhi* (1630), 11.22a–24a.

110. *Haiyan xian tujing* (1624), 6.31b–32b.

111. Lü Kun, *Xinwu Lü xiansheng shizhen lu*, 465–67.

112. See Gu Yanwu, *Tianxia junguo libing shu*, 16.2b–4b.

113. Given the late Ming urban reforms, the decision of the Qing, another conquest dynasty, not to impose urban taxation is an issue worth further investigation. A few clues may be found in the dynastic transition. As *fanhao yin* was adopted more and more during the late Ming reforms, in a desperate effort to survive internal rebellions and external attacks, the Ming court in 1636 officially imposed urban real estate taxes to raise military funds. Yet according to Wu Shen's memorial ("Fanghao de shang wu duo zheng pai zi rao shu"), it was widely regarded as exploitive—certainly not part of the Single Whip reform—and met with strong opposition. The negative perception might partly explain why the conquering Manchu regime decided not to continue

urban taxes. In fact, such a proposal was raised in the early Qing by Wu Weihua 吳惟華, a onetime Ming official who served the Qing. Wu was condemned by the Kangxi emperor as greedy and exploitive and received a harsh sentence of exile (see "Wu Weihua lie zhuan," in Zhou Junfu, *Er chen zhuan*).

CHAPTER 2

1. The meaning of *cheng* should not be narrowly construed as civilian government sites. The Ming administrative system consisted of two parallel systems: civilian (*zhouxian* 州縣, prefectures and counties) and military (*weisuo* 衛所, guards and battalions), and according to Edward Farmer ("Hierarchy of Ming City Walls") both were aggressively walled during the Ming era. One of the case studies (Puzi) in this chapter involves such a military city.

2. The special weight put on city-wall construction in the Ming dynasty was first noted by Frederick Mote in "Transformation of Nanking." Mote argued that the Ming obsession with walls reflects psychological insecurity after the Mongol rule. Edward Farmer further developed this view in "Hierarchy of Ming City Walls" with more systematic research; he attributed this development to the Ming's cultural conservatism in the wake of alien rule. The strong emphasis on wall construction in the Ming era becomes particularly evident in comparison to the Song and Yuan. According to Cheng Yinong ("Song, Yuan, yiji Mingdai"), the Song held a generally passive "no repair" policy toward city-wall construction except in extremely critical military areas. This policy was further developed into a formal ban on wall construction in the Yuan dynasty to facilitate the Mongols' alien rule. In the Ming era, the wall-construction policy was particularly forceful not only because of the consistent and firm policy position of the court but also because of the integration of wall construction into local officials' performance evaluations, which determined their promotion and career prospects. On the wall-construction policy and its implementation in specific areas in the Ming era, see Hsu Hong, "Mingdai Fujian de zhucheng yundong." Hsu's case study shows that there appeared to be three waves of city-wall building in the Ming dynasty: at the beginning right after the Ming took over power from the Mongols, in the sixteenth century in the wake of pirate attacks on the coastal areas, and at the end of the dynasty.

3. The pirates targeted coastal areas as well as areas that could be reached by water, including noncoastal cities such as Nanjing. Among the affected areas, Fujian and Zhejiang probably suffered the most and thus their wall-building

movement was particularly active. See Hsu Hong, "Mingdai Fujian de zhucheng yundong"; and Pang Xinping, "Kasei wakō katsuyakuki."

4. Mote, "Growth of Chinese Despotism"; Grimm, "State and Power in Juxtaposition"; Danjō Hiroshi, *Minchō sensei shihai.*

5. See Hucker, *Traditional Chinese State in Ming Times.* This view is also common among Chinese historians; see, e.g., Qian Mu, *Guoshi dagang,* 498–512.

6. This was made most explicit in the rite controversies during the Shizong and Shenzong reigns; see Ray Huang, *1587, A Year of No Significance.*

7. See "Introduction," in Esherick and Rankin, eds., *Chinese Local Elites*; and Shigeta, "Origins and Structure of Gentry Rule."

8. Brook, *The Chinese State,* esp. the Introduction and Conclusion; quotation from p. 13.

9. Ibid., 189.

10. Schneewind, *Community Schools*; quotation from the introduction, p. 5.

11. On the establishment of new counties/prefectures in the Ming in terms of the benefits to locals, such as higher quotas for the civil service examinations, improved local security, and better infrastructure to facilitate economic growth, see Bai Hua, *Mingdai zhouxian,* 52–74.

12. Han Zhongshu 韓仲叔, "Nancheng shuo" 難城説 (On the difficulty of building a wall), in *Gaochun xianzhi* (1683), 22.43b–45b.

13. Regional inspectors originally served as the "eyes and ears" of the emperor and reported directly to the court during their tours of duty as they monitored local governmental activities as well as accepted complaints from people. This position belonged to a unique Chinese inspection system (*jiancha* 監察) separate from the administration. Over the course of the Ming, however, their primary role gradually shifted from "inspecting" to "governing," and they became additional staff to the local administration; see Ogawa Takashi, *Mindai chihō kansatsu,* 19–36.

14. The 1573 edict designated officials, including regional inspectors, to be in charge of implementing the wall-construction policy; see *Ming Shenzong shilu* (1573), *juan* 2, 23–26. A full quotation and discussion of this edict can be found later in this section.

15. Judging from the timeline, the edict that prompted Xia's action might have been the one issued in 1573 (ibid., 23–26).

16. Pang Xinping, "Kasei wakō katsuyakuki," 39–42.

17. Hsu Hong, "Mingdai Fujian de zhucheng yundong."

18. There are more than three hundred entries in *Ming shilu* on wall construction. Although most address the situation in specific areas, some were general (re)announcements of the wall-construction policy. For example, in 1449, when Daizong assumed the throne after the kidnapping of Yingzong, he

issued an edict outlining his plans for his reign. The edict restated the importance of city walls and acknowledged the prevalent disrepair of city walls in the realm, which it attributed to a lack of oversight by local officials, and it urged local officials to repair the old walls. Officials in localities without walls were encouraged to propose construction plans to the court; see *Ming Yingzong shilu*, *juan* 186, 7323–24. The same happened in 1488 when Xiaozong assumed the throne (*Ming Xiaozong shilu*, *juan* 12, 276). In 1513, after receiving a memorial from Dong Ao 董鏊, the Zhengde emperor issued an edict ordering all unwalled cities to be walled (*Ming Wuzong shilu*, *juan* 98, 2054).

19. Tomaru Fukuju and Mogi Shūichirō, *Wakō kenkyū*.

20. *Ming Shenzong shilu* (1573), *juan* 2, 23–26.

21. Local initiatives have always played a central role in financing public works such as wall construction in imperial China; see Yang Lien-sheng, "Economic Aspects of Public Works," in idem, *Excursions in Sinology*, 191–248.

22. The presentation in local gazetteers was often affected by local politics, a phenomenon illustrated by *Xiaoshan xianzhi* (1935), 32.24a–24b. The gazetteer preserves a petition from 1568 complaining that a recent edition of the gazetteer deliberately referred to the petitioner's grandfather as a "local" (*yiren* 邑人) instead of as a "censor," his official title, in order to downplay the contribution of his family. For a fuller discussion of the development of local gazetteers in the Ming era, see Chapter 4.

23. Han Zhongshu, "Nan cheng shuo," in *Gaochun xianzhi* (1683), 22.43b–45b. Even though this piece is attributed to Han Zhongshu in all extant Gaochun gazetteers, Han Zhongshu made it clear that he was just summarizing the anti-wall petition written by Han Zhongxiao 韓仲孝, who was part of an activist group of Gaochun *shengyuan*. Therefore, although citations of this document in the notes credit Han Zhongshu as the author, my discussion focuses on the political lobbying by the *shengyuan* group headed by Han Zhongxiao.

24. Huang Bingshi, "Cheng Gaochun yi," in *Gaochun xianzhi* (1683), 22.51b–53b.

25. Although the 1606 gazetteer is no longer extant, the essays were reprinted in the 1683 edition used here.

26. Xiang Weicong, "Chongxiu *Gaochun xianzhi* xu," in *Gaochun xianzhi* (1683), 23.1a–3a.

27. For a description of local networks in Gaochun, see Chen Zuolin, *Jinling tongzhuan*, 19.1a–6a.

28. Huang Bingshi, "Cheng Gaochun yi," in *Gaochun xianzhi* (1683), 22.51b.

29. Xiang Weicong, "Jiancheng lun," in *Gaochun xianzhi* (1683), 22.50a.

30. The city wall was to be financed through the county office, and the expenses shared by all Gaochun residents, both inside and outside the county

seat. In the original Chinese texts, Gaochun county and Gaochun city can be distinguished only through their specific context. Basically, when discussing the wall-related expenses, the authors referred to Gaochun as a county and yet when debating the "wallability" of Gaochun, they tended to focus on the county capital, Gaochun city.

31. The locus classicus for this phrase is *Guoyu* 國語 ("Zhouyu" 周語): "Zhongxin chengcheng, zhongkou shuojin" 眾心成城, 眾口鑠金 (When the people's minds become walls, the people's words will melt gold). It emphasizes, in vivid terms, the importance to the ruler of winning the hearts and minds of his subjects.

32. Huang Bingshi, "Cheng Gaochun yi," in *Gaochun xianzhi* (1683), 22.51b–53b.

33. Xiang Weicong, "Jiancheng lun," in *Gaochun xianzhi* (1683), 22.50a.

34. Huang Bingshi, "Cheng Gaochun yi," in *Gaochun xianzhi* (1683), 22.51b.

35. Han Zhongshu, "Nancheng shuo," in *Gaochun xianzhi* (1683), 22.43b.

36. Ibid. Han's description is consistent with that of Xiang Weicong ("Jiancheng lun," in *Gaochun xianzhi* [1683]). Xiang emphasized not only the town-ish nature of Gaochun city but also the fact that there was no proper space to build a wall: "Once a town in Lishui county, Gaochun city faces a river to the south [i.e., Guanxi River, 官溪河; see Map 2.1], which later enters Lake Gucheng. To the east and west of the city all we can see is tilled polders. To the north are hills, where half of the land is occupied by tombs." Echoing Huang, whose point is discussed in the following paragraph, Xiang presented Gaochun's landscape as one defined by the water. Along the waterway lies the main residential and commercial area, whereas the elevated land is used as burial grounds (partially for *fengshui* reasons) and the rest turned into polders. Clearing a space for a wall would mean great economic and social losses for Gaochun residents.

37. Huang Bingshi, "Cheng Gaochun yi," in *Gaochun xianzhi* (1683), 22.51b–53b.

38. Ibid.

39. Ibid.

40. Ibid.

41. *Dimai* 地脈, a term in *fengshui* theory that describes the land contour as the vein of *qi* and life essence, which must not be disrupted.

42. Huang Bingshi, "Cheng Gaochun yi," in *Gaochun xianzhi* (1683), 22.51b–53b.

43. Tong Weisheng ("Gaochun xian jianxian") dates the designation of Gaochun as a county to 1491.

44. See Pang Xinping, "Kasei wakō katsuyakuki"; and Hsu Hong, "Mingdai Fujian de zhucheng yundong."

45. Lü Kun, "Zhancheng huowen" 展城或問 (Questions about wall expansion), in *Quweizhai ji*, 7.14b–29b.

46. *Wuxian zhi* (1642); see also the discussion of Suzhou's city walls in Yinong Xu, *Chinese City in Space and Time*.

47. Lü Kun, "Zhancheng huowen," in *Quweizhai ji*, 7.14b–29b. This essay was dated the first day of the first month of the lunar year corresponding roughly to 1601.

48. Lü Kun, "Yu gaixian xiangqin lun xiucheng" 與概縣鄉親論修城 (An open letter to my hometown fellows on the matter of city wall expansion), *Quweizhai ji*, 7.30a–34a.

49. Ibid., 7.32b.

50. Lü Kun, "Zhancheng huowen," in *Quweizhai ji*, 7.16b.

51. For a more detailed discussion of late Ming *gonglun* / "public opinion," see Chapter 1. Studies on the "civic society / public sphere" in late imperial China tend to focus on cities or economically advanced areas such as Jiangnan; see Brook and Frolic, *Civil Society in China*; Rowe, "Public Sphere in Modern China"; Wong, "Great Expectations"; and Bergère, "Civil Society." For more on the role of print media in late Ming public life, see Chapter 4.

52. *Shaoxing fuzhi* (1586), 2.6b–7a.

53. *Songjiang fuzhi* (1631), 19.1a–16b.

54. *Gaochun xianzhi* (1683), 15.7b–8a.

55. Ibid., 16.6b–7b.

56. Chen Zuolin, *Jinling tongzhuan*, 19.2a.

57. Han Bangxian, "Guangtongzhenba kao" 廣通鎮壩考 (A survey of the East Dam), in *Gaochun xianzhi* (1683), 22.32b–36a.

58. For the history of the Yanzhi River, see *Gaochun xianzhi* (1751), 4.3b–5a.

59. Hang Bangxian, "Gaochun shiyi," in *Gaochun xianzhi* (1683), 22.31b–32a.

60. Hang Bangxian, "Jianshui yi," in *Gaochun xianzhi* (1683), 8.21a–23a; idem, "Sitian yi," in *Gaochun xianzhi* (1683), 8.23a–25a.

61. Hang Bangxian, "Gaochun shiyi," in *Gaochun xianzhi* (1683), 22.31b–32a.

62. Chen Zuolin, *Jinling tongzhuan*, 19.1a–2a.

63. See "Fuyi kao" 賦役考 (Survey of taxes and levies), in *Gaochun xianzhi* (1683), 8.1a–30b.

64. See Huang Bingshi, "Cheng Gaochun yi," in *Gaochun xianzhi* (1683), 22.51b–53b.

65. *Jiangpu xianzhi* (1726), 2.6a–8b.

66. The grand commandant was the senior of three dignitaries who constituted the military regency council in control of Nanjing; see Hucker, *Dictionary
of Official Titles*.

67. *Jiangpu xianzhi* (1726), 1.26a.

68. *Jiangpu pisheng* (1891), 5.5b–6b.

69. In Nanjing, the two most critical positions were the grand commandant
and grand adjutant, both members of the triumvirate who were entrusted with
military control of Nanjing after 1420. Grand adjutant was normally a concurrent appointment for the Nanjing minister of war; see *Mingshi, juan 76*.

70. *Jiangpu xianzhi* (1726), 1.4a.

71. Lang Da 郎達, "Xunyanchayuan beijilue" 巡鹽察院碑記略 (Epigraph
on the office of the salt-control censor), in ibid., 8.128b–30a.

72. Zhu Jue 朱覺, "Hubu fensi gongshu ji" 戶部分司公署記 (Account of
the Branch Office of the Ministry of Revenue), in *Jiangpu xianzhi* (1726), 8.79a–
80a.

73. See "Wubeilzhi" 武備志 (On military defense), in *Jiangpu xianzhi* (1726),
3.1a–5b.

74. Jiao Hong 焦竑, "Kai Duijianghe ji" 開對江河記 (A record on the
dredging of the Duijiang River), 1594, in *Jiangpu xianzhi*, 8.98a–101a.

75. *Jiangpu xianzhi* (1726), 1.13a.

76. The Capital Training Divisions were large military encampments at the
two capitals to which troops belonging to guards (*wei* 衛) throughout the empire
were rotated for training and service as a kind of combat-ready reserve. By the
latter half of the Ming, they had ceased to function as effective fighting forces;
these troops were normally used as state construction crews or assigned to other
menial tasks, which was probably why they were part of the wall project.

77. *Jiangpu pisheng* (1891), 5.4a–9b.

78. Ibid., 5.5b–6b.

79. Ibid.

80. Zhang Bangzhi 張邦直, "Zhu Kuangkoushan tuyuan ji" 築曠口山土
垣記 (Account of the dirt-wall construction at Kuangkou mountatin), in *Jiangpu xianzhi* (1726), 8.82a–84a.

81. Jiang Bao 姜寶, "Jiangpu xincheng ji" 江浦新城記 (An essay on the new
Jiangpu city wall), 1580, in *Jiangpu xianzhi* (1726), 8.86a–88b; He Kuan 何寬,
"Jian Kuangkoushan cheng ji" 建曠口山城記 (An essay on the Kuangkou city
wall), 1580, in *Jiangpu xianzhi* (1726), 8.88b–92a. These essays are also collected in
Jiangpu pisheng (1891), 5.1a–4b.

82. Yu Menglin 余孟麟 in "Jian Wenminglo ji" 建文明樓記 commended
the magistrate: "As he conducted the construction with an efficient method-

ology and a fair distribution of labor, he accomplished the job with ease and received no public criticism" (quoted in *Jiangpu xianzhi* [1627], 8.92a–94b).

83. See Jiang Bao, "Jiangpu xincheng ji," and He Kuan, "Jian Kuangkou-shan cheng ji," in *Jiangpu xianzhi* (1726), 8.86a–88b and 88b–92a, respectively.

84. The acknowledgment list of Nanjing officials was compiled by Magistrate He on the completion of Jiangpu's city walls; see He Kuan, "Jian Kuang-koushan cheng ji," in *Jiangpu xianzhi* (1726), 8.88b–92a.

85. *Jiangpu pisheng* (1891), 3.7a–13a; *Luhe xianzhi* (1884), 1.19–24.

86. For a review of this line of Chinese scholarship, see Feuerwerker, "From 'Feudalism' to 'Capitalism'"; Li Wenzhi, *Wan Ming minbian*; and Fu Yiling, "Mingdai houqi Jiangnan chengzhen xiaceng shimin de fanfengjian yundong," in *Mingdai Jiangnan shimin jingji shitan*. Inspired by these late Ming social criticisms, some Japanese sinologists have also endeavored to determine how late Ming economic development created social or political conditions at odds with the once generally accepted notion of an all-powerful Chinese despotism. Historians like Tanaka Masatoshi, Saeki Yūichi, and Oyama Masaaki consider anti-rent and anti-tax movements in China as an indigenous form of class struggle under the conviction that without such struggles economic development could never take root in political reality. These scholars examine numerous cases in which people organized themselves at the grassroots level to make demands and voice their dissatisfaction. Like their Chinese colleagues, they concluded that the massive commercialization of the sixteenth century gave rise to new social relations capable of challenging traditional "feudalistic" authority. Representative works include Tanaka Masatoshi, "Popular Rebellions"; and Kobayashi Kazumi, "The Other Side of Rent and Tax Resistance Struggles." For a clear summary of the historiography in Japanese sinology, see the editors' introduction in Grove and Daniels, *State and Society in China*.

87. Zurndorfer, "Violence and Political Protest"; and Wakeman, "Rebellion and Revolution," also voice similar criticisms.

88. Kobayashi Kazumi, "The Other Side of Rent and Tax Resistance Struggles."

89. James Tong, *Disorder Under Heaven*, 194–97.

90. Ibid.

91. See Zurndorfer, "Violence and Political Protest," 317–19.

92. Wu Jen-shu, "Ming Qing chengshi minbian yanjiu."

93. Tong, *Disorder Under Heaven*, 155–57.

94. Ibid., 156.

95. Fang, *Auxiliary Administration*.

96. For the history of Yanzhi River, see *Gaochun xianzhi* (1751), 4.3b–5a.

97. Xu Gu 許穀, "Lishui xian gaijian bianmin xin cang ji" 溧水縣改建便民新倉記 (Account on the new granary in Lishui county), in *Gaochun xianzhi* (1683). G. William Skinner first made this argument based primarily on Qing sources, but a recent study of the Ming field administration confirms his findings: see Bai Hua, *Mingdai zhouxian*, 52–74.

98. Skinner's model introduces a spatial framework composed of three types of geographies: physiographic (based on natural topography), regional economic (based on Skinner's central-place model), and official-administrative (the province-prefecture-county hierarchy). Skinner's data show that the first two, the physiographic and macro-regional geographies, correspond closely. The formation of the third is rather complicated. The administrative hierarchy seems to have been superficially imposed by the state with a strong influence from the long-established tradition of field administration. On closer examination, Skinner found that the Qing government had in fact carefully crafted a balance between the physiographic and the economic geographies. Simply put, the state had two primary concerns when formulating the administrative hierarchy: revenues and military defense. Financial concerns led the administrative hierarchy to approximate the regional market geography: the place of a city in the economic hierarchy correlated with its capacity to generate revenue. The military defense function of a city was, by contrast, intrinsically related to its surrounding topography. Therefore, in core areas, administrative divisions coincided more with economic hierarchies, but in frontier regions, where defense was the primary concern, administrative systems were more strongly shaped by the natural topography. In other words, in order to achieve the two goals (revenue and security), the design of administrative hierarchy had to maintain a balance between economic and physiographic geographies. In practice, the Qing government employed a fourfold criterion to determine administrative appointments: *chong* 衝 (location, traffic intersection), *pi* 疲 (administrative difficulty), *fan* 繁 (short on tax quota), *nan* 難 (litigation and crime). This complicated scheme greatly enhanced the state's ability to adjust the administrative system to reconcile economic and physiographic geographies. Skinner observes that "the capstone of the system was the meticulous classification of capitals that faithfully reflected the core-periphery structure of regions, the capital's level in the hierarchy of economic central places, span of control, and the relative salience of distinctive administrative tasks." In light of this flexibility, Skinner concludes that "bureaucratic government may have imposed elements of formal uniformity on Chinese cities, but in practice, field administration expressed rather than suppressed functional differentiation within the city system." See Skinner, "Cities and the Hierarchy of Local Systems," in idem, ed., *City in Late Imperial China*, 275–77; and Liu Zhengyun, "'Chong, pi, fan, nan.'"

99. Kawakatsu Mamoru, *Min Shin kōnan shichin*, 73–142.

100. Traditional maps were often criticized as being badly proportioned and inaccurate. However, the cartographical techniques, at least in the Ming, had long been advanced enough to be able to produce proportionate grid maps, such as those in *Guangfangyu zhi* 廣方輿志. The reason that these maps did not prevail could only be ideological. For more on Ming maps, see Chapter 3.

101. See Huang Bingshi, "Cheng Gaochun yi," in *Gaochun xianzhi* (1683), 22.51b–53b.

102. For example, in the case of Ningyang county, its promotion into a county was perceived as a threat to the interest groups at Longyang, the mother county, and provoked a vehement fight. The *shengyuan* at Ningyang who had led the petition drive were stripped of their degrees. See Aoyama Ichirō, "Mingdai no shin ken."

103. Mori Masao, "Kōnan deruta no kyōchinshi"; see also idem, "Shindai Kōnan deruta no kyōchinshi"; and idem, "Ming-Qing shidai Jiangnan."

104. For a more detailed discussion of the development of local gazetteers, see Chapter 3.

105. The distinction between official and town gazetteers, for example, is clearly articulated in the preface to *Pingwang zhenzhi* (1732), 3–4. Also see Mori Masao, "Ming-Qing shidai Jiangnan," 803–11.

106. According to Mori Masao ("Ming-Qing shidai Jiangnan"), such sentiments softened in the Qing as many town gazetteer editors came to see their work as a supplement to official gazetteers.

107. See Xu Mingshi 徐鳴時, "Preface to *Hengxi lu*," in "Za ji" 雜記 (miscellaneous notes), in *Hengxi lu* (1629), *juan* 5, 162. in Wang Ji's 王濟 preface to *Wuqing zhenzhi* (1601) also suggests a similar sentiment: "Our town Wuqing . . . its extravagance and grandeur is famous all over the Yangzi River area. In addition, the town bred renowned scholars one after another. However, all these economic or cultural achievements were overlooked by the county gazetteers. Is it because the distance between our town and the county capital suddenly made us an uncivilized settlement? Of course, from the county's perspective, our town appears insignificant; yet from our viewpoint, this piece of land is indeed grand."

108. See Hamashima Atsutoshi, *Sōkan shinkō*, 113–234.

109. See Tang Shouli's 唐守禮 postscript to *Wuqing zhenzhi* (1601), 212–13.

110. Skinner, ed., *City in Late Imperial China*, 17–23.

111. The most forceful rebuttal to the Weberian line of argument comes from the two-volume work on Hankow by William Rowe (*Hankow: Commerce and Society* and *Hankow: Conflict and Community*). The chosen city, Hankow, was one of the most prominent market towns in the Qing dynasty.

112. Faure, "What Made Foshan a Town?"

113. Kawakatsu Mamoru, *Min Shin kōnan shichin*; Chen Guocan, "Luelun Nan Song."

114. *Xunjian si* were set up for small areas distant from the county seat, extending the state authority down to the most grassroots level. It was headed by a police chief (*xunjian*), ranked 9a, and sometimes staffed entirely by subofficial functionaries. See Hucker, *Dictionary of Official Titles.*

115. Kawakatsu Mamoru (*Min Shin kōnan shichin*, 543–72) believes the cut in the number of *xunjian si* and *shuike siju* indicates the diminished importance of market towns in the Ming. Fuma Susuma ("Chūgoku kinsei toshi"), however, contends that it was part of the general policy to reduce commercial taxation all over the empire, not a specific measure against market towns.

116. Zhang Yan, "Qingdai shizhen"; Lin Shaoming, "Ming-Qing nian jian Jiangnan shizhen"; Chen Zhongping, "Song Yuan Ming Qing shiqi Jiangnan shizhen."

117. Zhang Yan, "Qingdai shizhen."

118. Kawakatsu, *Min Shin kōnan shichin*, 73–142.

119. For a literature review on the rise of Ming-Qing market towns, see Fan I-chun, "Ming-Qing Jiangnan."

120. Farmer, "Hierarchy of Ming City Walls."

121. Sen-dou Chang, "The Morphology of Walled Capitals."

122. For example, because of the neglect of wall construction in the Yuan era, by the beginning of the Ming dynasty most cities in north China were not walled. See Hsu Hong, "Mingdai Fujian de zhucheng yundong."

123. Song and Yuan policies on wall building, for example, were quite different; see note 2 to this chapter.

CHAPTER 3

1. Li-tsui Flora Fu, "Xie Shichen"; Yi Ruofen, "Lüyou, woyou yu shenyou."

2. In fact, some literati even argued that with the proper mindset, imaginary touring was a much more valuable cultural practice than physical travel. More discussion of this point is presented later in this chapter.

3. The two different editions of *Jinling tuyong* can be found in the rare book collection at the National Central Library, Taipei, Taiwan.

4. Although lineage study is an established field among Ming-Qing historians, the focus has been predominantly rural. Only recently have there appeared case studies on urban lineages, such as Inoue Tōru's work on Suzhou (*Chūgoku no sōzoku to kokka no reisei*, chap. 5) and Huang Haiyan's research on Guangzhou (*Zai chengshi yu xiangcun zhijian*). In contrast to their focus on the social organization of urban lineages, this chapter studies the cultural performance of

native identity of a group of Nanjing families and its influence on the greater Nanjing community.

5. One entry in Gu Qiyuan's *Kezuo zhuiyu* (6: 198–99), "Yayou bian" 雅遊編 (The elegant tour), documents the origin and publication of *Jinling yayou bian*.

6. See Gu Qiyuan, "Jinlingren Jinling zhuzhi" 金陵人金陵諸志 (Various Jinling gazetteers compiled by Jinling natives), in idem, *Kezuo zhuiyu*, 7.219. Similar distinctions were also made in another *biji* on Nanjing by a Nanjing native: Zhou Hui's *Jinling suoshi*. By applying this native criterion extensively, both Gu and Zhou were able to establish a series of genealogies for native Nanjing painters, poets, connoisseurs, high officials, etc. For more on this, see Chapter 4.

7. This list contains only extant works. Contemporary accounts have much more extensive lists of Nanjing natives and their works on Nanjing. Since late Ming Nanjing literati had a strong interest in reconstructing a genealogy of Nanjing natives who wrote about Nanjing, the sources are very rich. See Chapter 4.

8. For the relationship among the authors of *Jinling tuyong*, see below. The authors of the other listed works had ties with him.

9. See Brook, *Geographical Sources of Ming-Qing History*, 49–72. According to his comprehensive survey of geographical sources, the mid-Ming witnessed a surging interest in the "particularity of places," manifested in both visual and written forms. For confirmation of this observation, see Naquin, *Peking*, 249–58.

10. Lewis, "Cities and Capitals," in idem, *Construction of Space*, 135–88.

11. There are still many unanswered questions about this famous painting, including the identity of its creator, its subject, and its purpose. See Hsingyuan Tsao, "Unraveling the Mystery of *Qingming shanghe tu.*"

12. See Steinhardt, "Mapping the Chinese City."

13. See Steinhardt, *Chinese Imperial City Planning*, 93–108.

14. Wang Junhua 王俊華, preface to *Hongwu jingcheng tuzhi*. Wang served as a gentleman for rendering service (not a specific position but rather an honorary title, or *san'guan*) and as right admonisher in the Right Secretariat of the Heir Apparent; he also worked for the Household of the Heir Apparent. The edition in use was published in 1928 by Liu Yizheng 柳詒徵 (1880–1956).

15. For example, Chen Yi, when he was compiling a Nanjing gazetteer, was allowed to view *Hongwu jingcheng tuzhi*. Chen Yi's story is discussed in the next section.

16. This was the year Nanjing was officially designated the *jingshi* 京師 (the capital).

17. For example, as capital of Wu in the Three Kingdoms period; East Jin, Song, Qi, Liang, and Chen in the Six Dynasties; and Southern Tang in the Five Dynasties.

18. In 1373, after the completion of Zhongdu 中都 (modern Fengyang 鳳陽 in Anhui), in the sacrifice ceremony for the city god, Taizu addressed the reason for building a new capital. He was concerned that Nanjing was not centrally located and that this made it difficult for the court to take full control of the realm; see *Ming Taizu shilu* (1373), 80.1447. In addition to strategic concerns, a record in *Huang Ming yonghua leibian* cites Taizu's apprehension about Nanjing's past as a reason for his decision to build Zhongdu, "Jinling was the old [capital] site for the Six Dynasties; however, none of these regimes enjoyed a long life" ("Jinling, liuchao jiudi, guozuo bu yong" 金陵・六朝舊地，國祚 不永), in Deng Qiu, "Duyi" 都邑 (The capital), in idem, *Huang Ming yonghua leibian*, 80.2a.

19. Zhu Yuanzhang, "Yuejiang lou ji"; idem, "You Yuejiang lou ji."

20. Song Lian, "Yuejiang lou ji." The geomantic centrality of Nanjing was further augmented by Zhu's mausoleum (Xiaoling 孝陵), and the discourse of "royal air" took on a new twist in late Ming politics. See Luo Xiaoxiang, "'Jingling genben zhongdi.'"

21. Zhu Yuanzhang, "Yuejiang lou ji."

22. The only known exception is Nanjing in the Song. A Song map in *Jinding Jiankang zhi* (1261) depicts a protrusion on the upper left corner, but the city is still generally projected as a regular square with straight perpendicular sides as opposed to the irregular curves of the *Hongwu Atlas*. The title of this map, "Longpan huju" (Coiling dragon, crouching tiger), suggests an emphasis on Nanjing's natural terrain, hence the slight deviation from convention. Nanjing in the Song was only a prefectural seat and thus was less subject to the pressure to conform to the ideal urban form.

23. The extraordinary continuity and emphasis on symbolic function in the morphology of Chinese cities has frequently been noted by scholars. Arthur Wright ("Cosmology of the Chinese City") suggested that Chinese imperial cities presented an exception to the general patterns of other civilizations in which, as they developed, the "authority of the ancient beliefs wanes and secular concerns—economic, strategic, and political—come to dominate the location and design of cities." In contrast, Chinese cities were a product more of ideological than of practical concerns. Such spatial ideology is best illustrated in the planning of an imperial capital as a microcosm of the Chinese universe with all symbolic power converging on the throne. As the symbolic center of the empire, imperial capitals embodied political legitimacy on a grand scale. This argument, however, has been largely modified by recently excavated archeological evidence. Based on newly available sources, Nancy Steinhardt's work demonstrates both the continuity and the transformation of Chinese imperial city planning; see esp. her "Why Were Chang'an and Beijing So Differ-

ent?" and *Chinese Imperial City Planning*. Steinhardt acknowledges the extraordinary continuity in Chinese urban tradition. Common features in imperial city planning include four-sided enclosures, gates, defensive projections, clearly articulated and directed space, orientation and alignment in accordance with cosmological order, ward systems, accessibility of water, vast size, huge populations, and a prescribed order of construction. It is remarkable that planners followed these basic prescriptions for city building to such an extent for over two millennia. Nevertheless, as Steinhardt points out, such seemingly impressive consistency might have been a product more of representation than of practice. Based on fresh archeological sources that have come to light in the past two decades, Steinhardt demonstrates that Chinese imperial plans were not exclusively modeled on a cosmological system but designed in response to a combination of factors. Most of them reflected pragmatic concerns such as drainage, topography, or military defense. Moreover, contrary to belief, there were three different models for imperial city planning, each with a history of more than two thousand years. However, in order to claim political legitimacy through adherence to an orthodox design, new regimes sometimes published idealized and fictitious capital plans, resulting in a myth of a universal Chinese imperial city plan.

24. *Ming Taizu shilu* (1366), 21.295.

25. See Hui-shu Lee, *Exquisite Moments*, 21–23.

26. Steinhardt, *Chinese Imperial City Planning*, 5.

27. Nancy Steinhardt (ibid.) argues that in China "city planning" has a twofold implication: it refers to the actual planning of spatial arrangement at the inception of a physical city, and it is also part of a representational program that affirms and asserts a new regime's ideological legitimacy. The latter often eclipses the former, and as a result, much of the on-the-ground innovation is not acknowledged.

28. The mountain and river map (Fig. 3.7) in the *Hongwu Atlas* demonstrates clearly how Hongwu pushed the city to its natural limits and had the capital defined by the surrounding landscape.

29. *Chongkan Jiangning fuzhi* (1736), 3.2a–b.

30. Yang Erzeng, *Xinjuan Hainei qiguan*.

31. See Wang Junhua, preface to *Hongwu jingcheng tuzhi*.

32. *Huang Ming yonghua leibian* records a conversation between Taizu and Liu Ji 劉基—Zhu's closest consultant prior to and after the founding of the Ming dynasty—about the peculiar siting of Nanjing's palace city. The foundation of the palace was initially set in the center of Nanjing. After Liu Ji pointed out the ill-fated association with the Six Dynasties, however, Taizu moved the palace to the eastern part of Nanjing and cited the *Yijing* passage "di chu hu zhen"

帝出乎震 (the emperor arises from the east) to justify this decision. See Deng Qiu, "Duyi," *Huang Ming yonghua leibian*, 80.3a–b. Although I cannot corroborate this entry in *Ming shilu*, a comparison with the other potential capital, Zhongdu, indicates that this might very well be accurate. Zhongdu was built before Nanjing and affected many aspects of Nanjing's planning. Yet the layout and placement of the palace in Zhongdu conformed strictly to the traditional paradigm. Thus, it is possible that the palace city in Nanjing was intentionally sited off-center for other symbolic concerns, such as the problematic association with the Six Dynasties. For more information on Zhongdu's plan, see Wang Jianying, *Ming Zhongdu yanjiu*; for a detailed discussion of the construction of Nanjing palace city and how Taizu reinterpreted the symbolic meaning of its unusual placement, see Hsu Hong, "Mingchu Nanjing huang-cheng."

33. In fact, all the monasteries and temples were administered under the state registry system. Since a state-issued certificate was required for anyone who wanted to join the monastery, the path between the secular and the religious was strictly regulated by the state through a very limited quota of passes. See He Xiaorong, *Mingdai Nanjing siyuan yianjiu*, 1–20.

34. *Ming Taizu shilu* (1382), 280.3099.

35. For example, the entertainment quarters had two tiers, one with official courtesans to entertain officials and merchants alike; the other to provide sex services open only to merchants. See Hsu Hong, "Mingchu Nanjing de dushi guihua," 94.

36. *Hongwu jingcheng tuzhi*, 7a.

37. Ibid., 6b.

38. Ibid., 8a.

39. Ibid., 8b, 5b.

40. According to Aoyama Sadao (*Tō-Sō jidai no kōtsū*), by the end of the Song, *zhi* had developed into a structured way, with a standardized table of contents, to represent a place. In the Ming period, gazetteers were further standardized in terms of compilation and contents. Not only were gazetteers systematically compiled by the state through local administrative units, but also the genre appeared to have become an essential venue for locals to register place-related information. For further discussion on this development and its ramification for cities, see Chapter 4.

41. This observation corresponds with that in Chang Che-chia, "Mingdai fangzhi zhong de ditu," which also categorizes maps in Ming gazetteers into the same three major categories.

42. Farmer, "Hierarchy of Ming City Walls."

43. This particular cultural perspective in Chinese maps, argues Chang Che-jia ("Mingdai fangzhi zhong de ditu"), can be contrasted with that of medieval European city maps, which were produced as if the city were viewed from a wide-angle, elevated perspective outside the city. His characterization of Ming maps is consistent with that in Nancy Steinhardt's comprehensive survey of Chinese city planning, "Mapping the Chinese City." She concludes, "The reality of the map of a Chinese city lay in the regal system it symbolized in which there was always a place for a ruler to sit facing south in the center" (33).

44. Liu Yizheng, "Chongkan ba" 重刊跋 (Preface) to the 1928 reprint of Chen Yi, *Jinling gujin tukao*, 36a.

45. Qian Qianyi characterized Nanjing's literary scene in the Ming era as having several stages; *Jinling sanjun* was part of the earliest; see "Jinling sheji zhushiren" 金陵社集諸詩人 (The poets at Nanjing gatherings), in Qian Qianyi, *Liechao shiji xiaozhuan, ding ji*, 502. This period also marked a golden age for art circles; see Shi Shouqian, "Langdang zhi feng."

46. Chen Yi, Preface to *Jinling gujin tukao*, 1a–b.

47. Ibid.

48. Chen Yi, *Jinling gujin tukao*, 8a–b, 10a–b, 12a–b.

49. Ibid., 33a–b.

50. Wang Hongru, Epilogue to the 1489 reprint of *Hongwu jingcheng tuzhi*.

51. Ibid.

52. Regarding the Ming dual-capital system, see Farmer, *Early Ming Government*.

53. See Aramiya Manabu, *Pekin sento no kenkyū*, 65–66. Aramiya argues that toward the end of the Hongwu reign there appeared to be some discussion of moving the capital north to Xi'an, of which Prince Jianwen was a major advocate. As a result, after Yongle's usurpation and Jianwen's exile (or death), all sources on this proposal were suppressed in official documents. When the theory of Hongwu's capital plan resurfaced in the mid-fifteenth century, the location of this new possible northern capital had become Beijing, instead of Xi'an, to validate the continuity between the Hongwu reign and the Yongle reign as well as the legitimacy of the latter.

54. Gui Youguang, "Ti *Hongwu jingcheng tuzhi* hou" 題洪武京城圖志後 (Inscription to *Hongwu jingcheng tuzhi*), included in the 1928 reprint of *Hongwu jingcheng tuzhi*; and also in Gui's collected works, *Zhenchuan ji*, 5.1b–2b.

55. Wang Qi, *Sancai tuhui*, 3.1034–35.

56. Yang Erzeng, *Xinjuan Hainei qiguan*, 2.7b–8a.

57. It is interesting that even though Chen Yi's atlas was made mainly to depict a Nanjing of the past, its map of Ming Nanjing was often appropriated

by Qing gazetteers as contemporary; see, e.g., *Jiangning xin zhi* (1748), *Shangyuan xianzhi* (1722), and *Shangyuan xianzhi* (1824).

58. Although scaled cartography had a long history in China, it was not until the nineteenth century that such a projection entered the mainstream. In a nineteenth-century Nanjing gazetteer, the editor explicitly criticized the local cartography of the past as being "ridiculous" and traced this failing to a Song gazetteer; see *Chongkan Jiangning fuzhi* (1811), "Yutu" 輿圖 (maps), 3.1a–9a.

59. Mote ("A Millennium of Chinese Urban History") argues that "place" in China was constituted by the textualization of space that created and recreated meaning for the past and present.

60. See Cahill, "Huangshan Paintings as Pilgrimage Pictures."

61. In Nanjing, for example, this trend led to a surge in the production of gazetteers of various kinds. In addition to the conventional gazetteers of administrative units, topographical and institutional gazetteers became popular after the sixteenth century. Three mountain gazetteers by Nanjing native authors, *Qixia xiaozhi* 棲霞小志 (Short record of Qixia Monastery), *Niushou shan zhi* 牛首山志 (Gazetteer of Mount Niushou), and *Xianhuayan zhi* 獻花岩志 (Gazetteer of Xianhua Grotto), fall into this emerging genre of topographical gazetteers. The trend also led to the publication of government institutional gazetteers, such as *Liubu zhi* 六部志 (Gazetteers of the Six Ministries), although out of the six only three survive: *Libu zhigao* 禮部志稿 (Gazetteer of the Nanjing Ministry of Rites, 1620), *Nanjing Hubuzhi* 南京戶部志 (Gazetteer of the Nanjing Ministry of Revenue, preface dated 1550), and *Nanjing Xingbuzhi* 南京刑部志 (Gazetteer of the Nanjing Ministry of Justice). Other extant institutional gazetteers include *Nanjing Taipusi zhi* 南京太僕寺誌 (Gazetteer of the Nanjing Court of the Imperial Stud), *Nanjing Guanglusi zhi* 南京光祿寺志 (Gazetteer of the Nanjing Court of Imperial Entertainment), *Longjiang chuanchang zhi* 龍江船廠志 (Gazetteer of the Longjiang Shipyard), *Jingxue zhi* 京學志 (Gazetteer of the prefectural school in the [Southern] Capital), and *Nanyong zhi* 南雍志 (Gazetteer of the Southern Academy). Other extant works include *Jinling fancha zhi* 金陵梵刹志 (Gazetteer of Buddhist monasteries in Nanjing), *Jinling xuanguan zhi* 金陵玄觀志 (Gazetteer of Daoist monasteries in Nanjing), *Houhu zhi* 後湖志 (Gazetteer of Xuanwu Lake), and *Linggu chanlin zhi* 靈谷禪林志 (Gazetteer of Linggu Chan Monastery).

62. On the late Ming reading public, see Brokaw and Chow, eds., *Printing and Book Culture.*

63. See Brook, *Geographical Sources of Ming-Qing*, esp. the Introduction, 49–72.

64. Zhao Jishi, "Shi yuan" 詩原 (Origin of poetry), in idem, *Jiyuan ji suo ji*, 129.

65. See Liscomb, "*The Eight Views of Beijing*"; Shi Shuqing, "Wang Fu *Beijing ba jing tu* yanjiu"; and White, "Topographical Painting."

66. For a more detailed discussion of these general guidebooks, see Meyer-Fong, "Seeing the Sights in Yangzhou."

67. Wu Jen-shu, "Wan Ming de lüyou."

68. See Meyer-Fong, "Seeing the Sights in Yangzhou," 213–16.

69. Brook, *Confusions of Pleasure*, 74–182; Wu Jen-shu, "Wan Ming de lüyou."

70. Meyer-Fong "Seeing the Sights in Yangzhou," 213.

71. For example, Chen Jiru, in his "Min you cao xu" 閩游草序 (Preface to the travelogue to the Min area) (reprinted in *Chen Meigong xiaopin*, 16–17), took great pains to establish the proprieties of *you*. Such clarification was important since—Chen cited the criticism of his friend Zhou Gongmei 周公美—many contemporary practices were not worthy of the name of *you*. For more detailed discussion, see Wu Jen-shu, "Wan Ming de lüyou."

72. Li Rihua (1565–1635) once commented: "There are no others as enchanted by the trend of touring as *shengyuan*"; (*Weishui xuan riji*, 6.385).

73. Xie Zhaozhi, "*Jin you cao* zi xu" 近遊草自序 (Preface to *Jin you cao*), in idem, *Xiaocao zhai ji*, 5.21a.

74. *Shanren*, "mountain eremites," had developed into a special social group by the late Ming. Many of them were well educated but had failed to pass the civil service examinations or secure official appointments. Relying on their literary skills and training in the Classics, some joined the retinues of prominent officials. Others achieved a certain level of autonomy through the prospering publishing industry at the time. Their alternative career path became a point of social contention, and *shanren* were the target of criticism and mockery. See Zhang Dejian, *Mingdai shanren wenxue yanjiu*; and idem, "Mingdai shanren qunti."

75. See Wu Jen-shu, "Wan Ming de lüyou"; and Meyer-Fong, "Seeing the Sights in Yangzhou."

76. Qian Qianyi, "Yuedong you cao yin" 越東游草引 (Preface to the travelogue of the eastern Yue area), in idem, *Muzhai chu xue ji*, 32.927–28.

77. The excessive production of scenic poetry was a widely recognized phenomenon. For a comment on the generally low quality of most such literary works at the time, see Shen Kai, "Qiyou manji xu" 奇遊漫記序 (Preface to the scattered notes on wondrous travel), in idem, *Huanxi ji*, 3.12a.

78. See Tang Xianzu, Preface to He Tang, *Mingshan shenggai ji*.

79. The most significant theory in the China field on the operation of social distinction in cultural connoisseurship was pioneered by Craig Clunas. In *Superfluous Things*, Clunas emphasizes the contended social boundaries between the bureaucratic elites and emulating merchants by analyzing late Ming discourses about the appreciation of objects. Clunas's work has provoked many

subsequent researches on the issue of taste and social boundaries. Although his view does apply to many cases, my findings here suggest that the contended social boundary as defined by the display of taste was much more complicated and requires a more nuanced approach. Above all, we should pay more attention to the internal stratification of the elite class. Zhang Dejian's study "Mingdai shanren qunti" on *shanren* is a good example. For a review of the issue of consumption and social class, see Wu Jen-shu, "Ming Qing xiaofei wenhua."

80. Wu Jen-shu, "Wan Ming de lüyou."

81. See *Xiangyan lueji* (1675), 1a, cited by Brook, *Geographical Sources of Ming-Qing History*, 38.

82. Ge Yinliang, *Jinling fancha zhi* (1627).

83. This trend was shared by other monastery gazetteers that also included travel literature (e.g., Sheng Shitai, *Niushou shan zhi*).

84. Indeed, the rendition of ten architectural maps clearly reflected such editorial principles. These images purported to illustrate temples designated as "large," with two exceptions—Hongji Temple 弘濟寺 and Qingliang Temple 清涼寺—included because of their outstanding scenery. This arrangement confirms that the purpose of these images was indeed twofold: facilitating monastery administration as well as enhancing the monasteries' appeal to both physical and virtual tourers. For example, the gazetteer maps of Hongji Temple, which was built next to the Yangzi River, offer a typical visualization of temples in this gazetteer. The image presents a full frontal view of the river, the mountain, the temple compound in between, as well as detailed close-ups of the property, which were rarely shown in other sources. In accord with this composition, the text labels indicate all registered buildings in the temple complex, its landed property (marked as *tian* 田, "farmland"), and all popular scenic sites to guide virtual or actual tourists. All main landmarks are efficiently signposted to navigate the viewer throughout the compound, with the main walkway labeled "the big road." Also prominently noted in this image is the Swallow Submerged Rock 燕子磯, a popular sight in Nanjing since the path to it opens onto a grand view of the river. In fact the temple itself also offered a commanding view to the Yangzi River and was a popular destination. Across the river was the major customs checkpoint for Nanjing, the Longjiang Customs Office 龍江關, which was considered a sight in itself. With so many famous attractions around the temple, it is not surprising that Ge Yinliang felt obliged to violate his own editorial principles and produced a separate image of the Hongji Temple for readers.

85. See Li-tsui Flora Fu, "Xie Shichen."

86. Yuan Zhongdao, "Song Shiyangzi xia di gui xing xu" 送石洋子下第歸省序 (Preface for Shiyangzi on his trip to visit his family), in idem, *Kexuezhai ji, juan* 9, 445.

87. Qian Qianyi, "Qin xiucai Gao" 秦秀才鎬, in idem, *Liechao shiji xiao-zhuan*, 682.

88. Kong Shangren, "Guo Kuangshan Guangling zeng yan xu" 郭匡山廣陵贈言序 (Preface to Guo Kuangshan's essay on Guangling), in idem, *Kong Shangren shiwen ji, juan* 6, 459–60.

89. Ibid., 459.

90. Zhong Xing, "Ti Linggu you juan" 題靈谷遊卷 (Inscription on the handscroll for the tour of Linggu), in idem, *Yinxiuxuan wenyu ji, tiba* 5b–6a.

91. Siggstedt, "Topographical Motifs."

92. Ibid.

93. Timothy Brook (*Geographical Sources of Ming-Qing History*, 55–64) suggests that the concentrated production of gazetteers and topographic art in six-teenth-century China reflects heightened sensitivity toward space and place. Moreover, a shared group of authors further indicates that topographical art and gazetteers were the products of a single cultural movement that exhibited strong interest in the particularity of places. Mette Siggstedt's case study of mid-Ming Suzhou, "Topographical Motifs," also confirms this observation.

94. Lin Jiaohong, "Wan Ming Huangshan"; Cahill, "Huangshan Paintings as Pilgrimage Pictures."

95. See McDermott, "The Making of a Chinese Mountain," 147.

96. Debevoise and Jang, "Topography and the Anhui School," 43–50.

97. Yao Ruxun, "You chengbei zhushan ji" 遊城北諸山記 (An essay on the tour of the mountains in northern Nanjing), in Zhu Zhifan, *Yushan bian*, 1a–7a.

98. Zhu Zhifan, *Yushan bian*, Epilogue, 20a.

99. Zhu Zhifan, ed., *Jinling tuyong*, Preface.

100. Yu Menglin et al., *Jinling yayou bian*, 9a–b.

101. Zhu Zhifan, ed., *Jinling tuyong*, 17b.

102. Ibid., 14b.

103. In "Place: Meditations on the Past of Chin-ling," Owen traces the de-velopment of the poetry on Nanjing over the course of several centuries in which images of the city were produced and embellished, leading up to the emergence of a dominant group of powerful poems. Given this virtually in-escapable legacy, he argues, writers of later generations were expected to speak of Nanjing through this particular group of received images.

104. Mei, "Mass-Production of Topographic Pictures."

105. This practice is said to have been particularly common among commercial presses in Suzhou; see Chiu Peng-sheng, "Mingdai Suzhou yingli chuban shiye."

106. In addition to the examples listed by Yun-ch'iu Mei ("Mass-Production of Topographic Pictures"), famous Nanjing native painters such as Hu Yukun 胡玉昆 also produced scenic paintings of Nanjing based on *Jinling tuyong* (James Cahill Collection, Berkeley Art Museum). For Hu Yukun, Zhou Lianggong, and the Nanjing school, see Kim, *The Life of a Patron*.

107. *Jiangning fuzhi* (1668). Zhou Lianggong's note indicated that Gao Cen produced more than 60 paintings for the project. However, only 38 are found in the gazetteer.

108. See Bol, "The 'Localist Turn' and 'Local Identity'"; and idem, "The Rise of Local History." For a fuller discussion of the development of local gazetteers in the Ming era, see Chapter 4.

109. Both James Cahill ("Huangshan Paintings as Pilgrimage Pictures") and Joseph P. McDermott ("The Making of a Chinese Mountain") observe the same trend in their studies. Cahill focuses on the development of Mount Huang images until the early seventeenth century, and McDermott continues the analysis though the modern period.

110. Cahill, "Huangshan Paintings as Pilgrimage Pictures," 279.

111. See Brook, *Geographical Sources of Ming-Qing History*, 49–72.

112. A prime example is the development of topographical paintings of Suzhou: visual practice to a great extent standardized the portrayal of its *jing*; see Siggstedt, "Topographical Motifs."

113. Cahill, "Huangshan Paintings as Pilgrimage Pictures," 279–80.

114. Zhu Zhifan, ed., *Jinling tuyong*, 31a.

115. Ibid., 11a.

116. Ibid., 27a, 39a, 16a.

117. This is clearly seen in the tradition of the *Qingming shanhe* scroll

118. Ma Ya-chen, "Citizen's Perspective Versus Imperial Perspective."

119. Wang Hongjun and Liu Ruzhong, "Mingdai hoqui Nanjing." For a reproduction of the painting, see Zhongguo lishi bowuguan, ed., *Hua xia zhi lu*, 90-2 and 90-3.

120. *Jiangning fuzhi* (1688), 2.28b–29a.

121. Ibid., 2.17b–18a.

122. See Hay, "Ming Palace and Tomb." Hay demonstrates that the two sites became favorite topics for late seventeenth- and early eighteenth-century painters as well as the Qing court because of the imbedded political symbolism.

123. This point is first made by Richard Vinograd ("Fan Ch'i") in his comparison of Fan Qi's landscape paintings with the images from *Jinling tuyong*.

Also, Tobie Meyer-Fong (*Building Culture in Early Qing Yangzhou*) points out the early Qing literary fashion of lamenting the ruin (metaphorical or physical) caused by the dynastic transition; this may have reflected an emotional attachment to late Ming prosperity similar to that observed in the Nanjing case.

124. Meyer-Fong, *Building Culture in Early Qing Yangzhou*; also idem, "Seeing the Sights in Yangzhou."

125. Meyer-Fong, "Seeing the Sights in Yangzhou."

126. See ibid.

127. *Chongkan Jiangning fuzhi* (1811), editorial note, 4a–b. A similar position was also expressed in *Shangyuan xianzhi* (1824).

128. *Sheshan zhi* (1790).

129. A typical example is the a gazetteer compiled by eighteenth-century Nanjing luminary Yuan Mei 袁枚, *Jiangning xin zhi* (1784). It includes twelve scenic images of Nanjing, all of which resonated with those from *Jinling tuyong*.

130. *Shangyuan xianzhi* (1721) is a case in point. It has twenty-four images of Nanjing scenes whose titles and compositions are modeled after *Jinling tuyong* and also highlights the records from the Southern Tours.

131. See, e.g., Wu Jen-shu, "Wan Ming de lüyou"; Brook, *Confusions of Pleasure*, 174–82; Clunas, *Pictures and Visuality*, 183–84; and Zheng Yan, *Zhongguo lüyou fazhanshi*, 2–3.

CHAPTER 4

1. Zhou Hui's *Shangbaizhai ketan* 尚白齋客談 (Chats with guests at the Shangbai studio) was later published as *Jinling suoshi* 金陵瑣事 (Trivia about Nanjing), *Xu Jinling suoshi* 續金陵瑣事 (Supplement to *Trivia About Nanjing*), and *Erxu Jinling suoshi* 二續金陵瑣事 (Second supplement to *Trivia About Nanjing*).

2. See Zhou Hui, *Jinling suoshi*, Preface dated 1610. The change in title rendered the collection less personal and more appealing to a wider audience interested in Nanjing. The concern with market perhaps stemmed from Zhou's financial difficulties, which almost prevented his work from being published. In fact, since Zhou could not afford to have his work published until long after he had finished the manuscript, one of his friends offered to "include" Zhou's collection in his own work. However, Zhou could not bring himself to give away his book and waited until Jiao Hong, a prominent cultural patron in late Ming Nanjing, offered to help publish it. Zhou's dire situation changed dramatically once the book came out and became a bestseller: two sequels appeared almost immediately. Now a famous and popular author, Zhou appropriated two unpublished manuscripts by other authors in his third sequel to *Jinling suoshi*: Chen Yi's *Xin mu bian* 訢慕編 (Book of admiration) and He Liang-

jun's 何良俊 *Jinling xianxian shiji* 金陵先賢詩集 (A collection of poetry by former worthies in Jinling).

3. Gu Qiyuan, *Kezuo zhuiyu*, Preface dated 1617. Gu Qiyuan in fact praised Zhou Hui's *Jinling suoshi* in his work (ibid., 292).

4. Gardner, "Modes of Thinking."

5. However, not all *ketan* conform to the original format. For example, both Nanjing *ketan* were edited by their authors, and many entries do not cite the original source.

6. Ji Yun et al., "Zajia" 雜家 (Miscellaneous schools), in idem, *Siku quanshu zongmu tiyao*, 120.1037.

7. On the standardization of local gazetteers in the Song, see Aoyama Sadao, *Tō-Sō jidai no kōtsū*. The earliest extant *zhi* reveal strong interests in novelty and religion. According to Aoyama, by the end of Song, *zhi* had evolved from *tujing* 圖經 (map guides), which were basically manuals for administrative purposes, into a structured way to represent a place in literary convention.

8. Ming Chengzu 明成祖 (r. 1402–24) issued two edicts regulating the compilation of local gazetteers, one in 1412 and the other in 1418. The 1412 edict is preserved in the Preface of *Shouchang xianzhi* (1586), which outlines the essential sections of local gazetteers: establishments, astronomy, jurisdiction, walls and moats, mountains and rivers, wards, towns and markets, local products, taxes and levies, social customs, population registry, schools, military stations, government offices, shrines and temples, bridges, ancient sites, biographies of local officials and luminaries, religious figures, miscellaneous notes, and local literature.

9. Although the format of local gazetteers was heavily dictated by administrative needs, locals still maintained a strong presence in their production. Even given an increasingly standardized format, filling in the prescribed categories was still a matter of subjective selection determined by the locals. For example, the section of local personages featured not just people with local affiliations but the ones whose political merit or virtuous practices imparted cultural prestige to the place. Peter Bol's research on the various editions of Wuzhou gazetteers provides a case in point. As the self-perception of the local literati community changed, the biography section underwent a remarkable revision between the 1480 and the 1578 editions. In a move to assert the literati's greater importance over religious clergy, hundreds of temples and monasteries went unmentioned in the latter edition; see Bol, "The Rise of Local History," 50–54. In supplying biographies of commendable local officials, prominent native sons, chaste women, and the like, local gazetteers created a host of genealogies for commemoration and thus articulated a sense of communal identity and local pride. With so much at stake, it is not surprising that the process was

often fraught with disputes and conflicts. Even the category of female chastity, one heavily regulated by the state, gave rise to controversies over whether certain women were entitled to inclusion in local gazetteers. One interesting, though somewhat extreme case relates the strenuous efforts of locals to advocate inclusion of "chaste courtesans"—high-class prostitutes who vowed to remain chaste after their primary clients died. The battle went on for years but to no avail; see Fei, "Cong dianfan dao guifan," 161–63. These examples indicate that the production of local gazetteers in effect opened a dialogue over the meaning of a locality: the state-prescribed categories (female chastity, filial piety, etc.) were populated through local interpretation.

10. According to Liu Zhiji (*Shi tong, juan* 10, "Zashu" 雜述 [Miscellaneous discussion]), *duyi bu* was intended to be the official documentation of capitals. The *Hongwu Atlas* discussed in Chapter 3 fell into this category.

11. Stephen West ("Interpretation of a Dream" and "Huanghou, zangli, youbing yu zhu") argues that the works that came after *Dongjing meng Hua lu* follow a more formulistic spatial structure, whereas the *Meng Hua lu* is perceived from the author's personal vantage point. In other words, the author of *Meng Hua lu* deconstructed the spatial order, and his recollections are closer to the mundane disorder of urban life; other texts more or less reflect the prescribed spatial hierarchy and cultural order.

12. Gu Qiyuan, Preface, *Kezou zhuiyu*, 1.

13. Wang Ying ("Gu Qiyuan shengping") argues that Gu Qiyuan's official career was not as short as scholars have believed. Gu served in Nanjing imperial university for almost a decade after he left Beijing. After this appointment, Gu retired in Nanjing despite repeated invitations from the court. Although legally Gu should have avoided serving positions in his hometown, Wang points out that this rule was not strictly enforced during the Wanli reign, and in fact, since the middle of the Ming dynasty, the rule of avoidance had ceased to apply to education-related positions.

14. In Dun yuan, Gu also built a pavilion named Qizhao ting 七召亭 (Pavilion of seven summons) to commemorate the seven times he declined to return to officialdom when summoned by the court (Goodrich and Fang, *Dictionary of Ming Biography*, 734–36). In contrast, the examination career of the author of *Jinling suoshi*, Zhou Hui, was much less successful. Contrary to Gu's early retirement and adamant refusal to return to office, Zhou Hui was never admitted to officialdom despite persistent efforts. Although his talent was greatly praised by contemporary luminaries such as Gu Qiyuan, Zhou never achieved any degree higher than *shengyuan*. After many failed attempts, Zhou gave up and focused on writing; *Jinling suoshi* became his best-known work. Although a popular author, Zhou was also well appreciated among elites for his

erudition. Yet the most recognized public personality of Zhou is one of an eremite (*yinshi* 隱士) who was able to savor his life despite the repeated frustration of failing the examinations (Gu Qiyuan, *Kezuo zhuiyu*, 292). The examination system had become so competitive by the late Ming that Zhou's story must have resonated with many of his peers and made him an alternative cultural icon. Yet despite the obvious distinction between social status and career paths, Zhou Hui appears to have been well connected to Gu's social circle, as indicated in the constant cross-references between the two Nanjing *ketan*.

15. For a general survey of Ming-Qing book culture, see McDermott, *A Social History of the Chinese Book*.

16. *Zhu* (host) and *ke* (guest) is a common trope in traditional discourses. For example, in the Song dynasty, it refers to landowners and landless tenants. In fact, for natives and sojourners, a more common paired term was *tu* 土 (native) vs. *ke* 客 (sojourner). Replacing *tu* with *zhu* lends added emphasis to Gu Qiyuan's status as a Nanjing native son and his vantage point in conceiving Nanjing's spatiality.

17. For a general survey of the varieties of different societies and associations in China, see Chen Baoliang, *Zhongguo de she yu hui*. Historians have noticed the unusually large number of societies formed in the late Ming. Although there are no conclusive data on the specific number of societies, some studies have pushed the number up to more than two hundred. For example, Guo Shaoyu, in "Mingdai de wenren jituan," in idem, *Zhaoyushi gudian wenxue lunji*, lists 176 literati societies, among which 115 dated to the late Ming. This number was later expanded to 213 in Li Shenghua, *Wan Ming shige yanjiu*. Although elite men and women ascribed lofty purposes to these gatherings (such as the writing of poetry or painting), ordinary folk simply gathered for the pleasure of drinking and feasting, as seen in the novel *Jin ping mei* 金瓶梅 (The plum in the golden vase). The monthly banquets at a local brothel held by Ximen Qing (the leading male character in the novel) and his *hui*-pals play a central role in this novel, which centers on the urban middle class, by supplying the occasions for many pacts, disputes, and business deals. Not only do the men take part in all sorts of social and religious societies, but courtesans also hold regular *hezihui* 盒子會 (box meetings). For example, in *Jin ping mei, juan* 45, one of Ximen Qing's concubines, Guijie (a former prostitute), hurries back to her mother's place for a *hezihui*. *Hezihui* were said to have been popular among Nanjing courtesans; see Zhou Hui, "Hezihui ci" 盒子會詞, *Xu Jinling suoshi*, 104a–5a; and Yu Huai, "Hezihui," in *Banqiao zaji*, 28–29. According to Chen Baoliang's survey, among all these clubs and societies, some served practical purposes, like guilds for sojourning merchants, whereas others were for entertainment, like *xiehui* 蟹會 (crab meetings), *lishe* 荔社 (litchi society meetings),

and *yinshe* 飲社 (drinking clubs). In one peculiar example, a group met regularly to recollect their dreams, and they subsequently produced a book titled *Mengjian* 夢鑒 (The appreciation of dreams).

18. Another famous work is *Kezuo xinwen* 客座新聞. Authored by a Suzhou cultural arbiter, Shen Zhou 沈周, the text consists of news and gossip offered by Shen's guests.

19. Lu Cai, *Yecheng kelun.*

20. Gu Qiyuan, "Chan guai" 產怪 (Bizarre births), *Kezuo zhuiyu*, 7.233.

21. Gu Qiyuan, "Fei dao" 飛盜 (Flying thief), *Kezuo zhuiyu*, 9.291.

22. Zhou Hui, "Wang Xiuer" 王繡二, *Xu Jinling suoshi*, 75b–76a.

23. For example, in Shen Zhou's *Kezuo xinwen*, although many anecdotes in the collections do refer to Shen's contemporaries, some items of "news" date in fact to the beginning of the dynasty.

24. For more discussion on the late Ming obsession with *qi*, see Qianshen Bai, *Fu Shan's World*, 16–20. The translation of Gu's quote is adapted from Bai's book. In fact, people in Nanjing were known for their obsession with *qi* in their excessive indulgence of novel and startling artworks. Despite its ubiquity, however, there appears to be no clear definition of the word. In fact, it was precisely this vagueness and fluidity that opened up new spaces of possibility for artistic, intellectual, and literary innovations. For a discussion about the development of the *qi* trend in art history, see Shi Shouqian, "You qiqu dao fugu."

25. Current events dramas proliferated in the seventeenth century; see Wu Jen-shu, "Ming Qing zhiji Jiangnan shishiju."

26. Chen Jiru, *Zhang zhe yan* 長者言 (Words from an elder), 6.

27. Xihu yuyin zhuren, *Huanxi yuanjia*, chap. 13, "Liang fang qi an zhong shuang cuo ren" 兩房妻暗中雙錯認 (Mistaken between two wives in the dark), 632. A similar episode involving news sellers can also be found in *Xingshi yinyuan zhuan* 醒世姻緣傳 (Tales of marriage destinies, chap. 54) where a news print costs about two coins. For a fuller discussion of the transmission of news in Ming-Qing cities, see Wang Hongtai, "Liudong yu hudong," Chap. 4.

28. Kong Shangren, "Yantai qiuxing sishi shou" 燕台秋興四十首 (Forty poems inspired by Yantai in the fall), note to the eighth poem, in *Kong Shangren shiwen ji*, 4.369.

29. See Wu Jen-shu, "Ming Qing zhiji Jiangnan shishiju"; and Wang Hongtai, in "Liudong yu hudong," chap. 4.

30. Ling's creation appeared to be very popular among his fellow exam takers. Ling related that he first wrote the stories "as a way of relieving the frustration that oppressed me . . . but whenever my [examination] colleagues visited me, they would ask me for one of my stories to read, and on finishing it,

would invariably slap the table and exclaim, 'What an amazing thing!' The news slipped out to a book merchant who begged me to let him publish the stories. So I copied them out, put them together, and assembled forty stories" (Ling Mengchu, Preface to *Er ke pai'an jingqi*; translation adapted from Hanan, *The Chinese Vernacular Story*, 144).

31. For example, Tan Jiading (*San yan Liang pai ziliao*) surveyed the origins of this collection and found that many were indeed based on real news stories.

32. Brook, "Printing in the Age of Information and the Wider Circulation of Official News," in idem, *Confusions of Pleasure*, 167–72.

33. Zhu Yunming, a famous Suzhou calligrapher, named as one of "The Four Talented Men of Suzhou" along with Tang Yin 唐寅, Wen Zhengming 文徵明, and Xu Zhenqing 徐禎卿; see Ji Yun et al., *Siku quanshu zongmu tiyao*, *juan* 144, "Xiaoshuojia lei cunmu," 1229.

34. Chen Liangmo, Preface to *Jianwen jixun* (1566), 551.

35. Qian Daxin, "Zazhu yi: zheng su" 雜著一正俗 (Miscellaneous writings, I, Rectifying customs), in idem, *Qianyantang wenji*, 17.282.

36. For a survey of commercial presses in Suzhou and their social influence, see Chiu Peng-sheng, "Mingdai Suzhou yingli chuban shiye."

37. See Lu Wenheng, *Se'an suibi*, 5.3b. Ling Mengchu in his preface to his famous collection of vernacular stories, *Pai'an jingqi* 拍案驚奇 (Slapping the table in amazement), made a similar moral statement. Ling deplored the belief that the only remarkable (or amazing) things are those outside the range of our eyes and ears, such as *niu gui she shen* 牛鬼蛇神, supernatural beings, phantasms, and the like. He argued that events based on daily life experiences— "from streets and back alleys"—constituted prime sources for literary creation. Unfortunately, vernacular fiction of his time, after a long period of peace and accompanying moral laxity, was often written by "vulgar delinquents just learning how to hold a brush," who were intent on defaming everything and everyone. Their fiction is either absurd or obscene, and Ling Mengchu recommended it be banned. The translation from the preface by Ling Mengchu is based on Hanan, *The Chinese Vernacular Story*, 145.

38. Wu Yuancui, *Linju manlu*, 3.445.

39. For a detailed discussion of this case, see Chapter 2.

40. Zhu Hong, *Zi zhi lu, juan xia*, 18.

41. Wang Hongtai, "Liudong yu hudong," chap. 4; Saeki Yūichi, "Minmatsu no Tō-shi no hen."

42. Zhou Hui, "Jun du" 菌毒 (Poison from mushrooms), *Jinling suoshi*, 3.163–64.

43. Gu Qiyuan, *Kezuo zhuiyu*, 3.106.

44. Gu Qiyuan, "Xuanwu lingqian" 玄武靈籤 (Efficacious divination sticks at the Temple of the Black Emperor), *Kezuo zhuiyu*, 7.232–33.

45. Zhou Hui, "Duan qiao gua" 斷橋掛 (An omen of a broken bridge) and "Gou chang zhu zhai" 狗償主債 (A dog returning a debt to its master), in *Jinling suoshi*, 3.153, 156–57, respectively.

46. Zhou Hui, "Shi bao" 識寶 (Spotting treasures), in *Jinling suoshi*, 3.154–56.

47. How the printing industry affected the ways by which late Ming people perceived their lived world is well studied by Wang Hongtai, "Liudong yu hudong." He suggests that the late Ming readers had in effect become spectators for this virtual reality made possible by the instant reproduction of current events in print and other forms of media such as drama.

48. Gu Qiyuan, "Wang Xiangmin gong buyiju" 王襄敏公不易居 (Sir Wang Xiangmin refused to move), *Kezuo zhuiyu*, 7.223.

49. Zhou Hui, "Jian yushi buqishen" 見御史不起身 (People who did not stand up in the presence of a censor), *Jinling suoshi*, 1.17a–b.

50. *Qingjiang xianzhi* (1642), "Fengsu," 1.34b.

51. For a detailed discussion of this transformation, see Kiang, *Cities of Aristocrats and Bureaucrats*.

52. On the development and decline of *xiang yinjiu li* in the late Ming, see Chiu Chung-lin, "Jing lao shi suoyi jian lao."

53. This thesis was first established by Japanese scholars, especially Atsushi Shigeta; see his "Origins and Structure of Gentry Rule."

54. Hamashima Atsutoshi, *Mindai Kōnan nōson*, 67–130.

55. For example, the reform-related documents collected in the *ketan* also served to testify the agreement reached between the state and the residents; see Chapter 1.

56. Peter Bol powerfully demonstrates in *"This Culture of Ours"* and *Neo-Confucianism in History* that the rise of Neo-Confucianism was, in part, a response to elite activism. It might be worthwhile to explore if the urban elite's activism as discussed in this section also provoked any form of intellectual development. For example, the many popular public lectures by Yangming school scholars held in cities (see Lü Miaofen, "Yangmingxue jianghui") might be an important phenomenon in this regard.

57. Zhou Hui, "Fei fei zi" 非非子, *Jinling suoshi*, 1.27b–28a.

58. According to Zhou's description, *zi* 子 might refer to Confucius. However, with the available information, it is unclear what the title 非非子 indicates.

59. Zhu Zhifan, "You chengbei zhushan ji" 遊城北諸山記 (Account of the journey to the mountains north of Nanjing), in idem, *Yushan bian*, 5a–6a.

60. *Hangzhou fuzhi* (1579), 19.1a–11a.

61. Fuma Susumu ("Chūgoku kinsei toshi") was the first to call attention to the differences between urban elites and rural gentry. In this brief symposium discussion, he used his research on Hangzhou as an example to show that urban elites had developed a different dynamic in mediating between state and society and hence their presence in cities should not be considered just an urban version of rural gentry dominance. Although he did not further elaborate the nature and ethos of urban elites, Fuma put forth a few important questions: Since landownership did not serve as the urban elite's power base, as it did in the case of rural gentry, what was at stake when urban elites mobilized locals and initiated political negotiations with the state? Was it something distinct from the traditional program of gentry benevolence such as charitable works and local management when the state ran short of resources? Although the entries in Nanjing *ketan* offer some clues, these questions call for more comprehensive case studies in order to build an in-depth understanding of urban social structure and power relationships.

62. Wang Fansen, "Qing chu shiren."

63. Gu Qiyuan, "Shishitai" 施食臺 (Terrace of food offerings), *Kezuo zhuiyu*, 2.39.

64. Clunas, *Superfluous Things*.

65. Included in *Kezuo zhuiyu*, this treatise is unattributed. Like most of the entries in the book, it is probably based (according to Gu Qiquan) on conversations among his friends. However, most later references (including gazetteers compiled in Gu's time) attribute this piece to Gu, and I follow this convention until new sources indicate otherwise. In any case, authorship does not affect the argument in this section since the focus is not on analyzing this treatise in a personal/biographic context but against the general discursive field of the late Ming. That is, rather than trace Gu's intellectual trajectory, I compare the ideas in this treatise with those in other contemporary texts.

66. The origin of the idea of "social custom" can be traced back two millennia; see Lewis, *Construction of Space in Early China*, chap. 4, "Regions and Customs."

67. Ban Gu, *Hanshu, juan* 28, "Dili zhi"; translation adapted from Lewis, *Construction of Space in Early China*, 190.

68. This qualitative classification scheme was also employed by the government to rank the level of difficulty in the field administration. For example, a 1566 edict mandated that the ranking of all administrative appointments be based on the following criteria combined: *daxiao* 大小 (large or small in terms of jurisdiction), *fanjian* 繁簡 (complicated or simple in terms of administration), *chongpi* 衝僻 (busy or remote location), and *nanyi* 難易 (difficulty or ease of governing locals) (Osawa Akihiro, "Chirisho to seisho," 475; see also Skinner,

"Cities and the Hierarchy of Local Systems," in idem, ed., *City in Late Imperial China*, 275–351).

69. This idea can be traced back to Ying Shao 應劭, *Fengsu tong* 風俗通 (Comprehensive meanings of wind-customs), "'Wind' means the cold or warmth of Heavenly energies, the difficulty or ease of Earthly terrain, the excellence or vileness of water and springs, the firmness or softness of grasses and trees. 'Custom' means the ways in which creatures with blood live through imitation of these features. Therefore the different sounds of languages and songs or the distinct forms of drummed dances and movements are sometimes straight and sometimes crooked, sometimes excellent and sometimes perverse. When the sage arises he balances and equalizes them, so they all return to what is correct. When the sage is abandoned they return to their original customs" (Lewis, *Construction of Space in Early China*, 190).

70. In a survey of Ming gazetteers, Hsu Hong found that the concern over corrupt social customs had become a national phenomenon by the sixteenth century; see Hsu Hong, "Mingdai houqi huabei shangpin jingji"; idem, "Mingmo shehui fengqi"; and Chiu Chung-lin, "Mingdai Beijing."

71. Such as Gu Qiyuan, "Su chi" 俗侈 (Luxurious customs); "Li zhi" 禮制 (Ritual regulation); and "Fushi" 服飾 (Dress and costumes); in *Kezuo zhuiyu*, 7.231–32, 9.287–90, 9.293, respectively.

72. E.g., *Gaochun xianzhi* (1683), 4.1a–3a; and *Jiangpu xianzhi* (1726), 1.21a–b.

73. The map in use is from Chen Yi, *Jinling gujin tukao*. The boundaries are drawn by the author based on descriptions in *Nanjing duchayuan zhi*.

74. Wakeland, "Metropolitan Administration in Ming China," 62–64.

75. In his biographical writings, Gu Qiyuan emphatically praised gentry women for not following contemporary fashions; see, e.g., "Pan ruren muzhiming" 潘儒人墓誌銘 (Epitaph for Mrs. Pan), in *Lanzhen caotang ji*, 33.22a–b; or "Chifeng ruren Guan shi muzhiming" 敕封儒人關氏墓誌銘 (Epitaph for Lady Guan), ibid., 33.29b–30a. In fact, Gu believed that the luxurious lifestyle of Nanjing women was the worst aspect of the corruption of social customs; see Gu Qiyuan, "Minli" 民利 (People's profit), *Kezuo zhuiyu*, 2.67.

76. *Wuxian zhi* (1642), 10.1b–3a.

77. *Hangzhou fuzhi* (1579), 19.4a–21b.

78. *Qingjiang xianzhi* (1642), "Fengsu," 1.34b.

79. In the late Ming context, *kemin* 客民 sometimes refers to the Hakka, an ethnic group who also had a strong presence in the Fujian area. However, judging from the context of this section, *ke* is not used as a proper noun for Hakka but serves as a generic term for all non-native outsiders, including the military population as well as immigrants from Zhangzhou and Tingzhou. This usage continued into the Qing. For example, in an essay about border defenses,

Yan Ruyu 嚴如煜 (1759–1826) pointed out that in forested areas of Sichuan, Shaanxi, and Hunan, where native residents were sparse, about two-tenths of the land relied on recruiting outside *kemin* to cultivate; see Yan Ruyu, "Celue" 策略 (Strategies), in idem, *San sheng bianfang bei lan*, 11.296.

80. The "Fengsu" section of the 1538 gazetteer is preserved in *Funing zhouzhi* (1593), 1.12b–13b.

81. *Funing zhouzhi* (1616), 2.14a–16a.

82. Ibid.

83. See Yang Guoan, "Zhu ke zhi jian."

84. *Yingshan xianzhi* (1576), *juan* 1, "Fengsu" (custom).

85. One telling example can be found in the armed fights between native-place groups that plagued southeastern China; see Lamley, "Hsieh-Tou."

86. *Hangzhou fuzhi* (1579), 19.11a–b. The editor pointed out that the most popular burial sites (probably owing to their excellent *fengshui* placement) just outside Hangzhou—Nanshan and Beishan—were now occupied by Huizhou merchants sojourning in the city. With their wealth as a weapon, Huizhou merchants successfully seized the better land and provoked a great number of lawsuits with locals as a result.

87. As far as the Ming government was concerned, there were only four types of people who left their registered locality: "escaping households," who abandoned their assignment of corvée labor; the "floating people," who were refugees from war or famine; people who sojourned in other places out of necessity; and finally people who migrated as mandated by the government. Under the heading "Fu ji" (Attached households), the *Mingshi* states that except for the forced migration planned by the government, migrants needed to apply for a permit on a regular basis and were eventually required to return to their native places. It in effect prohibited any form of voluntary migration in the Ming empire. See *Mingshi, juan* 77, "Shi huo" 食貨 1 (Monograph on food and commodities).

88. See Yang Guoan, "Zhu ke zhi jian."

89. *Mianyang zhouzhi* (1530) 9.12a–b.

90. There had been similar proposals before but the court refused to entertain the idea; see Liu Min, "Shilun Ming-Qing"; and *Ming Shenzong shilu* (1584), 154.2847–48.

91. Huang Zhifang, "Guojia rentong yu tuke chongtun."

92. Yang Rui, "Ti wei yishi shu."

93. See Shen Bang, "Liyi" 力役 (Corvée labor), *Wanshu zaji*, 50–52.

94. See Wang Zhenzhong, *Ming Qing huishang*; Wang Rigen, *Xiangtu zhi lian*; Long Denggao, "Cong kefan dao qiaoju"; Zhu Biheng, "Lun Ming Qing huishang"; and Xu Min, "Lun wan Ming shangren."

95. Lin Lian, "Zeng Jiezhuan Liu gong zhi Jiangxi zuoxia xu."

96. See the discussion of *Hongwu jingcheng tuzhi* in Chapter 3.

97. Fuma, "Mindai Nankin no toshi gyōsei," 245–47.

98. Gu Qiyuan, "Minli" 民利 (People's profit), *Kezuo zhuiyu*, 2.67.

99. Gu Qiyuan, "Lizheng" 力征 (On labor levies), *Kezuo zhuiyu*, 2.57.

100. See *Wanli Da Ming huidian* (1576), *juan* 19, "Liumin fuji renhu" 流民附籍人戶 (Floating population and attached households). Although Beijing was the most often cited precedent in official statutes, it was not the first to register sojourners. In 1506, officials in Wuhu 蕪湖 began to register sojourning merchants in order to equalize the levies between native and non-native merchants; see Wang Shimao 王世茂, "Keshang shezhi fuhu zhuance" 客商設置浮戶專冊 (Setting up a special "floating households" registry for sojourning merchants), in idem, *Shitu xuanjing, juan* 2.

101. *Taiping fuzhi* (1903), 12.26b; *Nanjing duchayuan zhi* (1623), *juan* 20, "Xunshi wucheng zhizhang" 巡視五城職掌 (The jurisdiction of the five wards).

102. *Ming Shenzong shilu* (1602), 367.6869–72.

103. Gu Yanwu, *Tianxia junguo libing shu*, 16.2b–4b.

104. Zhou Hui, "Yushi zoucha liuyi" 御史奏查流移 (A memorial for surveying the floating population by a censor), *Jinling suoshi*, 3.151a–52a. The memorial cited by Zhou Hui was dated 1530.

105. Wu Yingji, *Liudu jianwenlu*.

106. Wang Hongtai, "Liudong yu hudong," chap. 3.

107. Qian Qianyi, "Qi wang Sun Chengcai" 齊王孫承綵 (Lord Qi Sun Chengcai), in idem, *Liechao shiji xiaozhuan*, dingji shang, 551; Lu Shiyi, *Fushe jilue*.

108. Qian Qianyi, "Jinling sheji zhushiren" 金陵社集諸詩人 (Poets at Nanjing gatherings), in idem, *Liechao shiji xiaozhuan*, dingji shang, 502.

109. See Jerlian Tsao, "Remembering Suzhou"; Lin Liyue, "*Jianjiatang gao*"; idem, "Wan Ming 'chongshe'"; Chen Guodong, "You guan Lu Ji 'Jin she bian'"; Chao Xiaohong, "Jin ershi nian lai you guan Ming Qing 'shemi' zhi feng yanjiu."

110. Yu Yingshi, "Shishang hudong."

111. Zhou Hui, "Ying ju yi shan" 蠅聚一羶, in *Erxu Jinling suoshi*, 51a–b. Zhan Dongtu's (1519–1602) name was Jingfeng 景鳳; he earned a *jinshi* degree in 1567.

CONCLUSION

1. See Marmé, *Suzhou*. On the conspicuously low commercial taxes in the early Ming, see Iwai Shigeki, "Yōeki to zaisei no aida," pt. III; and Ray Huang, *Taxation and Governmental Finance*, chap. 6. Recently scholars such as Lin Feng ("Wanli kuang jian shui shi") even see the light commercial taxes as the root cause for the notorious *kuang shui* 礦稅 (mining taxes) of the Wanli reign.

2. For a general overview of the rich literature on *baojia* or *xiangyue*, see Heijdra, "Socio-Economic Development of Rural China." Sarah Schneewind's work on village schools, *Community Schools and the State in Ming China*, also shows that such local volunteerism often proceeded in tandem with local official sponsorship.

3. Brook, *Confusions of Pleasure*, "Introduction."

4. See Kawakatsu Mamoru, *Min Shin Kōnan shichin*, 117.

5. See Hamashima Atsutoshi, *Sōkan shinkō*.

6. See Cheng Yinong, "Song, Yuan, yiji Mingdai."

7. Other than the ethnic factor, the abuse of *fanghao yin* at the end of the Ming dynasty might also explain why the Qing rulers decided not to impose urban taxes (see note 114 to Chapter 1).

8. See Elliott, *The Manchu Way*, esp. "Manchu Cities," 89–128; and Ding Yizhuang, *Qingdai baqi zhufang yanjiu*.

9. Cheng Minsheng, "Lun Songdai de liudong renkou wenti." The legal rationale for the one-year rule (*Song shi*, 210.5b) appears to be directed at rural migrants. For cities, cases show that conversion to native status was permitted in urban census surveys conducted every three years; see Hu Jianhua, "Songdai chengshi liudong renkou."

10. For an overview of guilds in Ming-Qing eras, see Wang Rigen, *Xiangtu zhi lian*. For a specific case study of how these merchant organizations worked in the flourishing market economy in Suzhou, see Chiu Peng-sheng, "Shichang, falü yu renqing."

Works Cited

INSTITUTIONAL AND LOCAL GAZETTEERS

Chongkan Jiangning fuzhi (1811) 重刊江寧府志 (Gazetteer of Jiangning prefecture). Facsimile reprint of 1880 edition. Zhongguo fangzhi congshu. Taipei: Chengwen chubanshe, 1974.

Funing zhouzhi (1593) 福寧州志 (Gazetteer of Funing subprefecture). Xijian Zhongguo difangzhi huikan, 33. Beijing: Zhongguo shudian, 1992.

Funing zhouzhi (1616) 福寧州志 (Gazetteer of Funing subprefecture). Facsimile reprint of 1616 edition. Ribencang Zhongguo hanjian difangzhi congkan, 8. Beijing: Shumu wenxian chubanshe, 1990.

Gaochun xianzhi (1683) 高淳縣志 (Gazetteer of Gaochun county). Facsimile reprint of 1682 edition. Xijian Zhongguo difangzhi huikan, 12. Beijing: Zhongguo shudian, 1992.

Gaochun xianzhi (1751) 高淳縣志 (Gazetteer of Gaochun county). Facsimile reprint of Qianlong edition. Gugong zhenben congkan, 87. Haikou: Hainan chubanshe, 2001.

Ge Yinliang 葛寅亮, *jinshi* 1601. *Jinling fancha zhi* 金陵梵剎志 (Gazetteer of Buddhist monasteries in Nanjing). 1627. Reprinted—Zhenjiang: Jinshan jiang tian si, 1936.

Guangdong tong zhi (1602) 廣東通志 (Gazetteer of Guangdong province).

Haiyan xian tujing (1624) 海鹽縣圖經 (Gazetteer of Haiyan county). National Library, Taipei.

Hangzhou fuzhi (1579) 杭州府志 (Gazetteer of Hangzhou prefecture). Facsimile reprint of 1579 edition. Mingdai fangzhixuan. Taipei: Xuesheng shuju, 1965.

Hengxi lu (1629) 橫溪錄 (Record of Hengxi). Facsimile reprint of Ming edition. Huadong shifan daxue tushuguan cang xijian fangzhi congkan, 6. Beijing: Beijing tushu chubanshe, 2005.

Hongwu jingcheng tuzhi 洪武京城圖志 (The illustrated gazetteer of the Hongwu capital). Preface dated 1395. Reprinted and prefaced in 1928 by Liu Yizheng 柳詒徵 (1880–1956) based on a 1492 edition. The images are from another facscimile reprint, based on a Qing copy; see Beijing tuzhuguan guji zhenben congkan, 24. Beijing: Shumu wenxian chubanshe, 1988.

Houhu zhi 後湖志 (Gazetteer of Xuanwu Lake). 1514, 1549, and an expanded edition in 1611. Facsimile reprint of a handcopy. Nanjing: Guangling guji keyinshe, 1987.

Jianchang fuzhi (1613) 建昌府志 (Gazetter of Jianchang prefecture). National Diet Library, Tokyo.

Jiangning fuzhi (1668) 江寧府志 (Gazetteer of Jiangning prefecture). Microfilm.

Jiangning xin zhi (1748) 江寧新志 (New gazetteer of Jiangning county). Facsimile reprint of 1748 edition. Xijian Zhongguo difangshi huikan, 11.

Jiangpu pisheng (1891) 江浦埤乘 (Gazetteer of Jiangpu). Facsimile reprint of 1891 edition. Zhongguo difangzhi jicheng, 5. Nanjing: Jiangsu guji chubanshe, 1991.

Jiangpu xianzhi (1726) 江浦縣志 (Gazetteer of Jiangpu county). Facsimile reprint of 1726 edition. Gugong zhenben congkan, 87. Haikou: Hainan chubanshe, 2001.

Jiao Hong 焦竑. *Jingxue zhi* 京學志 (Gazetteer of the prefectural school in the [Southern] Capital). Facsimile reprint of 1603 edition. Taipei: Guofeng chubanshe, 1965.

Jiaxing xianzhi (1637) 嘉興縣志 (Gazetteer of Jiaxing county). Kunai shō, Tokyo.

Jingding Jiankang zhi (1261) 景定建康志 (Gazetteer of Jiangkang prefecture). Facsimile reprint of 1801 edition. Zhongguo fangzhi congshu. Taipei: Chengwen chubanshe, 1983.

Jinling xuanguan zhi 金陵玄觀志 (Gazetteer of Daoist monasteries in Nanjing). Reprinted—Guoxue tushuguan, 1937. Also, facsimile reprint of Ming edition. Xuxiu Siqu quanshu, 719. Shanghai: Guji chubanshe, 1997.

Libu zhigao 禮部志稿 (Gazetteer of the Nanjing Ministry of Rites). 1620. Jinying Wenyuange siku quanshu, 685. Taipei: Taiwan Shangwu yinshuguan, 1979.

Linggu chanlin zhi 靈谷禪林志 (Gazetteer of Linggu Chan Monastery). Facsimile reprint of 1886 edition. Zhongguo fosishizhi huikan. Taipei: Zongqing chubanshe, 1994.

Liyang xianzhi (1498) 溧陽縣志 (Gazetteer of Liyang county). Microfilm.

Longjiang chuanchang zhi 龍江船廠志 (Gazetteer of the Longjiang Shipyard). 1552. Xuanlantang congshu, 117–19. Taipei: Zhengzhong shuju, 1985.

Luhe xianzhi (1884) 六合縣志 (Gazetteer of Luhe county). Facsimile reprint of 1884 edition. Zhongguo difangzhi jicheng 中國地方志集成. Nanjing: Jiangsu guji chubanshe, 1991.

Mianyang zhouzhi (1530) 沔陽州志 (Gazetteer of Mianyang prefecture). Facsimile reprint of 1926 edition. Taipei: Chengwen chubanshe, 1975.

Nanchang fuzhi (1574) 南昌府志 (Gazetteer of Nanchang prefecture). Naikaku bunko, Tokyo.

Nanjing duchayuan zhi (1623) 南京都察院志 (Gazetteer of the Nanjing Censorate). Microfilm at Academia Sinica, Taiwan. Original copy at Naikaku bunko, Tokyo.

Nanjing Guanglusi zhi 南京光祿寺志 (Gazetteer of the Nanjing Court of Imperial Entertainment). 1596. Naikaku bunko, Tokyo.

Nanjing Hubuzhi 南京戶部志 (Gazetteer of the Nanjing Ministry of Revenue). 1550. Naikaku bunko, Tokyo.

Nanjing Taipusi zhi 南京太僕寺誌 (Gazetteer of the Nanjing Court of the Imperial Stud). Jiajing period (1521–66). Siqu quanshu cunmu congshu, 257. Tainan: Chuanyan chubanshe, 1996.

Nanjing Xingbuzhi 南京刑部志 (Gazetteer of the Nanjing Ministry of Justice). Library of Congress, Washington, DC.

Nanning fuzhi (1637) 南寧府志 (Gazetteer of Nanning prefecture). Naikaku bunko, Tokyo.

Nanshuzhi 南樞志 (Gazetteer of the Southern Pivot). Kyoto, Jinbunkan.

Nanyong zhi 南雍志 (Gazetteer of the Southern Academy). 1626. Microfilm. Washington, DC, Library of Congress.

Pingwang zhenzhi 平望鎮志 (1732) (Gazetteer of Pingwang town). Facsimile reprint of a handcopy. Zhongguo difangzhi jicheng: xiangzhenzhi zhuanji, 13. Shanghai: Shanghai shuju, 1992.

Qingjiang xianzhi (1642) 清江縣志 (Gazetteer of Qingjiang county). Facsimile reprint of Chongzhen edition. Siqu quanshu cunmu congshu, *shi* 212. Tainan: Zhuangyan chubanshe, 1996.

Qiongzhou fuzhi (1617) 瓊州府志 (Gazetteer of Qiongzhou prefecture). National Diet Library, Tokyo.

Quanzhou fuzhi (1612) 泉州府志 (Gazetteer of Quanzhou prefecture).

Shangyuan xianzhi (1721) 上元縣志 (Gazetteer of Shangyuan county). Naikaku bunko, Tokyo.

Shangyuan xianzhi (1824) 上元縣志 (Gazetteer of Shangyuan county). Facsimile reprint of 1824 edition. Taipei: Chengwen chubanshe, 1983.

Shaoxing fuzhi (1586) 紹興府志 (Gazetteer of Shaoxing prefecture). Microfilm prints.

Shaoxing fuzhi (1683) 紹興府志 (Gazetteer of Shaoxing prefecture). Microfilm prints.

Sheshan zhi 攝山志 (Gazetteer of Mount She). Facsimile reprint of 1790 edition. Zhongguo fosizhi, 34. Taipei: Mingwen shuju, 1980.

She zhi (1609) 歙志 (Gazetteer of She county). Sonkeikaku bunko, Tokyo.

Shouchang xianzhi (1586) 壽昌縣志 (Gazetteer of Shouchang county). Facsimile reprint of 1650 edition. Mingdai guben fangzhixuan. Beijing: Guojia tushuguan difangzhi he jiapu wenxian zhongxin, 2000.

Songjiang fuzhi (1630) 松江府志 (Gazetteer of Songjiang prefecture). Facsimile reprint of 1630 edition. Ribencang Zhongguo hanjian difangzhi congkan. Beijing: Shumu wenxian chubanshe, 1991.

Taiping fuzhi (1577) 太平府志 (Gazetteer of Taiping prefecture). Naikaku bunko, Tokyo.

Wuqing zhenzhi (1601) 烏青鎮志 (Gazetteer of Wuqing town). Facsimile reprint of 1601 edition. Zhongguo difangzhi jicheng: xiangzhenzhi zhuanji, 23. Shanghai: Shanghai shuju, 1992.

Wuxian zhi (1642) 吳縣志 (Gazetteer of Wu county). Facsimile reprint of 1642 edition. Tianyige cang Mingdai fangzhi xuankan xubian, 15. Shanghai: Shanghai shudian, 1990.

Xiaoshan xianzhi (1935) 蕭山縣志 (Gazetteer of Xiaoshan county). Facsimile reprint of 1935 edition. Zhongguo fangzhi congshu. Taipei: Chengwen chubanshe, 1983.

Xingning xianzhi (1637) 興寧縣志 (Gazetteer of Xingning county). National Diet Library, Tokyo.

Xinxiu Nanchang fuzhi (1588) 新修南昌府志 (New edition of gazetteer of Nanchang prefecture). Naikaku bunko, Tokyo.

Yingshan xianzhi (1576) 營山縣志. Facsimile reprint of 1576 edition. Tianyige Mingdai fangzhi xuankan xubian. Shanghai: Shanghai shuju, 1990.

Yiwu xianzhi (1640) 義烏縣志 (Gazetteer of Yiwu county). Naikaku bunko, Tokyo.

Yongjia xianzhi (1566) 永嘉縣志 (Gazetteer of Yongjia county). Sonkeikaku bunko, Tokyo.

Zhizheng Jinling xinzhi (1344) 至正金陵新志 (New gazetteer of Jinling). Facsimile reprint of 1344 edition. Zhongguo fangzhi congshu. Taipei: Chengwen chubanshe, 1983.

OTHER SOURCES

Aoyama Ichirō 青山一郎. "Mingdai no shin ken setchi to chiiki shakai" 明代の新県設置と地域社会 (The establishment of new counties and local society). *Shigaku zasshi* 史学雑誌 101, no. 2 (1992): 82–109.

Aoyama Sadao 青山定雄. *Tō-Sō jidai no kōtsū to chishi chizu no kenkyū* 唐宋時代の交通と地誌地圖の研究 (A study of the communication systems of Tang and Sung China and the development of their topographies and maps). Tokyo: Yoshikawa kōbunkan, 1963.

Aramiya Manabu 新宮学. *Pekin sento no kenkyū: kinsei Chūgoku no shuto iten* 北京遷都の研究: 近世中国の首都移転 (A historical study of the transfer of the capital to Beijing in the Ming dynasty). Tokyo: Kyūko shoin, 1995.

Arnade, Peter J.; Martha C. Howell; and Walter Simons. "Fertile Spaces: The Productivity of Urban Space in Northern Europe." *Journal of Interdisciplinary History* 32, no. 4 (2002): 515–48.

Bai Hua 白樺. *Mingdai zhouxian zhengzhi tizhi yanjiu* 明代州縣政治體制研究 (A study of the prefecture-county political governance in the Ming dynasty). Beijing: Zhongguo shehui kexue chubanshe, 2003.

Bai, Qianshen. *Fu Shan's World: The Transformation of Chinese Calligraphy in the Seventeenth Century.* Cambridge: Harvard University Asia Center, 2003.

Belsky, Richard. *Localities at the Center: Native Place, Space, and Power in Late Imperial Beijing.* Cambridge: Harvard University Asia Center, 2005.

Berg, Daria. "Marveling at the Wonders of the Metropolis." In *Town and Country in China: Identity and Perception,* ed. David Faure and Taotao Liu. New York: Palgrave, 2002, 17–40.

Bergère, Marie-Claire. "Civil Society and Urban Change in Republican China." *China Quarterly* 150 (1997): 309–28.

Bernhardt, Kathryn. *Rents, Taxes and Peasant Resistance: The Lower Yangzi Region, 1840–1950.* Stanford: Stanford University Press, 1992.

Bol, Peter K. "The 'Localist Turn' and 'Local Identity' in Later Imperial China." *Late Imperial China* 24, no. 2 (2003): 1–50.

———. "The Rise of Local History: History, Geography, and Culture in Southern Song and Yuan Wuzhou." *Harvard Journal of Asiatic Studies* 61, no. 1 (2001): 37–76.

———. "Society." In idem, *Neo-Confucianism in History.* Cambridge: Harvard University Asia Center, 2008, 218–69.

———. *"This Culture of Ours": Intellectual Transitions in T'ang and Sung China.* Stanford: Stanford University Press, 1992.

Bourgon, Jérôme. "Rights, Customs, and Civil Law Under the Late Qing and Early Republic (1900–1936)." In *Realms of Freedom in Modern China,* ed. William C. Kirby. Cambridge: Harvard University Press, 2004, 84–112.

———. "Uncivil Dialogue: Law and Custom Did Not Merge into Civil Law Under the Qing." *Late Imperial China* 23, no. 1 (2002): 50–90.

Britnell, Richard H. *The Commercialization of English Society, 1000–1500.* 2nd ed. Manchester: Manchester University Press, 1996.

Brokaw, Cynthia, and Kai-wing Chow, eds. *Printing and Book Culture in Late Imperial China.* Berkeley: University of California Press, 2004.

Brook, Timothy. *The Chinese State in Ming Society.* London: RoutledgeCurzon, 2005.

————. *The Confusions of Pleasure: Commerce and Culture in Ming China.* Berkeley: University of California Press, 1998.

————. *Geographical Sources of Ming-Qing History.* 1st edition. Ann Arbor: Center for Chinese Studies, University of Michigan, 1988.

————. "The Spatial Structure of Ming Local Administration." *Late Imperial China* 6, no. 1 (1985): 1–55.

Brook, Timothy, ed. *The Asiatic Mode of Production in China.* Armonk, NY: M. E. Sharpe, 1989.

Brook, Timothy, and B. Michael Frolic, eds. *Civil Society in China.* Boulder, CO: Westview Press, 1997.

Cahill, James. "Huangshan Paintings as Pilgrimage Pictures." In *Pilgrims and Sacred Sites in China*, ed. Susan Naquin and Chün-fang Yu. Berkeley: University of California Press, 1992, 246–92.

Cao Dazhang 曹大章 (1521–75). *Qinhuai shinübiao* 秦淮仕女表 (A list of Qinhuai ladies). Copy in rare book collection, Academia Sinica, Taipei.

Cartier, Carolyn. "Origins and Evolution of a Geographical Idea." *Modern China* 28, no. 1 (2002): 79–143.

Chang Che-chia 張哲嘉. "Mingdai fangzhi zhong de ditu" 明代方志中的地圖 (Maps in Ming gazetteers). In *Huazhong you hua: jindai Zhongguo de shijue biaoshu yu wenhua goutu* 畫中有話: 近代中國的視覺表述與文化構圖 (When images speak: visual representation and cultural mapping in modern China), ed. Huang Kewu 黃克武. Taipei: Academia Sinica, 2003, 179–212.

Chang, Sen-dou. "The Morphology of Walled Capitals." In *The City In Late Imperial China*, ed. G. William Skinner. Stanford: Stanford University Press, 1977, 75–100.

Chao Xiaohong 鈔曉鴻. "Jin ershi nian lai you guan Ming Qing 'shemi' zhi feng yanjiu pingshu" 近二十年來有關明清「奢靡」之風研究評述 (Review of studies in the past twenty years on conspicuous consumption during the Ming and Qing). *Zhongguo shi yanjiu dongtai* 中國史研究動態 2001, no. 10: 9–20.

Chen Baoliang 陳寶良. "Mingdai de baojia yu huojia" 明代的保甲與火甲 (The *baojia* and *huojia* in the Ming era). *Mingshi yanjiu* 明史研究 3 (1993): 59–66.

————. "Mingdai shehui liudong xing chu tan" 明代社會流動性初探 (A preliminary study of social mobility in the Ming dynasty). *Anhui shixue* 安徽史學 2005, no. 2: 18–24.

————. *Zhongguo de she yu hui* 中國的社與會 (The *she* and *hui* in China). Hangzhou: Zhejiang renmin chubanshe, 1996.

Chen Guocan 陳國燦. "Luelun Nan Song shiqi Jiangnan shizhen de shehui xingtai" 略論南宋時期江南市鎮的社會型態 (Local society in Jiangnan market towns in the Southern Song period). *Xueshu yuekan* 學術月刊 2001, no. 2: 59–65.

Chen Guodong 陳國棟. "You guan Lu Ji 'Jin she bian' zhi yanjiu suo sheji de xueli wenti: kua xuemen de yijian" 有關陸楫「禁奢辨」之研究所涉及的學理問題—跨學門的意見 (Issues regarding studies on Lu Ji's "Jin she bian": an interdisciplinary perspective). *Xinshixue* 新史學 5, no. 2 (1994): 159–79.

Chen Jiru 陳繼儒 (1558–1639). *Chen Meigong xiaopin* 陳眉公小品 (Shorter works of Chen Jiru). Beijing: Wenyi chubanshe, 1996.

———. *Zhang zhe yan* 長者言 (Words from an elder). In *Shuofu xu* 説郛續 (Sequel to *Environs of Fiction*). Shanghai: Shanghai guji chubanshe, 1980.

Chen Liangmo 陳良謨. *Jianwen jixun* 見聞紀訓. 1566. Facsimile reprint of 1579 edition. Xuxiu Siku quanshu, 1266. Shanghai: Shanghai guji chubanshe, 1995.

Chen Yi 陳沂. *Jinling gujin tukao* 金陵古今圖考 (Historical atlas of Nanjing). Preface 1516. Copy dated 1624 in National Central Library, Taipei, Rare Book Collection. The images are from a 1928 reprint by Liu Yizheng 柳詒徵 (1880–1956).

———. *Xianhuayan zhi* 獻花岩志 (Gazetteer of Xianhua Grotto). Preface by the author dated 1576; published and prefaced by Jiao Hong in 1603. Reprinted—Nanjing wenxian, no. 2. Nanjing: Tongzhiguan, 1947.

Chen Zhongping 陳忠平. "Mingqing shiqi Nanjing chengshi de fazhan yu yanbian" 明清時期南京城市的發展與演變 (The development of and changes in the city of Nanjing in the Ming and Qing dynasties). *Zhongguo shehui jingjishi yanjiu* 中國社會經濟史研究 1988, no. 1: 39–45.

———. "Song Yuan Ming Qing shiqi Jiangnan shizhen shehui zuzhi shulun" 宋元明清時期江南市鎮社會組織述論 (The social structure of market towns in the Jiangnan area during the Song, Yuan, Ming, and Qing eras). *Zhongguo shehui jingji shi yanjiu* 中國社會經濟史研究 1993, no. 1: 33–38.

Chen Zuolin 陳作霖. *Jinling tongji* 金陵通紀 (The comprehensive chronicle of Nanjing). 1904. Reprinted—Taipei: Chengwen chubanshe, 1970.

———. *Jinling tongzhuan* 金陵通傳 (The comprehensive biographies of Nanjing natives). 1904. Reprinted—Taipei: Chengwen chubanshe, 1970.

———. *Jinling xianzheng yanxinglu* 金陵先正言行錄. N.p.: Jiangchu shuju, n.d.

Cheng Minsheng 程民生. "Lun Songdai de liudong renkou wenti" 論宋代的流動人口問題 (The mobile population of the Song dynasty). *Xueshu yuekan* 學術月刊 2006, no. 7: 136–43.

Cheng Yinong 成一農. "Song, Yuan, yiji Mingdai qianzhongqi chengshi chengqiang zhengce de yanbian jiqi yuanyin" 宋、元以及明代前中期城市城牆政策的演變及其原因 (The evolution of city-wall policies in the Song, Yuan, and early to mid-Ming eras and its explanations). In *Zhong Ri gudai chengshi yanjiu* 中日古代城市研究 (Studies on ancient cities in China and Japan), ed. Nakamura Keiji 中村圭尔 and Xin Deyong 辛德勇. Beijing: Zhongguo shehui kexue chubanshe, 2004, 145–83.

Chevalier, Bernard. *Les bonnes villes: l'état et la société dans la France de la fin du XVe siècle*. Orléans: Paradigme, 1995.

Chiu Chung-lin 邱仲麟. "Jing lao shi suoyi jian lao: Mingdai xiang yinjiu li de bianqian ji qi yu difang shehui de hudong" 敬老適所以賤老: 明代鄉飲酒禮的變遷及其與地方社會的互動 (Veneration degrades into denigration: the permutation of the Ming dynasty community drinking rituals and their interplay with local society). *Shiyusuo jikan* 76, no. 1 (2005): 1–79.

———. "Mingdai Beijing shehui fengqi bianqian: lizhi yu jiazhigua de gaibian" 明代北京社會風氣變遷—禮制與價值觀的改變 (The changing social climate in Ming Beijing: changes in ritual and value). *Dalu zazhi* 大陸雜誌 88, no. 3 (1994): 1–15.

Chiu Peng-sheng 邱澎生. "Mingdai Suzhou yingli chuban shiye ji qi shehui xiaoying" 明代蘇州營利出版事業及其社會效應 (Commercial presses in Ming Suzhou and their social influence). *Jiuzhou xuekan* 九州學刊 5, no. 2 (1992): 139–59.

———. "Shichang, falü yu renqing: Ming-Qing Suzhou shangren tuanti tigong 'jiaoyi fuwu' de zhidu yu bianqian" 市場、法律與人情: 明清蘇州商人團體提供「交易服務」的制度與變遷 (Market, laws, and human nature: the institutional setup and transformation of transaction services provided by Ming-Qing Suzhou merchant organizations). In *Chūgoku no rekishi seikai: tōgō no shisutemu to tagen teki hatten* 中國の歷史世界—統合のシステムと多元的發展 (The Chinese historical world: unified systems and diversified developments), ed. Chūgoku shigakukai 中国史学会. Tōkyō shiritsu daigaku shuppanbu, 2002, 571–92.

Clunas, Craig. *Fruitful Sites: Garden Culture in Ming Dynasty China*. Durham, NC: Duke University Press, 1996.

———. *Pictures and Visuality in Early Modern China*. Princeton: Princeton University Press, 1997.

———. *Superfluous Things: Material Culture and Social Status in Early Modern China*. Urbana: University of Illinois Press, 1991.

Danjō Hiroshi 檀上寬. *Minchō sensei shihai no shiteki kōzō* 明朝專制支配の史的構造 (The historical structure of Ming despotism). Tokyo: Kyūko shoin, 1995.

Dardess, John. *Confucianism and Autocracy: Professsional Elites in the Founding of the Ming Dynasty*. Berkeley: University of California Press, 1983.

Debevoise, Jane, and Scarlett Jang. "Topography and the Anhui School." In *Shadows of Mt. Huang: Chinese Painting and Printing of the Anhui School*, ed. James Cahill. Berkeley: University Art Museum, 1981, 43–50.

Deng Qiu 鄧球 (*jinshi* 1535). *Huang Ming yonghua leibian* 皇明泳化類編 (Assorted records of the civilizing enterprise of the Ming dynasty). Facsimile reprint of Longjing era (1567–72) copy. Beijing: Shumu wenxian chubanshe, 1988.

Ding Bin 丁賓. *Ding Qinghui gong yiji* 丁清惠公遺集 (The posthumous collection of Ding Qinghui). 1638 preface. Reprinted in Siku jinhuishu congkan, *jibu* 44. Beijing: Beijing chubanshe, 2000.

Ding Yizhuang 定宜庄. *Qingdai baqi zhufang yanjiu* 清代八旗驻防研究 (Studies on the Eight Banner garrisons of the Qing dynasty). Liaoning: Minzu chubanshe, 2003.

Ding Yuanjian 丁元薦. *Zunzhuotang wenji* 尊拙堂文集 (Collection from the Zunzhuo Studio). Facsimile reprint of 1660 edition. *Siku quanshu cunmu congshu*, 170–1. Tainan: Zhuangyan chubanshe, 1995.

Dong Jianhong 董鑒泓. *Zhongguo chengshi jianshe fazhan shi* 中國城市建設發展史 (The history of Chinese urban development). Taipei: Minwen shuju, 1984.

Elliott, Mark C. *The Manchu Way: The Eight Banners and Ethnic Identity in Late Imperial China*. Stanford: Stanford University Press, 2001.

Elvin, Mark. "Chinese City Since the Sung Dynasty." In *Towns in Societies: Essays in Economic History and Historical Sociology*, ed. Philip Abrams and E. A. Wrigley. Cambridge: Cambridge University Press, 1978, 79–89.

———. "'Female Virtue' and the State in China." *Past and Present* 104 (1984); reprinted in idem, *Another History. Essays on China from a European Perspective*. Sydney: Wild Peony, 1996, 302–51.

Esherick, Joseph W., and Mary B. Rankin, eds. *Chinese Local Elites and Patterns of Dominance*. Berkeley: University of California Press, 1990.

Fan I-chun 范毅軍. "Ming-Qing Jiangnan shichang juluo shi yanjiu de huigu yu zhanwang" 明清江南市場聚落史研究的回顧與展望 (A review of the studies of Ming-Qing market settlements). *Xinshixue* 新史學 9, no. 3 (1998): 87–133.

Fang, Jun. "Auxiliary Administration: The Southern Capital of Ming China." Ph.D. diss., University of Toronto, 1995.

Farmer, Edward L. *Early Ming Government: The Evolution of Dual Capitals*. Cambridge: East Asian Research Center, Harvard University, 1976.

———. "The Hierarchy of Ming City Walls." In *City Walls: The Urban Enceinte in Global Perspective*, ed. James D. Tracy. Cambridge: Cambridge University Press, 2000, 461–87.

————. *Zhu Yuanzhang and Early Ming Legislation: The Reordering of Chinese Society Following the Era of Mongol Rule*. Leiden: E. J. Brill, 1995.

Farquhar, David M. *The Government of China Under Mongolian Rule: A Reference Guide*. Stuttgart: Steiner, 1990.

Faure, David. "What Made Foshan a Town? The Evolution of Rural-Urban Identities in Ming-Qing China." *Late Impeiral China* 11, no. 2 (1990): 1–31.

————. "What Weber Did Not Know: Towns and Economic Development in Ming and Qing China." In *Town and Country in China* (see next extry), 58–84.

Faure, David, and Taotao Liu, eds. *Town and Country in China: Identity and Perception*. New York: Palgrave, 2002.

Fei Siyen 費絲言. "Cong dianfan dao guifan" 從典範到規範 (The normalization of female chastity in Ming China). M.A. thesis, National Taiwan University, 1998.

Feuerwerker, Albert. "From 'Feudalism' to 'Capitalism' in Recent Historic Writing from Mainland China." *Journal of Asian Studies* 18, no. 1 (1958): 1070–116.

Fu Chunguan 傅春官. *Jinling lidai jianzhibiao* 金陵歷代建置表 (Chart of the historical development of Nanjing). 1897. Beijing: Zhonghua shuju, 1985.

Fu, Li-tsui Flora 傅立萃. "Xie Shichen de mingsheng guji sijing tu: jian tan Mingdai chongqi de chuangyou" 謝時臣的名勝古蹟四景圖—兼談明代中期的壯遊 (Paintings of four famous views by Xie Shichen: the vogue for travel in the second half of the Ming dynasty). *Guoli Taiwan daxue meishushi yanjiu jikan* 國立臺灣大學美術史研究集刊 / *Taida Journal of Art History* 4 (March 1997): 185–222.

Fu Yiling 傅衣凌. *Mingdai Jiangnan shimin jingji shitan* 明代江南市民經濟試探 (A preliminary survey of the Jiangnan urban economy). Shanghai: Shanghai renmin chubanshe, 1957.

Fuma Susumu 夫馬進. "Chūgoku kinsei toshi no shakai kōzō no kansuru mitsu no kentō" 中国近世都市の社会構造に関する三つの検討 (Three inquiries concerning Professor Kawakatsu's "Urban Social Structure in Modern China"). *Shichō* 史潮, n.s. 6 (1979): 91–98.

————. "Late Ming Urban Reform and the Popular Uprising in Hangzhou." In *Cities of Jiangnan in Late Imperial China*, ed. Linda Cooke Johnson. Albany: State University of New York Press, 1993, 47–80.

————. "Mindai Nankin no toshi gyōsei" 明代南京の都市行政 (Municipal administration in Ming Nanjing). In *Zenkindai ni okeru toshi to shakaisō* 前近代における都市と社会層 (Cities and social stratification in the premodern era), ed. Nakamura Kenjirō 中村賢二郎. Kyoto: Jinbun kagaku kenkyūjo, 1980, 245–97.

———. "Minmatsu han chihōkan shihen" 明末反地方官士變 (A student movement against local bureaucrats in the late Ming period). *Tōhō gakuhō* 東方学報 52 (1980): 595–622.

———. "Minmatsu han chihōkan shihen horon" 明末反地方官士変補論 (A supplement regarding a student movement against local bureaucrats in the late Ming period). *Toyama daigaku jinbungakubu kiyō* 富山大學人文學部紀要 4 (1981): 19–33.

———. "Minmatsu minpen to seiin: Kōnan no tosho ni okeru seron no keisei to seiin yakuwari" 明末民變と生員—江南の都市における世論の形成と生員役割 (The late Ming uprisings and *shengyuan*: urban public opinion in Jiangnan and the role of *shengyuan* in its formation). In *Chiiki shakai no shiten: chiiki shakai to rīdā* 地域社會の視点—地域社會リーダー, ed. Nagoya daigaku, Tōyō shigaku kenkyūshitsu 名古屋大学東洋史学研究室. Nagoya: Nagoya daigaku, Bunkakubu, 1982, 12–15.

———. "Minmatsu no toshi kaikaku to Kōshū minpen" 明末の都市改革と杭州民變 (Late Ming municipal reform and the Hangzhou uprising). *Tōhō gakuhō* 東方学報 49 (1977): 215–62.

Gardner, Daniel K. "Modes of Thinking and Modes of Discourse in the Sung: Some Thoughts on the *Yü-lu* (Recorded Conversations) Texts." *Journal of Asian Studies* 50, no. 3 (1991): 574–603.

Goodrich, L. Carrington, and Fang Chao-ying, eds. *Dictionary of Ming Biography, 1368–1644.* 2 vols. New York: Columbia University Press, 1976.

Grimm, Tilemann. "State and Power in Juxtaposition: An Assessment of Ming Despotism." In *The Scope of State Power in China*, ed. Stuart R. Schram. London: St. Martin's Press, 1985.

Grove, Linda, and Christian Daniels, eds. *State and Society in China: Japanese Perspectives on Ming-Qing Social and Economic History.* Tokyo: University of Tokyo Press, 1984.

Gu Qiyuan 顧起元 (1565–1628). *Kezuo zhuiyu* 客座贅語 (Superfluous chats from guests' seats). 1617. Reprinted—Beijing: Zhonghua shuju, 1987.

———. *Lanzhen caotang ji* 嬾眞草堂集 (Collection from the Lanzhen Studio). 1614. Reprinted—Taipei: Wenhai chubanshe, 1970.

Gu Yanwu 顧炎武. *Gutinglin shiwenji* 顧亭林詩文集 (The collected works of Gu Yanwu). Reprinted—Taipei: Hanjing wenhua, 1984.

———. *Tianxia junguo libing shu* 天下郡國利病書 (Book of the benefits and ills of the various states of the world). Original preface by Gu dated 1632. Facsimile reprint of Sibu congkan edition. Xuxiu Siku quanshu, 595–97.

Gui Youguang 歸有光. *Zhenchuan ji* 震川集 (Collected works of Gui Youguang). *Jingying Wenyuange siku quanshu*, 1289. Taipei: Taiwan Shangwu yinshuguan, 1979.

Guo Shaoyu 郭紹虞. *Zhaoyushi gudian wenxue lunji* 昭隅室古典文學論集 (A collection of essays on classical literature from the Zhaoyu Studio). Shanghai: Shanghai guji chubanshe, 1983.

Hai Rui 海瑞 (1514–87). *Hai Rui ji* 海瑞集 (Collected works of Hai Rui). 1624. Reprinted—Beijing: Zhonghua shuju, 1962.

Hamashima Atsutoshi 浜島敦俊. "Minbō kara gōshin e: 16–17 seiki no Kōnan shitaifu" '民望' から '郷紳-へ—十六, 七世紀の江南士大夫 (From *minwang* to *xiangshen*—Jiangnan literati of the sixteenth and seventeenth centuries). *Ōsaka daigaku Daigakuin Bungaku kenkyūka kiyō* 大坂大学院文学研究科紀要 41 (2001): 27–65.

———. *Mindai Kōnan nōson shakai no kenkyū* 明代江南農村社會の研究 (A study of Jiangnan rural society during the Ming dynasty). Tokyo: Tōkyō daigaku shuppankai, 1982.

———. *Sōkan shinkō: kinsei Kōnan nōson shakai to minkan shinkō* 総管信仰: 近世江南農村社会と民間信仰 (Belief in Zongguan: folk religion in rural society in Jiangnan during the Ming and Qing periods). Tokyo: Kenbun shuppan, 2001.

Han Guanghui 韓光輝. "Jindai zhu fu jie zhen chengshi lushi si yanjiu" 金代諸府節鎮城市錄事司研究 (Researches on the municipal administrative system in the Jin era). *Wenshi* 52 (2000): 37–51.

———. "Yuandai Zhongguo de jianzhi chengshi" 元代中國的建制城市 (Researches on municipal administrative cities in the Yuan dynasty). *Dili xuebao* 50, no. 4 (1995): 324–34.

Hanan, Patrick. *The Chinese Vernacular Story*. Cambridge: Harvard University Press, 1981.

Hargett, James M. "Song Dynasty Local Gazetteers and Their Place in the History of *Difangzhi* Writing." *Harvard Journal of Asiatic Studies* 56, no. 2 (1996): 405–42.

Harrison, Henrietta. "Village Identity in Rural North China." In *Town and Country in China: Identity and Perception*, ed. David Faure and Taotao Liu. New York: Palgrave, 2002, 85–106.

Hay, Jonathan. "Ming Palace and Tomb in Early Qing Jiangning: Dynastic Memory and the Openness of History." *Late Imperial China* 20, no. 1 (1999): 1–48.

He Tang 何鏜. *Mingshan shenggai ji* 名山勝概記 (Record of famous mountains and grand scenery). Late Ming edition. Copy at Library of Congress, Washington, DC.

He Xiaorong 何孝榮. *Mingdai Nanjing siyuan yanjiu* 明代南京寺院研究 (A study of Ming temples). Beijing: Zhongguo kexue chubanshe, 2000.

Hegel, R. E. *Reading Illustrated Fiction in Late Imperial China.* Stanford: Stanford University Press, 1998.

Heijdra, Martin. "The Socio-Economic Development of Rural China During the Ming." In *The Cambridge History of China,* vol. 8, *The Ming Dynasty, 1368–1644,* pt. II, ed. Denis Twitchett and F. W. Mote. Cambridge: Cambridge University Press, 1998, 417–587.

Hsu Hong 徐泓. "Mingchu Nanjing de dushi guihua yu renkou bianqian" 明初南京的都市規劃與人口變遷 (Urban planning and demographic changes in early Ming Nanjing). *Shihuo yuekan* 食貨月刊, n.s. 10, no. 3 (1980): 82–115.

――――. "Mingchu Nanjing huangcheng, gongcheng de guihua, pingmianbuju jiqi xiangzheng yiyi" 明初南京皇城、宮城的規劃，平面布局及其象徵意義 (The design and planning of imperial palaces and their symbolic meanings in early Ming Nanjing). *Taida jianzhu yu chengxiang yanjiu xuebao* 台大建築與城鄉研究學報 7 (1993): 79–96.

――――. "Mingdai Fujian de zhucheng yundong" 明代福建的築城運動 (The wall-building movement in Fujian during the Ming dynasty). *Jida xuebao* 暨大學報 3, no. 1 (1999): 25–76.

――――. "Mingdai houqi huabei shangpin jingji de fazhan yu shehui fengqi de bianqian" 明代後期華北商品經濟的發展與社會風氣的變遷 (The development of a commodity economy and social customs in northern China in the later half of the Ming dynasty). In the conference proceedings for the second *Zhongguo jindai jingjishi huiyi* 中國近代經濟史會議論文集. Taipei: Zhongyang yanjiuyuan jingji yanjiusuo 1989, 107–76.

――――. "Mingmo shehui fengqi de bianqian: yi Jiangzhe diqu weili" 明末社會風氣的變遷——以江浙地區為例 (Changes in late Ming social customs: a case study of the Jiangzhe area). *Dongnan wenhua* 24 (1986): 83–110.

Hu Jianhua 胡建華. "Songdai chengshi liudong renkou guanli tanxi" 宋代城市流動人口管理探析 (Analysis of the management of mobile urban population in the Song dynasty). *Yindu xuekan* 殷都學刊 1994, no. 2: 23–33.

Huang Haiyan 黃海妍. *Zai chengshi yu xiangcun zhijian: Qingdai yilai Guangzhou hezusi yanjiu* 在城市與鄉村之間：清代以來廣州合族祠研究 (Between cities and countryside: study on joint-lineage shrines in Guangzhou since the Qing dynasty). Beijing: Shenghuo, dushu, xinzhi sanlian shudian, 2008.

Huang, Philip C. C. "'Public Sphere' / 'Civil Society' in China?" *Modern China* 19, no. 2 (1993): 216–40.

Huang, Ray. *1587, A Year of no Significance: The Ming Dynasty in Decline.* New Haven: Yale University Press, 1981.

――――. *Taxation and Governmental Finance in Sixteenth-Century Ming China.* Cambridge: Cambridge University Press, 1975.

Huang Zhifan 黄志繁 "Guojia rentong yu tuke chongtu: Ming-Qing shiqi Gan nan de zuqun guanxi" 國家認同與土客衝突: 明清時期贛南的族群關係 (National identification and the conflict between natives and immigrants: relations between ethnic groups in southern Jiangxi during the Ming and Qing dynasties). *Zhongshan daxue xuebao* 2002, no. 4: 44–51.

Huangming tiaofashi leizuan 皇明條法事類纂 (Collections of itemized substatutes in the Ming dynasty). Beijing: Kexue chubanshe, 1994.

Hucker, Charles. *A Dictionary of Official Titles in Imperial China.* Stanford: Stanford University Press, 1985.

————. *The Ming Dynasty: Its Origins and Evolving Institutions.* Ann Arbor: Center for Chinese Studies, 1978.

————. *The Traditional Chinese State in Ming Times, 1368–1644.* Tucson: University of Arizona Press, 1961.

Hummel, Arthur W., ed. *Eminent Chinese of the Ch'ing Period (1644–1912).* 2 vols. Washington, DC: U.S. Government Printing Office, 1943–44.

Inoue Tōru 井上徹. *Chūgoku no sōzoku to kokka no reisei: sōhō shugi no shiten kara no bunseki* 中国の宗族と国家の礼制: 宗法主義の視点からの分析 (Chinese lineage and state rituals: analysis from the perspective of patriarchism). Tokyo: Kenbun shuppan, 2000.

Iwai Shigeki 岩井茂樹. "Chō Kyosei zaisei no kadai to hōhō" 張居正財政の課題と方法." In *Minmatsu Shin shoki no kenkyū* 明末清初期の研究 (Studies on the late Ming–early Qing period), ed. Iwami Hiroshi 岩見宏 and Taniguchi Kikuo 谷口規矩雄. Kyōto: Kyōto daigaku Jinbun kagaku kenkyūjo, 1989, 225–69.

————. "Chūgoku sensei kokka to zaisei" 中国専制国家と財政 (The despotic state of China and its finance). In *Chūseishi Kōza* 中世史講座 (Lectures on medieval history). Tokyo: Gakuseisha, 1992, 6: 273–310.

————. "Yōeki to zaisei no aida" 徭役と財政のあいだ (Between corvée and finance). 4 pts. *Keizai keiei ronsō* 經濟經營論叢, 28, no. 4 (1994): 1–58; 29, no. 1 (1995): 1–50; 29, no. 2 (1995): 1–68; 29, no. 3 (1995): 1–88.

Iwami Hiroshi 岩見宏. *Mindai yōeki seido no kenkyū* 明代徭役制度の研究 (Studies on the Ming corvée system). Kyoto: Dōhōsha, 1986.

Ji Yun 紀昀 et al. *Siku quanshu zongmu tiyao* 四庫全書總目提要 (General catalogue of the *Siku quanshu*, with descriptive notes). 1798. Reprinted—Taipei: Taiwan Shangwu yinshuguan, 1965.

Jiang Weilin 江爲霖. *Jinling baimei* 金陵百媚 (Hundred beauties in Nanjing). 1618. Copy in the Rare Book Collection, Naikaku bunko, Tokyo.

Jiao Hong 焦竑 (1541–1620). *Guochao xiancheng lu* 國朝獻徵錄 (Biographies of prominent people in the Ming dyansty). 1616. Facsimile reprint of 1616 edition. Taipei: Xuesheng shuju, 1984.

———. *Jinling jiushi* 金陵舊事 (Past events about Jinling). In *Jiaoshi bisheng* 焦氏筆乘 (Writings of Mr. Jiao). Reprinted—Taipei: Taiwan shangwu yinshuguan, 1966.

Jin Zhijun 金之俊. *Fu Wu xi lue* 撫吳檄略 (Manuscripts from my tenure as grand coordinator of the Wu area). In *Jin Wentong gong wenji* 金文通公集 (Collected works of Jin Wentong). Facsimile reprint of 1686 edition. Xuxiu Siku quanshu, 1392–93.

Johnson, David; Andrew J. Nathan; and Evelyn S. Rawski, eds. *Popular Culture in Late Imperial China*. Berkeley: University of California Press, 1985.

Johnson, Linda Cooke, ed. *Cities of Jiangnan in Late Imperial China*. Albany: State University of New York Press, 1993.

Kamachi Noriko. "Feudalism or Absolute Monarchism? Japanese Discourse on the Nature of State and Society in Late Imperial China." *Modern China* 16, no. 3 (1990): 330–70.

Kawakatsu Mamoru 川勝守. *Min Shin Kōnan shichin shakaishi kenkyū: kūkan to shakai keisei no rekishigaku* 明清江南市鎮社会史研究: 空間と社会形成の歴史学 (Social history of market towns in the Lower Yangtze Delta during the Ming and Qing periods: historical science based on space and the social formation). Tokyo: Kyūko shoin, 1999.

Kiang, Heng Chye. *Cities of Aristocrats and Bureaucrats: The Development of Medieval Chinese Cityscapes*. Honolulu: University of Hawai'i Press, 1999.

Kim, Hongnam. *The Life of a Patron: Zhou Lianggong (1612–1672) and the Painters of Seventeenth-Century China*. New York: China Institute in America, 1996.

Kishimoto Mio 岸本美緒. "Minmatsu Shinsho no chihō shakai to seron: Shōkō fu o chūshin to suru sobyō" 明末清初の地方社會と世論—松江府中心をとする素描 (Local society and public opinion in the late Ming: a sketch of the Songjiang area). *Rekishigaku kenkyū* 歴史學研究, no. 573 (1987): 131–40.

Ko, Dorothy. *Teachers of the Inner Chambers: Women and Culture in Seventeenth-Century China*. Stanford: Stanford University Press, 1994.

Kobayashi Kazumi. "The Other Side of Rent and Tax Resistance Struggles: Ideology and the Road to Rebellion." In *State and Society in China*, ed. Linda Grove and Christian Daniels. Tokyo: University of Tokyo Press, 1984, 215–43.

Kong Shangren 孔尚任. *Kong Shangren shiwen ji* 孔尚任詩文集 (Collection of poetry and essays by Kong Shangren). Reprinted—Beijing: Zhonghua shuju, 1962.

Kuhn, Philip A. Review of Susan Naquin, *Peking: Temples and City Life. American Historical Review* 107, no. 1 (2002): 167.

Kumamoto Takashi 熊本崇. "Sōsei 'jōkaku no hu' no hitotsu no kentō" 宋制「城郭之賦」の 一つの検討 (A review of Song urban taxation). *Shūkan tōyōgaku* 集刊東洋學 44 (1980): 88–97.

Kusano Yasushi 草野靖. "Sōdai no okuzei to chizei ni tsuite" 宋代の屋税と地税について (On the Song house and urban land taxes). *Shigaku zasshi* 史學雜誌 68, no. 4 (1959): 71–88.

Lamley, Harry J. "Hsieh-Tou: The Pathology of Violence in Southeast China." *Ching-shih wen-t'i* 3, no. 7 (1977): 1–39.

Lee, Hui-shu. *Exquisite Moments: West Lake and Southern Song Art*. New York: China Institute, 2001.

Lees, Lynn Hollen, and Paul M. Hohenberg. *The Making of Urban Europe, 1000–1950*. Cambridge: Harvard University Press, 1985.

Lewis, Mark Edward. *The Construction of Space in Early China*. Albany: State University of New York Press, 2006.

Li Rihua 李日華 (1565–1635). *Weishui xuan riji* 味水軒日記 (Diary at Weishui studio). Reprint, Shanghai: Shanghai yuandong chubanshe, 1996.

Li Shenghua 李聖華. *Wan Ming shige yanjiu* 晚明詩歌研究 (Studies on late Ming poetry). Beijing: Renmin wenxue chubanshe, 2002.

Li Wenzhi 李文治. *Wan Ming minbian* 晚明民變 (Late Ming uprisings). Shanghai: Shanghai shudian, 1989.

Liang Fangzhong (Liang Fang-chung) 梁方仲. *Liang Fangzhong jingjishi lunwenji* 梁方仲經濟史論文集 (Collected essays on economic history by Liang Fangzhong). Beijing: Zhonghua shuji, 1989.

———. *Mingdai liangzhang zhidu* 明代糧長制度 (The system of tax captains in the Ming dynasty). Shanghai: Shanghai renmin chubanshe, 1957.

———. *The Single Whip Method (I-t'iao-pien fa) of Taxation in China*. Trans. Wang Yu-chuan. Cambridge: Chinese Economic and Political Studies, Harvard University, 1956.

Lin Feng 林楓. "Wanli kuang jian shui shi yuanyin zaitan" 萬曆礦監稅使原因再探 (Further investigation into the reasons of Wan-li's eunuchs and army officers as tax-collectors and mining-supervisors). *Zhongguo shehui jingjishi yanjiu* 中國經濟史研究 2002, no. 1: 13–19.

Lin Jiaohong 林皎宏. "Wan Ming Huangshan luyou de xing qi" 晚明黄山旅游的興起 (The rise of tourism to Mt. Huang in the late Ming). *Shi yuan* 史原 19 (1993): 131–71.

Lin Lian 林嫌. "Zeng Jiezhuan Liu gong zhi Jiangxi zuoxia xu" 贈節齋劉公之江西左轄序 (Preface for Liu Jiezhuan to take office in Jiangxi). In *Ming jingshi wenbian* 明經世文編 (Ming documents on statecraft). Taipei: Zhonghua shuju, 1987, 313.3321.

Lin Liyue 林麗月. "*Jianjiatang gao* yu Lu Ji 'fan jinshe' sixiang zhi chuanyan" 《蒹葭堂稿》與陸楫「反禁奢」思想之傳衍 (*Jianjiatang gao* and the dissemination of Lu Ji's antisumptuary ideas). In *Mingren wenji yu Mingdai yanjiu* 明人文集與明代研究 (Anthologies from the Ming era and Ming studies), ed. Zhang Lian 張璉. Taipei: Mingdai yanjiu xuehui, 2002, 123–29.

———. "Wan Ming 'chongshe' sixiang yulun" 晚明「崇奢」思想隅論 (Thoughts on the late Ming's championing of the value of luxury). *Taiwan Shida lishi xuebao* 台灣師大歷史學報 19, no. 6 (June 1991): 215–34.

Lin Shaoming 林紹明. "Ming-Qing nian jian Jiangnan shizhen de xingzheng guanli" 明清年間江南市鎮的行政管理 (The administration of market towns in Jiangnan area during the Ming and Qing eras). *Huadong shifan daxue xuebao: zhexue shehuikexue ban* 華東師範大學學報 哲學社會科學版, 1987, no. 2: 93–95.

Ling Mengchu 凌濛初. *Er ke pai'an jingqi* 二刻拍案驚奇 (Slapping the table in amazement, second collection). Shanghai: Shanghai guji chubanshe, 1984.

Liscomb, Kathlyn. "The Eight Views of Beijing: Politics in Literati Art." *Artibus Asiae*, no. 491–92 (1988–89): 127–52.

Liu Min 劉敏. "Shilun Ming-Qing shiqi huji zhidu de bianhua" 試論明清時期戶籍制度的變化 (A preliminary survey of changes in the household-registration system during the Ming-Qing eras). *Zhongguo gudaishi luncong* 中國古代史論叢 1981, no. 2: 218–36.

Liu Zhengyun 劉錚雲. "'Chong, pi, fan, nan': Qingdai dao, fu, ting, zhou, xian dengji chutan" 「衝、疲、繁、難」:清代道、府、廳、州、縣等級初探 ("Frequented," "wearisome," "troublesome," "difficult": a study of the classification of administrative units in the Qing dynasty). *Zhongyang yanjiuyuan Lishi yuyan yanjiusuo jikan* 64, no. 1 (1993): 175–204.

Liu Zhiji 劉知幾 (661–721). *Shitong* 史通 (Generalities on history). 710. In Jingying Wenyuange siku quanshu 景印文淵閣四庫全書, 685. Taipei: Taiwan Shangwu yinshuguan, 1979.

Liu Zhiqin 劉志琴. "Chongxin renshi moshi shuaibian" 重新認識末世衰變 (A new understanding on the declining of an era). Preface to *Wan Ming shilun* 晚明史論 (Historical studies on the late Ming). Nanchang: Jiangxi gaoxiao chubanshe, 2003.

Liu Zhiwei 劉志偉. *Zai guojia yu shehui zhi jian: Ming Qing Guangdong lijia fuyi zhidu yanjiu* 在國家與社會之間: 明清廣東里甲賦役制度研究 (Between state and society: study on the tax and corvée system in Guangdong during the Ming-Qing period). Guangzhou: Zhongshan daxue chubanshe, 1997.

Long Denggao 龍登高. "Cong kefan dao qiaoju: chuantong shangren jingying fangshi de bianhua" 從客販到僑居: 傳統商人經營方式的變化 (From sojourning peddlers to residential merchants: changes in the management style of traditional merchants). *Zhongguo jingjishi yanjiu* 中國經濟史研究 1998, no. 2: 63–73.

Lu Cai 陸采. *Yecheng kelun* 冶城客論 (Guest talks at Nanjing). Facsimile reprint of a Qing copy now in the possession of Nanjing library. Siku quanshu cunmu congshu, 246. Tainan: Zhuangyan chubanshe, 1995.

Lü Kun 呂坤 (1536–1618). *Quweizhai ji* 去僞齋集 (Works from the Studio of Quwei). In *Lüzi yishu* 呂子遺書 (The posthumous collection of Lü Kun). 1827.

———. *Xinwu Lü xiansheng shizheng lu* 新吾呂先生實政錄 (Account of the administration of Mr. Lü from Xinwu). Facsimile reprint of late Ming edition in *Guanzhen shu jicheng* 官箴書集成 (Collection of administrative handbooks).

Lü Miaofen 呂妙芬. "Yangmingxue jianghui" 陽明學講會 (Public lectures and Yangming xue). *Xinshixue* 新史學 9, no. 2 (1998): 45–87.

Lu Shiyi 陸世儀. *Fushe jilue* 復社紀略 (Brief account of the Fushe). In *Biji xiaoshuo daguan* 筆記小説大觀 (Collection of miscellaneous notes and novels). Taipei: Xinxing shuju, 1984, 10.4, *juan* 2, 2097.

Lu Wenheng 陸文衡. *Se'an suibi* 嗇庵隨筆 (Casual notes from Se'an). Facsimile reprint of 1685 edition. Taipei: Guangwen shuju, 1969.

Luo Xiaoxiang 羅曉翔. "From Imperial City to Cosmopolitan Metropolis: Culture, Politics and State in Late Ming Nanjing." Ph.D. diss., Duke University, 2006.

———. "'Jinling genben zhongdi': Mingmo zhengzhi yujing zhong de fengshui guan" '金陵根本重地'—明末政治語境中的風水觀 ("Jinling is a fundamentally important place"—the geomantic viewpoint in the late Ming political context). *Zhongguo lishi dili luncong* 中國歷史地理論叢 23, no. 3 (2008): 22–29, 74.

———. "Mingdai Nanjing de fangxiang yu zipu: difang xingzheng yu chengshi shehui" 明代南京的坊廂與字鋪—地方行政與城市社會 (Lane and compartment system and bunks in Ming Nanjing: local administration and urban society). *Zhongguo shehui jingjishi yanjiu* 中國社會經濟史研究 2008, no. 4: 49–57.

Ma Yachen. "Citizen's Perspective Versus Imperial Perspective: Two Cityscapes of Nanjing." Unpublished paper, 2002, Stanford University.

———. "Picturing Suzhou: Visual Politics in the Making of Cityscapes in Eighteenth-Century China." Ph.D. diss., Stanford University, 2006.

Mann, Susan. *Local Merchants and the Chinese Bureaucracy, 1750–1950*. Stanford: Stanford University Press, 1987.

Marmé, Michael. *Suzhou: Where Goods of All the Provinces Converge*. Stanford: Stanford University Press, 2005.

McDermott, Joseph P. "The Making of a Chinese Mountain, Huangshan: Politics and Wealth in Chinese Art." *Asian Cultural Studies / Ajia bunka kenkyū* アジア文化研究 17 (1989): 145–76.

————. *A Social History of the Chinese Book: Books and Literati Culture in Late Imperial China*. Hongkong: Hongkong University Press, 2006.

Mei, Yun-ch'iu. "Mass-Production of Topographic Pictures in the Seventeenth-Century Exploration for Nanjing's Famous Sites." Unpublished paper, Stanford University, 2002.

Meyer-Fong, Tobie. *Building Culture in Early Qing Yangzhou*. Stanford: Stanford University Press, 2003.

————. "Seeing the Sights in Yangzhou from 1600 to the Present." In *When Images Speak: Visual Representations and Cultural Mapping in Modern China / Huazhong you hua: jindai Zhongguo de shijue biaoshu yu wenhua goutu* 畫中有話:近代中國的視覺表述與文化構圖. Taipei: Academia Sinica, 2003, 213–49.

Ming shi 明史 (Ming history). Taipei: Dingwen shuju, 1982.

Ming shilu 明實錄 (Veritable records of the Ming dynasty). Ed. Huang Zhang-jian 黄彰健. Taipei: Academia Sinica, 1984.

Mori Masao 森正夫. "Kōnan deruta no kyōchinshi ni tsuite: Ming gōhanki o chūshin ni" 江南デルタの郷鎮志について—明后半期を中心に (Late Ming town gazetteers in the Jiangnan Delta). In *Minmatsu Shinsho no shakai to bunka* 明末清初の社会と文化 (Society and culture in late Ming and early Qing periods), ed. Ono Kazuko 小野和子. Kyoto: Kyōto daigaku Jinbun kagaku kenkyūjo, 1996, 149–88.

————. "Ming-Qing shidai Jiangnan sanjiaozhou de xiangzhenshi yu diyu shehui: yi Qingdai wei zhongxin de kaocha" 明清時代江南三角洲的郷鎮志與地域社會—以清代為中心的考察 (Town gazetteers and local communities in the Jiangnan Delta during the Qing). In *Zhonghua minguo shi zhuanti lunwen ji* 中華民國史專題論文集 (Special essays on the history of the Republic of China), no. 5. Taipei: Academia Historica, 2000, 1: 787–821.

————. "Minmatsu ni okeru chitsujo hendō saikō" 明末における秩序変動再考 (A reconsideration of changes in the late Ming social order). *Chūgoku shakai to bunka* 中国社会と文化, no. 110 (1995): 3–27.

————. "Minmatsu no shakai kankei ni okeru chitsujo no hendō ni tsuite" 明末の社会関係における秩序の変動について (Changes in the hierarchies of social relations in the late Ming period). In *Nagoya daigaku Bungakubu sanjisshūnen kinen ronshū* 名古屋大学文学部三十年記念論集 (Essays in honor of the thirtieth anniversary of the foundation of the Humanities Division of Nagoya University). Nagoya: Nagoya daigaku Bungakubu, 1979, 135–59.

————. "Shindai Kōnan deruta no kyōchinshi to chiiki shakai" 清代江南デルタの郷鎮志と地域社會 (Town gazetteers and local communities of the Jiangnan delta in the Qing dynasty). *Tōyōshi kenkyū* 東洋史研究 58, no. 2 (1999): 82–119.

Mote, Frederick W. "The City in Traditional Chinese Civilization." In *Traditional China*, ed. James T. C. Liu and Wei-Ming Tu. Englewood Cliffs, NJ: Prentice-Hall, 1970, 48–49.

————. "The Growth of Chinese Despotism." *Oriens Extremus* 8 (1961): 1–41.

————. "A Millennium of Chinese Urban History: Form, Time and Space Concepts in Soochow." *Rice University Studies* 59, no. 4 (1977): 35–65.

————. "The Transformation of Nanking, 1350–1400." In *The City In Late Imperial China*, ed. G. William Skinner. Stanford: Stanford University Press, 1977, 101–53.

Mundy, John H., and Peter Riesenberg. *The Medieval Town*. Princeton, NJ: Van Nostrand, 1958.

Murphey, Rhoads. 1984. "City as a Mirror of Society: China, Tradition and Transformation." In *The City in Cultural Context*, ed. John A. Agnew, John Mercer, and David E. Sopher. Boston: Allen & Unwin, 1984.

Nakajima Yoshiaki 中島楽章. *Mindai gōson no funsō to chitsujo: Kishū monjo o shiryō to shite* 明代郷村の紛争と秩序: 徽州文書を史料として (Disputes and order in rural society during the Ming period: an analysis based on Huizhou documents). Tokyo: Kyūko shoin, 2002.

Naquin, Susan. *Peking: Temples and City Life, 1400–1900*. Berkeley: University of California Press, 2000.

Nicholas, David. *Town and Countryside: Social, Economic, and Political Tensions in Fourteenth-Century Flanders*. Bruges: De Tempel, 1971.

Norimatsu Akifumi 則松彰文. "Shindai chūki ni okeru shashi, hayari, shōhi: Kōnan chihō chūshin do" 清代中期における奢侈、流行、消費—江南地方中心ど (Luxury, fashion, and consumption in the mid-Qing period: a focus on the Jiangnan area). *Tōyō gakuhō* 東洋学報 80, no. 2 (1998): 31–58.

Ogawa Takashi 小川尚. *Mindai chihō kansatsu seido no kenkyū* 明代地方監察制度 (The system of local censors in the Ming era). Tokyo: Kyūko shoin, 1999.

Osawa Akihiro 大澤顯浩. "Chirisho to seisho" 地理書と政書 (Geographical books and administrative manuals). In *Minmatsu Shinsho no shakai to bunka* 明末清初の社會と文化 (Society and culture in late Ming and early Qing China), ed. Ono Kazuko 小野和子. Kyoto: Kyōtō daigaku Jinbun kagaku kenkyūjo, 1996, 457–501.

Otagi Matsuo 愛宕松男."Gendai toshi seido to sono kigen" 元代都市制度 と其の起源 (Yuan dynasty's municipal system and its origin). *Tōyōshi ken-kyū* 東洋史研究 3, no. 4 (1938): 1–28.

Owen, Stephen. "Place: Meditations on the Past of Chin-ling." *Harvard Journal of Asiatic Studies* 50, no. 2 (1990): 417–57.

Oyama Masaaki 小山正明. "Minmatsu Shinsho no dai tochi shoyū: toku ni Kōnan deruta chitai o chūshin ni shite" 明末清初の大土地所有: 特に江南デルタ地帯をちゅうしんにして (Large landownership in the Jiang-nan delta region during the late Ming–early Qing period). 2 pts. *Shigaku zasshi* 66, no. 12 (1957): 1–30; 67, no. 1 (1958): 50–72.

Pang Xinping 龐新平. "Kasei wakō katsuyakuki ni okeru chikujō" 嘉靖倭寇活躍期における築城 (Wall building during the peak of pirate attacks in the Jiajing reign [1522–66]). *Tōyō gakuhō* 東洋學報 75 (1994): 31–62.

Puett, Michael J. *To Become a God: Cosmology, Sacrifice, and Self-divinization in Early China*. Cambridge: Harvard University Asia Center, 2002.

Qi Biaojia 祁彪佳 (1602–45). *An Wu xi gao* 按吳檄稿 (Manuscripts from my tenure in the Wu area). Facsimile reprint of late Ming edition. Beijing tushuguan guji zhenben congkan, 48. Beijing: Shumu wenxian chubanshe, 1990.

Qian Daxin 錢大昕 (1728–1804). *Qianyantang wenji* 潛研堂文集 (Collected prose from the Qianyan Studio). Shanghai: Shanghai guji chubanshe, 1989.

Qian Mu 錢穆. *Guoshi dagang* 國史大綱 (An outline of Chinese history). 1940. Reprinted—Taipei: Shangwu chubanshe, 1988.

Qian Qianyi 錢謙益 (1582–1664). *Liechao shiji xiaozhuan* 列朝詩集小傳 (Biographical sketches of poets of the Ming dynasty). Taipei: Mingwen shuju, 1991.

———. *Muzhai chu xue ji* 牧齋初學集 (Collection of Qian Muzhai). Facsimile reprint of Chongzhen edition. Xuxiu Siku quanshu, 1390. Shanghai: Shang-hai guji chubanshe, 1995.

Rawski, Evelyn. "Economic and Social Foundations of Late Imperial Culture." In *Popular Culture in Late Imperial China*, ed. David Johnson, Andrew J. Na-than, and Evelyn S. Rawski. Berkeley: University of California Press, 1985, 3–33.

Ren Jincheng 任金城. "*Guangyu tu* zai Zhongguo dituxue shi shang de diwei jiqi yingxiang" 廣輿圖在中國地圖學史上的地位及其影響 (The contri-bution of *Guangyu tu* to the history of Chinese cartography and its impact). In *Zhongguo gudai dituji: Ming* 中國古代地圖集—明 (An atlas of ancient maps in China: Ming Dynasty [1368–1644]). Beijing: Cultural Relics Publish-ing House, 1994, 73–78.

Reynolds, Susan. *Kingdoms and Communities in Western Europe, 900–1300*. New York: Oxford University Press, 1984.

Rowe, William T. "Approaches to Modern Chinese Social History." In *Reliving the Past: The World of Social History*, ed. Olivier Zunz. Chapel Hill: University of North Carolina Press, 1985, 236–96.

———. *Hankow: Commerce and Society in a Chinese City, 1796–1889*. Stanford: Stanford University Press, 1984.

———. *Hankow: Conflict and Community in a Chinese City, 1796–1895*. Stanford: Stanford University Press, 1989.

———. "Modern Chinese Social History in Comparative Perspective." In *Heritage of China: Contemporary Perspectives on Chinese Civilization*, ed. Paul S. Ropp. Berkeley: University of California Press, 1990, 242–62.

———. "The Public Sphere in Modern China." *Modern China* 16, no. 3 (1990): 309–29.

Rubin, Miri. "Religious Culture in Town and Country: Reflections on a Great Divide." In *Church and City 1000–1500: Essays in Honour of Christopher Brooke*, ed. David Abulafia, Michael Franklin, and Miri Rubin. Cambridge: Cambridge University Press, 1992, 3–220.

Saeki Yūichi 佐伯有一. "Minmatsu no Tō-shi no hen: iwayuru 'nuhen' no seikaku ni kanrenshite" 明末の董氏の変: いわゆる「奴変」のせいかくに関連して (The Dong family rebellion in the late Ming: the nature of so-called bondservant rebellions). *Tōyōshi kenkyū* 16, no. 1 (1957): 26–57.

Saeki Yūichi 佐伯有一 and Tanaka Masatoshi 田中正俊. "Jūgo seiki ni okeru Fukken no nōmin hanran" 十五世紀に於ける福建の農民叛乱 (Peasant rebellion in fifteenth-century Fujian). *Rekishigaku kenkyū*, no. 167 (1954): 1–11.

Santangelo, Paolo. "Urban Society in Late Imperial Suzhou." In *Cities of Jiangnan in Late Imperial China*, ed. Linda Cooke Johnson. Albany: State University of New York Press, 1993, 81–116.

Schneewind, Sarah. *Community Schools and the State in Ming China*. Stanford: Stanford University Press, 2006.

———. "Visions and Revisions: Village Policies of the Ming Founder in Seven Phases." *T'oung Pao* 87 (2002): 1–43.

Shen Bang 沈榜. *Wanshu zaji* 宛署雜記 (Miscellaneous notes from the Wanping county office). 1593. Reprinted—Beijing: Beijing chubanshe, 1961.

Shen Kai 沈愷. *Huanxi ji* 環溪集. Facsimile reprint of 1571 edition. Siqu quanshu cunmu congshu 四庫全書存目叢書 4. Tainan: Zhuangan chubanshe, 1997.

Shen Zhou 沈周 (1427–1509). *Kezuo xinwe* 客座新聞 (News from guest seats). In Biji xiaoshuo daguan 筆記小説大觀, no. 40.10. Taipei: Xinxing shuju, 1985.

Sheng Shitai 盛時泰. *Niushou shan zhi* 牛首山志 (Gazetteer of Mount Niushou). 1577. Reprinted in Nanjing wenxian, no. 1. Nanjing: Tongzhiguan, 1947.

———. *Qixia xiaozhi* 棲霞小志 (Short record of Qixia Monastery). 1578. Reprinted in Nanjing wenxian, no. 2. Nanjing: Tongzhiguan, 1947.

Shi Jian 史鑑 (1434–96). *Xicun ji* 西村集 (Collections from West Village). Jingying Wenyuange siku quanshu, 1259. Taipei: Taiwan Shangwu yinshuguan, 1979.

Shi Shouqian 石守謙. "Langdang zhi feng: Mingdai zhongqi Nanjing de baimiao renwuhua" 浪蕩之風—明代中期南京的白描人物畫 (The dissolute style of portraiture in mid-Ming Nanjing). *Guoli Taiwan daxue meishushi yanjiu jikan* 國立臺灣大學美術史研究集刊 1 (1994): 39–61.

———. "You qiqu dao fugu: shiqi shiji Jinling huihua de yige qiemian" 由奇趣到復古—十七世紀金陵繪畫的一個切面 (From fantastic novelty to the revival of the ancient style: a facet of Nanjing paintings in the seventeenth century), *Gugong xueshu jikan* 故宮學術季刊 15, no. 4 (1998): 33–76.

Shi Shuqing 史樹清. "Wang Fu *Beijing ba jing* tu yanjiu" 王紱北京八景圖研究 (A study of Wang Fu's painting of *Eight Views of Beijing*). *Wenwu* 1981, no. 5: 78–85.

Shigeta, Atsushi. "The Origin and Structure of Gentry Rule." In *State and Society in China: Japanese Perspectives on Ming-Qing Social and Economic History*, ed. Linda Grove and Christian Daniels. Tokyo: University of Tokyo Press, 1984, 335–85. Trans. from *Jinbun kenkyū* 人文研究 22, no. 4 (1971).

Siggstedt, Mette. "Topographical Motifs in Middle Ming Su-chou: An Iconographical Implosion." In *Qu yu yu wang lu: jin qian nian lai Zhongguo meishushi yanjiu guoji xueshu yantaohui lunwenji* 區域與網路—近千年來中國美術史研究國際學術研討會論文集 (Proceedings of the Conference on Region and Network in Chinese Art History for the Past Thousand Years). Taipei: National Taiwan University, Graduate Program of Art History, 2001, 223–67.

Skinner, G. William, ed. *The City in Late Imperial China*. Stanford: Stanford University Press, 1977.

Song Lian 宋濂 (1310–81). "Yuejiang lou ji" 閱江樓記 (Record of the River-Viewing Pavilion). In *Wenxian ji* 文憲集 (Collected works of Song Wenxian), 3.1a–2b. Reprinted in Siku quanshu huiyao. Taipei: Shijie shuju, 1986.

Spence, Jonathan. "The Energies of Ming Life." 1981. Reprinted in idem, *Chinese Roundabout*. New York: Norton Press, 1992, 101–8.

Stabel, Peter. *Dwarfs Among Giants: The Flemish Urban Network in the Late Middle Ages*. Louvain: Garant, 1997.

Steinhardt, Nancy Shatzman. *Chinese Imperial City Planning*. Honolulu: University of Hawai'i Press, 1999.

———. "Mapping the Chinese City: The Image and the Reality." In *Envisioning the City: Six Studies in Urban Cartography*, ed. by David Buisseret. Chicago: University of Chicago Press, 1998, 1–33.

———. "Why Were Chang'an and Beijing So Different?" *Journal of the Society of Architectural Historians* 45, no. 4 (1986): 339–57.

Sun Chengze 孫承澤 (1592–1676). *Chunming mengyu lu* 春明夢餘錄. Facsimile reprint of 1883 edition—Hongkong: Longmen shuju, 1965.

Sun Hsi, Angela Ning-jy. "Social and Economic Status of the Merchant Class of the Ming Dynasty, 1368–1644." Ph.D. diss., University of Illinois, 1972.

Tan Jiading 譚嘉定, ed. *San yan Liang pai ziliao* 三言兩拍資料 (Sources of the *San yan Liang pai*). Taipei: Weimin shuju, 1983.

Tan Qixiang 譚其驤. *Zhongguo lishi ditu ji* 中國歷史地圖集 (Historical atlas of China). Shanghai: Xinhua, 1987.

Tanaka Masatoshi. "Popular Rebellions, Rent Resistance, and Bondservant Rebellions in the Late Ming." In *State and Society in China*, ed. Linda Grove and Christian Daniels. Tokyo: University of Tokyo Press, 1984, 165–214.

Tang Lizong 唐立宗. *Zai "daoqu" yu "zhengqu" zhi jian: Mingdai Min Yue Gan Xiang jiaojie de zhixu biandong yu difang xingzheng yanhua* 在「盜區」與「政區」之間—明代閩粵贛湘交界的秩序變動與地方行政演化 (Between the bandit zones and administrative areas: the changing order and local administration in the border areas between Fujian, Guangdong, Jiangxi, and Hunan during the Ming era). Taipei: Guoli Taiwan daxue chuban weiyuanhui, 2002.

Taniguchi Kikuo 谷口規矩雄. *Mindai yōeki seidoshi kenkyū* 明代徭役制度史の研究 (Studies on the history of the corvée system in the Ming dynasty). Kyoto: Dōhōsha, 1998.

Tomaru Fukuju 登丸福壽 and Mogi Shūichirō 茂木秀一郎. *Wakō kenkyū* 倭寇研究 (A study on pirates). Tokyo: Chūō kōronsha, 1942.

Tong, James. *Disorder Under Heaven: Collective Violence in the Ming Dynasty*. Stanford: Stanford University Press, 1991.

Tong Weisheng 童維生. "Gaochun xian jianxian de shijian" 高淳縣建縣的時間 (The year Gaochun officially became a county). *Nanjing shizhi* 南京史志 1988, no. 4: 39–40.

Tsao, Hsingyuan. "Unraveling the Mystery of *Qingming shanghe tu*." *Journal of Sung and Yuan Studies* 33 (2003): 155–80.

Tsao, Jerlian. "Remembering Suzhou: Urbanism in Late Imperial China." Ph.D. diss., University of California, Berkeley, 1992.

Umehara Kaoru 梅原郁. "Sōdai toshi no zeifu" 宋代都市の税賦 (The tax system in the Song dynasty). *Tōyōshi kenkyū* 東洋史研究 28, no. 4 (1970): 42–74.

Vinograd, Richard. "Fan Ch'i (1616–After 1694): Place-Making and the Semiotics of Sight in Seventeenth-Century Nanching." *Taida Journal of Art History* 14 (2003): 129–57.

von Glahn, Richard. *Fountain of Fortune: Money and Monetary Policy in China, 1000–1700.* Berkeley: University of California Press, 1996.

———. "Municipal Reform and Urban Social Conflict in Late Ming Jiangnan." *Journal of Asian Studies* 50, no. 2 (1991): 280–307.

———. "Myth and Reality of China's Seventeenth-Century Monetary Crisis." *Journal of Economic History* 56, no. 2 (1996): 429–54.

Wakeland, Joanne Clare. "Metropolitan Administration in Ming China: Sixteenth Cecntury Peking." Ph.D. diss., University of Michigan, 1982.

Wakeman, Frederic, Jr. "Boundaries of the Public Sphere in Ming and Qing China." *Dædalus* 127, no. 3 (1998): 167–89.

———. "China and the Seventeenth-Century Crisis." *Late Imperial China* 7, no. 1 (1986): 7–26.

———. "The Civil Society and Public Sphere Debate: Western Reflections on Chinese Political Culture." *Modern China* 19, no. 2 (1993): 124–36.

———. "Rebellion and Revolution: The Study of Popular Movements in Chinese History." *Journal of Asian Studies* 36, no. 2 (1977): 201–37.

Wang Fansen 王汎森. "Qing chu shiren de huizui xintai yu xiaoji xingwei" 清初士人的悔罪心態與消極行爲 (The mentality of guilt and passive resistance among early Qing literati). In *Guoshi fuhai kaixin lu* 國史浮海開新錄 (A new vision of Chinese history), ed. Zhou Zhiping 周質平 and Willard J. Peterson. Taipei: Lianjing chubanshe, 2002, 405–54.

Wang Gen 王艮. *Wang Xinzhai quan ji* 王心齋全集 (Complete works of Wang Xinzhai). Taipei: Guangwen shuju, 1987.

Wang Hongjun 王宏鈞 and Liu Ruzhong 劉如仲. "Mingdai houqi Nanjing chengshi jingji de fanrong he shehui shenghuo de bianhua: Ming ren hui *Nandu fanhui tujuan* de chubu yanjiu" 明代後期南京城市經濟的繁榮和社會生活的變化—明人繪南都繁會圖卷的初步研究 (Urban economic prosperity and change in social life of Nanjing in the late Ming: preliminary research on *Thriving Southern Capital* by an anonymous Ming painter). *Zhongguo lishi bowuguan guankan* 中國歷史博物館館刊, 1979, no. 1: 99–106. For a reproduction of the painting, see *Huaxia zhi lu* 華夏之路. Beijing: Chaohua chubanshe, 1997, 4: 90–2–3.

Wang Hongtai 王鴻泰. "Liudong yu hudong: you Ming Qing jian chengshi shenghuo de texing tance gongzhong changyu de kaizhan" 流動與互動—由明清間城市生活的特性探測公眾場域的開展 (Mobility and interaction: the emerging public sphere in urban life in Ming-Qing China). Ph.D. diss., National Taiwan University, 1998.

Wang Ji 王畿. *Longxi Wang xiansheng quanji* 龍谿王先生全集 (Complete works of Wang Longxi). Facsimile reprint of 1587 edition. Siku quanshu cunmu congshu, 98.

Wang Jianying 王劍英. *Ming Zhongdu yanjiu* 明中都研究 (Study on Ming Zhongdu). Beijing: Zhongguo qingnian chubanshe, 2005.

Wang Qi 王圻 (1530–1615). *Sancai tuhui* 三才圖會 (Comprehensive illustrated encyclopedia). 1607. Facsimile reprint of 1607 edition. Taipei: Chengwen chubanshe, 1970.

————. *Xu Wenxian tongkao* 續文獻通考 (Sequel to *General History of Institutions and Critical Examination of Documents and Studies*). 1602. Reprinted—Beijing: Xiandai chubanshe, 1991.

Wang Qingcheng 王慶成. "Wan Qing Huabei de jishi he jishi quan" 晚清華北的集市和集市圈 (North China's rural markets and marketing areas in the late Qing period). *Jindai shi yanjiu* 近代史研究, 2004, no. 4: 2–69.

Wang Rigen 王日根. *Xiangtu zhi lian: Ming-Qing huiguan yu shehui* 鄉土之鏈—明清會館與社會 (The link of the land: merchant guilds and society during the Ming-Qing era). Tianjin: Tianjin renmin chubanshe, 1996.

Wang Shimao 王世茂. *Shitu xuanjing* 仕途懸鏡 (A hanging mirror for career officials). Late Ming edition. Microfilm copy, Academia Sinica, Taipei.

Wang Ying 王穎. "Gu Qiyuan shengping xin kao" 顧起元生平新考 (New study of Gu Qiyuan's life and career). *Yuwen xuekan* (*gaojiao ban*) 語文學刊高教版 2006, no. 11: 54–56.

Wang Yuming 王裕明. "Mingdai zongjia zhezhi kaoshu" 明代總甲設置考述 (Survey of the *zongjia* system in the Ming era). *Zhongguo shi yanjiu* 中国史研究 2006, no. 1: 145–60.

Wang Yunhai 王雲海 and Zhang Dezong 張德宗. "Songdai fangguo hudeng de huafen" 宋代坊郭戶等的劃分 (The classification of urban households in the Song dynasty). *Shixue yuekan* 史學月刊 1985, no. 6: 33–37.

Wang Zhenzhong 王振忠. *Ming Qing Huishang yu Huai Yang shehui bianqian* 明清徽商与淮揚社會變遷 (Huizhou merchants and social changes in the Huai River–Yangzhou area during the Ming-Qing era). Beijing: Shenghuo, dushu, xinzhi sanlian shudian, 1996.

Wanli Da Ming huidian (1588) 萬曆大明會典 (Collected statutes of the Ming dynasty). Yangzhou: Guangling guji keyinshe, 1989.

West, Stephen H. "Huanghou, zangli, youbing yu zhu: *Dongjing meng hua lu* he dushi wenxue de xingqi" 皇后、葬禮、油餅與豬—東京夢華錄和都市文學的興起 (Empresses and funerals, pancakes and pigs: *Dreaming a Dream of Splendors Past* and the origins of urban literature). In *Wenxue, wenhua, yu shibian* 文學、文化、與世變 (Literature, culture, and world change), ed. Li Fengmao 李豐楙. Taipei: Academia Sinica, 2002, 197–218.

————. "The Interpretation of a Dream: The Sources, Influence, and Evaluation of the *Dongjing meng hua lu*." *T'oung Pao* 71 (1985): 63–108.

White, Marie Julia. "Topographical Painting in Early-Ming China: *Eight Scenes of Peking* by Wang Fu." M.A. thesis, University of California at Berkeley, 1983.

Wittfogel, Karl A. *Oriental Despotism: A Comparative Study of Total Power*. New Haven: Yale University Press, 1957.

Wong, R. Bin. *China Transformed: Historical Change and the Limits of European Experience*. Ithaca, NY: Cornell University Press, 1997.

————. "Great Expectations: The 'Public Sphere' and the Search for Modern Times in Chinese History." *Chūgoku shigaku* 中國史學 3 (1993): 7–50.

Wright, Arthur F. "The Cosmology of the Chinese City." In *The City in Late Imperial China*, ed. G. William Skinner. Stanford: Stanford University Press, 1977, 33–73.

Wu Jen-shu 巫仁恕. "Jieqing, xinyang yu kangzheng: Ming Qing chenghuang xinyang yu chengshi qunzhong de jiti kangyi xingwei" 節慶、信仰與抗爭—明清城隍信仰與城市群眾的集體抗議行為 (Festivals, religious belief, and protests: city god worship and urban collective action during the Ming-Qing eras). *Zhongyang yanjiuyuan Jindaishi yanjiusuo jikan* 中央研究院近代史研究所集刊, no. 34 (2000): 145–210.

————. "Mingdai pingmin fushi de liuxing yu shidafu de fanying" 明代平民服飾的流行與士大夫的反應 (Fashions in clothing among the common people in the Ming dynasty and literati responses). *Shinshixue* 新史學 10, no. 3 (1999): 55–110.

————. "Ming mo Qing chu chengshi shougong ye gongren de jiti kangyi xingdong: yi Suzhou cheng weitantao zhongxin" 明末清初城市手工業工人的集體抗議行動—以蘇州城為探討中心 (Collective protests among handicraft workers in late Ming, early Qing Suzhou). *Zhongyang yanjiuyuan Jindaishi yanjiusuo jikan* 中央研究院近代史研究所集刊, no. 25 (1998): 47–88.

————. "Ming Qing chengshi minbian de jiti xingdong moshi jiqi yingxiang" 明清城市民變的集體行動模式及其影響 (The pattern and influence of collective actions in Ming-Qing cities). In *Jinshi Zhongguo zhi chuantong yu shuibian: Liu Guangjing yuanshi qishiwu sui zhushou lunwen ji* 近世中國之傳統與蛻變: 劉廣京院士七十五歲祝壽論文集 (Tradition and transformation in modern China: in honor of the seventy-fifth birthday of Academician Liu Kuang-ching). Taibei: Zhongyang yanjiuyuan Jindaishi yanjiusuo, 1998, 229–58.

————. "Ming Qing chengshi minbian yanjiu: chuantong Zhongguo chengshi qunzhong jiti liudong zhi fenxi" 明清城市民變研究—傳統中國城市群眾集體行動之分析 (Popular protest in Ming and Qing cities: collective action in traditional Chinese cities). Ph.D. diss., National Taiwan University, 1996.

———. "Ming Qing xiaofei wenhua yanjiu de xin qujing yu xin wenti" 明清消費文化研究的新取徑與新問題 (New approaches to and new issues in the consumption culture of the Ming-Qing period). *Xinshixue* 新史學 17, no. 4 (2006): 217–54.

———. "Ming Qing zhi ji Jiangnan shishiju de fazhan jiqi suo fanying de shehui xingtai" 明清之際江南時事劇的發展及其所反映的社會心態 (The development of Jiangnan *shishiju* during the Ming-Qing transition and social mentalities reflected in them). *Zhongyang yanjiuyuan Jindaishi yanjiusuo jikan* 中央研究院近代史研究所集刊, no. 31 (1999): 1–48.

———. "Wan Ming de lüyou fengqi yu shidaifu xintai" 晚明的旅遊風氣與士大夫心態 (Travel and gentry mentalities in the late Ming). In *Ming-Qing yilai Jiangnan shehui yu wenhua lunji* 明清以來江南社會與文化論集 (Collected essays on society and culture in Ming and Qing Jiangnan), ed. Xiong Yuezhi 熊月之 and Xiong Bingzhen 熊秉眞. Shanghai: Shanghai shehui kexueyuan chubanshe, 2004, 225–55.

Wu Shen 吳甡. "Fanghao de xiang wu duo zheng pai zi rao shu" 房號得餉無多徵派滋擾疏 (Memorial on urban real estate tax, especially the little revenue gain and great abuse it generated). In idem, *Chaian shu ji* 柴菴疏集 (Collection of memorials from Chaian), 16.3a–5a. Reprinted in Siku jinhuishu congkan, *jibu*, 44. Beijing: Beijing chubanshe, 2000.

Wu Tao 吳滔. "Luelun Ming Qing Nanjing diqu de shizhen fazhan" 略論明清南京地區的市鎮發展 (A general discussion on the development of cities and towns in the Nanjing area in the Ming and Qing dynasties). *Zhongguo nongshi* 中國農史 18, no. 3 (1999): 32–42.

Wu Yingji 吳應箕 (1594–1645). *Liudu jianwenlu* 留都見聞錄 (What I saw and heard in the Southern Capital). 1680. In *Guichi xianzhe yishu* 貴池先哲遺書, 1920. Reprinted—Taipei: Yiwen yinshuguan, 1961.

Wu Yuancui 伍袁萃. *Linju manlu* 林居漫錄 (Idle notes from the residence in the woods). Facsimile reprint of Qing handcopy. Siku quanshu cunmu congshu, 242. Tainan: Zhuangyan wenhua chubanshe, 1995.

Xie Zhaozhi 謝肇淛 (1567–1624). *Xiaocao zhai ji* 小草齋集 (Collection from the Xiaocao Studio). Facsimile reprint of Wanli copy. Xuxiu Siku quanshu, 1367. Shanghai: Shanghai guji chubanshe, 1995.

Xihu yuyin zhuren 西湖漁隱主人. *Huanxi yuanjia* 歡喜冤家 (The happy foes). 1640. Reprinted in *Zhongguo gudai zhenxiben xiaoshuo* 中國古代珍稀本小說 (Rare works of traditional Chinese fiction), vol. 2. Shengyang: Chunfeng wenyi, 1994.

Xiong, Victor Cunrui. *Sui-Tang Chang'an—A Study in the Urban History of Medieval China*. Ann Arbor: Center for Chinese Studies, University of Michigan, 2000.

Xu Min 許敏. "Lun wan Ming shangren qiaoyu dingju hua quxiang yu shehui bianqian" 論晚明商人僑寓定居化趨向與社會變遷 (Discussion of trends among late Ming merchants to sojourn or settle down and social change). *Jianghai xuekan* 江海学刊 2002, no. 1: 134–41.

Xu, Yinong. *The Chinese City in Space and Time: The Development of Urban Form in Suzhou*. Honolulu: University of Hawai'i Press, 2000.

Yan Ruyu 嚴如煜. *San sheng bianfang beilan* 三省邊防備覽 (Overview of border defenses in the three provinces). Facsimile reprint of Daoguang copy. Xuxiu Siqu quanshu, 732. Shanghai: Shanghai guji chubanshe, 1997.

Yanagida Setsuko 柳田節子. "Sōdai toshi no kotōsei" 宋代都市の戸等制 (The ranking of households in Song cities). In *Sō Gen shakai keizaishi kenkyū* 宋元社会経済史研究 (Song and Yuan economic and social historical studies). Tokyo: Sōbunsha, 1995.

Yang Erzeng 楊爾曾. *Xinjuan hainei qiguan* 新鐫海内奇觀 (Fantastic spectacles within the realm). 1609. Reprinted—Changsha: Hunan meishu chubanshe, 1999.

Yang Guoan 楊國安. "Zhu ke zhi jian: Ming dai Lianghu diqu tuzhu yu liuyu de maodun yu chongtu" 主客之間: 明代兩湖地區土著與流寓的矛盾與衝突 (Between hosts and guests: contradictions and conflicts between natives and sojourners in the Lianghu area during the Ming era). *Zhongguo nongshi* 中國農史 2004, no. 1: 81–87.

Yang Lien-sheng. *Excursions in Sinology*. Cambridge: Harvard University Press, 1969.

Yang Rui 楊睿. "Ti wei yishi shu" 提爲議事疏 (A memorial on proposed matters for discussion). In *Ming jingshi wenbian* (Ming documents on statecraft), 92.1a–3a. Xuxiu siku quanshu, 1655. Shanghai: Guji chubanshe, 1995.

Yi Ruofen 衣若芬. "Lüyou, woyou yu shenyou: Mingdai wenren ti 'Xiaoxiang' shanshui hua shi de wenhua sikao" 旅遊、臥遊與神遊—明代文人題「瀟湘」山水畫詩的文化思考 (Travel, armchair travel, and spiritual travel: the cultural thinking behind the inscriptions on Xiaoxiang landscape paintings in the Ming era). In *Ming Qing wenxue yu sixiang zhong zhi zhuti yishi yu shehui* 明清文學與思想中之主體意識與社會 (Subjectivity and society in Ming-Qing literature and thought), ed. Wang Ailing 王璦玲. Taipei: Academia Sinica, 2004, 17–92.

Yu Huai 余懷 (1617–?). *Banqiao zaji* 板橋雜記 (Miscellaneous records for the wooden bridge). Preface dated 1705. Reprinted—Nanjing: Jiangsu wenyi chubanshe, 1987.

Yu Menglin 余孟麟, Gu Qiyuan 顧起元, Zhu Zhifan 朱之蕃, and Jiao Hong 焦竑. *Jinling yayou bian* 金陵雅遊編 (The elegant tour of Nanjing). 1624. Copy at the National Central Library, Taipei, Rare Book Collection.

Yu Yingshi 余英時. "Shishang hudong yu ruxue zhuanxiang" 士商互動與儒學轉向. 1997. Reprinted in idem, *Xiandai ruxue de huigu yu zhanwang* (see below), 3–52.

———. *Xiandai ruxue de huigu yu zhanwang* 現代儒學的回顧與展望 (Retrospect and prospect of modern Confucianism). Beijing: Sanlian shuju, 2004.

Yuan, Tsing. "Urban Riots and Disturbances." In *From Ming to Ch'ing: Conquest, Region, and Continuity in Seventeenth-Century China*, ed. Jonathan D. Spence and John E. Wills, Jr. New Haven: Yale University Press, 1979, 279–320.

Yuan Zhongdao 袁中道. *Kexuezhai ji* 珂雪齋集. Reprint, Shanghai: Shanghai guji chubanshe, 1989.

Zeng Ji 曾極. *Jinling baiyong* 金陵百詠 (A hundred poems about Jinling). Reprinted—Taipei: Taiwan Shangwu yinshiguan, 1983.

Zhang Dejian 張德建. "Mingdai shanren qunti de shengcheng yanbian jiqi wenhua yiyi" 明代山人群體的生成演變及其文化意義 (The formation and development of the "mountain hermits" community and its cultural significance in the Ming dynasty). *Zhongguo wenhua yanjiu* 中國文化研究 2003, no. 2 (2003): 80–90.

———. *Mingdai shanren wenxue yanjiu* 明代山人文學研究 (Study of "mountain hermits" literature). Changsha: Hunan renmin chubanshe, 2005.

Zhang Yan 張研. "Qingdai shizhen guanli chu tan" 清代市鎮管理初探 (A preliminary study of the administration of market towns in the Qing dynasty). *Qingshi yanjiu* 清史研究 1999, no. 1: 39–52.

Zhang Yongming 張永明 (1499–1566). *Zhang Zhuangxi wenji* 張莊僖文集 (Collected works of Zhang Zhuangxi). Yingyin Wenyuange Siku quanshu, 1277. Taipei: Shangwu yinshuguan, 1983.

Zhao Jishi 趙吉士. *Jiyuan ji suo ji* 寄園寄所寄 (Delivered from the Ji Garden). Lidai biji xiaoshuo jicheng 歷代筆記小説集成. 94. Shijiazhuang: Hebei jiaoyu chubanshe, 1996.

Zhao Shiyu. "Town and Country Representation as Seen in Temple Fairs." In *Town and Country in China: Identity and Perception*, ed. David Faure and Taotao Liu. New York: Palgrave, 2002, 41–57.

Zheng Yan 鄭焱. *Zhongguo lüyou fazhanshi* 中國旅遊發展史 (The history of travel in China). Changsha: Hunan jiaoyu chubanshe, 2000.

Zhong Xing 鍾惺. *Yinxiuxuan wenyu ji* 隱秀軒文餘集 (Collected work from the Yinxiu studio). Reprinted in Siku jinhuishu congkan, 46.

Zhongguo lishi bowuguan 中國歷史博物館, ed. *Hua xia zhi lu* 華夏之路. Beijing: Chaohua chubanshe, 1997.

Zhou Baoying 周寶俠. *Jinling lansheng shikao* 金陵覽勝詩考 (A collection of scenic poems about Nanjing). 1821. Reprinted—Yangzhou: Guangling guji chubanshe, 1987.

Zhou Hui 周暉. *Jinling suoshi* 金陵瑣事 (Trivia about Nanjing); *Xu Jinling suoshi* 續金陵瑣事 (Supplement to *Trivia About Nanjing*); and *Erxu Jinling suoshi* 二續金陵瑣事 (Second supplement to *Trivia About Nanjing*). 1610. Reprinted—Beijing: Wenxue guji kanxingshe, 1955.

Zhou Junfu 周駿富, ed. *Er chen zhuan* 貳臣傳 (Biographies of turncoat officials). Taipei: Mingwen shuju, 1985.

Zhou Zhibin 周志斌. "Luelun wan Ming Nanjing de shangye" 略論晚明南京的商業 (A general discussion of commerce in late Ming Nanjing). *Xuehai* 學海 1994, no. 4: 78–82.

Zhu Biheng 祝碧衡. "Lun Ming Qing Huishang zai Zhejiang Qu, Yan er fu de huodong" 论明清徽商在浙江衢、嚴二府的活动 (Activities of Huizhou merchants in Qu and Yan prefectures in Zhejiang during the Ming-Qing era). *Zhongguo shehui jingjishi yanjiu* 中國社會經濟史研究 2000, no. 3: 10–19.

Zhu Guozhen 朱國禎. *Zhu Wensu gong ji* 朱文肅公集 (Collected works of Zhu Wensu). Facsimile reprint of a Qing copy. Xuxiu Siku quanshu, 1366.

Zhu Hong 袾宏. *Zi zhi lu* 自知錄 (Record of self-knowledge). Reprinting of Ming Wanli copy (1572–1615), in Ming Jiaxing dazang jing 明嘉興大藏經 (Ming Jiaxing Buddhist canon), vol. 32.

Zhu Yuanzhang 朱元璋 (1328–98). "Yuejiang lou ji" 閱江樓記 (Record of the River-Viewing Pavilion) and "You Yuejiang lou ji" 又閱江樓記 (Another record of the River-Viewing Pavilion). In *Ming Taizu wenji* 明太祖文集 (Collected works of Zhu Yuanzhang), *juan* 14. Reprinted in Jingyin Wenyuange Siku quanshu, 1223. Taipei: Taiwan Shangwu yinshuguan, 1979.

Zhu Zhifan 朱之蕃 (1564–?). *Yushan bian* 雨山編 (A compilation from rainy mountains). 1600. Copy in the Naikaku bunko, Tokyo, Rare Book Collection.

Zhu Zhifan 朱之蕃, ed. *Jinling tuyong* 金陵圖詠 (Illustrated odes on Nanjing). 1623 and 1624. Copies in the National Central Library, Taipei, Rare Book Collection.

Zurndorfer, Harriet. "A Guide to the 'New' Chinese History: Recent Publications Concerning Chinese Social and Economic Development before 1800." *International Review of Social History* 33 (1988): 148–201.

———. "Not Bound to China: Étienne Balazs, Fernand Braudel and the Politics of the Study of Chinese History in Post-War France." *Past and Present* 185, no. 1 (2004): 189–221.

————. "Old and New Visions of Ming Society and Culture." *T'oung Pao* 88, no. 1–3 (2002): 151–69.

————. "Violence and Political Protest in Ming and Qing China." *International Review of Social History* 28 (1983): 304–19.

absentee landlords, 16, 37, 47, 206, 252

anti-wall protest, 93–94; in Gaochun, 77, 80, 82–93, 101–2, 109–13, 241, 289*n*23; in Jiangpu, 77, 103–13

Aramiya Manabu 新宮学, 301*n*53

architecture, 14, 19, 123, 269*n*26

autocracy, 6

autonomy, 49, 77, 238, 247; of market towns, 119, 249; public sphere, 249, 273*n*51; urban autonomy, 11, 13, 20–24, 26, 267*n*21, 273*n*54, 276*n*8

baojia 保甲 (mutual security system), 70, 245, 275*n*2, 318*n*2

baozhang 保長, see *baojia* 保甲

Beijing, 22–24, 150, 158, 215, 285*n*96; precedents, 52, 67, 215, 232, 280*n*55, 281*n*56, 282*n*61, 317*n*100. *See also* Nanjing

bianshen 編審 (inspection and registration), 43–44, 47

biji 筆記, 195, 198, 297*n*6

bingmasi 兵馬司 (warden's offices), 215

Bol, Peter K., 277*n*17, 280*n*52, 308*n*9, 313*n*56

Brook, Timothy, 78, 150, 172, 265*n*4, 273*n*51, 297*n*9, 305*n*93

Buddhism, 6, 199

bu rucheng 不入城, 209

Cao Xuequan 曹學佺, 151

capitalism, sprouts of, 6, 266*n*4, 269*n*24, 280*n*50

Capital Training Divisions, 105, 292*n*76

censor, 70, 101, 104, 210; borough censor, 53–54, 215; of Nanjing Censorate, 68, 101, 105, 107, 109, 205–6

census, 37, 135, 202–3, 232, 318*n*9

chai wai zhi chai 差外之差, 71

Chang Che-chia 張哲嘉, 300*n*41

Chang'an 長安, 205

Chang'an kehua 長安客話, 190

Chao Yue 晁説 (Song), 189; *Chaoshi keyu* 晁氏客語, 189

Chen Jiru 陳繼儒 (1558–1639), 196, 303*n*71

Chen Liangmo 陳良謨 (1482–1572), 198

Chen Shan 陳善 (fl. 1579), 224–25

Chen Yi 陳沂 (1469–1538), 126–28, 141–47, 163–64, 297*n*5, 301*n*57, 307*n*2

Chen Yuling 陳毓靈, 83

cheng 城 (city), 76, 79, 102, 287*n*1

chengguo zhi fu 城郭之賦, 32

chenghuangmiao 城隍廟 (city god temples), 118, 241, 298*n*18

Chenghua reign 成化 (1464–87), 163

Chinese civilization, 6, 11–12, 14, 25, 121, 123, 131, 230

chongshe lun 崇奢論, 235

Chunqiu 春秋, 84

Chunxi reign 淳熙 (1174–89), 119

city images, 20, 27, 125, 138, 185–87

City in Late Imperial China, The (G. W. Skinner), 115, 268*n*23, 277*n*11, 294*n*98, 315*n*68

city maps, 131, 135–37, 141, 301*n*43

cityscape, 19; of Nanjing, 2–3, 231; of Nanjing Metropolitan Area, 76–77, 113; paintings, 177–78, 272*n*43

civil service examinations, 15, 117, 146, 153, 157–58, 170–71, 236, 303*n*74; successful candidates, 160, 189, 202, 210

class conflict, 110–11, 279*n*42

Clunas, Craig, 127, 303*n*79

collective action, 15, 56, 101, 110–12, 200, 240, 271*n*33

commercial tax, 120, 233, 296*n*115, 317*n*1

Confucianism, 6, 199

connoisseurship, 209, 211–12, 237, 297*n*6, 303*n*79

conquest dynasty, 33, 186, 253, 277*n*12, 286*n*113

Da Gao 大誥, 37

Da Ming huidian 大明會典, 112, 283*n*65

Da Ming yitong mingsheng zhi 大明一統名勝志 (Cao Xuequan 曹學佺), 151

Daoism, 6, 199

Deng Chuwang 鄧楚望, 98

despotism, 77, 267*n*21, 293*n*86

difang gongyi 地方公議 (local public opinion), 46, 279*n*41

difang zhi 地方志 (local gazetteers), 82, 96, 117–18, 171, 289*n*22, 302*n*61, 308*n*9; standardization, 138–40, 189–90, 213, 308*nn*7–8. See also *fengsu*

Dijing jingwu lue 帝京景物略, 190

ding 丁, 45, 59–60, 230

Ding Bin 丁賓, 281*n*61; biography, 52, 284*n*90; consensus-building, 34, 49, 51–56, 67, 71–72, 75, 282*n*63

Ding Rijin 丁日近, 79

Ding Yuanjian 丁元薦 (1563–1628), 61, 283*n*79

Dong Ao 董鏊, 289*n*18

Dong Qichang 董其昌 (1555–1636), 200

Dongjing meng Hua lu 東京夢華錄, 130, 190–91, 309*n*11

Dun yuan 遯園 (Garden of escape), 192, 309*n*14

duyi bu 都邑簿, 190, 309*n*10

East Dam 東壩, 98–102, 113–14, 116–17

Eight Scenes of Beijing (*Beijing bajing* 北京八景), 150

Elders (*laoren* 老人) system, 36

Eurocentrism, 247

fanghao yin 房號銀, 72–73, 318*n*7. See also urban property tax

fangxiang yi 坊廂役 (ward corvée), 57–59, 63, 64–68, 71, 282*n*65, 284*n*88, 284*n*90, 285*n*99; *fangjia* 坊甲, 276*n*5

Fangyu shenglan 方輿勝覽 (Zhu Mu 祝穆), 152

Farmer, Edward L., 140, 287*nn*1–2, 301*n*52

Farong 法融 (594–667), 163

Faure, David, 17–18, 120, 269*n*24, 271*n*40

feichai 飛差 (extraordinary official duties), 30, 66, 68, 70, 276*n*4

Feng Menglong 馮夢龍, 197, 236

Feng Yuancheng 馮元成, 153

fengsu 風俗 (social customs), 193, 212–27, 233, 238, 242–43, 250–51, 315*n*69

feudalism, 110, 293*n*86

Four Books, 198

frugal governance, 63–64, 67, 73, 132

Fu Yiling 傅衣凌 266*n*14, 293*n*86

Fuma Susumu 夫馬進, 277*n*15, 279*n*39, 279*n*41, 280*n*45, 286*n*107, 296*n*115, 314*n*61

Gao Cen 高岑, 171, 183, 306*n*107

Ge Yinliang 葛寅亮, 156, 304*n*84

Grand Canal, 102, 114, 184, 233

Gu Guofu 顧國甫, 191–92

Gu Qiyuan 顧起元, 18, 55, 65, 126–29, 166, 188, 297*n*6, 315*n*75; biography, 309*nn*13–14; Nanjing *huojia* reform, 281*n*61, 282*n*63, 285*n*99. See also *Jinling yayou bian* 金陵雅遊編; *Kezuo zhuiyu* 客座贅語

Gu Yanwu 顧炎武, 276*n*6, 281*n*61

Guang Mao 光懋, 45

Guangtong Dam 廣通壩, *see* East Dam 東壩

Gui Youguang 歸有光 (1507–71), 146

Guifan 閨範 (Lü Kun 呂坤), 94

guiji 詭寄 (fraudulent trusteeships), 47

guilds, 23, 112, 255, 310*n*17, 318*n*10; Max Weber, 21, 267*n*21, 272*n*48, 273*n*54, 276*n*8

Guo Gaoxu 郭臬旭, 158

guo zi jian 國子監 (Imperial University), 165, 194, 210, 233, 309*n*13

Hai Rui 海瑞, 68–70, 281*n*58, 281*n*60, 285*n*94

Hainei qiguan 海內奇觀 (Yang Erzeng 楊爾增), 19, 134, 146, 151, 195

Haiyan 海鹽 county, 44

Hamashima Atsutoshi 浜島敦俊, 251, 279*n*42, 280*n*45, 283*n*68, 283*n*76, 283*nn*79–80

Han Bangben 韓邦本, 100

Han Bangxian 韓邦憲, 98–100

Han Bin 韓斌, 99

Han Shuyang 韓叔陽, 98

Han Zhongshu 韓仲叔, 83–92, 289*n*23

Han Zhongxiao 韓仲孝, 83–92, 98, 289*n*23

Han Zhongyong 韓仲雍, 98

Hangzhou, 19, 71, 158, 209, 224, 282*n*64, 286*n*107

He Liangjun 何良俊, 307*n*2

He Tang 何鏜, 151, 154

Hongji Temple 弘濟寺, 304*n*84

Hongwu jingcheng tuzhi 洪武京城圖志, 127–49 *passim*, 185, 187, 297*n*15, 298*n*22, 299*n*28, 309*n*10

Hongzhi reign 弘治 (1488–1505), 65, 104

household registration, 30, 50, 63, 70, 228–33, 276*n*5, 316*n*87

Hsu Hong 徐泓, 265*n*7, 287*n*2, 288*n*3, 296*n*122, 300*n*32, 300*n*35, 315*n*70

Hu Pengju 胡彭舉, 160

Hu Yukun 胡玉昆, 183, 306*n*106

Huang Bingshi 黃秉石, 83–92, 102

Huang Kezuan 黃克纘, 105

Huang, Philip C. C., 22, 274*n*58

huang ce 黃册 (Yellow Register),
277*n*16

Huanxi yuanjia 歡喜冤家, 197

huihui (Muslims), 202

Huitongguan 會同館 (Office of
Convergence), 53

huojia 火甲, 275*n*2, 275*n*4, 276*n*5,
284*n*88, 285*n*99, 285*n*102; abuse of,
29–30, 63–64, 68–72; Beijing,
280*n*55, 285*n*96; Nanjing reform,
35, 51–52, 56–57, 208, 266*n*16,
276*n*8, 281*nn*60–61. See also
fangxiang yi 坊廂役

Huzhou 湖州, 43–44, 60–61

Iwai Shigeki 岩井茂樹, 278*n*22,
279*n*30, 285*n*97, 317*n*1

jianghu 匠户, 30

Jiangnan, 2–3, 80, 99, 118, 184, 207;
financial reform, 41, 71, 278*n*23,
279*n*42

Jiankang 建康, 142

jiansheng 監生 (university student),
194, 202, 233, 260

Jianye 建業, 132, 142, 144, 146

jianzhen guan 監鎮官 (town-
supervising officials), 120

Jiao Hong 焦竑 (1541–1620), 126,
128–29, 164, 166, 170, 297*n*8,
307*n*2; Nanjing *huojia* reform, 55,
281*n*61, 282*n*63. See also *Jinling
yayou bian*

jiesheng zhishuo 節省之説, 64

Jiming Temple 雞鳴寺, 210

Jin Zhijun 金之俊, 48

jing 景 (prospects), 19, 149–51, 164–75,
185; *yongjing* 詠景 (textual and visual appreciation of scenes), 18–20

Jingtai reign 景泰 (1450–56), 58

Jin'gu qiguan 今古奇觀, 195

Jingxue zhi 京學志 (Jiao Hong 焦竑),
129, 302*n*61

Jinling 金陵 (Golden hills), 76, 132,
144, 298*n*18

Jinling baimei 金陵百媚, 222

Jinling fancha zhi 金陵梵剎志
(Ge Yinliang 葛寅亮), 156,
302*n*61

Jinling gujin tukao 金陵古今圖考
(Chen Yi 陳沂), 126–28, 141–44,
185, 187

Jinling jiushi 金陵舊事 (Jiao Hong
焦竑), 129

Jinling quanpin 金陵泉品 (Sheng Shitai 盛時泰), 129

Jinling sanjun 金陵三俊 (Three
prodigies of Nanjing), 141, 141*n*45

"Jinling sheji zhushiren" 金陵社集
諸詩人 (Qian Qianyi 錢謙益),
301*n*45

Jinling suoshi 金陵瑣事 (Zhou Hui
周暉), 129, 188–93, 201, 204, 212,
235, 243, 281*n*61, 297*n*6, 307*nn*1–2,
308*n*3; *Erxu Jinling suoshi* 二續
金陵瑣事, 307*n*1, 309*n*14; *Shangbaizhai ketan* 尚白齋客談, 188,
307*n*1; *Xu Jinling suoshi* 續金陵
瑣事, 195, 275*n*4, 307*n*1

Jinling xianxian shiji 金陵先賢詩集
(He Liangjun 何良浚), 188*n*2

Jinling xuanguan zhi 金陵玄觀志,
149*n*61

Jinling yayou bian 金陵雅遊編 (Yu
Menglin 余孟麟, Gu Qiyuan 顧
起元, Zhu Zhifan 朱之蕃, Jiao
Hong 焦竑), 126, 128, 155, 166–69

Jin ping mei 金瓶梅, 310*n*17

jinshen gongyi 縉紳公議 (public opinion of the gentry), 47. See also

difang gongyi 地方公議; *xiangshen* 鄉紳: public opinion of

jinshi 進士 (metropolitan graduates), 146, 192, 205, 210, 317*n*111

Jiqing, 133

junyao 均徭 (equalized labor service), 38, 56, 58–59, 286*n*105

Kaifeng 開封, 131, 190

Kawakatsu Mamoru 川勝守, 115, 296*n*115

ke 客 (guests/sojourners), 193, 212, 215, 228, 242, 244, 251, 310*n*16, 315*n*79; guest households, 229–30

ketan 客談 (conversations with guests), 4, 7–8, 188–212, 237, 242–44, 308*n*5; late Ming development, 196; market competition, 198; origin of genre, 189

Kezuo zhuiyu 客座贅語 (Gu Qiyuan 顧起元), 129, 188–95, 204, 214, 243, 251, 314*n*65

Kishimoto Mio 岸本美緒, 279*n*39, 280*n*45

Kong Shangren 孔尚任 (1648–1718), 157–60, 197

Kuang Ye 鄺埜 (fl. 1437), 65

Lake Gucheng, 290*n*36

Lake Hou 後湖, 133, 135, 202; *Houhu zhi* 後湖志, 302*n*61

land tax (*tianfu* 田賦), 30, 39–40, 57, 59–60, 62, 73–74, 229–31, 278*n*24. See also *chengguo zhi fu* 城郭之賦

Li Changgeng 李長庚, 280*n*54

Li Tingji 李廷機, 281*n*56

liang 糧, 45, 59–60

Liang Fangzhong (Liang Fang-chung) 梁方仲, 276*n*7, 278*nn*23–24, 279*n*30, 279*n*33

liangzhang 糧長 (tax captains), 36, 40

lichai 力差 (labor service), 38, 59

Liechao shiji xiaozhuan 列朝詩集小傳 (Qian Qianyi 錢謙益), 301*n*45

lijia 里甲 (Village Tithing), 35–37, 39–40, 42, 47; vs. *baojia*, 64, 71, 276*n*5; vs. *fangxiang*, 57, 65, 277*n*16, 282*n*65, 284*n*92

Lin Lian 林爌, 230

Lin'an 臨安, 133

lineage, 225, 296*n*4

Ling Mengchu 凌濛初, 197, 312*n*30, 312*n*37

Linggusi 靈谷寺, 160, 302*n*61

Linqing 臨清, 73

Lishui 溧水, 92–93, 97, 102, 114, 117

Liu Guangji 劉光濟, 60

Liu Ji 劉基, 299*n*32

Liu Mingxiao 劉鳴曉, 29

Liu Yizheng 柳詒徵 (1880–1956), 141

Liu Zhiwei 劉志偉, 278*n*22, 285*n*95

liumin 流民 (floating population), 226, 229–30, 232–33, 243–44, 316*n*87, 317*n*100

lizhang 里長 (village heads), 36–37, 40, 47–48, 84

lobby, 77–78, 99, 112, 162, 238, 241, 289*n*23

Longjiang 龍江, 302*n*61, 304*n*84

longpan huju 龍盤虎踞, 134, 298*n*22

Longqing reign (1567–72), 67

longue durée, 11–13, 26, 50, 248, 255

Lu Cai 陸采, 194, 198

Lü Kun 呂坤 (1536–1618), 71, 73, 94–95, 199, 275*n*2

Lu Wenheng 陸文衡, 199

Luhe county 六合, 76, 109, 123

Lushi si 錄事司 (Municipal Affairs Office), 32–33, 253, 277*n*12

Manchu, 10, 70, 171, 182, 186, 254, 287*n*114

market towns, see *zhen* 鎮

Marxism, 110

Master Gudao 古道師, 163

medieval urban revolution, 14, 119, 205, 255

mentan 門攤 (store franchise fees), 73

Meyer-Fong, Tobie, 19, 151–52, 184, 303*n*66, 307*n*123

mianshen 面審 (personal inspections), 44

migration control, 50, 193, 228–29, 238, 244, 252, 254–55

Ming Chengzu 明成祖 (Yongle 永樂; r. 1402–24), 2, 64, 146, 150, 301*n*53, 308*n*8

Ming Shenzong 明神宗 (Wanli 萬曆; r. 1572–1620), 81, 106, 230, 288*n*6, 309*n*13, 317*n*1

Ming Shizong 明世宗 (Jiajing 嘉靖; r. 1522–66), 96, 107, 234, 288*n*6

Mingshan shenggai ji 名山勝概記 (He Tang 何鏜), 151, 154

mingsheng 名勝, 150, 172. See also *jing* 景

Mingshi 明史, 280*n*53, 292*n*69, 316*n*87

Mingwen xuanqi 明文選奇, 195

minimal governance, ideal of, 36, 38, 40, 63

Ministry of Revenue, 45, 65, 70, 104, 211; Hubu fensi 戶部分司, 103; *Nanjing Hubuzhi* 南京戶部志, 302*n*61

Ministry of Rites, 105, 131, 156; *Libu zhigao* 禮部志稿, 302*n*61

Ministry of War, 81, 103–4, 105, 107–8, 292*n*69

Ministry of Works, 65, 230

modernity, 6, 11–12, 21, 121, 266*n*15, 269*n*24, 280*n*50

Moling 秣陵, 141, 144

Moling ji 秣陵集, 141

Mori Masao 森正夫, 265*n*8, 295*nn*105–6

Mount Huang 黃山, 162–64, 306*n*109

Mount Zutang 祖堂, 168

municipal governance, 32, 253

Nanchang 南昌 prefecture, 58–59

Nandu 南都 (Southern Metropolis), 3, 176, 187, 218, 233, 236

Nandu fanhui tu 南都繁會圖, 177

Nanjing: as auxiliary capital, 64–66, 69, 113–14; as primary capital of the Ming dynasty, 76–77, 99, 288*n*18, 299*n*32; transfer of court in 1421, 2–3, 145–47, 150, 231, 246, 301*n*53

Nanjing Metropolitan Area (Yingtian prefecture 應天府), 2–3, 69, 76–77, 102–4, 107, 109, 115–16, 207

Nanjing school painters, 171, 306*n*106

Nanjing shoubei 南京守備 (grand commandant), 103

Nanyong zhi 南雍志, 302*n*61

nan zhili 南直隸 (Southern Metropolitan Area), 76, 99

Naquin, Susan, 22–23, 266*n*18, 274*nn*65–66, 297*n*9

native-place identity, 15, 20, 23–24, 222, 229, 267*n*21, 272*n*48

native-place lodges, 23–24

Neo-Confucianism, 6, 313*n*56

Ni Yue 倪岳 (1444–1501), 205–6

nianyi pu 年誼譜, 160

Niushou shan 牛首山 (Mount Niushou), 163, 168–69
Niushou shan zhi 牛首山志, 129, 302*n*61, 304*n*83

Otagi Matsuo 愛宕松男, 277*n*12
Owen, Stephen, 170, 305*n*103

Pai'an jingqi 拍案驚奇 (Ling Meng-chu 凌濛初), 195, 199*n*37; *Er ke pai'an jingqi* 二刻拍案驚奇, 197, 197*n*30
paimen 排門, 30, 70, 285*n*99
Pan Zhiheng 潘之恆 (1556–1622), 162
Peach Blossom Fan (Kong Shangren 孔尚任), 158, 197
pirate, 77, 80–81, 85, 93–94, 96, 107, 287*n*3
poll tax, 59, 60*n*73. See also *ding*
pu 鋪, 29–30, 53–54, 72, 275*n*3, 276*n*8
public: general, 42, 46–49, 75, 162, 199, 215; reading, 4, 124, 149, 166, 200, 237, 243
public granaries, 245
public media, 42
public opinion, 6, 46–51, 95, 207–8, 249, 279*n*39, 279*n*41. See also under *xiangshen* 鄉紳
public spaces, 15, 21–24, 26, 186, 270*n*32, 274*n*66
public sphere, 20–25, 249, 272–74
puhang 鋪行, 281*n*56
Pumen 普門, 162
Puzi 浦子, 103–6, 287*n*1

qi 奇, 195–96, 198, 311*n*24
Qi Biaojia 祁彪佳, 41
Qian Qianyi 錢謙益 (1582–1664), 47, 153, 157; Nanjing, 234, 236, 301*n*45

Qing dynasty, 5, 11, 119, 180–87, 209, 286*n*113, 294*nn*97–98; continued from Ming, 14–15, 266*n*18, 269*n*26, 270*n*27, 270*n*32, 271*n*33. *See also under* urban administration; wall-construction policy
Qingliang Temple 清涼寺, 304*n*84
Qingming shanghe tu 清明上河圖, 130–31, 178
qingshui bofu 輕稅薄賦 (low tax / light corvée), 63
Qinhuai pleasure quarters, 197, 220, 222, 234
Qinhuai River, 173, 180
Qinhuai shinübiao 秦淮仕女表, 222
Qintianshan guan xiang tai 欽天山觀象台 (Nanjing Imperial Observatory), 203–4
Qiongzhou 瓊州 prefecture, 59, 71
Qixia xiaozhi 棲霞小志, 129, 302*n*61

Rowe, William T., 20–21, 255, 267*n*20, 268*n*23, 269*n*26, 271*n*34; civil society and public sphere debate, 272*n*48, 273*n*49, 273*n*54, 274*n*58, 291*n*51
Ru meng lu 如夢錄, 190

Sancai tuhui 三才圖會 (Wang Qi 王圻), 146
Santangelo, Paolo, 271*n*34
Sanyan 三言 (Feng Menglong 馮夢龍), 197
Schneewind, Sarah, 78, 318*n*2
self-governing rural communities: collapse, 39–40, 57, 64–65, 71, 282*n*65, 284*n*92; original ideal, 35–37, 42, 47, 276*n*5, 277*n*16
Shangyuan, 45, 65, 217, 221

shanren 山人 (mountain inhabitants), 18, 153, 303*n*74

Shen Bang 沈榜 (1540–97), 230, 275*n*2, 281*n*56

Shen Zhou 沈周 (1427–1509), 160–61, 198, 272*n*43, 311*n*18, 311*n*23

Sheng Shitai 盛時泰 (fl. 1552–60), 129, 304*n*83

shengjing tu 勝景圖, 172

shengyuan 生員, 46, 66, 83–84, 153, 289*n*23, 295*n*102, 309*n*14

Sheshan zhi 攝山志, 187

shiduanjin fa 十段錦法, 278*n*23

shimin gongyi 市民公議 (urban public opinion), 208

shiren gongyi 士人公議, 46, 279*n*41. See also *difang gongyi* 地方公議

Shishang yaolan 士商要覽, 152

shishi xi 時事戲 (current events plays), 94–95, 196, 199

sightseeing, 159, 161, 167, 250; cultured sightseeing, 8, 149–56, 169–70, 184, 186, 243

silver economy, 4, 7, 31, 39, 50

Single Whip reform, 98–99, 229–30, 245, 248–49; overview and criticism, 30–35, 38–40, 50–51, 253, 278*n*4, 279*n*30, 286*n*113; urban dimension, 59–64, 73–75, 230, 245

Skinner, G. William, 11–13, 25–26, 115, 119, 239; model, 267*n*23, 277*n*11, 294*nn*97–98

social landscape, 23, 225

social networking, 157–64, 186, 194, 242, 310*n*17. See also social tourism

social practices, 16, 18–20, 22–23, 26, 238, 250, 271*n*40

social tourism, 156–65, 171, 183, 185–86, 234, 243–44, 254

Song dynasty, 5, 115–20, 130–31, 133, 138, 150, 189, 254, 300*n*40; Nanjing, 298*n*22, 302*n*58; taxes and corvée, 32–33, 73, 277*n*17, 280*n*52, 282*n*64, 310*n*16, 318*n*9. See also *under* urban administration; wall-construction policy

Song Lian 宋濂, 132

Song Yiwang 宋儀望, 62

Songjiang 松江, 62, 97, 286*n*109

Southern Tours, 185–87, 307*n*130

spatial experiences, 20, 25, 124, 149, 172, 187

spatial imagination, 125, 130, 172

state-society dichotomy, 22, 51, 112, 274*n*58

Steinhardt, Nancy Shatzman, 133, 298*n*23, 299*n*27, 301*n*43

sumptuary laws, 225

Sun Chengze 孫承澤 (1592–1676), 64

Suzhou, 15, 19, 94, 118, 223–24, 296*n*4, 318*n*10; publishing industry, 198–99, 234–35, 306*n*105; sights and sightseeing, 158, 160–61, 170, 234, 272*n*43, 305*n*93; tax reform, 58, 62, 71

Tang Xianzu 湯顯祖, 154

Taoan mengyi 陶庵夢憶 (Zhang Dai 張岱), 19*n*43

tax bureaus (*shuike si* 稅課司), 120, 283*n*65, 296*n*115. See also commercial tax

tianfangqi 田房契 (stamp tax), 73

tianfu 田賦, see land tax

Tong, James W., 111–12

tong hun yi 銅渾儀 (copper armillary sphere), 203

tongyou 同游, 158–60

tourism, 151–52. *See also* social tourism

urban administration: Song, 11, 32, 240–41, 253; Yuan, 32–33, 253; Ming, 7–8, 33–35, 191, 230, 232, 240, 247, 249, 253; Qing, 253–54, 318*n*7

urban bourgeoisie, 120, 273*n*51

urban community, 20–21, 237, 267*n*21, 272*n*48, 273*n*49; of Nanjing, 3, 11–12, 200–201, 205–8

urban identity, 16–17, 272*n*48, 276*n*8

urbanism, 10–14, 25–27, 121, 247, 252, 255, 269*n*24

urbanity, 13, 18, 20, 25, 182, 250

urban morphology, 121, 241, 298*n*23

urban planning, 2, 27, 136, 145, 205, 270*n*27, 298*n*23, 299*n*32

urban property tax, 32, 72–73, 232–33, 253, 286*n*107, 286*n*113; invention of, 7–8, 29, 35, 56, 61, 241

urban public, 15, 31, 51–52, 56, 72, 204. *See also* public

urban riot/uprising, 7, 15, 68, 71, 111, 248, 286*n*107

urban-rural continuum, 13–14, 16–19, 25, 269*n*26, 270*n*27, 272*n*45

urban-rural divide, 14, 268*n*23, 272*n*45; in administrative practice, 16–17, 240–41, 251, 269*n*26; cultural paradigm, 20, 25, 269*n*26, 270*n*27; elite identity, 209, 224, 238, 269*n*26; in tax reform, 34–35, 39, 63, 73, 75

urban society, 19, 23–25, 193, 204, 235, 242–46, 250, 255, 269*n*26, 270*n*32; of Nanjing, 8, 221, 237, 266*n*16

urban space: as analytical category, 2, 12–13, 26, 239; as lived space, 3–4, 193, 221; regulation of, 25, 110; representation of, 125, 140, 162, 172–76, 190

village schools, 245, 318*n*2

Vinograd, Richard, 306*n*123

von Glahn, Richard, 265*n*3, 277*n*15, 279*n*42, 285*n*104

Wakeman, Frederic, Jr., 22, 272*n*48, 273*n*54, 274*n*58, 274*n*61, 293*n*87

wall-construction policy, 79–81, 85, 96, 106, 113, 248, 288*n*14, 288*n*18; Song, Yuan, and Qing, 77, 253–54, 287*n*2

wall protest, 7, 79, 82, 97, 101, 112–13, 240–41

wall tax, 86–87

Wang Fu 王紱 (1362–1416), 150

Wang Hongru 王鴻儒 (?–1519), 145

Wang Hongtai 王鴻泰, 270*n*32, 311*n*27, 313*n*47

Wang Huanru 王煥如 (fl. 1642), 223, 225

Wang Junhua 王俊華, 297*n*14

Wang Qi 王圻 (1530–1615), 281*n*55, 286*n*105

Wang Shixing 王士性 (1547–98), 157

Wang Shizhen 王世貞 (1526–90), 235

Wang Xiangzhi 王象之, 152

Wang Yiqi 王以旂, 205–6

Weber, Max, 11–14, 20–26, 119, 247, 267*nn*20–22, 276*n*8, 295*n*111

wei 衛 (Guards), 103, 104, 108, 287*n*1, 292*n*76

Wen Zhengming 文徵明, 161, 312*n*33

West, Stephen H., 309*n*11

Wong, R. Bin, 273*n*53, 274*n*55, 274*n*57, 291*n*51

woyou 臥遊, 124, 151, 154–56, 166–67

Wu Jen-shu 巫仁恕, 111, 271*n*33, 303*n*71, 304*n*79, 196*n*25

Wu Yingji 吳應箕, 233–34, 236

Wuqing zhen 烏青鎮, 119, 248, 295*n*107

Xia Daxun 夏大勳, 80–81

Xiang Weicong 項維聰, 83–84, 88, 91, 97–98, 290*n*36

xiangshen 鄉紳 (gentry), 22, 78, 92, 101, 113, 120; exemption privilege for, 30, 47–49, 61–63, 71, 73, 281*n*58, 283*nn*79–80; origin, 47; public opinion of, 46–49, 84, 208–9, 279*n*41; urbanization of, 8, 16, 120, 193, 204–8, 209–11, 237, 250, 314*n*61

xiang yinjiu li 鄉飲酒禮 (village libation ceremony), 205, 313*n*52

xiangyue 鄉約 (village compact), 49, 205, 245, 318*n*2

xiangzhen zhi 鄉鎮志, 117–18

Xianhua Grotto 獻花岩, 163–64, 168

Xianhuayan zhi 獻花岩志 (Chen Yi 陳沂), 128, 302*n*61

Xiaoling 孝陵, 183, 306*n*122

xiaopin 小品 (vignette-style writings), 157

xiaoshuo 小説 (vernacular stories), 6–7, 192, 196, 197–200, 236–37, 312*n*37

Xie Zhaozhi 謝肇淛 (1567–1624), 153

Xingshi yinyuan zhuan 醒世姻緣傳, 18, 311*n*27

Xin mu bian 訢慕編 (Chen Yi 陳沂), 188*n*2

xinwen 新聞 (news), 4, 192, 194–201, 237

Xu Xiake 徐霞客 (1587–1641), 157

Xuande reign 宣德 (1426–35), 58

Xuanwu lake, *see* Lake Hou

xun'an yushi 巡按御史 (regional inspectors): city wall construction, 79, 81, 101, 109, 288*n*3; financial reform, 41–42, 46, 59, 67, 73

xunfu 巡撫 (grand coordinators), 59, 81

xunjian 巡檢 (police chief), 296*n*114

xunjian si 巡檢司 (police stations), 120, 296*nn*114–15

xunlan 巡欄 (police bureaus), 283*n*65

Xu Wenxian tongkao 續文獻通考 (Wang Qi 王圻), 281*n*55, 286*n*105

Yan Ruyu 嚴如煜 (1759–1826), 316*n*79

Yang Erzeng 楊爾增, 151

Yangzhou, 3, 19, 158, 184–85, 250, 268*n*23

yanmen lunpai 沿門輪派, see *paimen* 排門

Yanzhi River 胭脂河 (Rouge Canal), 99, 114, 116

Yao Ruxun 姚汝循 (1535–97), 165

Ye Xianggao 葉向高 (1559–1627), 155

Yecheng kelun 冶城客論 (Lu Cai 陸采), 194, 198

yi 役 (labor service), 30, 39. See also *fangxiang yi* 坊廂役

yi 意 (mindset), 154–55

Yijian zhi 夷堅志 (Hong Mai), 200

Yijing 易經 (Book of changes), 84, 299*n*32

yinchai 銀差 (fixed cash payment), 38, 59

Yingtian prefecture 應天府, *see* Nanjing Metropolitan Area

yitian 役田 (corvée fields), 62, 73, 286*n*109

yitian yicang 義田義倉 (charity lands and granaries), 98

yizhiyoudan 易知由單 (easy-to-understand slip), 41

you 游 (touring), 151–56, 156–59, 303*n*71

Yu Menglin 余孟麟, 107–8, 126, 128, 166, 292*n*82

Yuan dynasty, 11, 32–33, 77, 138, 251, 253–54, 287*n*2, 296*n*122; Nanjing, 133, 146. *See also* urban administration; wall-construction policy

Yuan Mei 袁枚, 307*n*129

Yuan Zhongdao 袁中道 (1570–1623), 157

Yudi jisheng 輿地紀勝 (Wang Xiangzhi 王象之), 152

Yuejiang lou 閱江樓 (River-viewing pavilion), 132, 146; "Yuejiang lou ji" 閱江樓記, 146

Zhan Dongtu 詹東圖 (1519–1602), 235, 317*n*111

Zhang Dai 張岱, 19*n*43

Zhang Juzheng 張居正 (1525–82), 63, 280*n*53

Zhao Shanji 趙善繼 (fl. 1570s), 66–67, 72, 284*n*88

zhen 鎮 (market towns), 8, 17, 76–77, 79, 102, 115–21, 248–49, 253, 270*n*27

zhen chenghuang 鎮城隍 (town gods), 241

Zhengde reign 正德 (1506–21), 231, 289*n*18

Zhengtong reign 正統 (1436–49), 67

zhili 直隸, 76. See also *nan zhili* 南直隸

Zhong Xing 鍾惺 (1574–1624), 160

Zhou Hui 周暉, 129, 188, 206, 233, 281*n*61, 297*n*6, 307*nn*1–2, 309*n*14

Zhou Lianggong 周亮工 (1612–72), 171, 306*nn*106–7

zhu 主 (hosts/locals), 193, 215, 228, 242, 244, 251, 310*n*16

Zhu Guozhen 朱國楨, 43, 61

Zhu Hong 祩宏 (1535–1615), 199

Zhu Mu 祝穆, 152

Zhu Yuanzhang (1328–98, r. 1368–98): Nanjing, 2–4, 132–38, 143–46, 187, 191, 210, 275*n*4, 298*n*18, 299*n*32; Nanjing Metropolitan Area, 76–77, 103; social vision, 26–27, 31–38, 42, 51, 66, 254, 277*n*17, 278*n*22

Zhu Yunming 祝允明 (1460–1526), 198, 312*n*33

Zhu Zhifan 朱之蕃 (1564–?), 124–30, 141, 151, 165–66, 170, 208. See also *Jinling yayou bian*

zhuangyuan 狀元 (optimus), 170

zifeng tougui 自封投櫃 (self-seal and self-deposit), 40, 55

Zizhi lu 自知錄 (Zhu Hong 祩宏), 199

Zongguan 總管, 251–52

zongjia huofu 總甲火夫, 29, 70–71, 275*n*2, 285*n*102. See also *huojia* 火甲

Zou She 鄒喆, 183

Zurndorfer, Harriet, 110–11

Harvard East Asian Monographs
(*out-of-print)

*1. Liang Fang-chung, *The Single-Whip Method of Taxation in China*

*2. Harold C. Hinton, *The Grain Tribute System of China, 1845–1911*

3. Ellsworth C. Carlson, *The Kaiping Mines, 1877–1912*

*4. Chao Kuo-chün, *Agrarian Policies of Mainland China: A Documentary Study, 1949–1956*

*5. Edgar Snow, *Random Notes on Red China, 1936–1945*

*6. Edwin George Beal, Jr., *The Origin of Likin, 1835–1864*

7. Chao Kuo-chün, *Economic Planning and Organization in Mainland China: A Documentary Study, 1949–1957*

*8. John K. Fairbank, *Ching Documents: An Introductory Syllabus*

*9. Helen Yin and Yi-chang Yin, *Economic Statistics of Mainland China, 1949–1957*

10. Wolfgang Franke, *The Reform and Abolition of the Traditional Chinese Examination System*

11. Albert Feuerwerker and S. Cheng, *Chinese Communist Studies of Modern Chinese History*

12. C. John Stanley, *Late Ching Finance: Hu Kuang-yung as an Innovator*

13. S. M. Meng, *The Tsungli Yamen: Its Organization and Functions*

*14. Ssu-yü Teng, *Historiography of the Taiping Rebellion*

15. Chun-Jo Liu, *Controversies in Modern Chinese Intellectual History: An Analytic Bibliography of Periodical Articles, Mainly of the May Fourth and Post-May Fourth Era*

*16. Edward J. M. Rhoads, *The Chinese Red Army, 1927–1963: An Annotated Bibliography*

*17. Andrew J. Nathan, *A History of the China International Famine Relief Commission*

*18. Frank H. H. King (ed.) and Prescott Clarke, *A Research Guide to China-Coast Newspapers, 1822–1911*

*19. Ellis Joffe, *Party and Army: Professionalism and Political Control in the Chinese Officer Corps, 1949–1964*

*20. Toshio G. Tsukahira, *Feudal Control in Tokugawa Japan: The Sankin Kōtai System*

*21. Kwang-Ching Liu, ed., *American Missionaries in China: Papers from Harvard Seminars*

*22. George Moseley, *A Sino-Soviet Cultural Frontier: The Ili Kazakh Autonomous Chou*

23. Carl F. Nathan, *Plague Prevention and Politics in Manchuria, 1910–1931*
*24. Adrian Arthur Bennett, *John Fryer: The Introduction of Western Science and Technology into Nineteenth-Century China*
*25. Donald J. Friedman, *The Road from Isolation: The Campaign of the American Committee for Non-Participation in Japanese Aggression, 1938–1941*
*26. Edward LeFevour, *Western Enterprise in Late Ching China: A Selective Survey of Jardine, Matheson and Company's Operations, 1842–1895*
27. Charles Neuhauser, *Third World Politics: China and the Afro-Asian People's Solidarity Organization, 1957–1967*
*28. Kungtu C. Sun, assisted by Ralph W. Huenemann, *The Economic Development of Manchuria in the First Half of the Twentieth Century*
*29. Shahid Javed Burki, *A Study of Chinese Communes, 1965*
30. John Carter Vincent, *The Extraterritorial System in China: Final Phase*
31. Madeleine Chi, *China Diplomacy, 1914–1918*
*32. Clifton Jackson Phillips, *Protestant America and the Pagan World: The First Half Century of the American Board of Commissioners for Foreign Missions, 1810–1860*
*33. James Pusey, *Wu Han: Attacking the Present Through the Past*
*34. Ying-wan Cheng, *Postal Communication in China and Its Modernization, 1860–1896*
35. Tuvia Blumenthal, *Saving in Postwar Japan*
36. Peter Frost, *The Bakumatsu Currency Crisis*
37. Stephen C. Lockwood, *Augustine Heard and Company, 1858–1862*
38. Robert R. Campbell, *James Duncan Campbell: A Memoir by His Son*
39. Jerome Alan Cohen, ed., *The Dynamics of China's Foreign Relations*
40. V. V. Vishnyakova-Akimova, *Two Years in Revolutionary China, 1925–1927*, trans. Steven L. Levine
41. Meron Medzini, *French Policy in Japan During the Closing Years of the Tokugawa Regime*
42. Ezra Vogel, Margie Sargent, Vivienne B. Shue, Thomas Jay Mathews, and Deborah S. Davis, *The Cultural Revolution in the Provinces*
43. Sidney A. Forsythe, *An American Missionary Community in China, 1895–1905*
*44. Benjamin I. Schwartz, ed., *Reflections on the May Fourth Movement.: A Symposium*
*45. Ching Young Choe, *The Rule of the Taewŏngun, 1864–1873: Restoration in Yi Korea*
46. W. P. J. Hall, *A Bibliographical Guide to Japanese Research on the Chinese Economy, 1958–1970*
47. Jack J. Gerson, *Horatio Nelson Lay and Sino-British Relations, 1854–1864*
48. Paul Richard Bohr, *Famine and the Missionary: Timothy Richard as Relief Administrator and Advocate of National Reform*
49. Endymion Wilkinson, *The History of Imperial China: A Research Guide*
50. Britten Dean, *China and Great Britain: The Diplomacy of Commercial Relations, 1860–1864*
51. Ellsworth C. Carlson, *The Foochow Missionaries, 1847–1880*
52. Yeh-chien Wang, *An Estimate of the Land-Tax Collection in China, 1753 and 1908*
53. Richard M. Pfeffer, *Understanding Business Contracts in China, 1949–1963*

*54. Han-sheng Chuan and Richard Kraus, *Mid-Ching Rice Markets and Trade: An Essay in Price History*

55. Ranbir Vohra, *Lao She and the Chinese Revolution*

56. Liang-lin Hsiao, *China's Foreign Trade Statistics, 1864–1949*

*57. Lee-hsia Hsu Ting, *Government Control of the Press in Modern China, 1900–1949*

*58. Edward W. Wagner, *The Literati Purges: Political Conflict in Early Yi Korea*

*59. Joungwon A. Kim, *Divided Korea: The Politics of Development, 1945–1972*

60. Noriko Kamachi, John K. Fairbank, and Chūzō Ichiko, *Japanese Studies of Modern China Since 1953: A Bibliographical Guide to Historical and Social-Science Research on the Nineteenth and Twentieth Centuries, Supplementary Volume for 1953–1969*

61. Donald A. Gibbs and Yun-chen Li, *A Bibliography of Studies and Translations of Modern Chinese Literature, 1918–1942*

62. Robert H. Silin, *Leadership and Values: The Organization of Large-Scale Taiwanese Enterprises*

63. David Pong, *A Critical Guide to the Kwangtung Provincial Archives Deposited at the Public Record Office of London*

*64. Fred W. Drake, *China Charts the World: Hsu Chi-yü and His Geography of 1848*

*65. William A. Brown and Urgrunge Onon, translators and annotators, *History of the Mongolian People's Republic*

66. Edward L. Farmer, *Early Ming Government: The Evolution of Dual Capitals*

*67. Ralph C. Croizier, *Koxinga and Chinese Nationalism: History, Myth, and the Hero*

*68. William J. Tyler, tr., *The Psychological World of Natsume Sōseki*, by Doi Takeo

69. Eric Widmer, *The Russian Ecclesiastical Mission in Peking During the Eighteenth Century*

*70. Charlton M. Lewis, *Prologue to the Chinese Revolution: The Transformation of Ideas and Institutions in Hunan Province, 1891–1907*

71. Preston Torbert, *The Ching Imperial Household Department: A Study of Its Organization and Principal Functions, 1662–1796*

72. Paul A. Cohen and John E. Schrecker, eds., *Reform in Nineteenth-Century China*

73. Jon Sigurdson, *Rural Industrialism in China*

74. Kang Chao, *The Development of Cotton Textile Production in China*

75. Valentin Rabe, *The Home Base of American China Missions, 1880–1920*

*76. Sarasin Viraphol, *Tribute and Profit: Sino-Siamese Trade, 1652–1853*

77. Ch'i-ch'ing Hsiao, *The Military Establishment of the Yuan Dynasty*

78. Meishi Tsai, *Contemporary Chinese Novels and Short Stories, 1949–1974: An Annotated Bibliography*

*79. Wellington K. K. Chan, *Merchants, Mandarins and Modern Enterprise in Late Ching China*

80. Endymion Wilkinson, *Landlord and Labor in Late Imperial China: Case Studies from Shandong by Jing Su and Luo Lun*

*81. Barry Keenan, *The Dewey Experiment in China: Educational Reform and Political Power in the Early Republic*

*82. George A. Hayden, *Crime and Punishment in Medieval Chinese Drama: Three Judge Pao Plays*

*83. Sang-Chul Suh, *Growth and Structural Changes in the Korean Economy, 1910–1940*

84. J. W. Dower, *Empire and Aftermath: Yoshida Shigeru and the Japanese Experience, 1878–1954*

85. Martin Collcutt, *Five Mountains: The Rinzai Zen Monastic Institution in Medieval Japan*

86. Kwang Suk Kim and Michael Roemer, *Growth and Structural Transformation*

87. Anne O. Krueger, *The Developmental Role of the Foreign Sector and Aid*

*88. Edwin S. Mills and Byung-Nak Song, *Urbanization and Urban Problems*

89. Sung Hwan Ban, Pal Yong Moon, and Dwight H. Perkins, *Rural Development*

*90. Noel F. McGinn, Donald R. Snodgrass, Yung Bong Kim, Shin-Bok Kim, and Quee-Young Kim, *Education and Development in Korea*

*91. Leroy P. Jones and Il SaKong, *Government, Business, and Entrepreneurship in Economic Development: The Korean Case*

92. Edward S. Mason, Dwight H. Perkins, Kwang Suk Kim, David C. Cole, Mahn Je Kim et al., *The Economic and Social Modernization of the Republic of Korea*

93. Robert Repetto, Tai Hwan Kwon, Son-Ung Kim, Dae Young Kim, John E. Sloboda, and Peter J. Donaldson, *Economic Development, Population Policy, and Demographic Transition in the Republic of Korea*

94. Parks M. Coble, Jr., *The Shanghai Capitalists and the Nationalist Government, 1927–1937*

95. Noriko Kamachi, *Reform in China: Huang Tsun-hsien and the Japanese Model*

96. Richard Wich, *Sino-Soviet Crisis Politics: A Study of Political Change and Communication*

97. Lillian M. Li, *China's Silk Trade: Traditional Industry in the Modern World, 1842–1937*

98. R. David Arkush, *Fei Xiaotong and Sociology in Revolutionary China*

*99. Kenneth Alan Grossberg, *Japan's Renaissance: The Politics of the Muromachi Bakufu*

100. James Reeve Pusey, *China and Charles Darwin*

101. Hoyt Cleveland Tillman, *Utilitarian Confucianism: Chen Liang's Challenge to Chu Hsi*

102. Thomas A. Stanley, *Ōsugi Sakae, Anarchist in Taishō Japan: The Creativity of the Ego*

103. Jonathan K. Ocko, *Bureaucratic Reform in Provincial China: Ting Jih-ch'ang in Restoration Kiangsu, 1867–1870*

104. James Reed, *The Missionary Mind and American East Asia Policy, 1911–1915*

105. Neil L. Waters, *Japan's Local Pragmatists: The Transition from Bakumatsu to Meiji in the Kawasaki Region*

106. David C. Cole and Yung Chul Park, *Financial Development in Korea, 1945–1978*

107. Roy Bahl, Chuk Kyo Kim, and Chong Kee Park, *Public Finances During the Korean Modernization Process*

108. William D. Wray, *Mitsubishi and the N.Y.K, 1870–1914: Business Strategy in the Japanese Shipping Industry*

109. Ralph William Huenemann, *The Dragon and the Iron Horse: The Economics of Railroads in China, 1876–1937*

*110. Benjamin A. Elman, *From Philosophy to Philology: Intellectual and Social Aspects of Change in Late Imperial China*

111. Jane Kate Leonard, *Wei Yüan and China's Rediscovery of the Maritime World*

112. Luke S. K. Kwong, *A Mosaic of the Hundred Days:. Personalities, Politics, and Ideas of 1898*

*113. John E. Wills, Jr., *Embassies and Illusions: Dutch and Portuguese Envoys to K'ang-hsi, 1666–1687*

114. Joshua A. Fogel, *Politics and Sinology: The Case of Naitō Konan (1866–1934)*

*115. Jeffrey C. Kinkley, ed., *After Mao: Chinese Literature and Society, 1978–1981*

116. C. Andrew Gerstle, *Circles of Fantasy: Convention in the Plays of Chikamatsu*

117. Andrew Gordon, *The Evolution of Labor Relations in Japan: Heavy Industry, 1853–1955*

*118. Daniel K. Gardner, *Chu Hsi and the "Ta Hsueh": Neo-Confucian Reflection on the Confucian Canon*

119. Christine Guth Kanda, *Shinzō: Hachiman Imagery and Its Development*

*120. Robert Borgen, *Sugawara no Michizane and the Early Heian Court*

121. Chang-tai Hung, *Going to the People: Chinese Intellectual and Folk Literature, 1918–1937*

*122. Michael A. Cusumano, *The Japanese Automobile Industry: Technology and Management at Nissan and Toyota*

123. Richard von Glahn, *The Country of Streams and Grottoes: Expansion, Settlement, and the Civilizing of the Sichuan Frontier in Song Times*

124. Steven D. Carter, *The Road to Komatsubara: A Classical Reading of the Renga Hyakuin*

125. Katherine F. Bruner, John K. Fairbank, and Richard T. Smith, *Entering China's Service: Robert Hart's Journals, 1854–1863*

126. Bob Tadashi Wakabayashi, *Anti-Foreignism and Western Learning in Early-Modern Japan: The "New Theses" of 1825*

127. Atsuko Hirai, *Individualism and Socialism: The Life and Thought of Kawai Eijirō (1891–1944)*

128. Ellen Widmer, *The Margins of Utopia: "Shui-hu hou-chuan" and the Literature of Ming Loyalism*

129. R. Kent Guy, *The Emperor's Four Treasuries: Scholars and the State in the Late Chien-lung Era*

130. Peter C. Perdue, *Exhausting the Earth: State and Peasant in Hunan, 1500–1850*

131. Susan Chan Egan, *A Latterday Confucian: Reminiscences of William Hung (1893–1980)*

132. James T. C. Liu, *China Turning Inward: Intellectual-Political Changes in the Early Twelfth Century*

*133. Paul A. Cohen, *Between Tradition and Modernity: Wang T'ao and Reform in Late Ching China*

134. Kate Wildman Nakai, *Shogunal Politics: Arai Hakuseki and the Premises of Tokugawa Rule*

*135. Parks M. Coble, *Facing Japan: Chinese Politics and Japanese Imperialism, 1931–1937*

136. Jon L. Saari, *Legacies of Childhood: Growing Up Chinese in a Time of Crisis, 1890–1920*

137. Susan Downing Videen, *Tales of Heichū*

138. Heinz Morioka and Miyoko Sasaki, *Rakugo: The Popular Narrative Art of Japan*

139. Joshua A. Fogel, *Nakae Ushikichi in China: The Mourning of Spirit*

140. Alexander Barton Woodside, *Vietnam and the Chinese Model: A Comparative Study of Vietnamese and Chinese Government in the First Half of the Nineteenth Century*

*141. George Elison, *Deus Destroyed: The Image of Christianity in Early Modern Japan*

142. William D. Wray, ed., *Managing Industrial Enterprise: Cases from Japan's Prewar Experience*

*143. T'ung-tsu Ch'ü, *Local Government in China Under the Ching*

144. Marie Anchordoguy, *Computers, Inc.: Japan's Challenge to IBM*

145. Barbara Molony, *Technology and Investment: The Prewar Japanese Chemical Industry*

146. Mary Elizabeth Berry, *Hideyoshi*

147. Laura E. Hein, *Fueling Growth: The Energy Revolution and Economic Policy in Postwar Japan*

148. Wen-hsin Yeh, *The Alienated Academy: Culture and Politics in Republican China, 1919–1937*

149. Dru C. Gladney, *Muslim Chinese: Ethnic Nationalism in the People's Republic*

150. Merle Goldman and Paul A. Cohen, eds., *Ideas Across Cultures: Essays on Chinese Thought in Honor of Benjamin L. Schwartz*

151. James M. Polachek, *The Inner Opium War*

152. Gail Lee Bernstein, *Japanese Marxist: A Portrait of Kawakami Hajime, 1879–1946*

*153. Lloyd E. Eastman, *The Abortive Revolution: China Under Nationalist Rule, 1927–1937*

154. Mark Mason, *American Multinationals and Japan: The Political Economy of Japanese Capital Controls, 1899–1980*

155. Richard J. Smith, John K. Fairbank, and Katherine F. Bruner, *Robert Hart and China's Early Modernization: His Journals, 1863–1866*

156. George J. Tanabe, Jr., *Myōe the Dreamkeeper: Fantasy and Knowledge in Kamakura Buddhism*

157. William Wayne Farris, *Heavenly Warriors: The Evolution of Japan's Military, 500–1300*

158. Yu-ming Shaw, *An American Missionary in China: John Leighton Stuart and Chinese-American Relations*

159. James B. Palais, *Politics and Policy in Traditional Korea*

*160. Douglas Reynolds, *China, 1898–1912: The Xinzheng Revolution and Japan*

161. Roger R. Thompson, *China's Local Councils in the Age of Constitutional Reform, 1898–1911*

162. William Johnston, *The Modern Epidemic: History of Tuberculosis in Japan*

163. Constantine Nomikos Vaporis, *Breaking Barriers: Travel and the State in Early Modern Japan*

164. Irmela Hijiya-Kirschnereit, *Rituals of Self-Revelation: Shishōsetsu as Literary Genre and Socio-Cultural Phenomenon*

165. James C. Baxter, *The Meiji Unification Through the Lens of Ishikawa Prefecture*

166. Thomas R. H. Havens, *Architects of Affluence: The Tsutsumi Family and the Seibu-Saison Enterprises in Twentieth-Century Japan*

167. Anthony Hood Chambers, *The Secret Window: Ideal Worlds in Tanizaki's Fiction*

168. Steven J. Ericson, *The Sound of the Whistle: Railroads and the State in Meiji Japan*

169. Andrew Edmund Goble, *Kenmu: Go-Daigo's Revolution*

170. Denise Potrzeba Lett, *In Pursuit of Status: The Making of South Korea's "New" Urban Middle Class*

171. Mimi Hall Yiengpruksawan, *Hiraizumi: Buddhist Art and Regional Politics in Twelfth-Century Japan*

172. Charles Shirō Inouye, *The Similitude of Blossoms: A Critical Biography of Izumi Kyōka (1873–1939), Japanese Novelist and Playwright*

173. Aviad E. Raz, *Riding the Black Ship: Japan and Tokyo Disneyland*

174. Deborah J. Milly, *Poverty, Equality, and Growth: The Politics of Economic Need in Postwar Japan*

175. See Heng Teow, *Japan's Cultural Policy Toward China, 1918–1931: A Comparative Perspective*

176. Michael A. Fuller, *An Introduction to Literary Chinese*

177. Frederick R. Dickinson, *War and National Reinvention: Japan in the Great War, 1914–1919*

178. John Solt, *Shredding the Tapestry of Meaning: The Poetry and Poetics of Kitasono Katue (1902–1978)*

179. Edward Pratt, *Japan's Protoindustrial Elite: The Economic Foundations of the Gōnō*

180. Atsuko Sakaki, *Recontextualizing Texts: Narrative Performance in Modern Japanese Fiction*

181. Soon-Won Park, *Colonial Industrialization and Labor in Korea: The Onoda Cement Factory*

182. JaHyun Kim Haboush and Martina Deuchler, *Culture and the State in Late Chosŏn Korea*

183. John W. Chaffee, *Branches of Heaven: A History of the Imperial Clan of Sung China*

184. Gi-Wook Shin and Michael Robinson, eds., *Colonial Modernity in Korea*

185. Nam-lin Hur, *Prayer and Play in Late Tokugawa Japan: Asakusa Sensōji and Edo Society*

186. Kristin Stapleton, *Civilizing Chengdu: Chinese Urban Reform, 1895–1937*

187. Hyung Il Pai, *Constructing "Korean" Origins: A Critical Review of Archaeology, Historiography, and Racial Myth in Korean State-Formation Theories*

188. Brian D. Ruppert, *Jewel in the Ashes: Buddha Relics and Power in Early Medieval Japan*

189. Susan Daruvala, *Zhou Zuoren and an Alternative Chinese Response to Modernity*

*190. James Z. Lee, *The Political Economy of a Frontier: Southwest China, 1250–1850*

191. Kerry Smith, *A Time of Crisis: Japan, the Great Depression, and Rural Revitalization*

192. Michael Lewis, *Becoming Apart: National Power and Local Politics in Toyama, 1868–1945*

193. William C. Kirby, Man-houng Lin, James Chin Shih, and David A. Pietz, eds., *State and Economy in Republican China: A Handbook for Scholars*

194. Timothy S. George, *Minamata: Pollution and the Struggle for Democracy in Postwar Japan*

195. Billy K. L. So, *Prosperity, Region, and Institutions in Maritime China: The South Fukien Pattern, 946–1368*

196. Yoshihisa Tak Matsusaka, *The Making of Japanese Manchuria, 1904–1932*

Harvard East Asian Monographs

197. Maram Epstein, *Competing Discourses: Orthodoxy, Authenticity, and Engendered Meanings in Late Imperial Chinese Fiction*
198. Curtis J. Milhaupt, J. Mark Ramseyer, and Michael K. Young, eds. and comps., *Japanese Law in Context: Readings in Society, the Economy, and Politics*
199. Haruo Iguchi, *Unfinished Business: Ayukawa Yoshisuke and U.S.-Japan Relations, 1937–1952*
200. Scott Pearce, Audrey Spiro, and Patricia Ebrey, *Culture and Power in the Reconstitution of the Chinese Realm, 200–600*
201. Terry Kawashima, *Writing Margins: The Textual Construction of Gender in Heian and Kamakura Japan*
202. Martin W. Huang, *Desire and Fictional Narrative in Late Imperial China*
203. Robert S. Ross and Jiang Changbin, eds., *Re-examining the Cold War: U.S.-China Diplomacy, 1954–1973*
204. Guanhua Wang, *In Search of Justice: The 1905–1906 Chinese Anti-American Boycott*
205. David Schaberg, *A Patterned Past: Form and Thought in Early Chinese Historiography*
206. Christine Yano, *Tears of Longing: Nostalgia and the Nation in Japanese Popular Song*
207. Milena Doleželová-Velingerová and Oldřich Král, with Graham Sanders, eds., *The Appropriation of Cultural Capital: China's May Fourth Project*
208. Robert N. Huey, *The Making of 'Shinkokinshū'*
209. Lee Butler, *Emperor and Aristocracy in Japan, 1467–1680: Resilience and Renewal*
210. Suzanne Ogden, *Inklings of Democracy in China*
211. Kenneth J. Ruoff, *The People's Emperor: Democracy and the Japanese Monarchy, 1945–1995*
212. Haun Saussy, *Great Walls of Discourse and Other Adventures in Cultural China*
213. Aviad E. Raz, *Emotions at Work: Normative Control, Organizations, and Culture in Japan and America*
214. Rebecca E. Karl and Peter Zarrow, eds., *Rethinking the 1898 Reform Period: Political and Cultural Change in Late Qing China*
215. Kevin O'Rourke, *The Book of Korean Shijo*
216. Ezra F. Vogel, ed., *The Golden Age of the U.S.-China-Japan Triangle, 1972–1989*
217. Thomas A. Wilson, ed., *On Sacred Grounds: Culture, Society, Politics, and the Formation of the Cult of Confucius*
218. Donald S. Sutton, *Steps of Perfection: Exorcistic Performers and Chinese Religion in Twentieth-Century Taiwan*
219. Daqing Yang, *Technology of Empire: Telecommunications and Japanese Expansionism, 1895–1945*
220. Qianshen Bai, *Fu Shan's World: The Transformation of Chinese Calligraphy in the Seventeenth Century*
221. Paul Jakov Smith and Richard von Glahn, eds., *The Song-Yuan-Ming Transition in Chinese History*
222. Rania Huntington, *Alien Kind: Foxes and Late Imperial Chinese Narrative*
223. Jordan Sand, *House and Home in Modern Japan: Architecture, Domestic Space, and Bourgeois Culture, 1880–1930*

Harvard East Asian Monographs

224. Karl Gerth, *China Made: Consumer Culture and the Creation of the Nation*

225. Xiaoshan Yang, *Metamorphosis of the Private Sphere: Gardens and Objects in Tang-Song Poetry*

226. Barbara Mittler, *A Newspaper for China? Power, Identity, and Change in Shanghai's News Media, 1872–1912*

227. Joyce A. Madancy, *The Troublesome Legacy of Commissioner Lin: The Opium Trade and Opium Suppression in Fujian Province, 1820s to 1920s*

228. John Makeham, *Transmitters and Creators: Chinese Commentators and Commentaries on the Analects*

229. Elisabeth Köll, *From Cotton Mill to Business Empire: The Emergence of Regional Enterprises in Modern China*

230. Emma Teng, *Taiwan's Imagined Geography: Chinese Colonial Travel Writing and Pictures, 1683–1895*

231. Wilt Idema and Beata Grant, *The Red Brush: Writing Women of Imperial China*

232. Eric C. Rath, *The Ethos of Noh: Actors and Their Art*

233. Elizabeth Remick, *Building Local States: China During the Republican and Post-Mao Eras*

234. Lynn Struve, ed., *The Qing Formation in World-Historical Time*

235. D. Max Moerman, *Localizing Paradise: Kumano Pilgrimage and the Religious Landscape of Premodern Japan*

236. Antonia Finnane, *Speaking of Yangzhou: A Chinese City, 1550–1850*

237. Brian Platt, *Burning and Building: Schooling and State Formation in Japan, 1750–1890*

238. Gail Bernstein, Andrew Gordon, and Kate Wildman Nakai, eds., *Public Spheres, Private Lives in Modern Japan, 1600–1950: Essays in Honor of Albert Craig*

239. Wu Hung and Katherine R. Tsiang, *Body and Face in Chinese Visual Culture*

240. Stephen Dodd, *Writing Home: Representations of the Native Place in Modern Japanese Literature*

241. David Anthony Bello, *Opium and the Limits of Empire: Drug Prohibition in the Chinese Interior, 1729–1850*

242. Hosea Hirata, *Discourses of Seduction: History, Evil, Desire, and Modern Japanese Literature*

243. Kyung Moon Hwang, *Beyond Birth: Social Status in the Emergence of Modern Korea*

244. Brian R. Dott, *Identity Reflections: Pilgrimages to Mount Tai in Late Imperial China*

245. Mark McNally, *Proving the Way: Conflict and Practice in the History of Japanese Nativism*

246. Yongping Wu, *A Political Explanation of Economic Growth: State Survival, Bureaucratic Politics, and Private Enterprises in the Making of Taiwan's Economy, 1950–1985*

247. Kyu Hyun Kim, *The Age of Visions and Arguments: Parliamentarianism and the National Public Sphere in Early Meiji Japan*

248. Zvi Ben-Dor Benite, *The Dao of Muhammad: A Cultural History of Muslims in Late Imperial China*

249. David Der-wei Wang and Shang Wei, eds., *Dynastic Crisis and Cultural Innovation: From the Late Ming to the Late Qing and Beyond*

250. Wilt L. Idema, Wai-yee Li, and Ellen Widmer, eds., *Trauma and Transcendence in Early Qing Literature*

251. Barbara Molony and Kathleen Uno, eds., *Gendering Modern Japanese History*

252. Hiroshi Aoyagi, *Islands of Eight Million Smiles: Idol Performance and Symbolic Production in Contemporary Japan*

253. Wai-yee Li, *The Readability of the Past in Early Chinese Historiography*

254. William C. Kirby, Robert S. Ross, and Gong Li, eds., *Normalization of U.S.-China Relations: An International History*

255. Ellen Gardner Nakamura, *Practical Pursuits: Takano Chōei, Takahashi Keisaku, and Western Medicine in Nineteenth-Century Japan*

256. Jonathan W. Best, *A History of the Early Korean Kingdom of Paekche, together with an annotated translation of* The Paekche Annals *of the* Samguk sagi

257. Liang Pan, *The United Nations in Japan's Foreign and Security Policymaking, 1945–1992: National Security, Party Politics, and International Status*

258. Richard Belsky, *Localities at the Center: Native Place, Space, and Power in Late Imperial Beijing*

259. Zwia Lipkin, *"Useless to the State": "Social Problems" and Social Engineering in Nationalist Nanjing, 1927–1937*

260. William O. Gardner, *Advertising Tower: Japanese Modernism and Modernity in the 1920s*

261. Stephen Owen, *The Making of Early Chinese Classical Poetry*

262. Martin J. Powers, *Pattern and Person: Ornament, Society, and Self in Classical China*

263. Anna M. Shields, *Crafting a Collection: The Cultural Contexts and Poetic Practice of the* Huajian ji 花間集 *(Collection from Among the Flowers)*

264. Stephen Owen, *The Late Tang: Chinese Poetry of the Mid-Ninth Century (827–860)*

265. Sara L. Friedman, *Intimate Politics: Marriage, the Market, and State Power in Southeastern China*

266. Patricia Buckley Ebrey and Maggie Bickford, *Emperor Huizong and Late Northern Song China: The Politics of Culture and the Culture of Politics*

267. Sophie Volpp, *Worldly Stage: Theatricality in Seventeenth-Century China*

268. Ellen Widmer, *The Beauty and the Book: Women and Fiction in Nineteenth-Century China*

269. Steven B. Miles, *The Sea of Learning: Mobility and Identity in Nineteenth-Century Guangzhou*

270. Lin Man-houng, *China Upside Down: Currency, Society, and Ideologies, 1808–1856*

271. Ronald Egan, *The Problem of Beauty: Aesthetic Thought and Pursuits in Northern Song Dynasty China*

272. Mark Halperin, *Out of the Cloister: Literati Perspectives on Buddhism in Sung China, 960–1279*

273. Helen Dunstan, *State or Merchant? Political Economy and Political Process in 1740s China*

274. Sabina Knight, *The Heart of Time: Moral Agency in Twentieth-Century Chinese Fiction*

275. Timothy J. Van Compernolle, *The Uses of Memory: The Critique of Modernity in the Fiction of Higuchi Ichiyō*

276. Paul Rouzer, *A New Practical Primer of Literary Chinese*
277. Jonathan Zwicker, *Practices of the Sentimental Imagination: Melodrama, the Novel, and the Social Imaginary in Nineteenth-Century Japan*
278. Franziska Seraphim, *War Memory and Social Politics in Japan, 1945–2005*
279. Adam L. Kern, *Manga from the Floating World: Comicbook Culture and the* Kibyōshi *of Edo Japan*
280. Cynthia J. Brokaw, *Commerce in Culture: The Sibao Book Trade in the Qing and Republican Periods*
281. Eugene Y. Park, *Between Dreams and Reality: The Military Examination in Late Chosŏn Korea, 1600–1894*
282. Nam-lin Hur, *Death and Social Order in Tokugawa Japan: Buddhism, Anti-Christianity, and the* Danka *System*
283. Patricia M. Thornton, *Disciplining the State: Virtue, Violence, and State-Making in Modern China*
284. Vincent Goossaert, *The Taoists of Peking, 1800–1949: A Social History of Urban Clerics*
285. Peter Nickerson, *Taoism, Bureaucracy, and Popular Religion in Early Medieval China*
286. Charo B. D'Etcheverry, *Love After* The Tale of Genji: *Rewriting the World of the Shining Prince*
287. Michael G. Chang, *A Court on Horseback: Imperial Touring & the Construction of Qing Rule, 1680–1785*
288. Carol Richmond Tsang, *War and Faith: Ikkō Ikki in Late Muromachi Japan*
289. Hilde De Weerdt, *Competition over Content: Negotiating Standards for the Civil Service Examinations in Imperial China (1127–1279)*
290. Eve Zimmerman, *Out of the Alleyway: Nakagami Kenji and the Poetics of Outcaste Fiction*
291. Robert Culp, *Articulating Citizenship: Civic Education and Student Politics in Southeastern China, 1912–1940*
292. Richard J. Smethurst, *From Foot Soldier to Finance Minister: Takahashi Korekiyo, Japan's Keynes*
293. John E. Herman, *Amid the Clouds and Mist: China's Colonization of Guizhou, 1200–1700*
294. Tomoko Shiroyama, *China During the Great Depression: Market, State, and the World Economy, 1929–1937*
295. Kirk W. Larsen, *Tradition, Treaties and Trade: Qing Imperialism and Chosŏn Korea, 1850–1910*
296. Gregory Golley, *When Our Eyes No Longer See: Realism, Science, and Ecology in Japanese Literary Modernism*
297. Barbara Ambros, *Emplacing a Pilgrimage: The Ōyama Cult and Regional Religion in Early Modern Japan*
298. Rebecca Suter, *The Japanization of Modernity: Murakami Haruki between Japan and the United States*
299. Yuma Totani, *The Tokyo War Crimes Trial: The Pursuit of Justice in the Wake of World War II*

Harvard East Asian Monographs

300. Linda Isako Angst, *In a Dark Time: Memory, Community, and Gendered Nationalism in Postwar Okinawa*

301. David M. Robinson, ed., *Culture, Courtiers, and Competition: The Ming Court (1368–1644)*

302. Calvin Chen, *Some Assembly Required: Work, Community, and Politics in China's Rural Enterprises*

303. Sem Vermeersch, *The Power of the Buddhas: The Politics of Buddhism During the Koryŏ Dynasty (918–1392)*

304. Tina Lu, *Accidental Incest, Filial Cannibalism, and Other Peculiar Encounters in Late Imperial Chinese Literature*

305. Chang Woei Ong, *Men of Letters Within the Passes: Guanzhong Literati in Chinese History, 907–1911*

306. Wendy Swartz, *Reading Tao Yuanming: Shifting Paradigms of Historical Reception (427–1900)*

307. Peter K. Bol, *Neo-Confucianism in History*

308. Carlos Rojas, *The Naked Gaze: Reflections on Chinese Modernity*

309. Kelly H. Chong, *Deliverance and Submission: Evangelical Women and the Negotiation of Patriarchy in South Korea*

310. Rachel DiNitto, *Uchida Hyakken: A Critique of Modernity and Militarism in Prewar Japan*

311. Jeffrey Snyder-Reinke, *Dry Spells: State Rainmaking and Local Governance in Late Imperial China*

312. Jay Dautcher, *Down a Narrow Road: Identity and Masculinity in a Uyghur Community in Xinjiang China*

313. Xun Liu, *Daoist Modern: Innovation, Lay Practice, and the Community of Inner Alchemy in Republican Shanghai*

314. Jacob Eyferth, *Eating Rice from Bamboo Roots: The Social History of a Community of Handicraft Papermakers in Rural Sichuan, 1920–2000*

315. David Johnson, *Spectacle and Sacrifice: The Ritual Foundations of Village Life in North China*

316. James Robson, *Power of Place: The Religious Landscape of the Southern Sacred Peak (Nanyue 南嶽) in Medieval China*

317. Lori Watt, *When Empire Comes Home: Repatriation and Reintegration in Postwar Japan*

318. James Dorsey, *Critical Aesthetics: Kobayashi Hideo, Modernity, and Wartime Japan*

319. Christopher Bolton, *Sublime Voices: The Fictional Science and Scientific Fiction of Abe Kōbō*

320. Si-yen Fei, *Negotiating Urban Space: Urbanization and Late Ming Nanjing*